PROPERTY OF DUQUESNE

UNIVERSITY ARMY ROTC

BOOK # ___289___

Other

ARMY LINEAGE SERIES

AIR DEFENSE ARTILLERY

Compiled by
Janice E. McKenney

MILITARY INSTRVCTION

CENTER OF MILITARY HISTORY
UNITED STATES ARMY
WASHINGTON, D.C., 1985

U.S. Army Center of Military History

Brig. Gen. Douglas Kinnard, USA (Ret.), Chief of Military History

Chief Historian	David F. Trask
Chief, Historical Services Division	Col. David L. Lemon
Editor in Chief	John W. Elsberg

Library of Congress Cataloging in Publication Data

McKenney, Janice E., 1942-
  Air defense artillery.

  (Army lineage series)
  Includes bibliographies.
    1. Anti-aircraft artillery—United States—History.
  2. United States—Air defenses, Military—History.
  I. Title.   II. Series.
  UG733.M35 1984   358'.13'0973   84-14538

UG 733
.M35
1984

First Printing—CMH Pub 60–5

For sale by the Superintendent of Documents, U.S. Government Printing Office
Washington, D.C. 20402

Foreword

Air defense artillery units have a proud heritage dating back to the dawn of this country's history when the colonists erected fortifications and emplaced artillery pieces to defend against attack from the sea. Seacoast defense continued to be the primary mission of "foot" artillery units (as opposed to mounted field artillery units) until World War I, when a new dimension in warfare emerged—attack from the air. Through World War II, the Korean War, and Vietnam, air defense artillery units served as an indispensable part of the armed forces of the United States.

The lineages, honors, and heraldic items included in this volume should increase the historical awareness of air defense artillery soldiers as well as their pride in their units. Successful military organizations are founded upon the positive attitude of their members—soldiers with a strong sense of belonging to their unit and enthusiastic about its being their own. It is our hope that this volume will contribute to the espirit de corps of the air defense artillery.

Because of a desire to make the Army Lineage Series available to soldiers in the field as quickly as possible, this book does not contain the narrative history of the arm that previous volumes included. We hope that the volume will prove as useful and popular as earlier works in the series.

Washington, D.C.
1 December 1983

DOUGLAS KINNARD
Brigadier General, USA (Ret.)
Chief of Military History

SEP 0 4 1996

SEP 1 4 1995

Preface

Air defense artillery troops are those who fight with weapons and equipment designed to combat air targets from the ground. This volume on air defense artillery in the United States Army deals with the organization of such units at the level of regiments and below. Air defense artillery groups and brigades will be covered in a subsequent volume in the Army Lineage Series.

This volume gathers in compact form the official historical records of all air defense artillery regiments in the United States Army in order to perpetuate and publicize their traditions, honors, and heraldic entitlements. It includes the lineage and honors of the twenty-four Regular Army and five Army National Guard air defense artillery regiments in the force structure at the end of 1982. The lineages include the Regular Army and Army Reserve elements of each regiment that have been active since the inception of the Combat Arms Regimental System in 1957.

The lineage and honors certificate of a unit is an outline history in a highly stylized format. The unit lineages in this volume are adapted from the official certificates. The data has been compressed to save space, but the information is the same, which accounts for the technical language used. A Glossary of Lineage Terms appears at the end of the volume to assist the reader in understanding that language. The lineage begins with the official designation of the unit, followed by its special designation, as approved by the Center. The events in the life of a unit are restricted to a few specific actions, such as activation, inactivation, and redesignation. Campaigns and decorations for each battalion under the Combat Arms Regimental System include all the honors of the parent regiment. Asterisks appearing in the list of honors indicate the honors for which a particular unit is the *earning organization*. This distinction means that either the unit itself or a unit from which it is directly descended earned the honor. For batteries and detachments (those that have not been used to form battalions), only the honors for which the batteries or detachments are the *earning units* are listed. In these instances, asterisks are not used since all of the honors are earned. General orders announcing decorations are shown parenthetically for parent regiments and for those decorations of their components for which the elements are the *earning units.*

The Organizational History Branch is responsible for the determination of official unit lineages and honors, and the lineages that appear in this volume are the result of research done by many members of the branch, past and present. The compiler brought all the lineages up to date and prepared the unit bibliographies with the assistance of Mr. Charles E. Dornbusch's comprehensive bibliography entitled *Histories, Personal*

Narrative, United States Army (Cornwallville, N.Y.: Hope Farm Press, 1967) and the U.S. Army Military History Institute's similar work—compiled by Colonel George S. Pappas—entitled *United States Army Unit Histories* (Carlisle Barracks, 1971). Most of the unit histories cited are unofficial works that were prepared outside the Department of the Army. They are, nevertheless, valuable sources of additional information about the units.

Descriptions of coats of arms and distinctive insignia approved for air defense artillery regiments are included with the lineages. These descriptions and the color illustrations of the heraldic items were furnished by The Institute of Heraldry, U.S. Army; the compiler is especially grateful to Dr. Opal Landrum and Mrs. Adele Richey for their assistance. Ms. Barbara H. Gilbert of the Center's Editorial Branch prepared the manuscript for publication. Minor changes in heraldic material have been made to meet the need for brevity in this volume. At the beginning of the color illustrations is a brief account of the evolution of these items.

Since the Center of Military History is responsible for the determination and publication of unit lineages and honors under Army Regulation 870–5, comments are invited and should be addressed to the Center, Washington, D.C. 20314–0200.

Washington, D.C.   JANICE E. McKENNEY
1 December 1983

Contents

AIR DEFENSE ARTILLERY

Heraldic Items

Heraldic items for Army organizations reflect history, tradition, ideals, and accomplishments. Coats of arms, historic badges, and distinctive insignia have been so designed that each is distinctive to the organization for which approved. They serve as identifying devices, an inspiration, and an incentive for unity of purpose.

A coat of arms or a historic badge and a distinctive insignia are authorized for each regiment. The designs of these items are based on the lineages and battle honors of the organizations.

While the custom of bearing various symbols on shields, helmets, and flags existed in antiquity, heraldry was not introduced until the Middle Ages. The use of heraldic devices became more prevalent with the increased use of armor and the requirements for insignia to assist in distinguishing friend from foe on the battlefield. The symbols selected for use on these devices were commemorative of incidents of valor, mythological beasts, and, later, other symbols to which specific symbolism was ascribed. These heraldic bearings were placed on a surcoat worn over the armor, from which the term *coat of arms* was derived. Gradually a formal system of heraldry evolved, complete with rules for design, use, and display. These rules or principles were for the purpose of facilitating designs that would be distinctive and easily recognized. Present-day heraldic devices stem from this heraldic system which was established during the twelfth and thirteenth centuries.

A complete coat of arms consists of a shield, a crest, and a motto. The shield, the most important portion of the arms, contains the field or ground on which the charges are placed. The crest as originally used was placed upon the top of the helmet of the chief or leader to enable his followers to distinguish him during battle. The crest is placed upon a wreath of six skeins or twists composed of the principal metal and principal color of the shield, alternately, in the order named. This wreath (or torse) represents the piece of cloth which the knight twisted around the top of his helmet, and by means of which the actual crest was attached. Mottoes have been in use longer than coats of arms, many of the older ones having originated from war cries. They usually are of an idealistic nature and sometimes allude to a well-known event in the history of the organization.

Some organizations are authorized historic badges of a symbolic composition in lieu of coats of arms. These badges are not shield-shaped, but they include mottoes.

The elements of the coat of arms or the badge, as applicable, are embroidered on the organizational flag—the central element of which is the American eagle. The shield of the coat of arms is on the eagle's breast;

a scroll bearing the motto is held in his beak; and the crest is placed above his head. On flags of those organizations which have historic badges in lieu of coats of arms, the badge is placed above the eagle's head and the scroll bearing the motto is in his beak.

Distinctive insignia, manufactured in metal and enamel and worn on the uniform by all personnel of the regiment, usually are based on elements of the design of the coat of arms or historic badge. Thus the organizational flag (color) and the distinctive insignia include the same design elements.

Heraldic items today, as in the past, serve to distinguish specific organizations and their members.

1st Air Defense Artillery

2d Air Defense Artillery

3d Air Defense Artillery

4th Air Defense Artillery

VOLENS ET POTENS

5th Air Defense Artillery

6th Air Defense Artillery

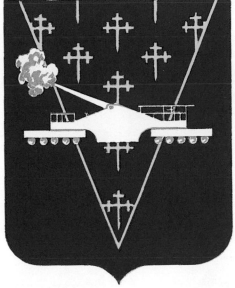

7th Air Defense Artillery

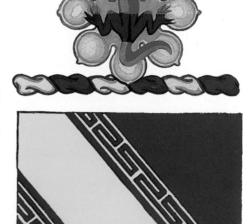

43d Air Defense Artillery

44th Air Defense Artillery

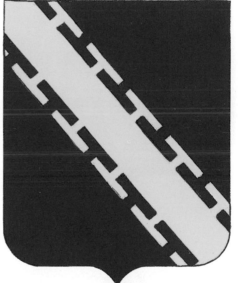

51st Air Defense Artillery

52d Air Defense Artillery

55th Air Defense Artillery

56th Air Defense Artillery

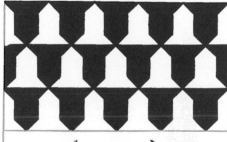

57th Air Defense Artillery

59th Air Defense Artillery

60th Air Defense Artillery

61st Air Defense Artillery

62d Air Defense Artillery

65th Air Defense Artillery

67th Air Defense Artillery

68th Air Defense Artillery

71st Air Defense Artillery

111th Air Defense Artillery

174th Air Defense Artillery

200th Air Defense Artillery

263d Air Defense Artillery

265th Air Defense Artillery

517th Air Defense Artillery

562d Air Defense Artillery

1st AIR DEFENSE ARTILLERY

HERALDIC ITEMS

COAT OF ARMS

Shield: Gules, two pallets argent, overall a cubit arm habited in the artillery uniform of 1861 erased holding aloft a burning torch or, between two of a snake vert, lipped and eyed of the third above and behind a prickly pear cactus all proper, fesswise.

Crest: On a wreath of the colors, argent and gules, a palmetto tree vert behind an arm embowed habited in the artillery uniform of 1861 issuing from the upper portion of an embattled tower and grasping a rammer staff fessways all or.

Motto: *Primus Inter Pares* (First Among Equals).

Symbolism: The shield is scarlet for artillery. With two white stripes, alluding to the campaign streamer of the War of 1812, the age of some of the units of the regiment is depicted. The snake and cactus, from the State Seal of Mexico, represent the Mexican War. The hand holding the torch of loyalty commemorates the defense of Fort Pickens, the only fort south of Fort Monroe that remained loyal to the federal government throughout the Civil War.

The arm and rammer staff rising out of a tower in front of a palmetto tree indicate participation in the Civil War at Fort Sumter. The palmetto tree is taken from the State Seal of South Carolina.

DISTINCTIVE INSIGNIA

The distinctive insignia is an adaptation of the crest and motto of the coat of arms.

LINEAGE AND HONORS

LINEAGE

Constituted 1 June 1821 in the Regular Army as the 1st Regiment of Artillery and organized from existing units with Headquarters at Fort Independence, Massachusetts. Regiment broken up 13 February 1901 and its elements reorganized and redesignated as separate numbered companies and batteries of Artillery Corps. Reconstituted 1 July 1924 in the Regular Army as the 1st Coast Artillery and partially organized with Headquarters at Fort de Lesseps, Canal Zone. (1st Battalion activated 1 June 1926 at Fort Randolph, Canal Zone; inactivated 31 July 1926 at Fort

Randolph, Canal Zone; 1st and 2d Battalions activated 15 April 1932 at
Forts Sherman and Randolph, Canal Zone, respectively; 3d Battalion
activated 15 March 1940 at Fort Randolph, Canal Zone; 1st and 2d
Battalions inactivated 30 March 1941 at Forts Randolph and Sherman,
Canal Zone, respectively; 1st and 2d Battalions activated 17 April 1942 at
Fort Sherman, Canal Zone.) Regiment broken up 1 November 1944 and
its elements reorganized and redesignated as follows: Headquarters and
Headquarters Battery as Headquarters and Headquarters Battery, 1st
Coast Artillery Group; remainder of regiment as the 1st Coast Artillery
Battalion.

Headquarters and Headquarters Battery, 1st Coast Artillery Group,
redesignated 2 January 1945 as Headquarters and Headquarters Battery,
Harbor Defenses of Cristobal. Inactivated 15 January 1947 at Fort Sherman, Canal Zone. Redesignated 21 June 1950 as Headquarters and Headquarters Battery, 1st Antiaircraft Artillery Group. Consolidated 18
November 1952 with Headquarters and Headquarters Battery, 1st Antiaircraft Artillery Group (*see* ANNEX), and consolidated unit designated as
Headquarters and Headquarters Battery, 1st Antiaircraft Artillery
Group. Activated 15 April 1953 in Germany. Inactivated 26 December
1957 in Germany.

1st Coast Artillery Battalion disbanded 1 February 1946 at Fort Sherman, Canal Zone. Reconstituted 21 June 1950 in the Regular Army and
redesignated as the 1st Coast Artillery, consisting of the 1st and 2d Battalions; 1st and 2d Battalions concurrently redesignated as the 1st and
54th Antiaircraft Battalions, respectively.

1st Antiaircraft Battalion redesignated 17 March 1955 as the 1st Antiaircraft Artillery Missile Battalion. Activated 15 April 1955 at Irwin,
Pennsylvania. Inactivated 1 September 1958 at Irwin, Pennsylvania.

54th Antiaircraft Battalion redesignated 15 December 1954 as the 54th
Antiaircraft Artillery Missile Battalion and activated at the U.S. Army
Chemical Center, Maryland. Inactivated 1 September 1958 at the U.S.
Army Chemical Center, Maryland.

Headquarters and Headquarters Battery, 1st Antiaircraft Artillery
Group; 1st and 54th Antiaircraft Artillery Missile Battalions; and 1st Field
Artillery Battalion (organized in 1907) consolidated, reorganized, and
redesignated 19 March 1959 as the 1st Artillery, a parent regiment under
the Combat Arms Regimental System.

1st Artillery (less former 1st Field Artillery Battalion) reorganized and
redesignated 1 September 1971 as the 1st Air Defense Artillery, a parent
regiment under the Combat Arms Regimental System (former 1st Field
Artillery Battalion concurrently reorganized and redesignated as the 1st
Field Artillery—hereafter separate lineage).

ANNEX

Constituted 5 August 1942 in the Army of the United States as Headquarters and Headquarters Battery, 1st Antiaircraft Artillery Automatic

Weapons Group. Activated 17 August 1942 at Fort Bliss, Texas. Redesignated 31 December 1943 as Headquarters and Headquarters Battery, 1st Antiaircraft Artillery Group. Disbanded 13 February 1945 in France. Reconstituted 18 November 1952 in the Regular Army.

CAMPAIGN PARTICIPATION CREDIT

War of 1812
  Canada

Indian Wars
  Seminoles
  Texas 1859

Mexican War
  Palo Alto
  Resaca de la Palma
  Monterey
  Vera Cruz
  Cerro Gordo
  Contreras
  Churubusco
  Chapultepec
  Tamaulipas 1846
  Vera Cruz 1847
  Mexico 1847

Civil War
  Sumter
  Bull Run
  Mississippi River
  Peninsula
  Manassas
  Antietam

  Fredericksburg
  Chancellorsville
  Gettysburg
  Wilderness
  Spotsylvania
  Cold Harbor
  Petersburg
  Shenandoah
  Appomattox
  Florida 1861
  Florida 1862
  Flordia 1864
  South Carolina 1862
  South Carolina 1863
  Virginia 1863
  Virginia 1864
  West Virginia 1863
  Louisiana 1864

World War II
  American Theater, Streamer without
    inscription
  Tunisia
  Sicily
  Rome-Arno
  Rhineland

DECORATIONS

  None.

1st BATTALION, 1st AIR DEFENSE ARTILLERY

RA
(nondivisional)

LINEAGE

Constituted 27 April 1798 in the Regular Army as a company in the 2d Regiment of Artillerists and Engineers. Organized in May 1798 as Capt. Lemuel Gates' Company, 2d Regiment of Artillerists and Engineers. Redesignated 3 March 1799 as Capt. Lemuel Gates' Company, 4th Battalion, 2d Regiment of Artillerists and Engineers. Redesignated 1 April 1802 as Capt. Lemuel Gates' Company, Regiment of Artillerists. Redesignated in 1807 as Capt. John Walbach's Company, Regiment of Artillerists. Redesignated 11 January 1812 as Capt. John Walbach's Company, 1st Regiment of Artillery. Redesignated 12 May 1814 as Bvt. Maj. John Walbach's Company, Corps of Artillery. Redesignated 17 May 1815 as Bvt. Maj. John Walbach's Company, Corps of Artillery, Northern Division. Redesignated 17 June 1816 as Company A, 2d Battalion, Corps of Artillery, Northern Division. Redesignated 1 June 1821 as Company I, 1st Regiment of Artillery.

Reorganized and redesignated 13 February 1901 as the 8th Company, Coast Artillery, Artillery Corps. Redesignated 2 February 1907 as the 8th Company, Coast Artillery Corps. Redesignated 1 July 1916 as the 9th Company, Fort Grant [Canal Zone]. Redesignated 31 August 1917 as the 9th Company, Coast Defenses of Balboa. Redesignated 30 June 1922 as the 8th Company, Coast Artillery Corps.

Redesignated 1 July 1924 as Battery A, 1st Coast Artillery, and inactivated in the Canal Zone. Activated 1 June 1926 at Fort Randolph, Canal Zone. Inactivated 31 July 1926 at Fort Randolph, Canal Zone. Activated 15 April 1932 at Fort Randolph, Canal Zone. Inactivated 30 March 1941 at Fort Randolph, Canal Zone. Activated 17 April 1942 at Fort Sherman, Canal Zone.

Reorganized and redesignated 1 November 1944 as Battery A, 1st Coast Artillery Battalion. Disbanded 1 February 1946 at Fort Sherman, Canal Zone. Reconstituted 21 June 1950 in the Regular Army as Battery A, 1st Coast Artillery; concurrently redesignated as Battery A, 1st Antiaircraft Battalion. Redesignated 17 March 1955 as Battery A, 1st Antiaircraft Artillery Missile Battalion. Activated 15 April 1955 at Irwin, Pennsylvania.

Inactivated 1 September 1958 at Irwin, Pennsylvania; concurrently consolidated with Headquarters and Headquarters Battery, 1st Howitzer Battalion, 1st Artillery (active) (organized in 1901), and consolidated unit designated as Headquarters and Headquarters Battery, 1st Howitzer Battalion, 1st Artillery (organic elements constituted and activated 15 May 1958). Redesignated 1 May 1966 as the 1st Battalion, 1st Artillery.

Redesignated (less former Headquarters and Headquarters Battery, 1st Howitzer Battalion, 1st Artillery) 1 September 1971 as the 1st Battalion, 1st Air Defense Artillery, and inactivated at West Point, New York (former Headquarters and Headquarters Battery, 1st Howitzer Battalion, 1st Artillery, concurrently reorganized and redesignated as the 1st Battalion, 1st Field Artillery—hereafter separate lineage). 1st Battalion, 1st Air Defense Artillery, activated 13 September 1972 in Germany.

CAMPAIGN PARTICIPATION CREDIT

War of 1812
   Canada

Indian Wars
   *Seminoles
   Texas 1859

Mexican War
   Palo Alto
   Resaca de la Palma
   Monterey
   *Vera Cruz
   *Cerro Gordo
   *Contreras
   *Churubusco
   *Molino del Rey
   *Chapultepec
   Tamaulipas 1846
   *Vera Cruz 1847
   Mexico 1847

Civil War
   Sumter
   *Bull Run
   Mississippi River
   *Peninsula
   Manassas
   *Antietam

   *Fredericksburg
   *Chancellorsville
   *Gettysburg
   *Wilderness
   *Spotsylvania
   *Cold Harbor
   *Petersburg
   Shenandoah
   *Appomattox
   Florida 1861
   Florida 1862
   Florida 1864
   *Virginia 1861
   *Virginia 1863
   Virginia 1864
   South Carolina 1862
   South Carolina 1863
   West Virginia 1863
   Louisiana 1864

World War II
   *American Theater, Streamer without
     inscription
   Tunisia
   Sicily
   Rome-Arno
   Rhineland

DECORATIONS

None.

2d BATTALION, 1st AIR DEFENSE ARTILLERY

RA
(nondivisional)

LINEAGE

Constituted 11 January 1812 in the Regular Army as a company in the 3d Regiment of Artillery. Organized in July 1812 as Capt. Ichabod B. Crane's Company, 3d Regiment of Artillery. Redesignated 12 May 1814 as Capt. Ichabod B. Crane's Company, Corps of Artillery. Redesignated 17 May 1815 as Capt. Ichabod B. Crane's Company, Corps of Artillery, Northern Division. Redesignated 17 June 1816 as Company B, 2d Battalion, Corps of Artillery, Northern Division. Redesignated 1 June 1821 as Company B, 1st Regiment of Artillery.

Reorganized and redesignated 13 February 1901 as the 2d Company, Coast Artillery, Artillery Corps. Redesignated 2 February 1907 as the 2d Company, Coast Artillery Corps. Redesignated 18 July 1916 as the 1st Company, Fort Ruger [Hawaii]. Redesignated 31 August 1917 as the 11th Company, Coast Defenses of Oahu. Redesignated in February 1921 as the 4th Company, Coast Defenses of Honolulu. Redesignated 30 June 1922 as the 2d Company, Coast Artillery Corps. Inactivated 1 July 1922 at Honolulu, Hawaii.

Redesignated 1 July 1924 as Battery B, 1st Coast Artillery. Activated 1 June 1926 at Fort Randolph, Canal Zone. Inactivated 31 July 1926 at Fort Randolph, Canal Zone. Activated 15 April 1932 at Fort Randolph, Canal Zone. Inactivated 30 March 1941 at Fort Sherman, Canal Zone. Activated 17 April 1942 at Fort Sherman, Canal Zone.

Reorganized and redesignated 1 November 1944 as Battery B, 1st Coast Artillery Battalion. Disbanded 1 February 1946 at Fort Sherman, Canal Zone. Reconstituted 21 June 1950 in the Regular Army as Battery B, 1st Coast Artillery; concurrently redesignated as Battery B, 1st Anti-aircraft Battalion. Redesignated 17 March 1955 as Battery B, 1st Anti-aircraft Artillery Missile Battalion. Activated 15 April 1955 at Irwin, Pennsylvania. Redesignated 26 October 1956 as Battery B, 74th Anti-aircraft Artillery Missile Battalion.

Inactivated 1 September 1958 at Pittsburgh, Pennsylvania; concurrently consolidated with Headquarters and Headquarters Battery, 2d Howitzer Battalion, 1st Artillery (active) (organized in 1901), and consolidated unit designated as Headquarters and Headquarters Battery, 2d Howitzer Battalion, 1st Artillery, an element of the 4th Infantry Division (organic elements constituted and activated 1 April 1957). Inactivated 1 October 1963 at Fort Lewis, Washington, and relieved from assignment to the 4th Infantry Division. Redesignated 14 July 1966 as the 2d Battalion, 1st Artillery. Activated 24 August 1966 at Fort Sill, Oklahoma.

Redesignated (less former Headquarters and Headquarters Battery, 2d Howitzer Battalion, 1st Artillery) 1 September 1971 as the 2d Battalion, 1st Air Defense Artillery, and inactivated at Fort Sill, Oklahoma (former

Headquarters and Headquarters Battery, 2d Howitzer Battalion, 1st Artillery, concurrently reorganized and redesignated as the 2d Battalion, 1st Field Artillery—hereafter separate lineage). 2d Battalion, 1st Air Defense Artillery, activated 13 September 1972 in Germany.

CAMPAIGN PARTICIPATION CREDIT

War of 1812
  *Canada

Indian Wars
  *Seminoles
   Texas 1859

Mexican War
  *Palo Alto
  *Resaca de la Palma
   Monterey
  *Vera Cruz
  *Cerro Gordo
  *Contreras
  *Churubusco
  *Chapultepec
  *Tamaulipas 1846
  *Vera Cruz 1847
  *Mexico 1847

Civil War
   Sumter
   Bull Run
   Mississippi River
   Peninsula
   Manassas
   Antietam

   Fredericksburg
   Chancellorsville
   Gettysburg
   Wilderness
   Spotsylvania
  *Cold Harbor
  *Petersburg
   Shenandoah
  *Appomattox
   Florida 1861
   Florida 1862
  *Florida 1864
  *South Carolina 1862
  *South Carolina 1863
   Virginia 1863
  *Virginia 1864
   West Virginia 1863
   Louisiana 1864

World War II
  *American Theater, Streamer without
     inscription
   Tunisia
   Sicily
   Rome-Arno
   Rhineland

DECORATIONS

None.

3d BATTALION, 1st AIR DEFENSE ARTILLERY

RA
(inactive)

LINEAGE

Organized in 1815 in the Regular Army at Plattsburgh Barracks, New York, as Capt. Francis Stribling's Company of Light Artillery (under the command of Lt. Nelson Freeland), Regiment of Light Artillery. Redesignated 1 May 1816 as Bvt. Maj. Alexander S. Brooks' Company of Light Artillery, Regiment of Light Artillery. Redesignated 22 May 1816 as Company C, Regiment of Light Artillery. Redesignated 1 June 1821 as Company C, 1st Regiment of Artillery.

Reorganized and redesignated 13 February 1901 as the 3d Company, Coast Artillery, Artillery Corps. Redesignated 2 February 1907 as the 3d Company, Coast Artillery Corps. Redesignated 1 July 1916 as the 2d Company, Fort Hamilton [New York]. Redesignated 31 August 1917 as the 2d Company, Coast Defenses of Southern New York.

Reorganized and redesignated 1 January 1918 as Battery C, 59th Artillery (Coast Artillery Corps). (Additionally designated 30 June 1922 as the 3d Company, Coast Artillery Corps; additional designation abolished 1 July 1924.) Inactivated 30 September 1922 at Fort Mills, Philippine Islands.

Redesignated 1 July 1924 as Battery C, 1st Coast Artillery. Activated 15 April 1932 at Fort Sherman, Canal Zone. Inactivated 30 March 1941 at Fort Sherman, Canal Zone. Activated 17 April 1942 at Fort Sherman, Canal Zone.

Reorganized and redesignated 1 November 1944 as Battery C, 1st Coast Artillery Battalion. Disbanded 1 February 1946 at Fort Sherman, Canal Zone. Reconstituted 21 June 1950 in the Regular Army as Battery C, 1st Coast Artillery; concurrently redesignated as Battery C, 1st Anti-aircraft Battalion. Redesignated 17 March 1955 as Battery C, 1st Anti-aircraft Artillery Missile Battalion. Activated 15 April 1955 at Irwin, Pennsylvania.

Consolidated 1 September 1958 with Battery C, 1st Field Artillery Battalion (organized in 1898), and consolidated unit reorganized and redesignated as Headquarters and Headquarters Battery, 3d Missile Battalion, 1st Artillery (organic elements constituted 12 August 1958 and activated 1 September 1958). Redesignated 20 December 1965 as the 3d Battalion, 1st Artillery.

Reorganized and redesignated (less former Battery C, 1st Field Artillery Battalion) 1 September 1971 as the 3d Battalion, 1st Air Defense Artillery (former Battery C, 1st Field Artillery Battalion concurrently redesignated as the 3d Battalion, 1st Field Artillery—hereafter separate lineage). 3d Battalion, 1st Air Defense Artillery, inactivated 30 August 1974 at Irwin, Pennsylvania.

CAMPAIGN PARTICIPATION CREDIT

War of 1812
Canada

Indian Wars
*Seminoles
*Texas 1859

Mexican War
Palo Alto
Resaca de la Palma
*Monterey
Vera Cruz
Cerro Gordo
Contreras
Churubusco
Chapultepec
Tamaulipas 1846
Vera Cruz 1847
Mexico 1847

Civil War
Sumter
Bull Run
Mississippi River
Manassas
Antietam
Fredericksburg
Chancellorsville
Gettysburg

Wilderness
Spotsylvania
Cold Harbor
*Petersburg
Shenandoah
Appomattox
Florida 1861
Florida 1862
Florida 1864
*North Carolina 1862
South Carolina 1862
*South Carolina 1863
Virginia 1863
Virginia 1864
West Virginia 1863
Louisiana 1864

World War I
*St. Mihiel
*Meuse-Argonne
*Lorraine 1918

World War II
*American Theater, Streamer without inscription
Tunisia
Sicily
Rome-Arno
Rhineland

DECORATIONS

None.

4th BATTALION, 1st AIR DEFENSE ARTILLERY

RA
(nondivisional)

LINEAGE

Organized in 1815 in the Regular Army at Fort Adams, Rhode Island, as Capt. John S. Peyton's Company of Light Artillery, Regiment of Light Artillery. Redesignated in March 1816 as Capt. John L. Eastman's Company of Light Artillery, Regiment of Light Artillery. Redesignated 22 May 1816 as Company G, Regiment of Light Artillery. Redesignated 1 June 1821 as Company D, 1st Regiment of Artillery.

Reorganized and redesignated 13 February 1901 as the 4th Company, Coast Artillery, Artillery Corps. Redesignated 2 February 1907 as the 4th Company, Coast Artillery Corps. Redesignated 5 August 1916 as the 13th Company, Fort Mills [Philippine Islands]. Redesignated 31 August 1917 as the 13th Company, Coast Defenses of Manila and Subic Bays. Redesignated 30 June 1922 as the 4th Company, Coast Artillery Corps.

Redesignated 1 July 1924 as Battery D, 1st Coast Artillery, and inactivated in the Philippine Islands. Activated 15 April 1932 at Fort Randolph, Canal Zone. Inactivated 30 March 1941 at Fort Randolph, Canal Zone.

Absorbed 1 November 1944 by the 1st Coast Artillery Battalion. (1st Coast Artillery [less Headquarters and Headquarters Battery] reorganized and redesignated 1 November 1944 as the 1st Coast Artillery Battalion; disbanded 1 February 1946 at Fort Sherman, Canal Zone.) Former Battery D, 1st Coast Artillery, reconstituted 21 June 1950 in the Regular Army and redesignated as Battery D, 1st Antiaircraft Battalion. Redesignated 17 March 1955 as Battery D, 1st Antiaircraft Artillery Missile Battalion. Activated 15 April 1955 at Irwin, Pennsylvania. Redesignated 26 October 1956 as Battery D, 74th Antiaircraft Artillery Missile Battalion.

Consolidated 1 September 1958 with Battery D, 1st Field Artillery (organized in 1792), and consolidated unit reorganized and redesignated as Headquarters and Headquarters Battery, 4th Missile Battalion, 1st Artillery (organic elements constituted 12 August 1958 and activated 1 September 1958). Redesignated 20 December 1965 as the 4th Battalion, 1st Artillery.

Reorganized and redesignated (less former Battery D, 1st Field Artillery) 1 September 1971 as the 4th Battalion, 1st Air Defense Artillery (former Battery D, 1st Field Artillery, concurrently redesignated as the 4th Battalion, 1st Field Artillery—hereafter separate lineage).

CAMPAIGN PARTICIPATION CREDIT

War of 1812
  Canada

Indian Wars
  *Seminoles
  Texas 1859

Mexican War
  *Palo Alto
  *Resaca de la Palma
  *Monterey
  Vera Cruz
  Cerro Gordo
  *Contreras
  *Churubusco
  *Chapultepec
  *Tamaulipas 1846
  *Vera Cruz 1847
  *Mexico 1847

Civil War
  Sumter
  Bull Run
  Mississippi River
  Peninsula
  Manassas
  Antietam

  Fredericksburg
  Chancellorsville
  Gettysburg
  *Wilderness
  Spotsylvania
  *Cold Harbor
  *Petersburg
  Shenandoah
  Appomattox
  Florida 1861
  Florida 1862
  Florida 1864
  *South Carolina 1862
  South Carolina 1863
  Virginia 1863
  *Virginia 1864
  West Virginia 1863
  Lousiana 1864

World War II
  *American Theater, Streamer without
    inscription
  Tunisia
  Sicily
  Rome-Arno
  Rhineland

DECORATIONS

None.

5th BATTALION, 1st AIR DEFENSE ARTILLERY

RA
(inactive)

LINEAGE

Constituted 3 March 1847 in the Regular Army as Company M, 1st Regiment of Artillery. Organized 1 October 1847.

Reorganized and redesignated 13 February 1901 as the 10th Company, Coast Artillery, Artillery Corps. Redesignated 2 February 1907 as the 10th Company, Coast Artillery Corps. Redesignated 18 July 1916 as the 1st Company, Fort DeRussy [Hawaii]. Redesignated 31 August 1917 as the 9th Company, Coast Defenses of Oahu. Redesignated 21 February 1921 as the 2d Company, Coast Defenses of Honolulu. Redesignated 30 June 1922 as the 10th Company, Coast Artillery Corps.

Reorganized and redesignated 1 July 1924 as Battery E, 1st Coast Artillery. Inactivated 30 March 1941 at Fort Sherman, Canal Zone. Activated 17 April 1942 at Fort Randolph, Canal Zone. Inactivated 20 August 1943 at Fort Randolph, Canal Zone.

Absorbed 1 November 1944 by the 1st Coast Artillery Battalion. (1st Coast Artillery [less Headquarters and Headquarters Battery] reorganized and redesignated 1 November 1944 as the 1st Coast Artillery Battalion; disbanded 1 February 1946 at Fort Sherman, Canal Zone.) Former Battery E, 1st Coast Artillery, reconstituted 21 June 1950 in the Regular Army and redesignated as Battery A, 54th Antiaircraft Battalion. Redesignated 15 December 1954 as Battery A, 54th Antiaircraft Artillery Missile Battalion, and activated at the U.S. Army Chemical Center, Maryland. Redesignated 1 August 1956 as Battery A, 602d Antiaircraft Artillery Missile Battalion.

Consolidated 1 September 1958 with Battery E, 1st Field Artillery (organized in 1812), and consolidated unit reorganized and redesignated as Headquarters and Headquarters Battery, 5th Missile Battalion, 1st Artillery (organic elements constituted 12 August 1958 and activated 1 September 1958). Redesignated 20 August 1965 as the 5th Battalion, 1st Artillery.

Reorganized and redesignated (less former Battery E, 1st Field Artillery) 1 September 1971 as the 5th Battalion, 1st Air Defense Artillery (former Battery E, 1st Field Artillery, concurrently redesignated as the 5th Battalion, 1st Field Artillery—hereafter separate lineage). 5th Battalion, 1st Air Defense Artillery, inactivated 13 September 1972 in Germany.

CAMPAIGN PARTICIPATION CREDIT

War of 1812
  Canada

Indian Wars
  Seminoles
  *Texas 1859

Mexican War
  Palo Alto
  Resaca de la Palma
  Monterey
  Cerro Gordo
  Contreras
  Churubusco
  Chapultepec
  Tamaulipas 1846
  Vera Cruz 1847
  Mexico 1847

Civil War
  Sumter
  Bull Run
  Mississippi River
  Peninsula
  Manassas
  Antietam
  Fredericksburg

  Chancellorsville
  Gettysburg
  Wilderness
  Spotsylvania
  *Cold Harbor
  *Petersburg
  Shenandoah
  *Appomattox
  Florida 1861
  Florida 1862
  *Florida 1864
  *South Carolina 1862
  South Carolina 1863
  Virginia 1863
  *Virginia 1864
  West Virginia 1863
  Louisiana 1864

World War II
  *American Theater, Streamer without
    inscription
  Tunisia
  Sicily
  Rome-Arno
  Rhineland

DECORATIONS

None.

6th BATTALION, 1st AIR DEFENSE ARTILLERY

RA
(inactive)

LINEAGE

Constituted 11 January 1812 in the Regular Army as a company in the 3d Regiment of Artillery. Organized in February 1812 as Capt. Robert G. Hite's Company, 3d Regiment of Artillery, at Governor's Island, New York. Redesignated 12 May 1814 as Capt. Robert G. Hite's Company, Corps of Artillery. Redesignated 17 May 1815 as Capt. Robert G. Hite's Company, Corps of Artillery, Northern Division. Redesignated 27 July 1815 as Bvt. Maj. James H. Boyle's Company, Corps of Artillery, Northern Division. Redesignated 12 March 1816 as Capt. Moses Swett's Company, Corps of Artillery, Northern Division. Redesignated 17 June 1816 as Company B, 4th Battalion, Corps of Artillery, Northern Division. Redesignated 1 June 1821 as Company F, 1st Regiment of Artillery.

Reorganized and redesignated 13 February 1901 as the 5th Company, Coast Artillery, Artillery Corps. Redesignated 2 February 1907 as the 5th Company, Coast Artillery Corps. Redesignated 1 July 1916 as the 2d Company, Fort Williams [Maine]. Redesignated 21 July 1917 as Battery H, 6th Provisional Regiment, Coast Artillery Corps. Redesignated 5 February 1918 as Battery H, 51st Artillery (Coast Artillery Corps). Redesignated 7 August 1918 as Battery F, 43d Artillery (Coast Artillery Corps). Inactivated 17 August 1921 at Camp Eustis, Virginia. (Additionally designated 1 June 1922 as the 5th Company, Coast Artillery Corps; additional designation abolished 1 July 1924.)

Redesignated 1 July 1924 as Battery F, 1st Coast Artillery. Activated 15 April 1932 at Fort Sherman, Canal Zone. Inactivated 30 March 1941 at Fort Sherman, Canal Zone. Activated 17 April 1942 at Fort Sherman, Canal Zone.

Absorbed 1 November 1944 by the 1st Coast Artillery Battalion. (1st Coast Artillery [less Headquarters and Headquarters Battery] reorganized and redesignated 1 November 1944 as the 1st Coast Artillery Battalion; disbanded 1 February 1946 at Fort Sherman, Canal Zone.) Former Battery F, 1st Coast Artillery, reconstituted 21 June 1950 in the Regular Army and redesignated as Battery B, 54th Antiaircraft Battalion. Redesignated 15 December 1954 as Battery B, 54th Antiaircraft Artillery Missile Battalion, and activated at the U.S. Army Chemical Center, Maryland. Inactivated 1 September 1958 at Cronhardt, Maryland.

Consolidated 17 March 1959 with Battery F, 1st Field Artillery (organized in 1861), and consolidated unit redesignated as Headquarters and Headquarters Battery, 6th Rocket Howitzer Battalion, 1st Artillery; concurrently withdrawn from the Regular Army, allotted to the Army Reserve, and assigned to the 79th Infantry Division (organic elements concurrently constituted). Battalion activated 6 April 1959 at Harrisburg, Pennsylvania. Inactivated 15 February 1963 at Harrisburg, Pennsylvania, and relieved from assignment to the 79th Infantry Division. Redesignated 24 November 1967 as the 6th Battalion, 1st Artillery; concurrently withdrawn from the Army Reserve, allotted to the Regular Army, assigned to the 6th Infantry Division, and activated at Fort Campbell, Kentucky. Inactivated 21 July 1969 at Fort Campbell, Kentucky, and relieved from assignment to the 6th Infantry Division.

Redesignated (less former Battery F, 1st Field Artillery) 1 September 1971 as the 6th Battalion, 1st Air Defense Artillery (former Battery F, 1st Field Artillery, concurrently redesignated as the 6th Battalion, 1st Field Artillery—hereafter separate lineage).

CAMPAIGN PARTICIPATION CREDIT

War of 1812
  *Canada

Indian Wars
  *Seminoles
  Texas 1859

Mexican War
  Palo Alto
  Resaca de la Palma
  Monterey
  *Vera Cruz
  *Cerro Gordo
  *Contreras
  *Churubusco
  *Chapultepec
  Tamaulipas 1846
  *Vera Cruz 1847
  *Mexico 1847

Civil War
  Sumter
  Bull Run
  *Mississippi River
  Peninsula
  Manassas
  Antietam
  Fredericksburg

Chancellorsville
Gettysburg
Wilderness
Spotsylvania
Cold Harbor
Petersburg
Shenandoah
Appomattox
*Florida 1861
*Florida 1862
Florida 1864
South Carolina 1862
South Carolina 1863
Virginia 1863
Virginia 1864
West Virginia 1863
*Louisiana 1864

World War I
  *St. Mihiel
  *Meuse-Argonne

World War II
  *American Theater, Streamer without inscription
  Tunisia
  Sicily
  Rome-Arno
  Rhineland

DECORATIONS

None.

7th BATTALION, 1st AIR DEFENSE ARTILLERY

AR
(inactive)

LINEAGE

Organized in 1814 in the Regular Army as Lt. Francis Stribling's Company of Light Artillery, Regiment of Light Artillery. Redesignated 30 June 1814 as Capt. Francis Stribling's Company of Light Artillery, Regiment of Light Artillery. Consolidated in June with Capt. Adam Larrabee's Company of Light Artillery, Regiment of Light Artillery (organized in 1814), and Capt. Thomas Ketcham's Company of Light Artillery, Regiment of Light Artillery (organized in 1814), and consolidated unit redesignated as Bvt. Lt. Col. Nathan Towson's Company of Light Artillery, Regiment of Light Artillery. Redesignated 22 May 1816 as Company D, Regiment of Light Artillery. Redesignated 1 June 1821 as Company H, 1st Regiment of Artillery.

Reorganized and redesignated 13 February 1901 as the 7th Company, Coast Artillery, Artillery Corps. Redesignated 2 February 1907 as the 7th Company, Coast Artillery Corps. Redesignated 30 June 1916 as the 2d Company, Fort Banks [Massachusetts]. Redesignated 21 July 1917 as Battery K, 6th Provisional Regiment, Coast Artillery Corps. Redesignated 7 March 1918 as the 6th Battery, Howitzer Regiment, 30th Brigade, Coast Artillery Corps. Redesignated 7 August 1918 as Battery D, 44th Artillery (Coast Artillery Corps). (Additionally designated 1 June 1922 as the 7th Company, Coast Artillery Corps; additional designation abolished 1 July 1924.)

Reorganized and redesignated 1 July 1924 as Headquarters Battery, 1st Coast Artillery.

Reorganized and redesignated 1 November 1944 as Headquarters Battery, 1st Coast Artillery Group. Redesignated 2 January 1945 as Headquarters Battery, Harbor Defenses of Cristobal. Inactivated 15 January 1947 at Fort Sherman, Canal Zone. Redesignated 21 June 1950 as Headquarters Battery, 1st Antiaircraft Group. Consolidated 18 November 1952 with Headquarters Battery, 1st Antiaircraft Artillery Group (*see* ANNEX), and consolidated unit designated as Headquarters Battery, 1st Antiaircraft Artillery Group. Activated 15 April 1953 in Germany. Inactivated 26 December 1957 in Germany.

Consolidated 19 March 1959 with Headquarters Battery, 1st Field Artillery Battalion (organized in 1916), and consolidated unit redesignated as Headquarters and Headquarters Battery, 7th Howitzer Battalion, 1st Artillery; concurrently withdrawn from the Regular Army, allotted to the Army Reserve, and assigned to the 83d Infantry Division (organic elements concurrently constituted). Battalion activated 20 March 1959 with Headquarters at Cleveland, Ohio. Redesignated 15 April 1963 as the 7th Battalion, 1st Artillery. Inactivated 31 December 1965 at Cleveland, Ohio, and relieved from assignment to the 83d Infantry Division.

Redesignated (less former Headquarters Battery, 1st Field Artillery Battalion) 1 September 1971 as the 7th Battalion, 1st Air Defense Artillery (former Headquarters Battery, 1st Field Artillery Battalion, concurrently redesignated as the 7th Battalion, 1st Field Artillery—hereafter separate lineage).

ANNEX

Constituted 5 August 1942 in the Army of the United States as Headquarters Battery, 1st Antiaircraft Artillery Automatic Weapons Group. Activated 17 August 1942 at Fort Bliss, Texas. Redesignated 31 December 1943 as Headquarters Battery, 1st Antiaircraft Artillery Group. Disbanded 13 February 1945 in France. Reconstituted 18 November 1952 in the Regular Army.

CAMPAIGN PARTICIPATION CREDIT

War of 1812
  *Canada

Indian Wars
  *Seminoles
  Texas 1859

Mexican War
  Palo Alto
  Resaca de la Palma
  Monterey
  *Vera Cruz
  *Cerro Gordo
  *Contreras
  *Churubusco
  *Chapultepec
  Tamaulipas 1846
  *Vera Cruz 1847
  *Mexico 1847

Civil War
  *Sumter
  Bull Run
  Mississippi River
  *Peninsula
  Manassas
  Antietam
  *Fredericksburg
  *Chancellorsville
  *Gettysburg

  *Wilderness
  *Spotsylvania
  *Cold Harbor
  *Petersburg
  Shenandoah
  Appomattox
  Florida 1861
  Florida 1862
  Florida 1864
  South Carolina 1862
  South Carolina 1863
  *Virginia 1863
  Virginia 1864
  West Virginia 1863
  Louisiana 1864

World War I
  *St. Mihiel
  *Alsace 1918
  *Lorraine 1918

World War II
  *American Theater, Streamer without
    inscription
  *Tunisia
  *Sicily
  *Rome-Arno
  *Rhineland

DECORATIONS

None.

8th BATTALION, 1st AIR DEFENSE ARTILLERY

RA
(inactive)

LINEAGE

Constituted 2 March 1899 in the Regular Army as Battery N, 1st Regiment of Artillery. Organized in April 1899 at St. Francis Barracks, Florida.

Reorganized and redesignated 13 February 1901 as the 11th Company, Coast Artillery, Artillery Corps. Redesignated 2 February 1907 as the 11th Company, Coast Artillery Corps. Redesignated 5 August 1916 as the 9th Company, Fort Mills [Philippine Islands]. Redesignated 31 August 1917 as the 9th Company, Coast Defenses of Manila and Subic Bays. Redesignated 30 June 1922 as the 11th Company, Coast Artillery Corps.

Reorganized and redesignated 1 July 1924 as Battery G, 1st Coast Artillery. Inactivated 31 May 1926 at Fort Randolph, Canal Zone. Activated 1 November 1938 at Fort Sherman, Canal Zone.

Absorbed 1 November 1944 by the 1st Coast Artillery Battalion. (1st Coast Artillery [less Headquarters and Headquarters Battery] reorganized and redesignated 1 November 1944 as the 1st Coast Artillery Battalion; disbanded 1 February 1946 at Fort Sherman, Canal Zone.) Former Battery G, 1st Coast Artillery, reconstituted 21 June 1950 in the Regular Army and redesignated as Battery C, 54th Antiaircraft Battalion. Redesignated 15 December 1954 as Battery C, 54th Antiaircraft Artillery Missile Battalion, and activated at the U.S. Army Chemical Center, Maryland. Inactivated 1 September 1958 at Edgewood Arsenal, Maryland.

Consolidated 9 September 1960 with Battery G, 1st Field Artillery (organized in 1939), and consolidated unit redesignated as Headquarters and Headquarters Battery, 8th Missile Battalion, 1st Artillery (organic elements concurrently constituted). Battalion activated 24 September 1960 at Fort Bliss, Texas. Redesignated 30 June 1968 as the 8th Battalion, 1st Artillery.

Reorganized and redesignated (less former Battery G, 1st Field Artillery) 1 September 1971 as the 8th Battalion, 1st Air Defense Artillery (former Battery G, 1st Field Artillery, concurrently redesignated as the 8th Battalion, 1st Field Artillery—hereafter separate lineage). 8th Battalion, 1st Air Defense Artillery, inactivated 12 June 1973 at Oakland Army Air Base, California.

Campaign Participation Credit

War of 1812
Canada

Indian Wars
Seminoles
Texas 1859

Mexican War
Palo Alto
Resaca de la Palma
Monterey
Vera Cruz
Cerro Gordo
Contreras
Churubusco
Chapultepec
Tamaulipas 1846
Vera Cruz 1847
Mexico 1847

Civil War
Sumter
Bull Run
Mississippi River
Peninsula
Manassas
Antietam

Fredericksburg
Chancellorsville
Gettysburg
Wilderness
Spotsylvania
Cold Harbor
Petersburg
Shenandoah
Appomattox
Florida 1861
Florida 1862
Florida 1864
South Carolina 1862
South Carolina 1863
Virginia 1863
Virginia 1864
West Virginia 1863
Louisiana 1864

World War II
*American Theater, Streamer without
inscription
Tunisia
Sicily
Rome-Arno
Rhineland

Decorations

None.

9th BATTALION, 1st AIR DEFENSE ARTILLERY

RA
(inactive)

LINEAGE

Constituted 1 July 1924 in the Regular Army as Headquarters, 1st Battalion, 1st Coast Artillery. Activated 1 June 1926 at Fort Randolph, Canal Zone. Inactivated 31 July 1926 at Fort Randolph, Canal Zone. Activated 15 April 1932 at Fort Randolph, Canal Zone. (Headquarters Battery, 1st Battalion, 1st Coast Artillery, constituted 21 January 1935 in the Regular Army and activated at Fort Randolph, Canal Zone.) Headquarters and Headquarters Battery, 1st Battalion, 1st Coast Artillery, inactivated 30 March 1941 at Fort Sherman, Canal Zone. Activated 17 April 1942 at Fort Sherman, Canal Zone.

Consolidated 1 November 1944 with Headquarters and Headquarters Battery, 2d Battalion, 1st Coast Artillery (organized in 1932), and consolidated unit reorganized and redesignated as Headquarters and Headquarters Battery, 1st Coast Artillery Battalion. Disbanded 1 February 1946 at Fort Sherman, Canal Zone. Former Headquarters and Headquarters Battery, 1st Battalion, 1st Coast Artillery, reconstituted 21 June 1950 in the Regular Army and redesignated as Headquarters and Headquarters Battery, 1st Antiaircraft Battalion (former Headquarters and Headquarters Battery, 2d Battalion, 1st Coast Artillery, concurrently reconstituted in the Regular Army and redesignated as Headquarters and Headquarters Battery, 54th Antiaircraft Battalion—hereafter separate lineage). Redesignated 17 March 1955 as Headquarters and Headquarters Battery, 1st Antiaircraft Artillery Missile Battalion. Activated 15 April 1955 at Irwin, Pennsylvania. Inactivated 1 September 1958 at Irwin, Pennsylvania.

Consolidated 14 June 1961 with Headquarters and Headquarters Battery, 1st Battalion, 1st Field Artillery (organized in 1907), and consolidated unit redesignated as Headquarters and Headquarters Battery, 9th Howitzer Battalion, 1st Artillery (organic elements concurrently constituted). Battalion assigned 1 July 1961 to the 25th Infantry Division and activated in Hawaii. Relieved 17 July 1963 from assignment to the 25th Infantry Division. Inactivated 5 August 1963 in Hawaii. Redesignated 10 May 1967 as the 9th Battalion, 1st Artillery. Activated 25 August 1967 at Fort Carson, Colorado. Inactivated 26 August 1968 at Fort Carson, Colorado.

Redesignated (less former Headquarters and Headquarters Battery, 1st Battalion, 1st Field Artillery) 1 September 1971 as the 9th Battalion, 1st Air Defense Artillery (former Headquarters and Headquarters Battery, 1st Battalion, 1st Field Artillery, concurrently redesignated as the 9th Battalion, 1st Field Artillery—hereafter separate lineage).

Campaign Participation Credit

War of 1812
  Canada

Indian Wars
  Seminoles
  Texas 1859

Mexican War
  Palo Alto
  Resaca de la Palma
  Monterey
  Vera Cruz
  Cerro Gordo
  Contreras
  Churubusco
  Chapultepec
  Tamaulipas 1846
  Vera Cruz 1847
  Mexico 1847

Civil War
  Sumter
  Bull Run
  Mississippi River
  Peninsula
  Manassas
  Antietam

Fredericksburg
Chancellorsville
Gettysburg
Wilderness
Spotsylvania
Cold Harbor
Petersburg
Shenandoah
Appomattox
Florida 1861
Florida 1862
Florida 1864
South Carolina 1862
South Carolina 1863
Virginia 1863
Virginia 1864
West Virginia 1863
Louisiana 1864

World War II
  *American Theater, Streamer without
    inscription
  Tunisia
  Sicily
  Rome-Arno
  Rhineland

Decorations

None.

16th DETACHMENT, 1st AIR DEFENSE ARTILLERY

RA
(inactive)

LINEAGE

Constituted 1 July 1924 in the Regular Army as Headquarters, 3d Battalion, 1st Coast Artillery. (Headquarters Battery, 3d Battalion, 1st Coast Artillery, constituted 21 January 1935 in the Regular Army.) Headquarters and Headquarters Battery, 3d Battalion, 1st Coast Artillery, activated 15 March 1940 at Fort Randolph, Canal Zone. Disbanded 1 November 1944 at Fort Randolph, Canal Zone.

Reconstituted 12 August 1958 in the Regular Army and redesignated as the 16th Detachment, 1st Artillery. Activated 1 September 1958 in Germany. Inactivated 20 July 1960 in Germany. Redesignated 1 September 1971 as the 16th Detachment, 1st Air Defense Artillery.

CAMPAIGN PARTICIPATION CREDIT

None.

DECORATIONS

None.

1ST AIR DEFENSE ARTILLERY BIBLIOGRAPHY

Babcock, D.S. "History of Battery 'D,' 1st Field Artillery—1792–1934." *Field Artillery Journal* 24 (September 1934):483–504. Pertains to the former Battery E, 1st Regiment of Artillery.

Blossy, Henry J. "The Climb Toward Perfection." *Field Artillery Journal* 38 (September–October 1948):227–30. Contains information about Headquarters and Headquarters Battery, 1st Antiaircraft Artillery Group.

Dyer, Frederick. "1st Regiment of Artillery." *A Compendium of the War of the Rebellion.* New York: Thomas Yoseloff, 1959.

Finley, Charles R. "The Coast Artillery in Panama." *Coast Artillery Journal* 83 (1940):522–27.

Haskin, William Lawrence. "The First Regiment of Artillery, 1821–1876." *The Army of the United States.* Edited by Theophilus F. Rodenbough and William L. Haskin, 301–11. New York: Maynard, Merrill and Company, 1896. Originally published in *Journal of the Military Service Institution of the United States* 15 (1894):1321–31.

_____. *The History of the First Regiment of Artillery; From Organization in 1821 to January 1st, 1876.* Portland, Maine: B. Thurston and Company, 1879.

History of the 4th Infantry Division and Brief Histories of Its Components. Fort Lewis, Washington, 1958. Contains information about the current 2d Battalion, 1st Air Defense Artillery.

History of Organization, 1784–1926. San Antonio, Tex., 1926.

Reed, Louis. *Illustrated Review of the United States Army in Oahu, T.H.* Honolulu: Hawaiian Gazette Company, 1911.

Sprague, John T. *The Origin, Progress, and Conclusion of the Florida War.* New York: D. Appleton and Company, 1848. Reprint. Gainesville, Fla.: University of Florida Press, 1964.

Wilson, William H., John B. McClure, and John McLaren. *A History of the Sixth Company, Coast Artillery, Late Battery "G," First United States Artillery, 1808–1906*. Hampton: Houston Printing and Publishing Company, 1906.

2d AIR DEFENSE ARTILLERY

HERALDIC ITEMS

COAT OF ARMS

Shield: Paly of fifteen, gules and argent, two Indian arrows saltire-wise or, behind a serpent vert, lipped and eyed of the third, coiled around and above a prickly pear cactus proper.

Crest: On a wreath of the colors, argent and gules, an eagle close or sitting on and at the intersection of a saltire azure fimbriated argent.

Motto: *Fidus Ultra Finem* (Faithful Beyond the End).

Symbolism: The shield is scarlet for artillery. The fifteen stripes, representative of the United States national flag of 1814, allude to the battle of Fort McHenry in which a company of the regiment participated. The snake and cactus commemorate service in the Mexican War. The arrows refer to the Indian Wars.

The American eagle, centered on the saltire from the battle flag of the Confederacy, depicts the defense of Fort Pickens, the only fort south of Fort Monroe that remained loyal to the federal government throughout the Civil War.

DISTINCTIVE INSIGNIA

The distinctive insignia is an adaptation of the crest and motto of the coat of arms.

LINEAGE AND HONORS

LINEAGE

Constituted 1 June 1821 in the Regular Army as the 2d Regiment of Artillery and organized from existing units with Headquarters at Baltimore, Maryland. Regiment broken up 13 February 1901 and its elements reorganized and redesignated as separate numbered companies and batteries of Artillery Corps. Reconstituted 1 July 1924 in the Regular Army as the 2d Coast Artillery (Batteries E, G, and H active in the Canal Zone). (Battery C activated 30 April 1926 at Fort Sherman, Canal Zone; Battery G concurrently inactivated at Fort Sherman, Canal Zone; Batteries C, E, and H inactivated 15 April 1932 at Fort Sherman, Canal Zone.) Regimental headquarters and Batteries C, E, and H activated 30 April 1932 at Fort Monroe, Virginia. (Battery A activated 1 September 1935 at Fort Monroe, Virginia; Battery H concurrently inactivated at Fort Monroe, Virginia; Batteries B and D activated 1 November 1938 at Fort Monroe, Virginia; Battery F activated 1 February 1940 at Fort Monroe, Virginia; remainder of 1st and 2d Battalions activated 1 August 1940 at Fort Monroe, Virginia; Battery G activated 1 March 1941 at Fort Monroe, Virginia; remainder of regiment activated 30 April 1942 at Fort Monroe, Virginia.)

Regiment broken up 1 October 1944 and its elements reorganized and redesignated as follows: Headquarters and Headquarters Battery and Batteries A, B, C, G, H, and I as the 2d Coast Artillery Battalion; Batteries D, E, and F as elements of the 175th Coast Artillery Battalion (inactivated 20 July 1946 at Fort Monroe, Virginia). 2d Coast Artillery Battalion inactivated 1 April 1945 at Fort Monroe, Virginia. Activated 1 August 1946 at Fort Winfield Scott, California. Inactivated 25 November 1946 at Fort Winfield Scott, California.

Headquarters and Headquarters Detachment, 2d Coast Artillery Battalion, consolidated 28 June 1950 with Headquarters and Headquarters Battery, 2d Antiaircraft Artillery Group (*see* ANNEX 1), and consolidated unit designated as Headquarters and Headquarters Battery, 2d Antiaircraft Artillery Group. Activated 10 June 1951 at Camp Edwards, Massachusetts. Reorganized and redesignated 20 March 1958 as Headquarters and Headquarters Battery, 2d Artillery Group. Inactivated 15 December 1961 at Lockport Air Force Station, New York.

Headquarters and Headquarters Battery, 1st Battalion, 2d Coast Artillery, reconstituted 28 June 1950 in the Regular Army and redesignated as Headquarters and Headquarters Battery, 2d Antiaircraft Artillery Battalion; concurrently Battery A, Harbor Defenses of Chesapeake Bay (formerly Battery A, 2d Coast Artillery Battalion), Batteries B and C, 2d Coast Artillery Battalion, and Battery F, 2d Harbor Defenses of Chesapeake Bay (formerly Battery A, 175th Coast Artillery Battalion), redesignated as Batteries A, B, C, and D, 2d Antiaircraft Artillery Battalion, respectively. 2d Antiaircraft Artillery Battalion redesignated 27 February 1951 as the 2d Antiaircraft Artillery Automatic Weapons Battalion and assigned to the 1st Armored Division. Activated 7 March 1951 at Fort Bliss, Texas. Consolidated 20 March 1951 with the 434th Antiaircraft Artillery Automatic Weapons Battalion (*see* ANNEX 2), and consolidated unit designated as the 2d Antiaircraft Artillery Automatic Weapons Battalion. Redesignated 20 May 1953 as the 2d Antiaircraft Artillery Battalion. Inactivated 15 February 1957 at Fort Polk, Louisiana, and relieved from assignment to the 1st Armored Division.

Headquarters and Headquarters Battery, 2d Battalion, 2d Coast Artillery, reconstituted 28 June 1950 in the Regular Army and redesignated as Headquarters and Headquarters Battery, 12th Antiaircraft Artillery Battalion; concurrently Batteries B, C, D, and E, Harbor Defenses of Chesapeake Bay (formerly Batteries E, F, G, and H, 2d Coast Artillery), redesignated as Batteries A, B, C, and D, 12th Antiaircraft Artillery Battalion, respectively; battalion concurrently consolidated with the 136th Antiaircraft Artillery Gun Battalion (*see* ANNEX 3), and consolidated unit designated as the 12th Antiaircraft Artillery Battalion. Redesignated 13 March 1952 as the 12th Antiaircraft Artillery Gun Battalion. Activated

8 April 1952 at Fort Hancock, New Jersey. Redesignated 15 May 1953 as the 12th Antiaircraft Artillery Battalion. Inactivated 20 December 1957 at New York, New York.

Headquarters and Headquarters Battery, 3d Battalion, 2d Coast Artillery, reconstituted 28 June 1950 in the Regular Army; concurrently consolidated with Battery F, 2d Coast Artillery Battalion, Battery E, 175th Coast Artillery Battalion, and the 42d Antiaircraft Artillery Automatic Weapons Battalion (active) (*see* ANNEX 4), and consolidated unit designated as the 42d Antiaircraft Artillery Automatic Weapons Battalion, an element of the 9th Infantry Division. Redesignated 25 May 1954 as the 42d Antiaircraft Artillery Battalion. Inactivated 1 December 1957 at Fort Carson, Colorado, and relieved from assignment to the 9th Infantry Division.

Headquarters and Headquarters Battery, 2d Artillery Group; 2d, 12th, and 42d Antiaircraft Artillery Battalions; and 2d Field Artillery Battalion (organized in 1907) consolidated, reorganized, and redesignated 15 December 1961 as the 2d Artillery, a parent regiment under the Combat Arms Regimental System.

2d Artillery (less former 2d Field Artillery Battalion) reorganized and redesignated as the 2d Air Defense Artillery, a parent regiment under the Combat Arms Regimental System (former 2d Field Artillery Battalion concurrently reorganized and redesignated as the 2d Field Artillery—hereafter separate lineage).

ANNEX 1

Constituted 5 August 1942 in the Army of the United States as Headquarters and Headquarters Battery, 2d Antiaircraft Artillery Automatic Weapons Group. Activated 17 August 1942 at Fort Bliss, Texas. Redesignated 26 May 1943 as Headquarters and Headquarters Battery, 2d Antiaircraft Artillery Group. Inactivated 26 October 1945 at Camp Kilmer, New Jersey.

ANNEX 2

Constituted 31 January 1942 in the Army of the United States as the 434th Coast Artillery Battalion. Activated 1 March 1942 at Camp Hulen, Texas. Redesignated 5 December 1943 as the 434th Antiaircraft Artillery Automatic Weapons Battalion. Disbanded 14 January 1945 in Italy. Reconstituted 20 March 1951 in the Regular Army.

ANNEX 3

Constituted 25 February 1943 in the Army of the United States as the 136th Antiaircraft Artillery Gun Battalion. Activated 15 June 1943 at Camp Edwards, Massachusetts. Inactivated 12 December 1945 at Camp Myles Standish, Massachusetts.

ANNEX 4

Constituted 25 February 1943 in the Army of the United States as the

795th Coast Artillery Battalion. Activated 20 April 1943 at Camp Stewart, Georgia. Redesignated 30 April 1943 as the 795th Antiaircraft Artillery Automatic Weapons Battalion. Inactivated 31 December 1945 in Germany. Redesignated 25 June 1948 as the 42d Antiaircraft Artillery Automatic Weapons Battalion and assigned to the 9th Infantry Division. Activated 12 July 1948 at Fort Dix, New Jersey.

CAMPAIGN PARTICIPATION CREDIT

War of 1812
  Canada

Indian Wars
  Seminoles

Mexican War
  Palo Alto
  Resaca de la Palma
  Monterey
  Vera Cruz
  Cerro Gordo
  Contreras
  Churubusco
  Molino del Rey
  Chapultepec
  Tamaulipas 1846
  Puebla 1847

Civil War
  Bull Run
  Peninsula
  Antietam
  Fredericksburg
  Chancellorsville
  Gettysburg
  Wilderness
  Spotsylvania
  Cold Harbor
  Petersburg
  Shenandoah
  Appomattox
  Florida 1861

  Florida 1862
  Virginia 1861
  Virginia 1862
  Virginia 1863
  Virginia 1865
  Maryland 1863

World War II
  Tunisia
  Naples-Foggia
  Anzio
  Rome-Arno
  Normandy
  Northern France
  North Apennines
  Rhineland
  Ardennes-Alsace
  Central Europe
  England 1944

Vietnam
  Counteroffensive, Phase II
  Counteroffensive, Phase III
  Tet Counteroffensive
  Counteroffensive, Phase IV
  Counteroffensive, Phase V
  Counteroffensive, Phase VI
  Tet 69/Counteroffensive
  Summer–fall 1969
  Winter–spring 1970
  Sanctuary Counteroffensive
  Counteroffensive, Phase VII

DECORATIONS

Meritorious Unit Commendation, Streamer embroidered VIETNAM 1967–1968 (5th Battalion, 2d Artillery, cited; DA GO 70, 1969)

Air Force Outstanding Unit Award, Streamer embroidered KOREA 1978–1981 (1st Battalion, 2d Air Defense Artillery, cited; DA GO 8, 1982)

1st BATTALION, 2d AIR DEFENSE ARTILLERY

RA
(inactive)

LINEAGE

Constituted 27 April 1798 in the Regular Army as a company in the 2d Regiment of Artillerists and Engineers. Organized in June 1798 in Rhode Island as Capt. John Henry's Company, 2d Regiment of Artillerists and Engineers. Redesignated 3 March 1799 as Capt. John Henry's Company, 4th Battalion, 2d Regiment of Artillerists and Engineers. Redesignated in August 1800 as Capt. William Steele's Company, 4th Battalion, 2d Regiment of Artillerists and Engineers. (Captain Steele joined company in January 1801.) Consolidated 1 April 1802 with Capt. Lloyd Beall's Company, 3d Battalion, 2d Regiment of Artillerists and Engineers (constituted 27 April 1798 in the Regular Army and organized in 1799 at Georgetown, District of Columbia), and consolidated unit redesignated as Capt. Lloyd Beall's Company, Regiment of Artillerists. Redesignated in July 1810 as Capt. James House's Company, Regiment of Artillerists. Redesignated 11 January 1812 as Capt. James House's Company, 1st Regiment of Artillery. Redesignated 16 August 1813 as Capt. Julius F. Heileman's Company, 1st Regiment of Artillery. Redesignated 12 May 1814 as Capt. Julius F. Heileman's Company, Corps of Artillery. Redesignated 17 May 1815 as Capt. Julius F. Heileman's Company, Corps of Artillery, Northern Division. Redesignated 17 June 1816 as Company L, 1st Battalion, Corps of Artillery, Northern Division. Redesignated 1 June 1821 as Company D, 2d Regiment of Artillery.

Reorganized and redesignated 13 February 1901 as the 15th Company, Coast Artillery, Artillery Corps. Redesignated 2 February 1907 as the 15th Company, Coast Artillery Corps. Redesignated in July 1916 as the 3d Company, Fort Randolph [Canal Zone]. Redesignated 31 August 1917 as the 9th Company, Coast Defenses of Cristobal. Redesignated 30 June 1922 as the 15th Company, Coast Artillery Corps.

Redesignated 1 July 1924 as Battery D, 2d Coast Artillery, and inactivated at Cristobal, Canal Zone. Activated 1 November 1938 at Fort Monroe, Virginia.

Reorganized and redesignated 1 October 1944 as Battery A, 175th Coast Artillery Battalion. Redesignated 1 April 1945 as Battery F, Harbor Defenses of Chesapeake Bay. Inactivated 20 July 1946 at Fort Monroe, Virginia. Redesignated 28 June 1950 as Battery D, 2d Antiaircraft Artillery Battalion. Redesignated 27 February 1951 as Battery D, 2d Antiaircraft Artillery Automatic Weapons Battalion, an element of the 1st Armored Division. Activated 7 March 1951 at Fort Bliss, Texas. Consolidated 20 March 1951 with Battery D, 434th Antiaircraft Artillery Automatic Weapons Battalion (see ANNEX), and consolidated unit designated as Battery D, 2d Antiaircraft Artillery Automatic Weapons Battalion. Redesignated 20 May 1953 as Battery D, 2d Antiaircraft Artillery Battalion. Inactivated 15 February 1957 at Fort Polk, Louisiana, and relieved from assignment to the 1st Armored Division.

Consolidated 15 December 1961 with Headquarters and Headquarters Battery, 1st Howitzer Battalion, 2d Artillery (active) (organized in 1907), and consolidated unit designated as Headquarters and Headquarters Battery, 1st Howitzer Battalion, 2d Artillery, an element of the 8th Infantry Division (organic elements constituted and activated 1 August 1957). Redesignated 1 April 1963 as the 1st Battalion, 2d Artillery.

Redesignated (less former Headquarters and Headquarters Battery, 1st Howitzer Battalion, 2d Artillery) 1 September 1971 as the 1st Battalion, 2d Air Defense Artillery; concurrently inactivated in Germany and relieved from assignment to the 8th Infantry Division (former Headquarters and Headquarters Battery, 1st Howitzer Battalion, 2d Artillery, concurrently reorganized and redesignated as the 1st Battalion, 2d Field Artillery—hereafter separate lineage). 1st Battalion, 2d Air Defense Artillery, activated 13 September 1972 in Korea. Inactivated 15 July 1981 in Korea.

ANNEX

Constituted 31 January 1942 in the Army of the United States as Battery D, 434th Coast Artillery Battalion. Activated 1 March 1942 at Camp Hulen, Texas. Redesignated 5 December 1943 as Battery D, 434th Antiaircraft Artillery Automatic Weapons Battalion. Disbanded 14 January 1945 in Italy. Reconstituted 20 March 1951 in the Regular Army.

CAMPAIGN PARTICIPATION CREDIT

War of 1812
  Canada

Indian Wars
  *Seminoles
  *New Mexico 1855

Mexican War
  Palo Alto
  Resaca de la Palma
  Monterey
  *Vera Cruz
  *Cerro Gordo
  *Contreras
  *Churubusco
  *Molino del Rey
  *Chapultepec
  Tamaulipas 1846
  *Puebla 1847

Civil War
  *Bull Run
  *Peninsula
  *Antietam
  *Fredericksburg
  *Chancellorsville
  *Gettysburg

*Wilderness
*Spotsylvania
*Cold Harbor
*Petersburg
*Shenandoah
Appomattox
Florida 1861
Florida 1862
Virginia 1861
Virginia 1862
*Virginia 1863
Virginia 1865
*Maryland 1863

World War II
  *Tunisia
  *Naples-Foggia
  Anzio
  *Rome-Arno
  Normandy
  Northern France
  *North Apennines
  Rhineland
  Ardennes-Alsace
  Central Europe
  England 1944

DECORATIONS

    *Air Force Outstanding Unit Award, Streamer embroidered KOREA 1978-1981 (1st Battalion, 2d Air Defense Artillery, cited; DA GO 8, 1982)

2d BATTALION, 2d AIR DEFENSE ARTILLERY

RA
(nondivisional)

LINEAGE

Constituted 11 January 1812 in the Regular Army as a company in the 2d Regiment of Artillery. Organized in March 1812 as Bvt. Lt. Col. Nathan Towson's Company, 2d Regiment of Artillery. Redesignated 12 May 1814 as Bvt. Lt. Col. Nathan Towson's Company, Corps of Artillery. Redesignated 17 May 1815 as Bvt. Lt. Col. Nathan Towson's Company, Corps of Artillery, Northern Division. Redesignated in June 1815 as Capt. William Gates' Company, Corps of Artillery, Northern Division. Redesignated 17 June 1816 as Company I, 1st Battalion, Corps of Artillery, Northern Division. Redesignated 1 June 1821 as Company B, 2d Regiment of Artillery.

Reorganized and redesignated 13 February 1901 as the 13th Company, Coast Artillery, Artillery Corps. Redesignated 2 February 1907 as the 13th Company, Coast Artillery Corps. Redesignated 20 July 1916 as the 1st Company, Fort Miley [California]. Redesignated 31 August 1917 as the 18th Company, Coast Defenses of San Francisco. Redesignated 16 September 1918 as Battery E, 40th Artillery (Coast Artillery Corps). Redesignated 30 December 1918 as the 18th Company, Coast Defenses of San Francisco. Redesignated 1 June 1922 as the 13th Company, Coast Artillery Corps.

Redesignated 1 July 1924 as Battery B, 2d Coast Artillery, and inactivated at San Francisco, California. Activated 1 November 1938 at Fort Monroe, Virginia.

Reorganized and redesignated 1 October 1944 as Battery B, 2d Coast Artillery Battalion. Inactivated 1 July 1945 at Fort Monroe, Virginia. Activated 1 August 1946 at Fort Winfield Scott, California. Inactivated 25 November 1946 at Fort Winfield Scott, California. Redesignated 28 June 1950 as Battery B, 2d Antiaircraft Artillery Battalion. Redesignated 27 February 1951 as Battery B, 2d Antiaircraft Artillery Automatic Weapons Battalion, an element of the 1st Armored Division. Activated 7 March 1951 at Fort Bliss, Texas. Consolidated 20 March 1951 with Battery B, 434th Antiaircraft Artillery Automatic Weapons Battalion (*see* ANNEX), and consolidated unit designated as Battery B, 2d Antiaircraft Artillery Automatic Weapons Battalion. Redesignated 20 May 1953 as Battery B, 2d Antiaircraft Artillery Battalion. Inactivated 15 February 1957 at Fort Polk, Louisiana, and relieved from assignment to the 1st Armored Division.

Consolidated 15 December 1961 with Headquarters and Headquarters Battery, 2d Howitzer Battalion, 2d Artillery (active) (organized in 1901), and consolidated unit designated as Headquarters and Headquarters Battery, 2d Howitzer Battalion, 2d Artillery (organic elements constituted 2 June 1958 and activated 25 June 1958). Redesignated 15 March 1968 as the 2d Battalion, 2d Artillery.

Redesignated (less former Headquarters and Headquarters Battery, 2d Howitzer Battalion, 2d Artillery) 1 September 1971 as the 2d Battalion, 2d Air Defense Artillery, and inactivated at Fort Sill, Oklahoma (former Headquarters and Headquarters Battery, 2d Howitzer Battalion, 2d Artillery, concurrently reorganized and redesignated as the 2d Battalion, 2d Field Artillery—hereafter separate lineage). 2d Battalion, 2d Air Defense Artillery, activated 13 September 1972 in Germany.

ANNEX

Constituted 31 January 1942 in the Army of the United States as Battery B, 434th Coast Artillery Battalion. Activated 1 March 1942 at Camp Hulen, Texas. Redesignated 5 December 1943 as Battery B, 434th Antiaircraft Artillery Automatic Weapons Battalion. Disbanded 14 January 1945 in Italy. Reconstituted 20 March 1951 in the Regular Army.

CAMPAIGN PARTICIPATION CREDIT

War of 1812
    *Canada
    *Chippewa
    *Lundy's Lane

Indian Wars
    *Seminoles

Mexican War
    Palo Alto
    Resaca de la Palma
    Monterey
    *Vera Cruz
    *Cerro Gordo
    Contreras
    Churubusco
    Molino del Rey
    Chapultepec
    Tamaulipas 1846
    *Puebla 1847

Civil War
    Bull Run
    *Peninsula
    *Antietam
    *Fredericksburg
    *Chancellorsville
    *Gettysburg

*Wilderness
*Spotsylvania
*Cold Harbor
*Petersburg
*Shenandoah
 Appomattox
 Florida 1861
 Florida 1862
*North Carolina 1861
*Virginia 1861
*Virginia 1862
*Virginia 1863
 Virginia 1865
*Maryland 1863

World War II
    *Tunisia
    *Naples-Foggia
    *Anzio
    *Rome-Arno
    Normandy
    Northern France
    *North Apennines
    Rhineland
    Ardennes-Alsace
    Central Europe
    England 1944

DECORATIONS

None.

3d BATTALION, 2d AIR DEFENSE ARTILLERY

RA
(inactive)

LINEAGE

Constituted 27 April 1798 in the Regular Army as a company in the 2d Regiment of Artillerists and Engineers. Organized 14 July 1798 at Fort Fayette, Pennsylvania, as Capt. James Read's Company, 2d Regiment of Artillerists and Engineers. Redesignated 3 March 1799 as Capt. James Read's Company, 1st Battalion, 2d Regiment of Artillerists and Engineers. Redesignated 1 April 1802 as Capt. George W. Carmichael's Company, Regiment of Artillerists. Redesignated 6 March 1806 as Capt. James House's Company, Regiment of Artillerists. Redesignated 15 February 1807 as Capt. George Armistead's Company, Regiment of Artillerists. Redesignated 11 January 1812 as Capt. George Armistead's Company, 1st Regiment of Artillery. Redesignated 12 May 1814 as Capt. Thomas Bennett's Company, Corps of Artillery. Redesignated 17 May 1815 as Capt. Nathaniel N. Hall's Company, Corps of Artillery. Redesignated 17 May 1815 as Capt. Nathaniel N. Hall's Company, Corps of Artillery, Northern Division. Redesignated 17 June 1816 as Company H, 4th Battalion, Corps of Artillery, Northern Division. Redesignated 1 June 1821 as Company H, 2d Regiment of Artillery.

Reorganized and redesignated 13 February 1901 as the 18th Company, Coast Artillery, Artillery Corps. Redesignated 5 August 1916 as the 12th Company, Fort Mills [Philippine Islands]. Redesignated 31 August 1917 as the 12th Company, Coast Defenses of Manila and Subic Bays. Redesignated 30 June 1922 as the 18th Company, Coast Artillery Corps.

Reorganized and redesignated 1 July 1924 as Battery H, 2d Coast Artillery. Inactivated 15 April 1932 at Fort Sherman, Canal Zone. Activated 30 April 1932 at Fort Monroe, Virginia. Inactivated 1 September 1935 at Fort Monroe, Virginia. Activated 30 April 1942 at Fort Monroe, Virginia.

Reorganized and redesignated 1 October 1944 as Battery E, 2d Coast Artillery Battalion. Redesignated 1 April 1945 as Battery E, Harbor Defenses of Chesapeake Bay. Inactivated 20 July 1946 at Fort Story, Virginia. Consolidated 28 June 1950 with Battery D, 136th Antiaircraft Artillery Gun Battalion (*see* ANNEX), and consolidated unit redesignated as Battery D, 12th Antiaircraft Artillery Battalion. Redesignated 13 March 1952 as Battery D, 12th Antiaircraft Artillery Gun Battalion. Activated 8 April 1952 at Fort Hancock, New Jersey. Redesignated 15 August 1953 as Battery D, 12th Antiaircraft Artillery Battalion. Inactivated 20 December 1957 at Fort Hancock, New Jersey.

Redesignated 11 February 1958 as Headquarters and Headquarters Battery, 3d Automatic Weapons Battalion, 2d Artillery (organic elements concurrently constituted). Battalion activated 17 March 1958 at Fort Riley, Kansas. Inactivated 5 May 1959 at Fort Riley, Kansas. Redesignated

3 February 1962 as the 3d Battalion, 2d Artillery, and assigned to the 1st Armored Division. Activated 1 March 1962 at Fort Hood, Texas. Inactivated 25 March 1969 at Fort Hood, Texas, and relieved from assignment to the 1st Armored Division. Redesignated 1 September 1971 as the 3d Battalion, 2d Air Defense Artillery.

ANNEX

Constituted 25 February 1943 in the Army of the United States as Battery D, 136th Antiaircraft Artillery Gun Battalion. Activated 15 June 1943 at Camp Edwards, Massachusetts. Inactivated 12 December 1945 at Camp Myles Standish, Massachusetts.

CAMPAIGN PARTICIPATION CREDIT

War of 1812
  Canada

Indian Wars
  *Seminoles

Mexican War
  Palo Alto
  Resaca de la Palma
  Monterey
  *Vera Cruz
  *Cerro Gordo
  *Contreras
  *Churubusco
  *Molino del Rey
  *Chapultepec
  Tamaulipas 1846
  *Puebla 1847

Civil War
  Bull Run
  Peninsula
  Antietam
  Fredericksburg
  Chancellorsville
  Gettysburg
  Wilderness

  Spotsylvania
  Cold Harbor
  Petersburg
  Shenandoah
  Appomattox
  *Florida 1861
  *Florida 1862
  Virginia 1861
  Virginia 1862
  Virginia 1863
  Virginia 1865
  Maryland 1863

World War II
  Tunisia
  Naples-Foggia
  Anzio
  Rome-Arno
  Normandy
  *Northern France
  North Apennines
  *Rhineland
  *Ardennes-Alsace
  *Central Europe
  England 1944

DECORATIONS

    *Belgian Fourragere 1940 (136th Antiaircraft Artillery Gun Battalion cited; DA GO 43, 1950)

      *Cited in the Order of the Day of the Belgian Army for action in defense of ANTWERP (136th Antiaircraft Artillery Gun Battalion cited; DA GO 43, 1950)

      *Cited in the Order of the Day of the Belgian Army for action in defense of ANTWERP HARBOR (136th Antiaircraft Artillery Gun Battalion cited; DA GO 43, 1950)

4th HOWITZER BATTALION, 2d AIR DEFENSE ARTILLERY

AR
(inactive)

LINEAGE

Organized in 1810 in the Regular Army at Fort Washington, Maryland, as Capt. Lloyd Beall's Company, Regiment of Artillerists. Redesignated 11 January 1812 as Capt. Lloyd Beall's Company, 1st Regiment of Artillery. Redesignated in 1813 as Capt. Samuel T. Dyson's Company, 1st Regiment of Artillery (under the command of 3d Lt. Moses M. Russell). Redesignated in 1814 as Capt. Frederick Evans' Company, 1st Regiment of Artillery. Redesignated 12 May 1814 as Capt. Frederick Evans' Company, Corps of Artillery. Redesignated 17 May 1815 as Capt. Isaac Roach, Jr.'s Company, Corps of Artillery, Northern Division. Redesignated in 1815 as Capt. James Reed's Company, Corps of Artillery, Northern Division (under the command of Capt. Thomas Randall). Redesignated 17 June 1816 as Company C, 3d Battalion, Corps of Artillery, Northern Division. Redesignated 1 June 1821 as Company C, 2d Regiment of Artillery.

Reorganized and redesignated 13 February 1901 as the 14th Company, Coast Artillery, Artillery Corps. Redesignated 2 February 1907 as the 14th Company, Coast Artillery Corps. Redesignated 30 June 1916 as the 1st Company, Fort Greble [Rhode Island]. Redesignated 31 August 1917 as the 7th Company, Coast Defenses of Narragansett Bay. Redesignated 1 June 1922 as the 14th Company, Coast Artillery Corps.

Redesignated 1 July 1924 as Battery C, 2d Coast Artillery, and inactivated at Fort Greble, Rhode Island. Activated 30 April 1926 at Fort Sherman, Canal Zone. Inactivated 15 April 1932 at Fort Sherman, Canal Zone. Activated 30 April 1932 at Fort Monroe, Virginia.

Reorganized and redesignated 1 October 1944 as Battery C, 2d Coast Artillery Battalion. Inactivated 1 April 1945 at Fort Monroe, Virginia. Activated 1 August 1946 at Fort Winfield Scott, California. Inactivated 25 November 1946 at Fort Winfield Scott, California. Redesignated 28 June 1950 as Battery C, 2d Antiaircraft Artillery Battalion. Redesignated 27 April 1951 as Battery C, 2d Antiaircraft Artillery Automatic Weapons Battalion, an element of the 1st Armored Division. Activated 7 March 1951 at Fort Bliss, Texas. Consolidated 20 March 1951 with Battery C, 434th Antiaircraft Artillery Automatic Weapons Battalion (*see* ANNEX), and consolidated unit designated as Battery C, 2d Antiaircraft Artillery Automatic Weapons Battalion. Redesignated 20 May 1953 as Battery C, 2d Antiaircraft Artillery Battalion. Inactivated 15 February 1957 at Fort Polk, Louisiana, and relieved from assignment to the 1st Armored Division.

Consolidated 29 April 1959 with Battery C, 2d Field Artillery Battalion (organized in 1907), and consolidated unit redesignated as Headquarters and Headquarters Battery, 4th Howitzer Battalion, 2d Artillery; concurrently withdrawn from the Regular Army, allotted to the Army Reserve, and assigned to the 96th Infantry Division (organic elements concurrently constituted). Battalion activated 1 June 1959 with Headquarters at Twin Falls, Idaho. Inactivated 15 March 1963 at Twin Falls, Idaho, and relieved from assignment to the 96th Infantry Division.

Redesignated (less former Battery C, 2d Field Artillery Battalion) 1 September 1971 as the 4th Howitzer Battalion, 2d Air Defense Artillery (former Battery C, 2d Field Artillery Battalion, concurrently redesignated as the 4th Howitzer Battalion, 2d Field Artillery—hereafter separate lineage).

ANNEX

Constituted 31 January 1942 in the Army of the United States as Battery C, 434th Coast Artillery Battalion. Activated 1 March 1942 at Camp Hulen, Texas. Redesignated 5 December 1943 as Battery C, 434th Antiaircraft Artillery Automatic Weapons Battalion. Disbanded 14 January 1945 in Italy. Reconstituted 20 March 1951 in the Regular Army.

CAMPAIGN PARTICIPATION CREDIT

War of 1812
   Canada
   *McHenry

Indian Wars
   *Seminoles

Mexican War
   *Palo Alto
   *Resaca de la Palma
   Monterey
   *Vera Cruz
   *Cerro Gordo
   *Contreras
   *Churubusco
   *Molino del Rey
   *Chapultepec
   *Tamaulipas 1846
   *Puebla 1847

Civil War
   Bull Run
   Peninsula
   Antietam
   Fredericksburg
   Chancellorsville
   Gettysburg
   Wilderness

Spotsylvania
Cold Harbor
Petersburg
Shenandoah
Appomattox
*Florida 1861
*Florida 1862
Virginia 1861
Virginia 1862
Virginia 1863
Virginia 1865
*Louisiana 1863
Maryland 1863

World War II
   *Tunisia
   *Naples-Foggia
   *Anzio
   *Rome-Arno
   Normandy
   Northern France
   *North Apennines
   Rhineland
   Ardennes-Alsace
   Central Europe
   England 1944

DECORATIONS

None.

5th BATTALION, 2d AIR DEFENSE ARTILLERY

RA
(inactive)

LINEAGE

Constituted 3 March 1847 in the Regular Army as Company M, 2d Regiment of Artillery. Organized 12 March 1847.

Reorganized and redesignated 13 February 1901 as the 22d Company, Coast Artillery, Artillery Corps. Redesignated 2 February 1907 as the 22d Company, Coast Artillery Corps. Redesignated 6 July 1916 as the 1st Company, Fort Barrancas [Florida]. Redesignated 31 August 1917 as the 5th Company, Coast Defenses of Pensacola. Redesignated 1 August 1920 as the 3d Company, Coast Defenses of Pensacola. Redesignated 1 June 1922 as the 22d Company, Coast Artillery Corps.

Redesignated 1 July 1924 as Battery A, 2d Coast Artillery, and inactivated at Pensacola, Florida. Activated 1 September 1935 at Fort Monroe, Virginia.

Reorganized and redesignated 1 October 1944 as Battery A, 2d Coast Artillery Battalion. Redesignated 1 April 1945 as Battery A, Harbor Defenses of Chesapeake Bay. Inactivated 20 July 1946 at Fort Story, Virginia. Redesignated 28 June 1950 as Battery A, 2d Antiaircraft Artillery Battalion. Redesignated 27 February 1951 as Battery A, 2d Antiaircraft Artillery Automatic Weapons Battalion, an element of the 1st Armored Division. Activated 7 March 1951 at Fort Bliss, Texas. Consolidated 20 March 1951 with Battery A, 434th Antiaircraft Artillery Automatic Weapons Battalion (*see* ANNEX), and consolidated unit designated as Battery A, 2d Antiaircraft Artillery Automatic Weapons Battalion. Redesignated 20 May 1953 as Battery A, 2d Antiaircraft Artillery Battalion. Inactivated 15 February 1957 at Fort Polk, Louisiana, and relieved from assignment to the 1st Armored Division.

Redesignated 20 August 1958 as Headquarters and Headquarters Battery, 5th Automatic Weapons Battalion, 2d Artillery (organic elements concurrently constituted). Battalion activated 1 September 1958 in Germany. Inactivated 21 March 1960 in Germany. (Headquarters and Headquarters Battery, 5th Automatic Weapons Battalion, 2d Artillery, consolidated 15 December 1961 with Battery A, 2d Field Artillery Battalion [organized in 1901], and consolidated unit designated as Headquarters and Headquarters Battery, 5th Automatic Weapons Battalion, 2d Artillery.) Redesignated 25 April 1966 as the 5th Battalion, 2d Artillery. Inactivated 23 June 1971 at Fort Lewis, Washington. Redesignated (less former Battery A, 2d Field Artillery Battalion) 1 September 1971 as the 5th Battalion, 2d Air Defense Artillery (former Battery A, 2d Field Artillery Battalion, concurrently redesignated as the 5th Battalion, 2d Field Artillery—hereafter separate lineage).

Constituted 31 January 1942 in the Army of the United States as Battery A, 434th Coast Artillery Battalion. Activated 1 March 1942 at Camp Hulen, Texas. Redesignated 5 December 1943 as Battery A, 434th Antiaircraft Artillery Automatic Weapons Battalion. Disbanded 14 January 1945 in Italy. Reconstituted 20 March 1951 in the Regular Army.

CAMPAIGN PARTICIPATION CREDIT

War of 1812
  Canada

Indian Wars
  Seminoles

Mexican War
  Palo Alto
  Resaca de la Palma
  Monterey
  Vera Cruz
  Cerro Gordo
  Contreras
  Churubusco
  Molino del Rey
  Chapultepec
  Tamaulipas 1846
  Puebla 1847

Civil War
  *Bull Run
  *Peninsula
  *Antietam
  *Fredericksburg
  *Chancellorsville
  *Gettysburg
  *Wilderness
  *Spotsylvania
  Cold Harbor
  *Petersburg
  *Shenandoah
  *Appomattox
  Florida 1861
  Florida 1862

  Virginia 1861
  *Virginia 1862
  *Virginia 1863
  *Virginia 1865
  *Maryland 1862
  *Maryland 1863

World War II
  *Tunisia
  *Naples-Foggia
  Anzio
  *Rome-Arno
  Normandy
  Northern France
  *North Apennines
  Rhineland
  Ardennes-Alsace
  Central Europe
  England 1944

Vietnam
  *Counteroffensive, Phase II
  *Counteroffensive, Phase III
  *Tet Counteroffensive
  *Counteroffensive, Phase IV
  *Counteroffensive, Phase V
  *Counteroffensive, Phase VI
  *Tet 69/Counteroffensive
  *Summer–fall 1969
  *Winter–spring 1970
  *Sanctuary Counteroffensive
  *Counteroffensive, Phase VII

DECORATIONS

*Meritorious Unit Commendation, Streamer embroidered VIETNAM 1967–1968 (5th Battalion, 2d Artillery, cited; DA GO 70, 1969)

*Republic of Vietnam Cross of Gallantry with Palm, Streamer embroidered VIETNAM 1966–1967 (Headquarters and Headquarters Battery, 5th Battalion, 2d Artillery, and Battery C, 5th Battalion, 2d Artillery, cited; DA GO 31, 1969, as amended by DA GO 43, 1969. Battery A, 5th Battalion, 2d Artillery, cited; DA GO 21, 1969, as amended by DA GO 38, 1970. Battery B, 5th Battalion, 2d Artillery, cited; DA GO 48, 1971)

*Republic of Vietnam Cross of Gallantry with Palm, Streamer embroidered VIETNAM 1967–1969 (5th Battalion, 2d Artillery, cited; DA GO 60, 1969)

*Republic of Vietnam Civil Action Honor Medal, First Class, Streamer embroidered VIETNAM 1966–1971 (5th Battalion, 2d Artillery, cited; DA GO 51, 1971, as amended by DA GO 54, 1974. Battery A, 5th Battalion, 2d Artillery, cited; DA GO 53, 1970. Battery C, 5th Battalion, 2d Artillery, cited; DA GO 59, 1969)

Battery A additionally entitled to Valorous Unit Award, Streamer embroidered VIETNAM 1968–1969 (Batteries A and B, 5th Battalion, 2d Artillery, cited; DA GO 43, 1970)

Battery B additionally entitled to Valorous Unit Award, Streamer embroidered VIETNAM 1968–1969 (Batteries A and B, 5th Battalion, 2d Artillery, cited; DA GO 43, 1970), and Republic of Vietnam Cross of Gallantry with Palm, Streamer embroidered VIETNAM 1969–1970 (Battery B, 5th Battalion, 2d Artillery, cited; DA GO 5, 1973)

Battery C additionally entitled to Republic of Vietnam Cross of Gallantry with Palm, Streamer embroidered VIETNAM 1969 (Battery C, 5th Battalion, 2d Artillery, cited; DA GO 59, 1969)

Battery D additionally entitled to Meritorious Unit Commendation, Streamer embroidered VIETNAM 1968–1969 (Battery D, 5th Battalion, 2d Artillery, cited; DA GO 59, 1969)

6th MISSILE BATTALION, 2d AIR DEFENSE ARTILLERY

RA
(inactive)

LINEAGE

Constituted 11 January 1812 in the Regular Army as a company in the 3d Regiment of Artillery. Organized in September 1812 as Capt. Thomas Stockton's Company, 3d Regiment of Artillery. Redesignated 1 October 1813 as Capt. Benjamin K. Pierce's Company, 3d Regiment of Artillery. Redesignated 12 May 1814 as Capt. Benjamin K. Pierce's Company, Corps of Artillery. Redesignated 17 May 1815 as Capt. Benjamin K. Pierce's Company, Corps of Artillery, Northern Division. Redesignated 17 June 1816 as Company O, 1st Battalion, Corps of Artillery, Northern Division. Redesignated 1 June 1821 as Company I, 2d Regiment of Artillery.

Reorganized and redesignated 13 February 1901 as the 19th Company, Coast Artillery, Artillery Corps. Redesignated 2 February 1907 as the 19th Company, Coast Artillery Corps. Redesignated 7 September 1916 as the 1st Company, Fort Caswell [North Carolina]. Redesignated 31 August 1917 as the 1st Company, Coast Defenses of Cape Fear. Redesignated 1 June 1922 as the 19th Company, Coast Artillery Corps.

Redesignated 1 July 1924 as Battery I, 2d Coast Artillery, and inactivated at Fort Caswell, North Carolina. Activated 30 April 1942 at Fort Monroe, Virginia.

Reorganized and redesignated 1 October 1944 as Battery F, 2d Coast Artillery Battalion. Inactivated 1 April 1945 at Little Creek, Virginia. Consolidated 28 June 1950 with Battery A, 42d Antiaircraft Artillery Automatic Weapons Battalion (active) (*see* ANNEX), and consolidated unit designated as Battery A, 42d Antiaircraft Artillery Automatic Weapons Battalion, an element of the 9th Infantry Division. Redesignated 25 May 1954 as Battery A, 42d Antiaircraft Artillery Battalion. Inactivated 1 December 1957 at Fort Carson, Colorado, and relieved from assignment to the 9th Infantry Division.

Redesignated 11 February 1958 as Headquarters and Headquarters Battery, 6th Automatic Weapons Battalion, 2d Artillery (organic elements concurrently constituted). Battalion activated 24 February 1958 at Fort Hood, Texas. Inactivated 25 September 1958 at Fort Hood, Texas. Redesignated 4 April 1960 as the 6th Missile Battalion, 2d Artillery. Activated 20 April 1960 at Walker Air Force Base, New Mexico. Inactivated 25 June 1960 at Walker Air Force Base, New Mexico. Redesignated 1 September 1971 as the 6th Missile Battalion, 2d Air Defense Artillery.

ANNEX

Constituted 25 February 1943 in the Army of the United States as Battery A, 795th Coast Artillery Battalion. Activated 20 April 1943 at Camp Stewart, Georgia. Redesignated 30 April 1943 as Battery A,

795th Antiaircraft Artillery Automatic Weapons Battalion. Inactivated 31 December 1945 in Germany. Redesignated 25 June 1948 as Battery A, 42d Antiaircraft Artillery Automatic Weapons Battalion, an element of the 9th Infantry Division. Activated 12 July 1948 at Fort Dix, New Jersey.

CAMPAIGN PARTICIPATION CREDIT

War of 1812
  *Canada

Indian Wars
  Seminoles

Mexican War
  Palo Alto
  Resaca de la Palma
  Monterey
  *Vera Cruz
  *Cerro Gordo
  *Contreras
  *Churubusco
  *Molino del Rey
  *Chapultepec
  Tamaulipas 1846
  *Puebla 1847

Civil War
  Bull Run
  Peninsula
  Antietam
  Fredericksburg
  Chancellorsville
  Gettysburg
  Wilderness

Spotsylvania
Cold Harbor
Petersburg
Shenandoah
Appomattox
Florida 1861
Florida 1862
Virginia 1861
Virginia 1862
Virginia 1863
Virginia 1865
Maryland 1863

World War II
  Tunisia
  Naples-Foggia
  Anzio
  Rome-Arno
  *Normandy
  *Northern France
  North Apennines
  *Rhineland
  Ardennes-Alsace
  *Central Europe
  England 1944

DECORATIONS

  None.

7th BATTALION, 2d AIR DEFENSE ARTILLERY

RA
(inactive)

LINEAGE

Constituted 1 June 1821 in the Regular Army as Company E, 2d Regiment of Artillery. Organized in July 1821 at Pittsburgh, Pennsylvania.

Reorganized and redesignated 13 February 1901 as the 16th Company, Coast Artillery, Artillery Corps. Redesignated 2 February 1907 as the 16th Company, Coast Artillery Corps. Redesignated in July 1916 as the 5th Company, Fort Sherman [Canal Zone]. Redesignated 31 August 1917 as the 5th Company, Coast Defenses of Cristobal. Redesignated 30 June 1922 as the 16th Company, Coast Artillery Corps.

Reorganized and redesignated 1 July 1924 as Battery E, 2d Coast Artillery. Inactivated 15 April 1932 at Fort Sherman, Canal Zone. Activated 30 April 1932 at Fort Monroe, Virginia.

Reorganized and redesignated 1 October 1944 as Battery B, 175th Coast Artillery Battalion. Redesignated 1 April 1945 as Battery B, Harbor Defenses of Chesapeake Bay. Inactivated 20 July 1946 at Fort Story, Virginia. Consolidated 28 June 1950 with Battery A, 136th Antiaircraft Artillery Gun Battalion (*see* ANNEX), and consolidated unit redesignated as Battery A, 12th Antiaircraft Artillery Battalion. Redesignated 13 March 1952 as Battery A, 12th Antiaircraft Artillery Gun Battalion. Activated 8 April 1952 at Fort Hancock, New Jersey. Redesignated 15 April 1953 as Battery A, 12th Antiaircraft Artillery Battalion. Inactivated 20 December 1957 at Fort Hancock, New Jersey.

Redesignated 1 November 1960 as Headquarters and Headquarters Battery, 7th Missile Battalion, 2d Artillery (organic elements concurrently constituted). Battalion activated 27 November 1960 at Fort Bliss, Texas. (Headquarters and Headquarters Battery, 7th Missile Battalion, 2d Artillery, consolidated 15 December 1961 with Battery E, 2d Field Artillery [organized in 1907], and consolidated unit designated as Headquarters and Headquarters Battery, 7th Missile Battalion, 2d Artillery.) Redesignated 10 January 1966 as the 7th Battalion, 2d Artillery.

Reorganized and redesignated (less former Battery E, 2d Field Artillery) 1 September 1971 as the 7th Battalion, 2d Air Defense Artillery (former Battery E, 2d Field Artillery, concurrently redesignated as the 7th Battalion, 2d Field Artillery—hereafter separate lineage). 7th Battalion, 2d Air Defense Artillery, inactivated 13 September 1972 in Korea.

ANNEX

Constituted 25 February 1943 in the Army of the United States as Battery A, 136th Antiaircraft Artillery Gun Battalion. Activated 15 June 1943 at Camp Edwards, Massachusetts. Inactivated 12 December 1945 at Camp Myles Standish, Massachusetts.

CAMPAIGN PARTICIPATION CREDIT

War of 1812
  Canada

Indian Wars
  *Seminoles

Mexican War
  Palo Alto
  Resaca de la Palma
  Monterey
  Vera Cruz
  Cerro Gordo
  Contreras
  Churubusco
  Molino del Rey
  Chapultepec
  Tamaulipas 1846
  Puebla 1847

Civil War
  *Bull Run
  *Peninsula
  *Manassas
  *Antietam
  *Fredericksburg
  Chancellorsville
  Gettysburg
  Wilderness
  Spotsylvania
  Cold Harbor

  Petersburg
  Shenandoah
  Appomattox
  Florida 1861
  Florida 1862
  Virginia 1861
  Virginia 1862
  Virginia 1863
  Virginia 1865
  Maryland 1863
  *Mississippi 1863
  *Tennessee 1863

War With Spain
  *Santiago

World War II
  Tunisia
  Naples-Foggia
  Anzio
  Rome-Arno
  Normandy
  *Northern France
  North Apennines
  *Rhineland
  *Ardennes-Alsace
  *Central Europe
  England 1944

DECORATIONS

  *Belgian Fourragere 1940 (136th Antiaircraft Artillery Gun Battalion cited; DA GO 43, 1950)

  *Cited in the Order of the Day of the Belgian Army for action in defense of ANTWERP (136th Antiaircraft Artillery Gun Battalion cited; DA GO 43, 1950)

  *Cited in the Order of the Day of the Belgian Army for action in defense of ANTWERP HARBOR (136th Antiaircraft Artillery Gun Battalion cited; DA GO 43, 1950)

16th DETACHMENT, 2d AIR DEFENSE ARTILLERY

RA
(inactive)

LINEAGE

Constituted 25 February 1943 in the Army of the United States as Battery C, 795th Coast Artillery Battalion. Activated 20 April 1943 at Camp Stewart, Georgia. Redesignated 30 April 1943 as Battery C, 795th Antiaircraft Artillery Automatic Weapons Battalion. Inactivated 31 December 1945 in Germany. Redesignated 25 June 1948 as Battery C, 42d Antiaircraft Artillery Automatic Weapons Battalion, an element of the 9th Infantry Division. Activated 12 July 1948 at Fort Dix, New Jersey. Allotted 28 June 1950 to the Regular Army. Redesignated 25 May 1954 as Battery C, 42d Antiaircraft Artillery Battalion. Inactivated 1 December 1957 at Fort Carson, Colorado, and relieved from assignment to the 9th Infantry Division.

Redesignated 7 August 1958 as the 16th Detachment, 2d Artillery. Activated 25 August 1958 in Korea. Inactivated 25 January 1959 in Korea. Redesignated 1 September 1971 as the 16th Detachment, 2d Air Defense Artillery.

CAMPAIGN PARTICIPATION CREDIT

World War II-EAME
  Normandy
  Northern France
  Rhineland
  Central Europe

DECORATIONS

None.

2D AIR DEFENSE ARTILLERY BIBLIOGRAPHY

Birkhimer, William E., et al. "Historical Sketch of the Second United States Artillery." *Journal of the Military Service Institution of the United States* 14 (1893):1040–42.

Dyer, Frederick. "2d Regiment of Artillery." *A Compendium of the War of the Rebellion.* New York: Thomas Yoseloff, 1959.

8th Infantry Division, 50th Anniversary. Germany, 1968. Contains information about the 1st Battalion, 2d Air Defense Artillery.

Finley, Charles R. "The Coast Artillery in Panama." *Coast Artillery Journal* 83 (1940):522–27.

1st Armored Division, Fort Hood, Texas. Baton Rouge: Army and Navy Publishing Company, 1963. Contains information about the 3d Battalion, 2d Air Defense Artillery.

The Historical Record of the 136th Antiaircraft Artillery Gun Battalion (Mobile). Antwerp: De Vos-Van Kleef, 1945.

Lossing, Benson John. *Memoir of Lieutenant Colonel John T. Greble of the United States Army*. Philadelphia, 1870.

Murphy, John G. "Activities of the Ninth Army Antiaircraft Artillery." *Antiaircraft Artillery Journal* 90 (May 1949):3–13.

Ott, David Ewing. *Field Artillery, 1954–1973*. Vietnam Studies. Washington: Government Printing Office, 1975. Contains information about the 5th Battalion, 2d Air Defense Artillery.

Reilly, James. "An Artilleryman's Story." *Journal of the Military Service Institution of the United States* 33 (1903): 438–46.

Rice, Josiah. *A Cannoneer in Navajo Country: Journal of Private Josiah M. Rice, 1851*. Edited by Richard H. Dillon. Denver: Old West Publishing Company, 1970.

Simpson, W.A. "The Second Regiment of Artillery." *The Army of the United States*. Edited by Theophilus F. Rodenbough and William L. Haskin, 312–27. New York: Maynard, Merrill and Company, 1896.

Sprague, John T. *The Origin, Progress, and Conclusion of the Florida War*. New York: D. Appleton and Company, 1848. Reprint. Gainesville, Fla.: University of Florida Press, 1964.

Weaver, Erasmus M. "History of the 2d Artillery." *Journal of the Military Service Institution of the United States* 14 (1893):1258–60.

3d AIR DEFENSE ARTILLERY

HERALDIC ITEMS

COAT OF ARMS

Shield: Or, on a chevron gules above an imperial Chinese dragon of the like armed azure three mullets argent, on a chief of the second two pallets of the fourth an arrow in fess counterchanged.

Crest: Out of a mural crown or masoned gules a garland the dexter branch cactus the sinister palm proper encircling a sun in splendor argent.

Motto: *Non Cedo Ferio* (I Yield Not, I Strike).

Symbolism: Scarlet is used for artillery. The two white stripes on the scarlet chief, the colors of the campaign streamers for the War of 1812, commemorate the participation of several companies of the regiment. The arrow alludes to the Indian Wars. The chevron and stars indicate service in the Civil War. The stars also refer to the numerical designation of the regiment. The dragon represents service in China; the claws and teeth are blue to indicate that elements of the regiment served in the China Relief Expedition as infantry.

The mural crown, cactus, and palm signify the regiment's participation in the Mexican War and elements of the regiment in the Philippine Insurrection. The sun in its glory commemorates the laurels earned by the regiment during its days of glory.

DISTINCTIVE INSIGNIA

The distinctive insignia is an adaptation of the crest and motto of the coat of arms.

LINEAGE AND HONORS

LINEAGE

Constituted 1 June 1821 in the Regular Army as the 3d Regiment of Artillery and organized from existing units with Headquarters at Fort Washington, Maryland. Regiment broken up 13 February 1901 and its elements reorganized and redesignated as separate numbered companies and batteries of Artillery Corps. Reconstituted 1 July 1924 in the Regular Army as the 3d Coast Artillery and organized (less Batteries C, F, and G) with Headquarters at Fort MacArthur, California. (Batteries A and B inactivated 1 March 1930 at San Pedro and Fort MacArthur, California,

51

respectively; Batteries A and F activated 1 July 1939 at Fort MacArthur, California, and Fort Stevens, Oregon, respectively; Batteries D and F inactivated 1 February 1940 at Fort Rosecrans, California, and Fort Stevens, Oregon, respectively; Batteries C, D, and F activated 2 December 1940 at Fort Rosecrans and Fort MacArthur, California; Battery G activated 1 June 1941 at Los Angeles, California; Battery G inactivated 29 August 1941 at Los Angeles, California; Battery G activated 14 February 1942 at Fort MacArthur, California.) Regiment broken up 18 October 1944 and its elements reorganized and redesignated as follows: Headquarters and Headquarters Battery as Battery B, 521st Coast Artillery Battalion; 1st, 2d, and 3d Battalions as the 520th, 521st, and 522d Coast Artillery Battalions, respectively.

Battery B, 521st Coast Artillery Battalion, disbanded 15 September 1945 at Fort MacArthur, California. Reconstituted 28 June 1950 in the Regular Army and redesignated as Headquarters and Headquarters Battery, 3d Antiaircraft Artillery Group. Activated 11 June 1951 at Camp Stewart, Georgia. Redesignated 20 March 1958 as Headquarters and Headquarters Battery, 3d Artillery Group. Inactivated 15 December 1961 at Norfolk, Virginia.

520th Coast Artillery Battalion redesignated 1 December 1944 as the 3d Coast Artillery Battalion. Disbanded 15 September 1945 at Fort MacArthur, California. Reconstituted 20 January 1950 in the Regular Army; concurrently consolidated with the 3d Antiaircraft Artillery Automatic Weapons Battalion (active) (*see* ANNEX 1), and consolidated unit designated as the 3d Antiaircraft Artillery Automatic Weapons Battalion, an element of the 3d Infantry Division. Redesignated 15 April 1953 as the 3d Antiaircraft Artillery Battalion. Inactivated 1 July 1957 at Fort Benning, Georgia, and relieved from assignment to the 3d Infantry Division.

521st Coast Artillery Battalion disbanded 15 September 1945 at Fort MacArthur, California. Reconstituted 28 June 1950 in the Regular Army and redesignated as the 18th Antiaircraft Artillery Battalion. Redesignated 13 March 1952 as the 18th Antiaircraft Artillery Gun Battalion. Activated 2 May 1952 at Fort Custer, Michigan. Redesignated 24 July 1953 as the 18th Antiaircraft Artillery Battalion. Redesignated 15 June 1957 as the 18th Antiaircraft Artillery Missile Battalion. Inactivated 1 September 1958 at Detroit, Michigan.

522d Coast Artillery Battalion disbanded 15 September 1945 at Huntington Beach, California. Reconstituted 28 June 1950 in the Regular Army; concurrently consolidated with the 43d Antiaircraft Artillery Automatic Weapons Battalion (active) (*see* ANNEX 2), and consolidated unit designated as the 43d Antiaircraft Artillery Automatic Weapons Battalion, an element of the 10th Infantry Division. Redesignated 15 June 1954 as the 43d Antiaircraft Artillery Battalion. Relieved 16 May 1957 from assignment to the 10th Infantry Division. Inactivated 14 November 1957 in Germany.

Headquarters and Headquarters Battery, 3d Artillery Group; 18th

Antiaircraft Artillery Missile Battalion; 3d and 43d Antiaircraft Artillery Battalions; and 3d Armored Field Artillery Battalion (organized in 1907) consolidated, reorganized, and redesignated 15 December 1961 as the 3d Artillery, a parent regiment under the Combat Arms Regimental System.

3d Artillery (less former 3d Armored Field Artillery Battalion) reorganized and redesignated 1 September 1971 as the 3d Air Defense Artillery, a parent regiment under the Combat Arms Regimental System (former 3d Armored Field Artillery Battalion concurrently reorganized and redesignated as the 3d Field Artillery—hereafter separate lineage).

ANNEX 1

Constituted 6 July 1942 in the Army of the United States as the 534th Coast Artillery Battalion. Activated 15 July 1942 at Fort Bliss, Texas. Redesignated 12 December 1943 as the 534th Antiaircraft Artillery Automatic Weapons Battalion. Inactivated 19 October 1945 at Camp Patrick Henry, Virginia. Redesignated 9 December 1948 as the 3d Antiaircraft Artillery Automatic Weapons Battalion and allotted to the Regular Army. Activated 15 January 1949 at Fort Bliss, Texas. Assigned 22 November 1949 to the 3d Infantry Division.

ANNEX 2

Constituted 5 May 1942 in the Army of the United States as the 2d Battalion, 504th Coast Artillery. Activated 1 July 1942 at Camp Hulen, Texas.

Reorganized and redesignated 20 January 1943 as the 630th Coast Artillery Battalion. Redesignated 12 December 1943 as the 630th Antiaircraft Artillery Automatic Weapons Battalion. Inactivated 26 September 1945 in Italy. Redesignated 18 June 1948 as the 43d Antiaircraft Artillery Automatic Weapons Battalion and assigned to the 10th Infantry Division. Activated 1 July 1948 at Fort Riley, Kansas.

CAMPAIGN PARTICIPATION CREDIT

War of 1812
  Canada

Indian Wars
  Seminoles
  Washington 1858

Mexican War
  Palo Alto
  Resaca de la Palma
  Monterey
  Buena Vista
  Vera Cruz
  Cerro Gordo
  Contreras
  Churubusco
  Molino del Rey
  Chapultepec
  Puebla 1847

Civil War
  Peninsula
  Antietam
  Fredericksburg
  Chancellorsville
  Gettysburg
  Wilderness

  Spotsylvania
  Petersburg
  Shenandoah
  Mississippi 1863
  Tennessee 1863
  Tennessee 1864
  Virginia 1863

World War II
  Naples-Foggia (with arrowhead)
  Anzio (with arrowhead)
  Rome-Arno
  Southern France (with arrowhead)
  North Apennines
  Ardennes-Alsace
  Central Europe
  Po Valley

Korean War
  CCF intervention
  First UN counteroffensive
  CCF spring offensive
  UN summer-fall offensive
  Second Korean winter
  Korea, summer-fall 1952
  Third Korean winter
  Korea, summer 1953

DECORATIONS

Meritorious Unit Commendation, Streamer embroidered EUROPEAN THEATER (630th Antiaircraft Artillery Automatic Weapons Battalion cited; GO 103, Headquarters, Fifth Army, 19 August 1945)

1st BATTALION, 3d AIR DEFENSE ARTILLERY

RA
(101st Airborne Division)

LINEAGE

Constituted 27 April 1798 in the Regular Army as a company in the 2d Regiment of Artillerists and Engineers. Organized in 1799 as Capt. John Lillie's Company, 2d Regiment of Artillerists and Engineers. Redesignated 1 April 1802 as Capt. George Izard's Company, Regiment of Artillerists. Redesignated in June 1803 as Capt. Howell Cobb's Company, Regiment of Artillerists. Redesignated 1 February 1806 as Capt. William Yates' Company, Regiment of Artillerists. Redesignated in 1807 as Capt. Addison B. Armistead's Company, Regiment of Artillerists. Redesignated 11 January 1812 as Capt. Addison B. Armistead's Company, 2d Regiment of Artillery. Redesignated 12 May 1814 as a company in the Corps of Artillery. Redesignated 17 May 1815 as a company in the Corps of Artillery, Southern Division. Redesignated 21 August 1816 as Company I, 1st Battalion, Corps of Artillery, Southern Division. Consolidated 1 June 1821 with Company I, Regiment of Light Artillery (*see* ANNEX 1), and consolidated unit redesignated as Company E, 3d Regiment of Artillery.

Reorganized and redesignated 13 February 1901 as the 28th Company, Coast Artillery, Artillery Corps. Redesignated 2 February 1907 as the 28th Company, Coast Artillery Corps. Redesignated 12 July 1916 as the 1st Company, Fort Rosecrans [California]. Redesignated 31 August 1917 as the 1st Company, Coast Defenses of San Diego. Consolidated 13 October 1919 with the 2d Company, Coast Defenses of San Diego (*see* ANNEX 2), and consolidated unit designated as the 1st Company, Coast Defenses of San Diego. Redesignated 1 June 1922 as the 28th Company, Coast Artillery Corps.

Reorganized and redesignated 1 July 1924 as Battery E, 3d Coast Artillery.

Reorganized and redesignated 18 October 1944 as Battery A, 520th Coast Artillery Battalion. Redesignated 1 December 1944 as Battery A, 3d Coast Artillery Battalion. Redesignated 15 September 1945 as Battery B, Harbor Defenses of Los Angeles. Inactivated 30 June 1946 at Fort Mac-Arthur, California. Consolidated 20 January 1950 with Battery A, 3d Antiaircraft Artillery Automatic Weapons Battalion (active) (*see* ANNEX 3), and consolidated unit designated as Battery A, 3d Antiaircraft Artillery Automatic Weapons Battalion, an element of the 3d Infantry Division. Redesignated 15 April 1953 as Battery A, 3d Antiaircraft Artillery Battalion. Inactivated 1 July 1957 at Fort Benning, Georgia, and relieved from assignment to the 3d Infantry Division.

Consolidated 1 January 1960 with Headquarters and Headquarters Battery, 1st Howitzer Battalion, 3d Artillery (active) (organized in 1794), and consolidated unit designated as Headquarters and Headquarters

Battery, 1st Howitzer Battalion, 3d Artillery, an element of the 2d Armored Division (organic elements constituted 21 June 1957 and activated 1 July 1957). Redesignated 1 December 1963 as the 1st Battalion, 3d Artillery.

Redesignated (less former Headquarters and Headquarters Battery, 1st Howitzer Battalion, 3d Artillery) 1 September 1971 as the 1st Battalion, 3d Air Defense Artillery; concurrently inactivated in Germany and relieved from assignment to the 2d Armored Division (former Headquarters and Headquarters Battery, 1st Howitzer Battalion, 3d Artillery, concurrently reorganized and redesignated as the 1st Battalion, 3d Field Artillery—hereafter separate lineage). 1st Battalion, 3d Air Defense Artillery, activated 10 July 1972 at Fort Bliss, Texas. Assigned 4 December 1972 to the 101st Airborne Division.

ANNEX 1

Organized in 1813 in the Regular Army at Greenbush, New York, as Capt. George W. Melven's Company of Light Artillery, Regiment of Light Artillery. Redesignated in 1815 as Bvt. Lt. Col. Nathan Towson's Company of Light Artillery (under the command of 2d Lt. George E. Wells), Regiment of Light Artillery. Redesignated in 1815 as Capt. Henry K. Craig's Company of Light Artillery, Regiment of Light Artillery. Redesignated 22 May 1816 as Company I, Regiment of Light Artillery.

ANNEX 2

Organized 23 May 1917 in the Regular Army as the 4th Company, Fort Rosecrans [California]. Redesignated 31 August 1917 as the 4th Company, Coast Defenses of San Diego. Redesignated 1 January 1918 as the 2d Company, Coast Defenses of San Diego.

ANNEX 3

Constituted 6 July 1942 in the Army of the United States as Battery A, 534th Coast Artillery Battalion. Activated 15 July 1942 at Fort Bliss, Texas. Redesignated 12 December 1943 as Battery A, 534th Antiaircraft Artillery Automatic Weapons Battalion. Inactivated 19 October 1945 at Camp Patrick Henry, Virginia. Redesignated 9 December 1948 as Battery A, 3d Antiaircraft Artillery Automatic Weapons Battalion, and allotted to the Regular Army. Activated 15 January 1949 as an element of the 3d Infantry Division.

CAMPAIGN PARTICIPATION CREDIT

War of 1812
  *Canada

Indian Wars
  *Seminoles
  Washington 1858

Mexican War
  Palo Alto
  Resaca de la Palma
  *Monterey
  *Buena Vista
  Vera Cruz
  Cerro Gordo
  Contreras
  Churubusco
  Molino del Rey
  Chapultepec
  *Tamaulipas 1846
  Puebla 1847

Civil War
  *Bull Run
  Peninsula
  Antietam
  Fredericksburg
  Chancellorsville
  Gettysburg
  Wilderness
  Spotsylvania
  *Petersburg
  Shenandoah

*South Carolina 1862
*South Carolina 1863
  Mississippi 1863
  Tennessee 1863
  Tennessee 1864
  Virginia 1863
*Virginia 1864
*Florida 1864
*North Carolina 1865

World War II
  *Naples-Foggia (with arrowhead)
  *Anzio (with arrowhead)
  *Rome-Arno
  *Southern France (with arrowhead)
  North Apennines
  *Ardennes-Alsace
  *Central Europe
  Po Valley

Korean War
  *CCF intervention
  *First UN counteroffensive
  *CCF spring offensive
  *UN summer-fall offensive
  *Second Korean winter
  *Korea, summer-fall 1952
  *Third Korean winter
  *Korea, summer 1953

DECORATIONS

Meritorious Unit Commendation, Streamer embroidered EUROPEAN
THEATER

*Republic of Korea Presidential Unit Citation, Streamer embroidered
UIJONGBU CORRIDOR (3d Antiaircraft Artillery Battalion cited;
DA GO 20, 1953)

*Republic of Korea Presidential Unit Citation, Streamer embroidered
IRON TRIANGLE (3d Antiaircraft Artillery Battalion cited; DA GO 29,
1954)

*Chryssoun Aristion Andrias (Bravery Gold Medal of Greece),
Streamer embroidered KOREA (3d Antiaircraft Artillery Battalion cited;
DA GO 2, 1956)

2d BATTALION, 3d AIR DEFENSE ARTILLERY

RA
(inactive)

LINEAGE

Constituted 11 January 1812 in the Regular Army as a company in the 3d Regiment of Artillery. Organized in July 1812 at Sacket's Harbor, New York, as Capt. Roger Jones' Company, 3d Regiment of Artillery. Redesignated in February 1814 as Capt. A.C.W. Fanning's Company, 3d Regiment of Artillery. Redesignated 12 May 1814 as Capt. A.C.W. Fanning's Company, Corps of Artillery. Redesignated in 1815 as Capt. Roger Jones' Company, Corps of Artillery, Northern Division. Redesignated 17 June 1816 as Company E, 3d Battalion, Corps of Artillery, Northern Division. Redesignated 1 June 1821 as Company A, 3d Regiment of Artillery.

Reorganized and redesignated 13 February 1901 as the 25th Company, Coast Artillery, Artillery Corps. Redesignated 2 February 1907 as the 25th Company, Coast Artillery Corps. Redesignated in July 1916 as the 2d Company, Fort Miley [California]. Redesignated 31 August 1917 as the 19th Company, Coast Defenses of San Francisco. Redesignated 25 October 1918 as Battery C, 18th Artillery (Coast Artillery Corps). Redesignated 2 December 1918 as the 19th Company, Coast Defenses of San Francisco. Redesignated 1 June 1922 as the 25th Company, Coast Artillery Corps.

Reorganized and redesignated 1 July 1924 as Battery A, 3d Coast Artillery. Inactivated 1 March 1930 at San Pedro, California. Activated 1 July 1939 at Fort MacArthur, California.

Reorganized and redesignated 18 October 1944 as Battery C, 520th Coast Artillery Battalion. Redesignated 1 December 1944 as Battery C, 3d Coast Artillery Battalion. Disbanded 15 September 1945 at Fort Mac-Arthur, California. Reconstituted 20 January 1950 in the Regular Army; concurrently consolidated with Battery C, 3d Antiaircraft Artillery Automatic Weapons Battalion (active) (*see* ANNEX), and consolidated unit designated as Battery C, 3d Antiaircraft Artillery Automatic Weapons Battalion, an element of the 3d Infantry Division. Redesignated 15 April 1953 as Battery C, 3d Antiaircraft Artillery Battalion. Inactivated 1 July 1957 at Fort Benning, Georgia, and relieved from assignment to the 3d Infantry Division.

Consolidated 1 January 1960 with Headquarters and Headquarters Battery, 2d Howitzer Battalion, 3d Artillery (active) (organized in 1812), and consolidated unit designated as Headquarters and Headquarters Battery, 2d Howitzer Battalion, 3d Artillery, an element of the 3d Armored Division (organic elements constituted 30 August 1957 and activated 1 October 1957). Redesignated 1 September 1963 as the 2d Battalion, 3d Artillery.

Redesignated (less former Headquarters and Headquarters Battery, 2d Howitzer Battalion, 3d Artillery) 1 September 1971 as the 2d Battalion,

3d Air Defense Artillery; concurrently inactivated in Germany and relieved from assignment to the 3d Armored Division (former Headquarters and Headquarters Battery, 2d Howitzer Battalion, 3d Artillery, concurrently reorganized and redesignated as the 2d Battalion, 3d Field Artillery—hereafter separate lineage). 2d Battalion, 3d Air Defense Artillery, activated 13 September 1972 at Selfridge Air Force Base, Michigan. Inactivated 30 September 1974 at Selfridge Air Force Base, Michigan.

ANNEX

Constituted 6 July 1942 in the Army of the United States as Battery C, 534th Coast Artillery Battalion. Activated 15 July 1942 at Fort Bliss, Texas. Redesignated 12 December 1943 as Battery C, 534th Antiaircraft Artillery Automatic Weapons Battalion. Inactivated 19 October 1945 at Camp Patrick Henry, Virginia. Redesignated 9 December 1948 as Battery C, 3d Antiaircraft Artillery Automatic Weapons Battalion, and allotted to the Regular Army. Activated 15 January 1949 at Fort Bliss, Texas, as an element of the 3d Infantry Division.

CAMPAIGN PARTICIPATION CREDIT

War of 1812
  *Canada

Indian Wars
  *Seminoles
  *Washington 1858

Mexican War
  *Palo Alto
  *Resaca de la Palma
  *Monterey
  Buena Vista
  *Vera Cruz
  *Cerro Gordo
  Contreras
  Churubusco
  Molino del Rey
  Chapultepec
  *Puebla 1847
  *Tlaxcala 1847

Civil War
  Peninsula
  Antietem
  Fredericksburg
  Chancellorsville
  Gettysburg
  Wilderness
  Spotsylvania
  Petersburg

  Shenandoah
  Mississippi 1863
  Tennessee 1863
  Tennessee 1864
  Virginia 1863

China Relief Expedition
  *Streamer without inscription

Philippine Insurrection
  *Streamer without inscription

World War II
  *Naples-Foggia (with arrowhead)
  *Anzio (with arrowhead)
  *Rome-Arno
  *Southern France (with arrowhead)
  North Apennines
  *Ardennes-Alsace
  *Central Europe
  Po Valley

Korean War
  *CCF intervention
  *First UN counteroffensive
  *CCF spring offensive
  *UN summer–fall offensive
  *Second Korean winter
  *Korea, summer–fall 1952
  *Third Korean winter
  *Korea, summer 1953

DECORATIONS

Meritorious Unit Commendation, Streamer embroidered EUROPEAN THEATER

*Republic of Korea Presidential Unit Citation, Streamer embroidered UIJONGBU CORRIDOR (3d Antiaircraft Artillery Battalion cited; DA GO 20, 1953)

*Republic of Korea Presidential Unit Citation, Streamer embroidered IRON TRIANGLE (3d Antiaircraft Artillery Battalion cited; DA GO 29, 1954)

*Chryssoun Aristion Andrias (Bravery Gold Medal of Greece), Streamer embroidered KOREA (3d Antiaircraft Artillery Battalion cited; DA GO 2, 1956)

3d BATTALION, 3d AIR DEFENSE ARTILLERY

RA
(inactive)

LINEAGE

Constituted 11 January 1812 in the Regular Army as a company in the 2d Regiment of Artillery. Organized in April 1812 at Petersburg, Virginia, as Capt. George W. Russell's Company, 2d Regiment of Artillery. Redesignated 12 May 1814 as Capt. George W. Russell's Company, Corps of Artillery. Redesignated in late 1814 as Capt. John S. Peyton's Company, Corps of Artillery. Redesignated 17 May 1815 as Capt. John S. Peyton's Company, Corps of Artillery, Southern Division (commanded by 2d Lt. Peter A. Dennis). Redesignated in September 1815 as Capt. Hippolite H. Villard's Company, Corps of Artillery, Southern Division. Redesignated 21 August 1816 as Company O, 2d Battalion, Corps of Artillery, Southern Division. Redesignated 1 June 1821 as Company I, 3d Regiment of Artillery.

Reorganized and redesignated 13 February 1901 as the 31st Company, Coast Artillery, Artillery Corps. Redesignated 2 February 1907 as the 31st Company, Coast Artillery Corps. Redesignated in September 1916 as the 2d Company, Fort Caswell [North Carolina]. Redesignated 19 July 1917 as Battery L, 8th Provisional Regiment, Coast Artillery Corps. Redesignated 5 February 1918 as Battery L, 53d Artillery (Coast Artillery Corps). Redesignated 6 August 1918 as Battery E, 53d Artillery (Coast Artillery Corps). (Additionally designated 1 June 1922 as the 31st Company, Coast Artillery Corps; additional designation abolished 1 July 1924.)

Redesignated 1 July 1924 as Battery C, 3d Coast Artillery, and inactivated at San Diego, California. Activated 2 December 1940 at Fort Rosecrans, California.

Reorganized and redesignated 18 October 1944 as Battery A, 522d Coast Artillery Battalion. Redesignated 15 September 1945 as Battery D, Harbor Defenses of Los Angeles. Inactivated 30 June 1946 at Fort MacArthur, California. Redesignated 28 June 1950 as Battery A, 18th Antiaircraft Artillery Battalion. Redesignated 13 March 1952 as Battery A, 18th Antiaircraft Artillery Gun Battalion. Activated 2 May 1952 at Fort Custer, Michigan. Redesignated 24 July 1953 as Battery A, 18th Antiaircraft Artillery Battalion. Redesignated 15 June 1957 as Battery B, 504th Antiaircraft Artillery Missile Battalion. Inactivated 1 September 1958 at Newport, Michigan.

Consolidated 1 January 1960 with Headquarters and Headquarters Battery, 3d Howitzer Battalion, 3d Artillery (active) (organized in 1861), and consolidated unit designated as Headquarters and Headquarters Battery, 3d Howitzer Battalion, 3d Artillery (organic elements constituted 2 June 1958 and activated 25 June 1958). Redesignated 1 July 1968 as the 3d Battalion, 3d Artillery. Inactivated 30 June 1971 at Fort Knox, Kentucky.

Redesignated (less former Headquarters and Headquarters Battery, 3d Howitzer Battalion, 3d Artillery) 1 September 1971 as the 3d Battalion,

3d Air Defense Artillery (former Headquarters and Headquarters Battery, 3d Howitzer Battalion, 3d Artillery, concurrently redesignated as the 3d Battalion, 3d Field Artillery—hereafter separate lineage).

CAMPAIGN PARTICIPATION CREDIT

War of 1812
  Canada

Indian Wars
  *Seminoles
  Washington 1858

Mexican War
  *Palo Alto
  *Resaca de la Palma
  Monterey
  Buena Vista
  Vera Cruz
  Cerro Gordo
  *Contreras
  *Churubusco
  *Molino del Rey
  *Chapultepec
  *Vera Cruz 1847
  Puebla 1847

Civil War
  Peninsula
  Antietam
  Fredericksburg
  Chancellorsville
  Gettysburg
  Wilderness
  Spotsylvania
  Petersburg
  Shenandoah
  Mississippi 1863
  Tennessee 1863

Tennessee 1864
Virginia 1863

China Relief Expedition
  *Streamer without inscription

Philippine Insurrection
  *Streamer with inscription

World War I
  *St. Mihiel
  *Meuse-Argonne
  *Lorraine 1918

World War II
  Naples-Foggia (with arrowhead)
  Anzio (with arrowhead)
  Rome-Arno
  Southern France (with arrowhead)
  North Apennines
  Ardennes-Alsace
  Central Europe
  Po Valley

Korean War
  CCF intervention
  First UN counteroffensive
  CCF spring offensive
  UN summer-fall offensive
  Second Korean winter
  Korea, summer–fall 1952
  Third Korean winter
  Korea, summer 1953

DECORATIONS

Meritorious Unit Commendation, Streamer embroidered EUROPEAN THEATER

4th BATTALION, 3d AIR DEFENSE ARTILLERY

RA
(inactive)

LINEAGE

Constituted 9 May 1794 in the Regular Army as the 3d Company, 4th Battalion, Corps of Artillerists and Engineers. Organized 7 August 1794 at West Point, New York, as Capt. Michael Kalteisen's 3d Company, 4th Battalion, Corps of Artillerists and Engineers. Redesignated 27 April 1798 as Capt. Michael Kalteisen's Company, 2d Battalion, 1st Regiment of Artillerists and Engineers. Redesignated 1 April 1802 as Capt. Michael Kalteisen's Company, Regiment of Artillerists. Redesignated 3 November 1807 as Capt. George Peter's Company, Regiment of Artillerists. Redesignated in May 1808 as Capt. Clarence Mulford's Company, Regiment of Artillerists. Redesignated 11 January 1812 as Capt. Clarence Mulford's Company (under the command of 2d Lt. Samuel Champlain), 1st Regiment of Artillery. Redesignated in February 1812 as Capt. William Wilson's Company, 1st Regiment of Artillery. Redesignated 12 May 1814 as Capt. William Wilson's Company, Corps of Artillery. Redesignated 17 May 1815 as Capt. William Wilson's Company, Corps of Artillery, Southern Division. Redesignated 21 August 1816 as Company B, 2d Battalion, Corps of Artillery, Southern Division. Redesignated 1 June 1821 as Company B, 3d Regiment of Artillery.

Reorganized and redesignated 13 February 1901 as the 26th Company, Coast Artillery, Artillery Corps. Redesignated 2 February 1907 as the 26th Company, Coast Artillery Corps. Redesignated 16 July 1916 as the 1st Company, Fort Flagler [Washington]. Redesignated 31 August 1917 as the 13th Company, Coast Defenses of Puget Sound. Redesignated 1 June 1922 as the 26th Company, Coast Artillery Corps.

Reorganized and redesignated 1 July 1924 as Battery B, 3d Coast Artillery. Inactivated 1 March 1930 at Fort MacArthur, California. Activated 1 July 1940 at Fort MacArthur, California.

Reorganized and redesignated 18 October 1944 as Battery B, 520th Coast Artillery Battalion. Redesignated 1 December 1944 as Battery B, 3d Coast Artillery Battalion. Redesignated 15 September 1945 as Battery C, Harbor Defenses of Los Angeles. Inactivated 30 June 1946 at Fort MacArthur, California. Consolidated 27 February 1950 with Battery B, 3d Antiaircraft Artillery Automatic Weapons Battalion (active) (*see* ANNEX), and consolidated unit designated as Battery B, 3d Antiaircraft Artillery Automatic Weapons Battalion, an element of the 3d Infantry Division. Redesignated 15 April 1953 as Battery B, 3d Antiaircraft Artillery Battalion. Inactivated 1 July 1957 at Fort Benning, Georgia, and relieved from assignment to the 3d Infantry Division.

Redesignated 12 August 1958 as Headquarters and Headquarters Battery, 4th Missile Battalion, 3d Artillery (organic elements concurrently constituted). Battalion activated 1 September 1958 at Detroit, Michigan. (Headquarters and Headquarters Battery, 4th Missile Battalion, 3d Artillery, consolidated 1 January 1960 with Battery B, 3d Armored Field Artillery Battalion [organized in 1898], and consolidated unit designated as Headquarters and Headquarters Battery, 4th Missile Battalion, 3d Artillery.) Inactivated 23 December 1960 at Detroit, Michigan. Redesignated 22 January 1962 as the 4th Battalion, 3d Artillery, and assigned to the lst Armored Division. Activated 3 February 1962 at Fort Hood, Texas. Inactivated 5 May 1971 at Fort Hood, Texas, and relieved from assignment to the 1st Armored Division.

Redesignated (less former Battery B, 3d Armored Field Artillery Battalion) 1 September 1971 as the 4th Battalion, 3d Air Defense Artillery (former Battery B, 3d Armored Field Artillery Battalion, concurrently redesignated as the 4th Battalion, 3d Field Artillery—hereafter separate lineage).

ANNEX

Constituted 6 July 1942 in the Army of the United States as Battery B, 534th Coast Artillery Battalion. Activated 15 July 1942 at Fort Bliss, Texas. Redesignated 12 December 1943 as Battery B, 534th Antiaircraft Artillery Automatic Weapons Battalion. Inactivated 19 October 1945 at Camp Patrick Henry, Virginia. Redesignated 9 December 1948 as Battery B, 3d Antiaircraft Artillery Automatic Weapons Battalion, and allotted to the Regular Army. Activated 15 January 1949 at Fort Bliss, Texas, as an element of the 3d Infantry Division.

CAMPAIGN PARTICIPATION CREDIT

War of 1812
  Canada

Indian Wars
  *Seminoles
  *Oregon 1856
  *Washington 1858

Mexican War
  Palo Alto
  Resaca de la Palma
  *Monterey
  Buena Vista
  *Vera Cruz
  *Cerro Gordo
  *Contreras
  *Churubusco
  *Molino del Rey
  *Chapultepec
  *Puebla 1847

Civil War
  Peninsula
  Antietam
  Fredericksburg
  Chancellorsville
  Gettysburg
  Wilderness

Spotsylvania
Petersburg
Shenandoah
Mississippi 1863
Tennessee 1863
Tennessee 1864
Virginia 1863

World War II
  *Naples-Foggia (with arrowhead)
  *Anzio (with arrowhead)
  *Rome-Arno
  *Southern France (with arrowhead)
  North Apennines
  *Ardennes-Alsace
  *Central Europe
  Po Valley

Korean War
  *CCF intervention
  *First UN counteroffensive
  *CCF spring offensive
  *UN summer-fall offensive
  *Second Korean winter
  *Korea, summer–fall 1952
  *Third Korean winter
  *Korea, summer 1953

DECORATIONS

Meritorious Unit Commendation, Streamer embroidered EUROPEAN THEATER

*Republic of Korea Presidential Unit Citation, Streamer embroidered UIJONGBU CORRIDOR (3d Antiaircraft Artillery Battalion cited; DA GO 20, 1953)

*Republic of Korea Presidential Unit Citation, Streamer embroidered IRON TRIANGLE (3d Antiaircraft Artillery Battalion cited; DA GO 29, 1954)

*Chryssoun Aristion Andrias (Bravery Gold Medal of Greece), Streamer embroidered KOREA (3d Antiaircraft Artillery Battalion cited; DA GO 2, 1956)

5th BATTALION, 3d AIR DEFENSE ARTILLERY

RA
(inactive)

LINEAGE

Constituted 9 May 1794 in the Regular Army as the 4th Company, 2d Battalion, Corps of Artillerists and Engineers. Organized in August 1794 at West Point, New York, as Capt. Donald G. Mitchell's 4th Company, 2d Battalion, Corps of Artillerists and Engineers. Redesignated 27 April 1798 as Capt. Donald G. Mitchell's Company, 3d Battalion, 1st Regiment of Artillerists and Engineers. Redesignated 6 August 1798 as Capt. Nehemiah Freeman's Company, 3d Battalion, 1st Regiment of Artillerists and Engineers. Redesignated 1 April 1802 as Capt. Richard S. Blackburn's Company, Regiment of Artillerists. Redesignated 30 April 1803 as Capt. John Saunder's Company, Regiment of Artillerists. Redesignated 3 June 1809 as Capt. William Wilson's Company, Regiment of Artillerists. Redesignated 11 January 1812 as Capt. William Wilson's Company, 1st Regiment of Artillery. Redesignated 29 February 1812 as Capt. Hannibal M. Allen's Company, 1st Regiment of Artillery. Redesignated 16 August 1813 as Capt. Hopley Yeaton's Company, 1st Regiment of Artillery. Redesignated 12 May 1814 as Capt. Hopley Yeaton's Company, Corps of Artillery. Redesignated 17 May 1815 as Capt. Hopley Yeaton's Company, Corps of Artillery, Southern Division. Redesignated 21 August 1816 as Company K, 2d Battalion, Corps of Artillery, Southern Division. Redesignated 1 August 1821 as Company D, 3d Regiment of Artillery.

Reorganized and redesignated 13 February 1901 as the 27th Company, Coast Artillery, Artillery Corps. Redesignated 2 February 1907 as the 27th Company, Coast Artillery Corps. Redesignated in July 1916 as the 7th Company, Fort Winfield Scott [California]. Redesignated 31 August 1917 as the 7th Company, Coast Defenses of San Francisco. Redesignated 22 December 1917 as the 4th Separate Antiaircraft Battery. Disbanded 22 January 1919 at Fort Totten, New York. Reconstituted 1 June 1922 in the Regular Army; concurrently consolidated with the 3d Company, Coast Defenses of Los Angeles (active) (organized 1 February 1918 at Los Angeles), and consolidated unit redesignated as the 27th Company, Coast Artillery Corps.

Reorganized and redesignated 1 July 1924 as Battery D, 3d Coast Artillery. Inactivated 1 February 1940 at Fort Rosecrans, California. Activated 2 December 1940 at Fort MacArthur, California. Inactivated 1 October 1942 at Fort MacArthur, California. Disbanded 18 October 1944.

Reconstituted 27 February 1950 in the Regular Army; concurrently consolidated with Battery D, 3d Antiaircraft Artillery Automatic Weapons Battalion (active) (*see* ANNEX), and consolidated unit designated as Battery D, 3d Antiaircraft Artillery Automatic Weapons Battalion, an element of the 3d Infantry Division. Redesignated 15 April 1953 as Battery D, 3d Antiaircraft Artillery Battalion. Inactivated 1 July 1957 at Fort Benning, Georgia, and relieved from assignment to the 3d Infantry Division.

Redesignated 12 August 1958 as Headquarters and Headquarters Battery, 5th Missile Battalion, 3d Artillery (organic elements concurrently constituted). Battalion activated 1 September 1958 at Pittsburgh, Pennsylvania. (Headquarters and Headquarters Battery, 5th Missile Battalion, 3d Artillery, consolidated 1 January 1960 with Battery D, 3d Field Artillery [organized in 1798], and consolidated unit designated as Headquarters and Headquarters Battery, 5th Missile Battalion, 3d Artillery.) Inactivated 18 October 1963 at Oakdale, Pennsylvania. Redesignated 24 November 1967 as the 5th Battalion, 3d Artillery, assigned to the 6th Infantry Division, and activated at Fort Campbell, Kentucky. Inactivated 24 July 1968 at Fort Campbell, Kentucky, and relieved from assignment to the 6th Infantry Division.

Redesignated (less former Battery D, 3d Field Artillery) 1 September 1971 as the 5th Battalion, 3d Air Defense Artillery (former Battery D, 3d Field Artillery, concurrently redesignated as the 5th Battalion, 3d Field Artillery—hereafter separate lineage).

ANNEX

Constituted 6 July 1942 in the Army of the United States as Battery D, 534th Coast Artillery Battalion. Activated 15 July 1942 at Fort Bliss, Texas. Redesignated 12 December 1943 as Battery D, 534th Antiaircraft Artillery Automatic Weapons Battalion. Inactivated 19 October 1945 at Camp Patrick Henry, Virginia. Redesignated 9 December 1948 as Battery D, 3d Antiaircraft Artillery Automatic Weapons Battalion, and allotted to the Regular Army. Activated 15 January 1949 at Fort Bliss, Texas, as an element of the 3d Infantry Division.

CAMPAIGN PARTICIPATION CREDIT

War of 1812
  Canada

Indian Wars
  *Seminoles
  Washington 1858

Mexican War
  Palo Alto
  Resaca de la Palma
  Monterey
  Buena Vista
  *Vera Cruz
  *Cerro Gordo
  Contreras
  Churubusco
  Molino del Rey
  Chapultepec
  Puebla 1847

Civil War
  Peninsula
  Antietam
  Fredericksburg
  Chancellorsville
  Gettysburg
  Wilderness
  Spotsylvania
  Petersburg
  Shenandoah

Mississippi 1863
Tennessee 1863
Tennessee 1864
Virginia 1863

China Relief Expedition
  *Streamer without inscription

Philippine Insurrection
  *Streamer without inscription

World War II
  *Naples-Foggia (with arrowhead)
  *Anzio (with arrowhead)
  *Rome-Arno
  *Southern France (with arrowhead)
  North Apennines
  *Ardennes-Alsace
  *Central Europe
  Po Valley

Korean War
  *CCF intervention
  *First UN counteroffensive
  *CCF spring offensive
  *UN summer–fall offensive
  *Second Korean winter
  *Korea, summer–fall 1952
  *Third Korean winter
  *Korea, summer 1953

DECORATIONS

Meritorious Unit Commendation, Streamer embroidered EUROPEAN THEATER

*Republic of Korea Presidential Unit Citation, Streamer embroidered UIJONGBU CORRIDOR (3d Antiaircraft Artillery Battalion cited; DA GO 20, 1953)

*Republic of Korea Presidential Unit Citation, Streamer embroidered IRON TRIANGLE (3d Antiaircraft Artillery Battalion cited; DA GO 29, 1954)

*Chryssoun Aristion Andrias (Bravery Gold Medal of Greece), Streamer embroidered KOREA (3d Antiaircraft Artillery Battalion cited; DA GO 2, 1956)

6th MISSILE BATTALION, 3d AIR DEFENSE ARTILLERY

RA
(inactive)

LINEAGE

Constituted 3 March 1847 in the Regular Army as Company M, 3d Regiment of Artillery. Organized 1 October 1847.

Reorganized and redesignated 13 February 1901 as the 34th Company, Coast Artillery, Artillery Corps. Redesignated 2 February 1907 as the 34th Company, Coast Artillery Corps. Redesignated in July 1916 as the 1st Company, Fort Stevens [Oregon]. Redesignated 31 August 1917 as the 1st Company, Coast Defenses of the Columbia. Redesignated 1 June 1922 as the 34th Company, Coast Artillery Corps.

Redesignated 1 July 1924 as Battery F, 3d Coast Artillery, and inactivated at Fort Stevens, Oregon. Activated 1 July 1939 at Fort Stevens, Oregon. Inactivated 1 February 1940 at Fort Stevens, Oregon. Activated 2 December 1940 at Fort MacArthur, California.

Reorganized and redesignated 18 October 1944 as Battery C, 522d Coast Artillery Battalion. Disbanded 15 September 1945 at Fort Mac-Arthur, California. Reconstituted 28 June 1950 in the Regular Army; concurrently consolidated with Battery C, 43d Antiaircraft Artillery Automatic Weapons Battalion (active) (*see* ANNEX), and consolidated unit designated as Battery C, 43d Antiaircraft Artillery Automatic Weapons Battalion, an element of the 10th Infantry Division. Redesignated 15 June 1954 as Battery C, 43d Antiaircraft Artillery Battalion. (43d Antiaircraft Artillery Battalion relieved 16 May 1957 from assignment to the 10th Infantry Division.) Inactivated 14 November 1957 in Germany.

Redesignated 12 August 1958 as Headquarters and Headquarters Battery, 6th Missile Battalion, 3d Artillery (organic elements concurrently constituted). Battalion activated 1 September 1958 at Arlington Heights, Illinois. (Headquarters and Headquarters Battery, 6th Missile Battalion, 3d Artillery, consolidated 1 January 1960 with Battery F, 3d Field Artillery [organized in 1898], and consolidated unit designated as Headquarters and Headquarters Battery, 6th Missile Battalion, 3d Artillery.) Inactivated 1 June 1965 at Chicago, Illinois.

Redesignated (less former Battery F, 3d Field Artillery) 1 September 1971 as the 6th Missile Battalion, 3d Air Defense Artillery (former Battery F, 3d Field Artillery, concurrently redesignated as the 6th Missile Battalion, 3d Field Artillery—hereafter separate lineage).

ANNEX

Constituted 5 May 1942 in the Army of the United States as Battery G, 504th Coast Artillery. Activated 1 July 1942 at Camp Hulen, Texas.

Reorganized and redesignated 20 January 1943 as Battery C, 630th Coast Artillery Battalion. Redesignated 12 December 1943 as Battery C,

630th Antiaircraft Artillery Automatic Weapons Battalion. Inactivated 26 September 1945 in Italy. Redesignated 18 June 1948 as Battery C, 43d Antiaircraft Artillery Automatic Weapons Battalion, an element of the 10th Infantry Division. Activated 1 July 1948 at Fort Riley, Kansas.

CAMPAIGN PARTICIPATION CREDIT

War of 1812
  Canada

Indian Wars
  Seminoles
  *California 1850
  *Washington 1858

Mexican War
  Palo Alto
  Resaca de la Palma
  Monterey
  Buena Vista
  Vera Cruz
  Cerro Gordo
  Contreras
  Churubusco
  Molino del Rey
  Chapultepec
  Puebla 1847

Civil War
  *Peninsula
  *Antietam
  *Fredericksburg
  Chancellorsville
  Gettysburg
  *Wilderness

Spotsylvania
Petersburg
Shenandoah
*Mississippi 1863
*Tennessee 1863
*Tennessee 1864
Virginia 1863

World War II
  *Naples-Foggia (with arrowhead)
  Anzio (with arrowhead)
  *Rome-Arno
  Southern France (with arrowhead)
  *North Apennines
  Ardennes-Alsace
  Central Europe
  *Po Valley

Korean War
  CCF intervention
  First UN counteroffensive
  CCF spring offensive
  UN summer–fall offensive
  Second Korean winter
  Korea, summer–fall 1952
  Third Korean winter
  Korea, summer 1953

DECORATIONS

*Meritorious Unit Commendation, Streamer embroidered EUROPEAN THEATER (630th Antiaircraft Artillery Automatic Weapons Battalion cited; GO 103, Headquarters, Fifth Army, 19 August 1945)

7th BATTALION, 3d AIR DEFENSE ARTILLERY

AR
(inactive)

LINEAGE

Constituted 2 March 1899 in the Regular Army as Battery N, 3d Regiment of Artillery. Organized in April 1899 at Angel Island, California.

Reorganized and redesignated 13 February 1901 as the 35th Company, Coast Artillery, Artillery Corps. Redesignated 2 February 1907 as the 35th Company, Coast Artillery Corps. Redesignated 1 July 1916 as the 1st Company, Fort Monroe [Virginia]. Redesignated 31 August 1917 as the 1st Company, Coast Defenses of Chesapeake Bay. Redesignated 1 June 1922 as the 35th Company, Coast Artillery Corps.

Redesignated 1 July 1924 as Battery G, 3d Coast Artillery, and inactivated at Fort Monroe, Virginia. Activated 1 June 1941 as Los Angeles, California. Inactivated 29 August 1941 at Los Angeles, California. Activated 14 February 1942 at Fort MacArthur, California.

Reorganized and redesignated 18 October 1944 as Battery A, 521st Coast Artillery Battalion. Redesignated 15 September 1945 as Battery E, Harbor Defenses of Los Angeles. Inactivated 30 June 1946 at Fort MacArthur, California. Redesignated 28 June 1950 as Battery B, 18th Antiaircraft Artillery Battalion. Redesignated 13 March 1952 as Battery B, 18th Antiaircraft Artillery Gun Battalion. Activated 2 May 1952 at Fort Custer, Michigan. Redesignated 24 July 1953 as Battery B, 18th Antiaircraft Artillery Battalion. Redesignated 15 June 1957 as Battery D, 85th Antiaircraft Artillery Missile Battalion. Inactivated 1 September 1958 at Newport, Michigan.

Redesignated 24 July 1959 as Headquarters and Headquarters Battery, 7th Howitzer Battalion, 3d Artillery; concurrently withdrawn from the Regular Army, allotted to the Army Reserve, and assigned to the Fifth United States Army (organic elements concurrently constituted). Battalion activated 1 October 1959 with Headquarters at Evanston, Illinois. Location of Headquarters changed 1 March 1963 to Chicago, Illinois. Redesignated 1 October 1963 as the 7th Battalion, 3d Artillery. Inactivated 1 September 1971 at Chicago, Illinois; concurrently redesignated as the 7th Battalion, 3d Air Defense Artillery.

Campaign Participation Credit

War of 1812
   Canada

Indian Wars
   Seminoles
   Washington 1858

Mexican War
   Palo Alto
   Resaca de la Palma
   Monterey
   Buena Vista
   Vera Cruz
   Cerro Gordo
   Contreras
   Churubusco
   Molino del Rey
   Chapultepec
   Puebla 1847

Civil War
   Peninsula
   Antietam
   Fredericksburg
   Chancellorsville
   Gettysburg
   Wilderness
   Spotsylvania
   Petersburg
   Shenandoah
   Mississippi 1863
   Tennessee 1863
   Tennessee 1864
   Virginia 1863

World War II
   Naples-Foggia (with arrowhead)
   Anzio (with arrowhead)
   Rome-Arno
   Southern France (with arrowhead)
   North Apennines
   Ardennes-Alsace
   Central Europe
   Po Valley

Korean War
   CCF intervention
   First UN counteroffensive
   CCF spring offensive
   UN summer–fall offensive
   Second Korean winter
   Korea, summer–fall 1952
   Third Korean winter
   Korea, summer 1953

Decorations

Meritorious Unit Commendation, Streamer embroidered EUROPEAN THEATER

8th BATTALION, 3d AIR DEFENSE ARTILLERY

RA
(inactive)

LINEAGE

Constituted 2 March 1899 in the Regular Army as Battery O, 3d Regiment of Artillery. Organized in 1899 at the Presidio of San Francisco, California.

Reorganized and redesignated 13 February 1901 as the 36th Company, Coast Artillery, Artillery Corps. Redesignated 2 February 1907 as the 36th Company, Coast Artillery Corps. Redesignated in July 1916 as the 5th Company, Fort Mills [Philippine Islands]. Redesignated 31 August 1917 as the 5th Company, Coast Defenses of Manila and Subic Bays. Redesignated 30 June 1922 as the 36th Company, Coast Artillery Corps.

Reorganized and redesignated 1 July 1924 as Headquarters Battery, 3d Coast Artillery.

Reorganized and redesignated 18 October 1944 as Battery B, 521st Coast Artillery Battalion. Disbanded 15 September 1945 at Fort Mac-Arthur, California.

Reconstituted 28 June 1950 in the Regular Army and redesignated as Headquarters Battery, 3d Antiaircraft Artillery Group. Activated 11 June 1951 at Camp Stewart, Georgia. Redesignated 20 March 1958 as Headquarters Battery, 3d Artillery Group.

Inactivated 15 December 1961 at Norfolk, Virginia; concurrently consolidated with Headquarters and Headquarters Battery, 8th Missile Battalion, 3d Artillery (active) (organized in 1916), and consolidated unit designated as Headquarters and Headquarters Battery, 8th Missile Battalion, 3d Artillery (organic elements constituted 16 January 1961 and activated 1 February 1961). Redesignated 30 June 1968 as the 8th Battalion, 3d Artillery.

Reorganized and redesignated (less former Headquarters and Headquarters Battery, 8th Missile Battalion, 3d Artillery) 1 September 1971 as the 8th Battalion, 3d Air Defense Artillery (former Headquarters and Headquarters Battery, 8th Missile Battalion, 3d Artillery, concurrently redesignated as the 8th Battalion, 3d Field Artillery—hereafter separate lineage). 8th Battalion, 3d Air Defense Artillery, inactivated 12 June 1973 at Oakland Army Base, California.

Campaign Participation Credit

War of 1812
Canada

Indian Wars
Seminoles
Washington 1858

Mexican War
Palo Alto
Resaca de la Palma
Monterey
Buena Vista
Vera Cruz
Cerro Gordo
Contreras
Churubusco
Molino del Rey
Chapultepec
Puebla 1847

Civil War
Peninsula
Antietam
Fredericksburg
Chancellorsville
Gettysburg
Wilderness
Spotsylvania
Petersburg
Shenandoah

Mississippi 1863
Tennessee 1863
Tennessee 1864
Virginia 1863

China Relief Expedition
*Streamer without inscription

Philippine Insurrection
*Streamer without inscription

World War II
Naples-Foggia (with arrowhead)
Anzio (with arrowhead)
Rome-Arno
Southern France (with arrowhead)
North Apennines
Ardennes-Alsace
Central Europe
Po Valley

Korean War
CCF intervention
First UN counteroffensive
CCF spring offensive
UN summer–fall offensive
Second Korean winter
Korea, summer–fall 1952
Third Korean winter
Korea, summer 1953

Decorations

Meritorious Unit Commendation, Streamer embroidered EUROPEAN
THEATER

16th DETACHMENT, 3d AIR DEFENSE ARTILLERY

RA
(inactive)

LINEAGE

Constituted 5 May 1942 in the Army of the United States as Headquarters Battery, 2d Battalion, 504th Coast Artillery. Activated 1 July 1942 at Camp Hulen, Texas. Reorganized and redesignated 20 January 1943 as Headquarters Battery, 630th Coast Artillery Battalion. Redesignated 12 December 1943 as Headquarters Battery, 630th Antiaircraft Artillery Automatic Weapons Battalion. Inactivated 26 September 1945 in Italy. Redesignated 18 June 1948 as Headquarters Battery, 43d Antiaircraft Artillery Automatic Weapons Battalion, an element of the 10th Infantry Division. Activated 1 July 1948 at Fort Riley, Kansas. Redesignated 15 June 1954 as Headquarters Battery, 43d Antiaircraft Artillery Battalion. (43d Antiaircraft Artillery Battalion relieved 16 May 1957 from assignment to the 10th Infantry Division.) Inactivated 14 November 1957 in Germany.

Redesignated 7 August 1958 as the 16th Detachment, 3d Artillery. Activated 1 September 1958 on Okinawa. Inactivated 25 October 1961 on Okinawa. Redesignated 1 September 1971 as the 16th Detachment, 3d Air Defense Artillery.

CAMPAIGN PARTICIPATION CREDIT

World War II–EAME
    Naples-Foggia (with arrowhead)
    Rome-Arno
    North Apennines
    Po Valley

DECORATIONS

Meritorious Unit Commendation for action in the EUROPEAN THEATER (630th Antiaircraft Artillery Automatic Weapons Battalion cited; GO 103, Headquarters, Fifth Army, 19 August 1945)

3D AIR DEFENSE ARTILLERY BIBLIOGRAPHY

Anderson, Robert. *An Artillery Officer in the Mexican War, 1846–7.* New York and London: G.P. Putnam's Sons, 1911.

Birkhimer, William E. "The Third Regiment of Artillery." *The Army of the United States.* Edited by Theophilus F. Rodenbough and William L. Haskin, 328–50. New York: Maynard, Merrill and Company, 1896. Originally published in *Journal of the Military Service Institution of the United States* 14 (1893):458–90.

Dutchak, Eugene, ed. *2d Armored Division, Fort Hood, Texas, 1961–1962.* Topeka: Josten Military Publications, 1962. Contains information about the 1st Battalion, 2d Air Defense Artillery.

Dyer, Frederick. "3d Regiment of Artillery." *A Compendium of the War of the*

Rebellion. New York: Thomas Yoseloff, 1959.

1st Armored Division, Fort Hood, Texas. Baton Rouge: Army and Navy Publishing Company, 1963. Contains information about the 4th Battalion, 3d Air Defense Artillery.

Halpern, Norman G. "A Battery's Flying Tackle." *Antiaircraft Artillery Journal* 94 (November–December 1951):15–16.

Harbor Defenses of Los Angeles, Fort MacArthur, 1941. Baton Rouge: Army and Navy Publishing Company, 1941.

Harbor Defenses of Los Angeles in World War II. Los Angeles, 1946.

Hawley, Donald C. *Third Coast Artillery.* San Pedro, Calif., 1942.

Kip, Lawrence. *Army Life on the Pacific; A Journal of the Expedition Against Northern Indians; The Tribes of the Coeur D'Alenes, Spokans, and Pelouzes, in the Summer of 1858.* Redfield, N.Y., 1859.

Mahon, John K. *History of the Second Seminole War, 1835–1842.* Gainesville: University of Florida Press, 1967.

Marquat, William F. "Automatic Artillery in Korea." *Antiaircraft Artillery Journal* 93 (November–December 1950):2–9; 94 (January–February 1951):2–12; (March–April 1951):2–5; (May–June 1951):2–6; (July–August 1951):2–9; (September–October 1951):2–5; (November–December 1951):2–6; 95 (January–February 1952):2–5; (March–April 1952):8–10; (May–June 1952):12–15.

Moomaw, Otho A. "Divisional Organic Antiaircraft Artillery: Sum and Substance." *Antiaircraft Artillery Journal* 96 (July 1953):2–7.

―――――. "Up Front with the 3d Antiaircraft Artillery." *Antiaircraft Artillery Journal* 96 (March 1953):20–21.

Nurre, H.J. *"D" Battery, 534th AAA (AW) Battalion.* Nuremburg, Germany, 1945.

2d Armored Division "Hell on Wheels," Fort Hood, Texas, 1965. Baton Rouge: Army and Navy Publishing Company, 1965. Contains information about the 1st Battalion, 3d Air Defense Artillery.

Sprague, John T. *The Origin, Progress, and Conclusion of the Florida War.* New York: D. Appleton and Company, 1848. Reprint. Gainesville, Fla.: University of Florida Press, 1964.

The Third Coast Artillery, A Historical Sketch. N.p., 1943.

4th AIR DEFENSE ARTILLERY

HERALDIC ITEMS

COAT OF ARMS

Shield: Gules, two pallets argent, on and over a fess vert between in chief overall five rays beveled counter beveled issuant fanwise blended from base blue through green and yellow to orange and in base a Lorraine Cross or, an escallop of the last charged with a Spanish castle of the first and between two cannon palewise of the second.

Crest: On a wreath of the colors, or and gules, a sheaf of twelve arrows argent behind a garb pierced by a fishhook fesswise, hook to sinister and base, or.

Motto: *Audacia* (By Daring Deeds).

Symbolism: The shield is scarlet for artillery and with the two white stripes, representative of the campaign streamer of the War of 1812, depicts the age of some of the units of the regiment. The green fess refers to Mexican War service, and the two silver cannon allude to those lost without dishonor and regained with glory during that war. The escallop, the emblem of St. James, with the Spanish castle, represents the battle of Santiago, Cuba, in which elements of the regiment participated. The Lorraine Cross signifies the service of a battery of the regiment in Lorraine during World War I. The five rays, indicative of the aurora borealis, denote the service of batteries of the regiment in Alaska.

The garb and fishook commemorate participation in the battle of Gettysburg in the wheat field, the fishhook being the shape of the federal battle line. The arrows denote the Indian campaigns.

DISTINCTIVE INSIGNIA

The distinctive insignia is an adaptation of the crest and motto of the coat of arms.

LINEAGE AND HONORS

LINEAGE

Constituted 1 June 1821 in the Regular Army as the 4th Regiment of Artillery and organized from new and existing units with Headquarters at Pensacola, Florida. Regiment broken up 13 February 1901 and its elements reorganized and redesignated as separate numbered companies and batteries of Artillery Corps. Reconstituted 1 July 1924 in the Regular Army as the 4th Coast Artillery. Activated 18 August 1924 (less Batteries B, E, and F) in the Canal Zone. (Battery C inactivated 31 July 1926 at Fort Amador, Canal Zone; Batteries B, C, and F activated 15 April 1932 at Fort Amador, Canal Zone; Battery E activated 1 February 1938 at Fort Amador, Canal Zone; Battery O activated 15 March 1940 in the Canal Zone; Batteries M and N activated 14 October 1940 in the Canal Zone; Battery L activated 27 January 1941 in the Canal Zone.) Regiment (less Headquarters and Headquarters Battery) disbanded 3 October 1944 in the Canal Zone.

Headquarters and Headquarters Battery, 4th Coast Artillery, reorganized and redesignated 1 November 1944 as Headquarters and Headquarters Battery, 4th Coast Artillery Group. Reorganized and redesignated 2 January 1945 as Headquarters and Headquarters Battery, Harbor Defenses of Balboa. Inactivated 15 January 1947 at Fort Amador, Canal Zone. Consolidated 28 June 1950 with Headquarters and Headquarters Battery, 4th Antiaircraft Artillery Group (*see* ANNEX 1), and consolidated unit designated as Headquarters and Headquarters Battery, 4th Antiaircraft Artillery Group. Activated 1 September 1951 at Ladd Air Force Base, Alaska. Inactivated 15 January 1958 at Ladd Air Force Base, Alaska.

Regiment (less Headquarters and Headquarters Battery) reconstituted 12 October 1944 in the Regular Army; concurrently consolidated with the 4th Coast Artillery Battalion (constituted 3 October 1944 in the Army of the United States) and consolidated unit designated as the 4th Coast Artillery Battalion. Activated 1 November 1944 in the Canal Zone. Disbanded (less Batteries A and D) 1 February 1946 in the Canal Zone (Batteries A and D concurrently redesignated as Batteries A and D, Harbor Defenses of Balboa; inactivated 15 January 1947 and 15 May 1950, respectively, in the Canal Zone). 4th Coast Artillery Battalion (less Batteries A and D) reconstituted 28 June 1950 in the Regular Army; concurrently battalion and Batteries A and D, Harbor Defenses of Balboa, redesignated as the 4th Coast Artillery (less Headquarters and Headquarters Battery).

1st Battalion, 4th Coast Artillery, consolidated 28 June 1950 with the 4th Antiaircraft Artillery Automatic Weapons Battalion (active) (*see* ANNEX 2), and consolidated unit designated as the 4th Antiaircraft Artillery Automatic Weapons Battalion. Redesignated 31 July 1950 as the 4th Antiaircraft Artillery Battalion. Inactivated 16 June 1957 in England.

2d Battalion, 4th Coast Artillery, redesignated 28 June 1950 as the 20th Antiaircraft Artillery Battalion. Redesignated 13 March 1952 as the 20th Antiaircraft Artillery Gun Battalion. Activated 8 May 1952 at Fort Lewis, Washington. Redesignated 1 May 1953 as the 20th Antiaircraft Artillery Battalion. Inactivated 20 December 1957 at Phantom Lake, Washington.

3d Battalion, 4th Coast Artillery, redesignated 28 June 1950 as the

44th Antiaircraft Artillery Battalion. Redesignated 1 April 1951 as the 44th Antiaircraft Artillery Gun Battalion and activated at Fort Stewart, Georgia. Redesignated 3 August 1953 as the 44th Antiaircraft Artillery Battalion. Redesignated 22 March 1955 as the 44th Antiaircraft Artillery Missile Battalion. Inactivated 1 September 1958 at Niagara Falls, New York.

Headquarters and Headquarters Battery, 4th Antiaircraft Artillery Group; 4th and 20th Antiaircraft Artillery Battalions; 44th Antiaircraft Artillery Missile Battalion; and 4th Field Artillery Battalion (organized in 1907) consolidated, reorganized, and redesignated as the 4th Artillery, a parent regiment under the Combat Arms Regimental System.

4th Artillery (less former 4th Field Artillery Battalion) reorganized and redesignated 1 September 1971 as the 4th Air Defense Artillery, a parent regiment under the Combat Arms Regimental System (former 4th Field Artillery Battalion concurrently reorganized and redesignated as the 4th Field Artillery—hereafter separate lineage).

ANNEX 1

Constituted 5 August 1942 in the Army of the United States as Headquarters and Headquarters Battery, 4th Antiaircraft Artillery Automatic Weapons Group. Activated 24 August 1942 at Camp Stewart, Georgia. Redesignated in the fall of 1943 as Headquarters and Headquarters Battery, 4th Antiaircraft Artillery Group. Disbanded 9 December 1944 in Italy. Reconstituted 28 June 1950 in the Regular Army.

ANNEX 2

Constituted 16 December 1940 in the Regular Army as the 3d Battalion, 95th Coast Artillery. Activated 17 April 1941 at Camp Davis, North Carolina.

Reorganized and redesignated 12 December 1943 as the 866th Antiaircraft Artillery Automatic Weapons Battalion. Inactivated 30 September 1946 on Luzon, Philippine Islands. Redesignated 13 October 1948 as the 4th Antiaircraft Artillery Automatic Weapons Battalion. Activated 15 January 1949 at Fort Bliss, Texas.

CAMPAIGN PARTICIPATION CREDIT

War of 1812
Louisiana 1815

Indian Wars
Creeks
Seminoles
Modocs
Little Big Horn
Nez Perces
Bannocks

Mexican War
Palo Alto
Resaca de la Palma
Monterey
Vera Cruz
Cerro Gordo
Contreras
Chapultepec
Tamaulipas 1846

Civil War
Peninsula
Shiloh
Valley
Manassas
Antietam
Fredericksburg
Murfreesborough
Chancellorsville
Gettysburg
Chickamauga
Chattanooga
Wilderness
Spotsylvania

Cold Harbor
Petersburg
Shenandoah
Nashville
Appomattox
Virginia 1861
Virginia 1862
Virginia 1863
Virginia 1864
Virginia 1865
Mississippi 1862

World War II
American Theater, Streamer without
inscription
Tunisia
Sicily
Naples-Foggia
Rome-Arno
Leyte
Ryukyus

Vietnam
Counteroffensive, Phase II
Counteroffensive, Phase III
Tet Counteroffensive
Counteroffensive, Phase IV
Counteroffensive, Phase V
Counteroffensive, Phase VI
Tet 69/Counteroffensive
Summer–fall 1969
Winter–spring 1970
Sanctuary Counteroffensive
Counteroffensive, Phase VII
Consolidation I

DECORATIONS

Presidential Unit Citation (Navy), Streamer embroidered VIETNAM 1967 (8th Battalion [less Battery B], 4th Artillery, cited; DA GO 32, 1973)

Valorous Unit Award, Streamer embroidered SAIGON (2d Battalion, 4th Artillery, cited; DA GO 43, 1970)

Meritorious Unit Commendation, Streamer embroidered VIETNAM 1968–1969 (8th Battalion, 4th Artillery, cited; DA GO 59, 1970)

1st BATTALION, 4th AIR DEFENSE ARTILLERY

RA

LINEAGE   (nondivisional)

Constituted 20 October 1786 in the Regular Army as Capt. Henry Burbeck's Company of Artillery and organized at West Point, New York. Redesignated 3 October 1787 as Capt. Henry Burbeck's 3d Company, Battalion of Artillery. Redesignated in 1792 as Capt. Daniel McLane's Company of Artillery of the 4th Sublegion, Legion of the United States. Redesignated 9 May 1794 as Capt. Daniel McLane's Company, 1st Battalion, Corps of Artillerists and Engineers. Redesignated 1 November 1797 as Capt. George Ingersoll's Company, 1st Battalion, Corps of Artillerists and Engineers. Redesignated 27 April 1798 as Capt. George Ingersoll's Company, 1st Battalion, 1st Regiment of Artillerists and Engineers. Consolidated 1 April 1802 with Capt. George Izard's Company, 1st Regiment of Artillerists and Engineers (*see* ANNEX 1), Capt. Frederick Frye's Company, 1st Battalion, 1st Regiment of Artillerists and Engineers (*see* ANNEX 2), and Capt. Peter Tallman's Company, 1st Regiment of Artillerists and Engineers (*see* ANNEX 3), and consolidated unit redesignated as Capt. Henry M. Muhlenberg's Company, Regiment of Artillerists. Redesignated 24 November 1804 as Capt. James B. Many's Company, Regiment of Artillerists. Redesignated 11 January 1812 as Capt. James B. Many's Company, 1st Regiment of Artillery. Redesignated 16 August 1813 as Capt. Thomas G. Murray's Company, 1st Regiment of Artillery. Redesignated 12 May 1814 as Capt. Thomas G. Murray's Company, Corps of Artillery. Redesignated 17 May 1815 as Capt. Thomas G. Murray's Company, Corps of Artillery, Southern Division. Redesignated 21 August 1816 as Company G, 3d Battalion, Corps of Artillery, Southern Division. Redesignated 1 June 1821 as Company D, 4th Regiment of Artillery.

Reorganized and redesignated 13 February 1901 as the 39th Company, Coast Artillery, Artillery Corps. Redesignated 2 February 1907 as the 39th Company, Coast Artillery Corps. Redesignated 30 June 1916 as the 1st Company, Fort Morgan [Alabama]. Redesignated 31 August 1917 as the 1st Company, Coast Defenses of Mobile. Inactivated 18 September 1921 at Fort Morgan, Alabama. Redesignated 1 June 1922 as the 39th Company, Coast Artillery Corps.

Redesignated 1 July 1924 as Battery D, 4th Coast Artillery. Activated 18 August 1924 at Fort Amador, Canal Zone. Disbanded 3 October 1944 in the Canal Zone.

Reconstituted 12 October 1944 in the Regular Army; concurrently consolidated with Battery D, 4th Coast Artillery Battalion (constituted 3 October 1944 in the Army of the United States), and consolidated unit designated as Battery D, 4th Coast Artillery Battalion. Activated 1 November 1944 at Fort Amador, Canal Zone. Redesignated 1 February 1946 as Battery D, Harbor Defenses of Balboa. Inactivated 15 May 1950 at Fort Amador, Canal Zone. Consolidated 28 June 1950 with Battery D, 4th Antiaircraft Artillery Automatic Weapons Battalion (active) (*see* ANNEX 4), and consolidated unit designated as Battery D, 4th Antiaircraft Artillery Automatic Weapons Battalion. Redesignated 31 July 1950 as Battery D, 4th Antiaircraft Artillery Battalion. Disbanded 15 November 1954 in England.

Reconstituted 12 August 1958 in the Regular Army; concurrently consolidated with Battery D, 4th Field Artillery (organized in 1901), and consolidated unit redesignated as Headquarters and Headquarters Battery, 1st Missile Battalion, 4th Artillery (organic elements concurrently constituted). Battalion activated 1 September 1958 at Niagara Falls, New York. Redesignated 20 December 1965 as the 1st Battalion, 4th Artillery. Inactivated 31 March 1970 at Niagara Falls, New York.

Redesignated (less former Battery D, 4th Field Artillery) 1 September 1971 as the 1st Battalion, 4th Air Defense Artillery (former Battery D, 4th Field Artillery, concurrently redesignated as the 1st Battalion, 4th Field Artillery—hereafter separate lineage). 1st Battalion, 4th Air Defense Artillery, activated 13 September 1972 at Fort Lawton, Washington. Inactivated 30 July 1974 at Fort Lawton, Washington. Activated 1 April 1979 at Fort Lewis, Washington.

ANNEX 1

Constituted 9 May 1794 in the Regular Army as the 1st Company, 2d Battalion, Corps of Artillerists and Engineers. Organized in June 1795 as Capt. Griffith J. McRee's 1st Company, 2d Battalion, Corps of Artillerists and Engineers. Redesignated in August 1796 as a company, 2d Battalion, Corps of Artillerists and Engineers (Captain McRee took command of Captain Wadsworth's Company in 1796—*see* ANNEX 3). Redesignated 27 April 1798 as a company, 1st Battalion, 1st Regiment of Artillerists and Engineers. Redesignated 9 March 1801 as Capt. Piercy S. Pope's Company, 1st Regiment of Artillerists and Engineers. Redesignated in 1801 as Capt. George Izard's Company, 1st Regiment of Artillerists and Engineers.

ANNEX 2

Constituted 27 April 1798 in the Regular Army as a company in the 1st Regiment of Artillerists and Engineers. Organized in July 1798 in Pennsylvania as Capt. John McClallen's Company, 1st Battalion, 1st Regiment of Artillerists and Engineers. Redesignated in 1799 as Capt. Frederick Frye's Company, 1st Battalion, 1st Regiment of Artillerists and Engineers.

ANNEX 3

Constituted 9 May 1794 in the Regular Army as the 2d Company, 3d Battalion, Corps of Artillerists and Engineers. Organized in June 1794 at West Point, New York, as Capt. Decius Wadsworth's 2d Company, 3d Battalion, Corps of Artillerists and Engineers. Redesignated 30 June 1796 as Lt. William Morris' 2d Company, 3d Battalion, Corps of Artillerists and Engineers. Redesignated in August 1796 as Capt. Griffith J. McRee's 3d Company, 3d Battalion, Corps of Artillerists and Engineers. Redesignated 27 April 1798 as Capt. Joseph Elliott's Company, 1st Regiment of Artillerists and Engineers. Redesignated 29 December 1800 as Capt. Peter Tallman's Company, 1st Regiment of Artillerists and Engineers.

ANNEX 4

Constituted 16 December 1940 in the Regular Army as Battery M, 95th Coast Artillery. Activated 17 April 1941 at Camp Davis, North Carolina.

Reorganized and redesignated 12 December 1943 as Battery D, 866th Antiaircraft Artillery Automatic Weapons Battalion. Inactivated 30 September 1946 on Luzon, Philippine Islands. Redesignated 13 October 1948 as Battery D, 4th Antiaircraft Artillery Automatic Weapons Battalion. Activated 15 January 1949 at Fort Bliss, Texas.

CAMPAIGN PARTICIPATION CREDIT

War of 1812
   *Louisiana 1815

Indian Wars
   *Creeks
   *Seminoles
   Modocs
   Little Big Horn
   *Nez Perces
   *Bannocks

Mexican War
   *Palo Alto
   *Resaca de la Palma
   Monterey
   *Vera Cruz
   *Cerro Gordo
   *Contreras
   *Chapultepec
   *Tamaulipas 1846

Civil War
   Peninsula
   Shiloh
   Valley
   Manassas
   Antietam
   Fredericksburg

Murfreesborough
Chancellorsville
Gettysburg
Chickamauga
Chattanooga
Wilderness
Spotsylvania
*Cold Harbor
*Petersburg
Shenandoah
Nashville
Appomattox
*Virginia 1861
*Virginia 1862
*Virginia 1863
*Virginia 1864
Virginia 1865
Mississippi 1862

World War II
   *American Theater, Streamer without
     inscription
   Tunisia
   Sicily
   Naples-Foggia
   Rome-Arno
   *Leyte
   *Ryukyus

DECORATIONS

*Philippine Presidential Unit Citation, Streamer embroidered 17 OCTOBER 1944 TO 4 JULY 1945 (866th Antiaircraft Artillery Automatic Weapons Battalion cited; DA GO 47, 1950)

2d BATTALION, 4th AIR DEFENSE ARTILLERY

RA
(inactive)

LINEAGE

Constituted 3 March 1847 in the Regular Army as Company M, 4th Regiment of Artillery. Organized 28 July 1847 at Fortress Monroe, Virginia.

Reorganized and redesignated 13 February 1901 as the 46th Company, Coast Artillery, Artillery Corps. Redesignated 2 February 1907 as the 46th Company, Coast Artillery Corps. Redesignated 12 July 1916 as the 3d Company, Fort Strong [Massachusetts]. Redesignated 21 July 1917 as Battery C, 6th Provisional Regiment, Coast Artillery Corps. Redesignated 5 February 1918 as Battery C, 51st Artillery (Coast Artillery Corps). Redesignated 7 August 1918 as Battery C, 43d Artillery (Coast Artillery Corps). Inactivated 16 August 1921 at Camp Eustis, Virginia. (Additionally designated 1 June 1922 as the 46th Company, Coast Artillery Corps; additional designation abolished 1 July 1924.)

Redesignated 1 July 1924 as Battery B, 4th Coast Artillery. Activated 15 April 1932 at Fort Amador, Canal Zone. Disbanded 3 October 1944 in the Canal Zone.

Reconstituted 12 October 1944 in the Regular Army; concurrently consolidated with Battery B, 4th Coast Artillery Battalion (constituted 3 October 1944 in the Army of the United States), and consolidated unit designated as Battery B, 4th Coast Artillery Battalion. Activated 1 November 1944 at Fort Amador, Canal Zone. Disbanded 1 February 1946 at Fort Amador, Canal Zone. Reconstituted 28 June 1950 in the Regular Army; concurrently consolidated with Battery B, 4th Antiaircraft Artillery Automatic Weapons Battalion (active) (*see* ANNEX), and consolidated unit designated as Battery B, 4th Antiaircraft Artillery Automatic Weapons Battalion. Redesignated 31 July 1950 as Battery B, 4th Antiaircraft Artillery Battalion. Inactivated 16 June 1957 in England.

Redesignated 1 December 1957 as Headquarters and Headquarters Battery, 2d Howitzer Battalion, 4th Artillery, assigned to the 9th Infantry Division, and activated at Fort Carson, Colorado (organic elements constituted 13 November 1957 and activated 1 December 1957). (Headquarters and Headquarters Battery, 2d Howitzer Battalion, 4th Artillery, consolidated 26 June 1958 with Battery B, 4th Field Artillery Battalion [organized in 1901], and consolidated unit designated as Headquarters and Headquarters Battery, 2d Howitzer Battalion, 4th Artillery.) Battalion inactivated 31 January 1962 at Fort Carson, Colorado. Redesignated 1 February 1966 as the 2d Battalion, 4th Artillery, and activated at Fort Riley, Kansas. Inactivated 13 October 1970 at Fort Lewis, Washington.

Redesignated (less former Battery B, 4th Field Artillery Battalion) 1 September 1971 as the 2d Battalion, 4th Air Defense Artillery, and relieved from assignment to the 9th Infantry Division (former Battery B, 4th Field Artillery Battalion, concurrently redesignated as the 2d Battalion, 4th Field Artillery—hereafter separate lineage).

ANNEX

Constituted 16 December 1940 in the Regular Army as Battery K, 95th Coast Artillery. Activated 17 April 1941 at Camp Davis, North Carolina.

Reorganized and redesignated 12 December 1943 as Battery B, 866th Antiaircraft Artillery Automatic Weapons Battalion. Inactivated 30 September 1946 in the Philippine Islands. Redesignated 13 October 1948 as Battery B, 4th Antiaircraft Artillery Automatic Weapons Battalion. Activated 15 January 1949 at Fort Bliss, Texas.

CAMPAIGN PARTICIPATION CREDIT

War of 1812
    Louisiana 1815

Indian Wars
    Creeks
    *Seminoles
    *Modocs
    Little Big Horn
    Nez Perces
    *Bannocks

Mexican War
    Palo Alto
    Resaca de la Palma
    Monterey
    Vera Cruz
    Cerro Gordo
    Contreras
    Chapultepec
    Tamaulipas 1846

Civil War
    Peninsula
    *Shiloh
    Valley
    Manassas
    Antietam
    Fredericksburg
    *Murfreesborough
    Chancellorsville
    Gettysburg
    *Chickamauga
    Chattanooga
    Wilderness
    Spotsylvania
    Cold Harbor
    Petersburg

    Shenandoah
    *Franklin
    *Nashville
    Appomattox
    Virginia 1861
    Virginia 1862
    Virginia 1863
    Virginia 1864
    Virginia 1865
    *Mississippi 1862

World War I
    *Lorraine 1918

World War II
    *American Theater, Streamer without
      inscription
    Tunisia
    Sicily
    Naples-Foggia
    Rome-Arno
    *Leyte
    *Ryukyus

Vietnam
    *Counteroffensive, Phase II
    *Counteroffensive, Phase III
    *Tet Counteroffensive
    *Counteroffensive, Phase IV
    *Counteroffensive, Phase V
    *Counteroffensive, Phase VI
    *Tet 69/Counteroffensive
    *Summer–fall 1969
    *Winter–spring 1970
    *Sanctuary Counteroffensive
    *Counteroffensive, Phase VII

DECORATIONS

*Valorous Unit Award, Streamer embroidered SAIGON (2d Battalion, 4th Artillery, cited; DA GO 43, 1970)

*Philippine Presidential Unit Citation, Streamer embroidered 17 OCTOBER 1944 TO 4 JULY 1945 (866th Antiaircraft Artillery Automatic

Weapons Battalion cited; DA GO 47, 1950)

*Republic of Vietnam Cross of Gallantry with Palm, Streamer embroidered VIETNAM 1966–1968 (2d Battalion, 4th Artillery, cited; DA GO 31, 1969, as amended)

*Republic of Vietnam Cross of Gallantry with Palm, Streamer embroidered VIETNAM 1968 (2d Battalion, 4th Artillery, cited; DA GO 31, 1969)

*Republic of Vietnam Cross of Gallantry with Palm, Streamer embroidered VIETNAM 1969 (2d Battalion, 4th Artillery, cited; DA GO 59, 1969)

*Republic of Vietnam Cross of Gallantry with Palm, Streamer embroidered VIETNAM 1969–1970 (2d Battalion, 4th Artillery, cited; DA GO 55, 1971)

*Republic of Vietnam Civil Action Honor Medal, First Class, Streamer embroidered VIETNAM 1966–1969 (2d Battalion, 4th Artillery, cited; DA GO 59, 1969)

*Republic of Vietnam Civil Action Honor Medal, First Class, Streamer embroidered VIETNAM 1969–1970 (2d Battalion, 4th Artillery, cited; DA GO 55, 1971)

Battery D additionally entitled to Valorous Unit Award, Streamer embroidered PARROT'S BEAK (Battery D, 2d Battalion, 4th Artillery, cited; DA GO 48, 1971)

3d BATTALION, 4th AIR DEFENSE ARTILLERY

RA
(82d Airborne Division)

LINEAGE

Constituted 11 January 1812 in the Regular Army as a company in the 2d Regiment of Artillery. Organized in May 1812 as Capt. James N. Barker's Company, 2d Regiment of Artillery. Consolidated in late 1813 with Capt. Spotswood Henry's Company, 2d Regiment of Artillery (organized in 1812), and consolidated unit designated as Capt. James N. Barker's Company, 2d Regiment of Artillery. Redesignated in December 1813 as Capt. Samuel B. Archer's Company, 2d Regiment of Artillery. Redesignated 12 May 1814 as Capt. Samuel B. Archer's Company, Corps of Artillery. Redesignated 17 May 1815 as Capt. Samuel B. Archer's Company, Corps of Artillery, Southern Division. Redesignated 21 August 1816 as Company D, 4th Battalion, Corps of Artillery, Southern Division. Redesignated 1 June 1821 as Company C, 4th Regiment of Artillery.

Reorganized and redesignated 13 February 1901 as the 38th Company, Coast Artillery, Artillery Corps. Redesignated 2 February 1907 as the 38th Company, Coast Artillery Corps. Redesignated 24 July 1916 as the 4th Company, Fort Winfield Scott [California]. Redesignated 29 March 1917 as the 1st Company, Fort MacArthur [California]. Redesignated 31 August 1917 as the 1st Company, Coast Defenses of Los Angeles. Redesignated in October 1917 as the 3d Separate Antiaircraft Battery. Demobilized 22 January 1919 at Fort Totten, New York. Reconstituted 1 June 1922 in the Regular Army and consolidated with the 2d Company, Coast Defenses of Los Angeles (active) (organized 1 February 1918 at Los Angeles; consolidated in 1922 with the 1st Company, Coast Defenses of Los Angeles [organized in January 1921 at Los Angeles]; and consolidated unit designated as the 2d Company, Coast Defenses of Los Angeles); consolidated unit concurrently redesignated as the 38th Company, Coast Artillery Corps, and inactivated at Los Angeles, California.

Redesignated 1 July 1924 as Battery C, 4th Coast Artillery. Activated 18 August 1924 at Fort Amador, Canal Zone. Inactivated 31 July 1926 at Fort Amador, Canal Zone. Activated 15 April 1932 at Fort Amador, Canal Zone.

Disbanded 1 November 1944 at Fort Kobbe, Canal Zone; concurrently reconstituted in the Regular Army, consolidated with Battery C, 4th Coast Artillery Battalion (constituted 3 October 1944 in the Army of the United States), consolidated unit designated as Battery C, 4th Coast Artillery Battalion, and activated at the Air Base, Seymour Island, Galapagos. Disbanded 1 February 1946 at Fort Amador, Canal Zone. Reconstituted 28 June 1950 in the Regular Army; concurrently consolidated with Battery C, 4th Antiaircraft Artillery Automatic Weapons Battalion (active) (*see* ANNEX), and consolidated unit designated as Battery C, 4th Antiaircraft Artillery Automatic Weapons Battalion. Inactivated 17 June 1957 in England.

Consolidated 25 June 1958 with Battery C, 4th Field Artillery Battalion (active) (organized in 1901), and consolidated unit reorganized and redesignated as Headquarters and Headquarters Battery, 3d Howitzer Battalion, 4th Artillery (organic elements constituted 2 June 1958 and activated 25 June 1958). Battalion inactivated 25 September 1958 at Fort Sill, Oklahoma. Assigned 15 March 1960 to the 2d Infantry Brigade. Activated 1 April 1960 at Fort Devens, Massachusetts. Inactivated 20 April 1962 at Fort Devens, Massachusetts, and relieved from assignment to the 2d Infantry Brigade.

Redesignated (less former Battery C, 4th Field Artillery Battalion) 1 September 1971 as the 3d Battalion, 4th Air Defense Artillery (former Battery C, 4th Field Artillery Battalion, concurrently redesignated as the 3d Battalion, 4th Field Artillery—hereafter separate lineage). 3d Battalion, 4th Air Defense Artillery, assigned 13 September 1972 to the 82d Airborne Division and activated at Fort Bragg, North Carolina.

ANNEX

Constituted 16 December 1940 in the Regular Army as Battery L, 95th Coast Artillery. Activated 17 April 1941 at Camp Davis, North Carolina.

Reorganized and redesignated 12 December 1943 as Battery C, 866th Antiaircraft Artillery Automatic Weapons Battalion. Inactivated 30 September 1946 at San Narciso, Luzon, Philippine Islands. Redesignated 13 October 1948 as Battery C, 4th Antiaircraft Artillery Automatic Weapons Battalion. Activated 15 January 1949 at Fort Bliss, Texas.

CAMPAIGN PARTICIPATION CREDIT

War of 1812
  *Canada
  Louisiana 1815

Barbary Wars
  *Streamer with bronze star (authorized
    by the U.S. Navy for actions against
    Algiers in 1815)

Indian Wars
  Creeks
  *Seminoles
  Modocs
  *Little Big Horn
  Nez Perces
  Bannocks

Mexican War
  Palo Alto
  Resaca de la Palma
  Monterey
  Vera Cruz
  Cerro Gordo
  *Contreras
  *Chapultepec
  Tamaulipas 1846

Civil War
  *Peninsula
  Shiloh
  Valley
  Manassas
  *Antietam
  *Fredericksburg
  Murfreesborough

  *Chancellorsville
  *Gettysburg
  Chickamauga
  Chattanooga
  *Wilderness
  *Spotsylvania
  Cold Harbor
  *Petersburg
  *Shenandoah
  Nashville
  *Appomattox
  Virginia 1861
  *Virginia 1862
  *Virginia 1863
  Virginia 1864
  *Virginia 1865
  Mississippi 1862

War With Spain
  *Puerto Rico

World War I
  *Streamer without inscription

World War II
  *American Theater, Streamer without
    inscription
  Tunisia
  Sicily
  Naples-Foggia
  Rome-Arno
  *Leyte
  *Ryukyus

DECORATIONS

*Philippine Presidential Unit Citation, Streamer embroidered 17 OCTOBER 1944 TO 4 JULY 1945 (866th Antiaircraft Artillery Automatic Weapons Battalion cited; DA GO 47, 1950)

4th BATTALION, 4th AIR DEFENSE ARTILLERY

RA
(inactive)

LINEAGE

Organized in the spring of 1821 in the Regular Army as Capt. John Erving's Company of Artillery. Redesignated 1 June 1821 as Company H, 4th Regiment of Artillery.

Reorganized and redesignated 13 February 1901 as the 42d Company, Coast Artillery, Artillery Corps. Redesignated 2 February 1907 as the 42d Company, Coast Artillery Corps. Redesignated 5 August 1916 as the 11th Company, Fort Mills [Philippine Islands]. Redesignated 31 August 1917 as the 11th Company, Coast Defenses of Manila and Subic Bays. Redesignated 30 June 1922 as the 42d Company, Coast Artillery Corps.

Redesignated 1 July 1924 as Battery H, 4th Coast Artillery, and inactivated in the Philippine Islands. Activated 18 August 1924 at Fort Amador, Canal Zone. Disbanded 3 October 1944 at Fort Clayton, Canal Zone.

Reconstituted 28 June 1950 in the Regular Army and redesignated as Battery D, 20th Antiaircraft Artillery Battalion. Redesignated 13 March 1952 as Battery D, 20th Antiaircraft Artillery Gun Battalion. Activated 8 May 1952 at Fort Lewis, Washington. Redesignated 1 May 1953 as Battery D, 20th Antiaircraft Artillery Battalion. Inactivated 20 December 1957 at Seattle, Washington.

Redesignated 12 August 1958 as Headquarters and Headquarters Battery, 4th Missile Battalion, 4th Artillery (organic elements concurrently constituted). Battalion activated 1 September 1958 at Poulsbo, Washington. Redesignated 20 December 1965 as the 4th Battalion, 4th Artillery. Redesignated 1 September 1971 as the 4th Battalion, 4th Air Defense Artillery. Inactivated 13 September 1972 at Fort Lawton, Washington.

Campaign Participation Credit

War of 1812
Louisiana 1815

Indian Wars
*Creeks
*Seminoles
Modocs
*Little Big Horn
Nez Perces
Bannocks

Mexican War
Palo Alto
Resaca de la Palma
*Monterey
*Vera Cruz
*Cerro Gordo
*Contreras
*Chapultepec
Tamaulipas 1846

Civil War
Peninsula
*Shiloh
Valley
Manassas
Antietam
Fredericksburg
*Murfreesborough
Chancellorsville
Gettysburg

*Chickmauga
Chattanooga
Wilderness
Spotsylvania
Cold Harbor
Petersburg
Shenandoah
Nashville
Appomattox
Virginia 1861
Virginia 1862
Virginia 1863
Virginia 1864
Virginia 1865
*Mississippi 1862
*Georgia 1864

War With Spain
*Santiago

World War II
*American Theater, Streamer without
inscription
Tunisia
Sicily
Naples-Foggia
Rome-Arno
Leyte
Ryukyus

Decorations

None.

5th BATTALION, 4th AIR DEFENSE ARTILLERY

RA
(inactive)

LINEAGE

Organized in May 1815 in the Regular Army at Fort Independence, Massachusetts, as Bvt. Lt. Col. Samuel D. Harris' Company, Regiment of Light Artillery. Redesignated 22 May 1816 as Company E, Regiment of Light Artillery. Redesignated 1 June 1821 as Company G, 4th Regiment of Artillery.

Reorganized and redesignated 13 February 1901 as the 41st Company, Coast Artillery, Artillery Corps. Redesignated 2 February 1907 as the 41st Company, Coast Artillery Corps. Redesignated 1 July 1916 as the 2d Company, Fort Monroe [Virginia]. Redesignated 31 August 1917 as the 2d Company, Coast Defenses of Chesapeake Bay. Redesignated 1 June 1922 as the 41st Company, Coast Artillery Corps.

Reorganized and redesignated 1 July 1924 as Battery G, 4th Coast Artillery. Disbanded 1 November 1944 at Fort Amador, Canal Zone.

Reconstituted 28 June 1950 in the Regular Army and redesignated as Battery C, 20th Antiaircraft Artillery Battalion. Redesignated 13 March 1952 as Battery C, 20th Antiaircraft Artillery Gun Battalion. Activated 8 May 1952 at Fort Lewis, Washington. Redesignated 1 May 1953 as Battery C, 20th Antiaircraft Artillery Battalion. Inactivated 20 December 1957 at Seattle, Washington.

Redesignated 12 August 1958 as Headquarters and Headquarters Battery, 5th Automatic Weapons Battalion, 4th Artillery (organic elements concurrently constituted). Battalion activated 1 September 1958 in Germany. Inactivated 10 August 1960 in Germany. Redesignated 19 February 1962 as the 5th Battalion, 4th Artillery, assigned to the 5th Infantry Division, and activated at Fort Carson, Colorado. Inactivated 17 August 1971 at Fort Carson, Colorado, and relieved from assignment to the 5th Infantry Division. Redesignated 1 September 1971 as the 5th Battalion, 4th Air Defense Artillery.

CAMPAIGN PARTICIPATION CREDIT

War of 1812
  Louisiana 1815

Indian Wars
  *Creeks
  *Seminoles
  Modocs
  Little Big Horn
  *Nez Perces
  *Bannocks
  *Nebraska 1855

Mexican War
  Palo Alto
  Resaca de la Palma
  *Monterey
  *Vera Cruz
  *Cerro Gordo
  *Contreras
  *Molino del Rey
  *Chapultepec
  Tamaulipas 1846

Civil War
  *Peninsula
  Shiloh
  Valley
  Manassas
  *Antietam
  *Fredericksburg
  Murfreesborough
  *Chancellorsville
  *Gettysburg
  Chickamauga
  *Chattanooga
  Wilderness

  Spotsylvania
  Cold Harbor
  Petersburg
  Shenandoah
  Nashville
  Appomattox
  *Virginia 1861
  Virginia 1862
  Virginia 1863
  Virginia 1864
  Virginia 1865
  Mississippi 1862

War With Spain
  *Santiago

World War II
  *American Theater, Streamer without
    inscription
  Tunisia
  Sicily
  Naples-Foggia
  Rome-Arno
  Leyte
  Ryukyus

Vietnam
  *Counteroffensive, Phase V
  *Counteroffensive, Phase VI
  *Tet 69/Counteroffensive
  *Summer–fall 1969
  *Winter–spring 1970
  *Sanctuary Counteroffensive
  *Countcroffensive, Phase VII
  *Consolidation I

DECORATIONS

*Republic of Vietnam Cross of Gallantry with Palm, Streamer embroidered VIETNAM 1968 (5th Battalion, 4th Artillery, cited; DA GO 43, 1970)

*Republic of Vietnam Cross of Gallantry with Palm, Streamer embroidered VIETNAM 1971 (5th Battalion, 4th Artillery, cited; DA GO 42, 1972)

6th BATTALION, 4th AIR DEFENSE ARTILLERY

AR
(inactive)

LINEAGE

Organized in 1816 in the Regular Army as Company M, 4th Battalion, Corps of Artillery, Southern Division. Redesignated 1 June 1821 as Company I, 4th Regiment of Artillery.

Reorganized and redesignated 13 February 1901 as the 43d Company, Coast Artillery, Artillery Corps. Redesignated 2 February 1907 as the 43d Company, Coast Artillery Corps. Redesignated 3 July 1916 as the 1st Company, Fort Terry [New York]. Redesignated 31 August 1917 as the 12th Company, Coast Defenses of Long Island Sound. Redesignated 2 December 1918 as the 8th Company, Coast Defenses of Long Island Sound. Redesignated 4 March 1921 as the 2d Company, Coast Defenses of Long Island Sound. Redesignated 17 December 1921 as the 5th Company, Coast Defenses of Long Island Sound. Redesignated 1 June 1922 as the 43d Company, Coast Artillery Corps.

Redesignated 1 July 1924 as Battery I, 4th Coast Artillery, and inactivated in the Coast Defenses of Long Island Sound. Activated 18 August 1924 at Fort Amador, Canal Zone. Disbanded 1 November 1944 at Fort Amador, Canal Zone.

Reconstituted 28 June 1950 in the Regular Army and redesignated as Battery A, 44th Antiaircraft Artillery Battalion. Redesignated 1 April 1951 as Battery A, 44th Antiaircraft Artillery Gun Battalion, and activated at Camp Stewart, Georgia. Redesignated 22 March 1955 as Battery A, 44th Antiaircraft Artillery Missile Battalion. Inactivated 1 September 1958 at Model City, New York.

Redesignated 31 March 1959 as Headquarters and Headquarters Battery, 6th Howitzer Battalion, 4th Artillery; concurrently withdrawn from the Regular Army, allotted to the Army Reserve, and assigned to the 63d Infantry Division (organic elements concurrently constituted). Battalion activated 1 May 1959 at Santa Monica, California. Redesignated 1 April 1963 as the 6th Battalion, 4th Artillery. Location of Headquarters changed 16 March 1964 to Playa del Rey, California. Inactivated 31 December 1965 at Playa del Rey, California, and relieved from assignment to the 63d Infantry Division. Redesignated 1 September 1971 as the 6th Battalion, 4th Air Defense Artillery.

CAMPAIGN PARTICIPATION CREDIT

War of 1812
   Louisiana 1815

Indian Wars
   *Creeks
   *Seminoles
   Modocs
   Little Big Horn
   Nez Perces
   Bannocks

Mexican War
   *Palo Alto
   *Resaca de la Palma
   *Monterey
   Vera Cruz
   Cerro Gordo
   Contreras
   Chapultepec
   *Tamaulipas 1846

Civil War
   Peninsula
   Shiloh
   Valley
   Manassas
   Antietam
   Fredericksburg
   Murfreesborough
   Chancellorsville
   Gettysburg
   *Chickamauga

*Chattanooga
Wilderness
Spotsylvania
Cold Harbor
Petersburg
Shenandoah
*Nashville
Appomattox
*Virginia 1861
Virginia 1862
Virginia 1863
Virginia 1864
Virginia 1865
*Mississippi 1862
*Kentucky 1862
*Tennessee 1863
*Tennessee 1864
*Alabama 1865
*Georgia 1865

World War II
   *American Theater, Streamer without
      inscription
   Tunisia
   Sicily
   Naples-Foggia
   Rome-Arno
   Leyte
   Ryukyus

DECORATIONS

None.

7th BATTALION, 4th AIR DEFENSE ARTILLERY

AR
(inactive)

LINEAGE

Constituted 5 July 1838 in the Regular Army as Company K, 4th Regiment of Artillery. Organized 24 July 1838 at Fort Columbus, New York.

Reorganized and redesignated 13 February 1901 as the 44th Company, Coast Artillery, Artillery Corps. Redesignated 2 February 1907 as the 44th Company, Coast Artillery Corps. Redesignated 1 July 1916 as the 1st Company, Fort Sherman [Canal Zone]. Redesignated 31 August 1917 as the 1st Company, Coast Defenses of Cristobal. Redesignated 30 June 1922 as the 44th Company, Coast Artillery Corps.

Redesignated 1 July 1924 as Battery K, 4th Coast Artillery, and inactivated in the Canal Zone. Activated 18 August 1924 at Fort Amador, Canal Zone. Disbanded 1 November 1944 at Fort Amador, Canal Zone.

Reconstituted 28 June 1950 in the Regular Army and redesignated as Battery B, 44th Antiaircraft Artillery Battalion. Redesignated 1 April 1951 as Battery B, 44th Antiaircraft Artillery Gun Battalion, and activated at Camp Stewart, Georgia. Redesignated 22 March 1955 as Battery B, 44th Antiaircraft Artillery Missile Battalion. Inactivated 1 September 1958 at Cambria, New York.

Redesignated 7 April 1959 as Headquarters and Headquarters Battery, 7th Howitzer Battalion, 4th Artillery; concurrently withdrawn from the Regular Army, allotted to the Army Reserve, and assigned to the 77th Infantry Division (organic elements concurrently constituted). Battalion activated 1 May 1959 at Fort Totten, New York. Redesignated 26 March 1963 as the 7th Battalion, 4th Artillery. Inactivated 30 December 1965 at Fort Totten, New York, and relieved from assignment to the 77th Infantry Division. Redesignated 1 September 1971 as the 7th Battalion, 4th Air Defense Artillery.

CAMPAIGN PARTICIPATION CREDIT

War of 1812
  Louisiana 1815

Indian Wars
  Creeks
  Seminoles
  *Modocs
  *Little Big Horn
  Nez Perces
  Bannocks

Mexican War
  Palo Alto
  Resaca de la Palma
  Monterey
  Vera Cruz
  Cerro Gordo
  Contreras
  Chapultepec
  Tamaulipas 1846

Civil War
  *Peninsula
  Shiloh
  Valley
  Manassas
  Antietam
  *Fredericksburg
  Murfreesborough
  *Chancellorsville
  *Gettysburg
  Chickamauga
  Chattanooga
  *Wilderness
  *Spotsylvania
  *Cold Harbor
  *Petersburg
  Shenandoah
  Nashville
  *Appomattox
  Virginia 1861
  *Virginia 1862
  *Virginia 1863
  Virginia 1864
  Virginia 1865
  Mississippi 1862

World War II
  *American Theater, Streamer without
    inscription
  Tunisia
  Sicily
  Naples-Foggia
  Rome-Arno
  Leyte
  Ryukyus

DECORATIONS

None.

8th BATTALION, 4th AIR DEFENSE ARTILLERY

RA
(inactive)

LINEAGE

Constituted 3 March 1847 in the Regular Army as Company L, 4th Regiment of Artillery. Organized 12 November 1847 at Fort Columbus, New York.

Reorganized and redesignated 13 February 1901 as the 45th Company, Coast Artillery, Artillery Corps. Redesignated 2 February 1907 as the 45th Company, Coast Artillery Corps. Redesignated 1 July 1916 as the 3d Company, Fort Grant [Canal Zone]. Redesignated 31 August 1917 as the 3d Company, Coast Defenses of Balboa. Redesignated 30 June 1922 as the 45th Company, Coast Artillery Corps.

Redesignated 1 July 1924 as Battery A, 4th Coast Artillery, and inactivated in the Canal Zone. Activated 18 August 1924 at Fort Amador, Canal Zone. Disbanded 3 October 1944 at Fort Amador, Canal Zone.

Reconstituted 12 October 1944 in the Regular Army; concurrently consolidated with Battery A, 4th Coast Artillery Battalion (constituted 3 October 1944 in the Army of the United States), and consolidated unit designated as Battery A, 4th Coast Artillery Battalion. Activated 1 November 1944 at Fort Amador, Canal Zone. Redesignated 1 February 1946 as Battery A, Harbor Defenses of Balboa. Inactivated 15 January 1947 at Fort Amador, Canal Zone. Consolidated 28 June 1950 with Battery A, 4th Antiaircraft Artillery Automatic Weapons Battalion (active) (*see* ANNEX), and consolidated unit designated as Battery A, 4th Antiaircraft Artillery Automatic Weapons Battalion. Redesignated 31 July 1950 as Battery A, 4th Antiaircraft Artillery Battalion. Inactivated 17 June 1957 in England.

Consolidated 4 April 1960 with Battery A, 4th Field Artillery Battalion (organized in 1901); consolidated unit redesignated as Headquarters and Headquarters Battery, 8th Howitzer Battalion, 4th Artillery, and assigned to the 1st Infantry Division (organic elements concurrently constituted). Battalion activated 20 April 1960 at Fort Riley, Kansas. Relieved 23 October 1963 from assignment to the 1st Infantry Division. Inactivated 2 January 1964 at Fort Sill, Oklahoma. Redesignated 20 December 1966 as the 8th Battalion, 4th Artillery. Activated 1 March 1967 at Fort Sill, Oklahoma.

Redesignated (less former Battery A, 4th Field Artillery Battalion) 1 September 1971 as the 8th Battalion, 4th Air Defense Artillery, and inactivated in Vietnam (former Battery A, 4th Field Artillery Battalion, concurrently reorganized and redesignated as the 8th Battalion, 4th Field Artillery—hereafter separate lineage).

ANNEX

Constituted 16 December 1940 in the Regular Army as Battery I, 95th Coast Artillery. Activated 17 April 1941 at Camp Davis, North Carolina.

Reorganized and redesignated 12 December 1943 as Battery A, 866th Antiaircraft Artillery Automatic Weapons Battalion. Inactivated 30 Sepember 1946 on Luzon, Philippine Islands. Redesignated 13 October 1948 as Battery A, 4th Antiaircraft Artillery Automatic Weapons Battalion. Activated 15 January 1949 at Fort Bliss, Texas.

CAMPAIGN PARTICIPATION CREDIT

War of 1812
  Louisiana 1815

Indian Wars
  Creeks
  *Seminoles
  Modocs
  Little Big Horn
  Nez Perces
  Bannocks

Mexican War
  Palo Alto
  Resaca de la Palma
  Monterey
  Vera Cruz
  Cerro Gordo
  Contreras
  Chapultepec
  Tamaulipas 1846

Civil War
  Peninsula
  Shiloh
  Vallcy
  Manassas
  Antietam
  Fredericksburg
  Murfreesborough
  Chancellorsville
  Gettysburg
  Chickamauga
  Chattanooga
  Wilderness
  Spotsylvania
  *Cold Habor

*Petersburg
Shenandoah
Nashville
Appomattox
*Virginia 1861
*Virginia 1862
*Virginia 1863
*Virginia 1864
Virginia 1865
Mississippi 1862
*North Carolina 1863

World War II
  *American Theater, Streamer without
    inscription
  Tunisia
  Sicily
  Naples-Foggia
  Rome-Arno
  *Leyte
  *Ryukyus

Vietnam
  *Counteroffensive, Phase III
  *Tet Counteroffensive
  *Counteroffensive, Phase IV
  *Counteroffensive, Phase V
  *Counteroffensive, Phase VI
  *Tet 69/Counteroffensive
  *Summer–fall 1969
  *Winter–spring 1970
  *Sanctuary Counteroffensive
  *Counteroffensive, Phase VII
  *Consolidation I

DECORATIONS

*Presidential Unit Citation (Navy), Streamer embroidered VIETNAM 1967 (8th Battalion [less Battery B], 4th Artillery, cited; DA GO 32, 1973)

*Meritorious Unit Commendation, Streamer embroidered VIETNAM 1968–1969 (8th Battalion, 4th Artillery, cited; DA GO 39, 1970)

*Philippine Presidential Unit Citation, Streamer embroidered 17 OCTOBER 1944 TO 4 JULY 1945 (866th Antiaircraft Artillery Automatic Weapons Battalion cited; DA GO 47, 1950)

*Republic of Vietnam Cross of Gallantry with Palm, Streamer embroidered VIETNAM 1971 (8th Battalion, 4th Artillery, cited; DA GO 6, 1974)

16th DETACHMENT, 4th AIR DEFENSE ARTILLERY

RA
(inactive)

LINEAGE

Constituted 1 July 1924 in the Regular Army as Headquarters, 2d Battalion, 4th Coast Artillery. Activated 18 August 1924 at Fort Amador, Canal Zone. Disbanded 1 November 1944 at Fort Amador, Canal Zone.

Reconstituted 28 June 1950 in the Regular Army and redesignated as Headquarters and Headquarters Battery, 20th Antiaircraft Artillery Battalion. Redesignated 13 March 1952 as Headquarters and Headquarters Battery, 20th Antiaircraft Artillery Gun Battalion. Activated 8 May 1952 at Fort Lewis, Washington. Redesignated 1 May 1953 as Headquarters and Headquarters Battery, 20th Antiaircraft Artillery Battalion. Inactivated 20 December 1957 at Phantom Lake, Washington.

Redesignated 5 August 1958 as the 16th Detachment, 4th Artillery. Activated 1 September 1958 at Fort Bliss, Texas. Inactivated 17 September 1962 at Fort Bliss, Texas. Redesignated 1 September 1971 as the 16th Detachment, 4th Air Defense Artillery.

CAMPAIGN PARTICIPATION CREDIT

None.

DECORATIONS

None.

4TH AIR DEFENSE ARTILLERY BIBLIOGRAPHY

"Activities of the 35th Antiaircraft Artillery Brigade." *Antiaircraft Artillery Journal* 93 (July 1950):31–32.

Buell, Augustus C. *The Cannoneer*. Washington: National Tribune, 1890.

Dyer, Alexander Brydie. *Historical Sketch of the Fourth U.S. Artillery*. Governor's Island, N.Y., 1890.

————. "The Fourth Regiment of Artillery." *The Army of the United States*. Edited by Theophilus F. Rodenbough and William L. Haskin, 351–75. New York: Maynard, Merrill and Company, 1896. Originally published in *Journal of the Military Service Institution of the United States* 11 (1890):843–67.

Dyer, Frederick. "4th Regiment of Artillery." *A Compendium of the War of the Rebellion*. New York: Thomas Yoseloff, 1959.

4th AAA, AW Battalion (M), Fort Bliss, Texas. Baton Rouge: Army and Navy Publishing Company, 1949.

Fuger, Frederick. "Cushing's Battery at Gettysburg." *Journal of the Military Service Institution of the United States* 41 (1907):405–10.

Gardner, Asa Bird. "Henry Burbeck: Brevet Brigadier-General United States Army—Founder of the United States Military Academy." *Magazine of American History* 9 (April 1883):251–66. Contains information about the current 1st Battalion, 4th Air Defense Artillery.

Ginsburg, A.R. "O'Brien's Bulldogs." *Field Artillery Journal* 27 (May-June 1937):182–87. Contains information about the current 5th Battalion, 4th Air Defense Artillery, and the former Battery B, 4th Regiment of Artillery.

McClellan, Edwin North. *History of the United States Marine Corps*. Washington: Historical Section, U.S. Marine Corps, 1931. Volume 2, pages 2–3, 8–9, contains information about the current 3d Battalion, 4th Air Defense Artillery.

Mahon, John K. *History of the Second Seminole War, 1835–1842*. Gainesville: University of Florida Press, 1967.

Michie, Peter Smith. *The Life and Letters of Emory Upton, Colonel of the Fourth Regiment of Artillery*. New York: D. Appleton and Company, 1885.

Official Register of the Fourth United States Artillery to April 1, 1866. Baltimore: J.B. Rose and Company, 1866.

Ott, David Ewing. *Field Artillery, 1954–1973*. Vietnam Studies. Washington: Government Printing Office, 1975. Contains information about the 2d and 8th Battalions, 4th Air Defense Artillery.

Reysen, Frank, ed. *9th Infantry Division, 1918–1968*. Vietnam: 9th Infantry Division, 1968. Contains information about the 2d Battalion, 4th Air Defense Artillery.

Roster of Commissioned Officers of the Fourth U.S. Artillery, From its Organization, June 1st, 1821, until the Regimental Organization was Discontinued February 2nd, 1901. Fort Monroe: Artillery School Press, 1901.

Sprague, John T. *The Origin, Progress, and Conclusion of the Florida War*. New York: D. Appleton and Company, 1848. Reprint. Gainesville, Fla.: University of Florida Press, 1964.

"The US Army in the Barbary Wars." *Air Defense* (July-September 1977): 36–37. Pertains to the current 3d Battalion, 4th Air Defense Artillery.

Weise, Carl, ed. *2nd Howitzer Battalion, 4th Artillery, 9th Infantry Division*. 2 vols. Dallas: Miller Publishing Company, 1958.

5th AIR DEFENSE ARTILLERY

HERALDIC ITEMS

COAT OF ARMS

Shield: Gules, a bend or charged with six cannon paleways in pairs sable, between in sinister chief a fishhook fessways, ring to dexter, barb to base, and in dexter base a Lorraine Cross, both of the second (or).

Crest: On a wreath of the colors, or and gules, upon a cannon wheel or partly surrounded by two palm branches vert the wheel grasped by two hands proper issuant chevronways from base, a bronze cannon paleways smoking of the last (proper).

Motto: *Volens et Potens* (Willing and Able).

Symbolism: The shield is scarlet for artillery. The fishhook, representative of the shape of the federal battle lines, alludes to the battle of Gettysburg. The cannon in pairs refer to the battle of New Market, 1864. The Lorraine Cross denotes service in Lorraine by an element of the regiment during World War I.

The crest represents the gallant service of Lt. Richard Metcalf's battery at Spotsylvania, 4–24 May 1864, when it charged earthworks firing its guns and then ran them up by hand to a new position, to the Bloody Angle, and fired repeatedly. This is purported to be the only recorded instance in the Civil War of a battery charging on breastworks.

DISTINCTIVE INSIGNIA

The distinctive insignia is the shield of the coat of arms.

LINEAGE AND HONORS

LINEAGE

Constituted 18 June 1861 in the Regular Army as the 5th Regiment of Artillery. Organized 4 July 1861 at Fort Greble, Pennsylvania. Regiment broken up 13 February 1901 and its elements reorganized and redesignated as separate numbered companies and batteries of Artillery Corps. Reconstituted 1 July 1924 in the Regular Army as the 5th Coast Artillery and partially organized with Headquarters at Fort Hamilton, New York. (Batteries A and B activated 1 August 1940 and 15 January 1941, respectively, at Fort Wadsworth, New York; Battery D activated 15 January

103

1941 at Fort Hamilton, New York.) Active elements of regiment inactivated 19 April 1944 at Camp Rucker, Alabama. Disbanded 26 June 1944.

Headquarters and Headquarters Battery, 5th Coast Artillery, reconstituted 28 June 1950 in the Regular Army; concurrently consolidated with Headquarters and Headquarters Battery, 5th Antiaircraft Artillery Group (active) (*see* ANNEX 1), and consolidated unit designated as Headquarters and Headquarters Battery, 5th Antiaircraft Artillery Group. Redesignated 20 March 1958 as Headquarters and Headquarters Battery, 5th Artillery Group. Inactivated 26 August 1960 at Camp Hanford, Washington.

1st Battalion, 5th Coast Artillery, reconstituted 28 June 1950 in the Regular Army.

2d Battalion, 5th Coast Artillery, reconstituted 28 June 1950 in the Regular Army; concurrently consolidated with the 214th Antiaircraft Artillery Gun Battalion (*see* ANNEX 2), and consolidated unit redesignated as the 24th Antiaircraft Artillery Battalion. Redesignated 13 March 1952 as the 24th Antiaircraft Artillery Gun Battalion. Activated 16 April 1952 in Korea. Inactivated 20 December 1954 in Korea. Redesignated 23 May 1955 as the 24th Antiaircraft Artillery Missile Battalion. Activated 1 June 1955 at Fort Banks, Massachusetts. Inactivated 1 September 1958 at Bedford, Massachusetts.

Headquarters and Headquarters Battery, 5th Artillery Group; 24th Antiaircraft Artillery Missile Battalion; 1st Battalion, 5th Coast Artillery; and 5th Field Artillery Battalion (organized in 1907) consolidated, reorganized, and redesignated 26 August 1960 as the 5th Artillery, a parent regiment under the Combat Arms Regimental System.

5th Artillery (less former 5th Field Artillery Battalion) reorganized and redesignated 1 September 1971 as the 5th Air Defense Artillery, a parent regiment under the Combat Arms Regimental System (former 5th Field Artillery Battalion concurrently reorganized and redesignated as the 5th Field Artillery—hereafter separate lineage).

ANNEX 1

Constituted 5 August 1942 in the Army of the United States as Headquarters and Headquarters Battery, 5th Antiaircraft Artillery Automatic Weapons Group. Activated 17 August 1942 at Camp Hulen, Texas. Redesignated 18 February 1944 as Headquarters and Headquarters Battery, 5th Antiaircraft Artillery Group. Inactivated 15 October 1945 at Camp Myles Standish, Massachusetts. Activated 1 August 1946 at Fort Bliss, Texas.

ANNEX 2

Constituted 5 May 1942 in the Army of the United States as the 1st Battalion, 504th Coast Artillery. Activated 1 July 1942 at Camp Hulen, Texas.

Reorganized and redesignated 20 January 1943 as the 214th Coast

Artillery Battalion. Redesignated 13 November 1943 as the 214th Anti-aircraft Artillery Gun Battalion. Inactivated 12 February 1946 at Camp Kilmer, New Jersey.

CAMPAIGN PARTICIPATION CREDIT

Civil War
Peninsula
Manassas
Antietam
Fredericksburg
Chancellorsville
Gettysburg
Wilderness
Spotsylvania
Cold Harbor
Petersburg
Shenandoah
Appomattox
Virginia 1862
Virginia 1863
Virginia 1864

World War II
Tunisia
Sicily
Naples-Foggia
Anzio
Rome-Arno

Southern France (with arrowhead)
Rhineland
Ardennes-Alsace
Central Europe

Korean War
Second Korean winter
Korea, summer-fall 1952
Third Korean winter
Korea, summer 1953

Vietnam
Defense
Counteroffensive
Counteroffensive, Phase II
Counteroffensive, Phase III
Tet Counteroffensive
Counteroffensive, Phase IV
Counteroffensive, Phase V
Counteroffensive, Phase VI
Tet 69/Counteroffensive
Summer–fall 1969
Winter–spring 1970

DECORATIONS

Meritorious Unit Commendation, Streamer embroidered VIETNAM 1966–1967 (1st Battalion, 5th Artillery, cited; DA GO 48, 1968).

Meritorious Unit Commendation, Streamer embroidered VIETNAM 1967–1968 (1st Battalion, 5th Artillery, cited; DA GO 39, 1970)

1st BATTALION, 5th AIR DEFENSE ARTILLERY

RA
(inactive)

LINEAGE

Constituted 18 June 1861 in the Regular Army as Battery L, 5th Regiment of Artillery. Organized 4 July 1861 at Fort Greble, Pennsylvania.

Reorganized and redesignated 13 February 1901 as the 56th Company, Coast Artillery, Artillery Corps. Redesignated 2 February 1907 as the 56th Company, Coast Artillery Corps. Redesignated 20 July 1916 as the 6th Company, Fort Hancock [New Jersey]. Redesignated 31 August 1917 as the 6th Company, Coast Defenses of Sandy Hook. Redesignated 1 June 1922 as the 56th Company, Coast Artillery Corps.

Redesignated 1 July 1924 as Battery D, 5th Coast Artillery, and inactivated in New Jersey. Activated 15 January 1941 at Fort Hamilton, New York. Inactivated 19 April 1944 at Camp Rucker, Alabama. Disbanded 26 June 1944. Reconstituted 28 June 1950 in the Regular Army.

Consolidated 26 August 1960 with Headquarters and Headquarters Battery, 1st Rocket Howitzer Battalion, 5th Artillery (active) (organized in 1776), and consolidated unit designated as Headquarters and Headquarters Battery, 1st Rocket Howitzer Battalion, 5th Artillery, an element of the 1st Infantry Division (organic elements constituted 8 February 1957 and activated 15 February 1957). Redesignated 21 January 1964 as the 1st Battalion, 5th Artillery.

Redesignated (less former Headquarters and Headquarters Battery, 1st Rocket Howitzer Battalion, 5th Artillery) 1 September 1971 as the 1st Battalion, 5th Air Defense Artillery; concurrently inactivated at Fort Riley, Kansas, and relieved from assignment to the 1st Infantry Division (former Headquarters and Headquarters Battery, 1st Rocket Howitzer Battalion, 5th Artillery, concurrently reorganized and redesignated as the 1st Battalion, 5th Field Artillery—hereafter separate lineage). 1st Battalion, 5th Air Defense Artillery, activated 13 September 1972 at Coventry, Rhode Island. Inactivated 30 October 1974 at Coventry, Rhode Island.

CAMPAIGN PARTICIPATION CREDIT

Civil War
- Peninsula
- Manassas
- Antietam
- Fredericksburg
- Chancellorsville
- Gettysburg
- Wilderness
- Spotsylvania
- Cold Harbor
- Petersburg
- *Shenandoah
- Appomattox
- Virginia 1862
- *Virginia 1863
- *Virginia 1864
- *Maryland 1864

World War II
- Tunisia
- Sicily
- Naples-Foggia
- Anzio
- Rome-Arno

- Southern France (with arrowhead)
- Rhineland
- Ardennes-Alsace
- Central Europe

Korean War
- Second Korean winter
- Korea, summer–fall 1952
- Third Korean winter
- Korea, summer 1953

Vietnam
- *Defense
- *Counteroffensive
- *Counteroffensive, Phase II
- *Counteroffensive, Phase III
- *Tet Counteroffensive
- *Counteroffensive, Phase IV
- *Counteroffensive, Phase V
- *Counteroffensive, Phase VI
- *Tet 69/Counteroffensive
- *Summer–fall 1969
- *Winter–spring 1970

DECORATIONS

*Meritorious Unit Commendation, Streamer embroidered VIETNAM 1966–1967 (1st Battalion, 5th Artillery, cited; DA GO 48, 1968)

*Meritorious Unit Commendation, Streamer embroidered VIETNAM 1967–1968 (1st Battalion, 5th Artillery, cited; DA GO 39, 1970)

*Republic of Vietnam Cross of Gallantry with Palm, Streamer embroidered VIETNAM 1965–1968 (1st Battalion, 5th Artillery, cited; DA GO 21, 1969)

*Republic of Vietnam Cross of Gallantry with Palm, Streamer embroidered VIETNAM 1969–1970 (1st Battalion, 5th Artillery, cited; DA GO 2, 1971)

*Republic of Vietnam Civil Action Honor Medal, First Class, Streamer embroidered VIETNAM 1965–1970 (1st Battalion, 5th Artillery, cited; DA GO 53, 1970)

2d BATTALION, 5th AIR DEFENSE ARTILLERY

RA
(2d Armored Division)

LINEAGE

Constituted 18 June 1861 in the Regular Army as Battery A, 5th Regiment of Artillery. Organized 4 July 1861 at Fort Greble, Pennsylvania.

Reorganized and redesignated 13 February 1901 as the 49th Company, Coast Artillery, Artillery Corps. Redesignated 2 February 1907 as the 49th Company, Coast Artillery Corps. Redesignated 1 July 1916 as the 3d Company, Fort Williams [Maine]. Redesignated 21 July 1917 as Battery G, 6th Provisional Regiment, Coast Artillery Corps. Redesignated 5 February 1918 as Battery G, 51st Artillery (Coast Artillery Corps). Redesignated 15 July 1918 as Battery D, 57th Artillery (Coast Artillery Corps). Disbanded 30 June 1921 at Camp Lewis, Washington. Reconstituted 1 June 1922 in the Regular Army; concurrently consolidated with Headquarters Company, Coast Defenses of Puget Sound (active) (organized in June 1921), and consolidated unit redesignated as the 49th Company, Coast Artillery Corps.

Redesignated 1 July 1924 as Battery A, 5th Coast Artillery, and inactivated in the Coast Defenses of Puget Sound. Activated 1 August 1940 at Fort Wadsworth, New York. Inactivated 19 April 1944 at Camp Rucker, Alabama. Disbanded 26 June 1944. Reconstituted 28 June 1950 in the Regular Army.

Consolidated 26 August 1960 with Headquarters and Headquarters Battery, 2d Howitzer Battalion, 5th Artillery (active) (organized in 1898), and consolidated unit designated as Headquarters and Headquarters Battery, 2d Howitzer Battalion, 5th Artillery (organic elements constituted 1 June 1958 and activated 25 June 1958). Redesignated 25 June 1964 as the 2d Battalion, 5th Artillery.

Redesignated (less former Headquarters and Headquarters Battery, 2d Howitzer Battalion, 5th Artillery) 1 September 1971 as the 2d Battalion, 5th Air Defense Artillery, and inactivated in Germany (former Headquarters and Headquarters Battery, 2d Howitzer Battalion, 5th Artillery, concurrently reorganized and redesignated as the 2d Battalion, 5th Field Artillery—hereafter separate lineage). 2d Battalion, 5th Air Defense Artillery, assigned 13 September 1972 to the 2d Armored Division and activated at Fort Hood, Texas.

Campaign Participation Credit

Civil War
  *Peninsula
   Manassas
  *Antietam
  *Fredericksburg
   Chancellorsville
   Gettysburg
   Wilderness
   Spotsylvania
  *Cold Harbor
  *Petersburg
   Shenandoah
   Appomattox
   Virginia 1862
  *Virginia 1863
  *Virginia 1864

World War I
  *St. Mihiel

  *Meuse-Argonne
  *Lorraine 1918

World War II
   Tunisia
   Sicily
   Naples-Foggia
   Anzio
   Rome-Arno
   Southern France (with arrowhead)
   Rhineland
   Ardennes-Alsace
   Central Europe

Korean War
   Second Korean winter
   Korea, summer–fall 1952
   Third Korean winter
   Korea, summer 1953

Decorations

None.

3d BATTALION, 5th AIR DEFENSE ARTILLERY

RA
(inactive)

LINEAGE

Constituted 18 June 1861 in the Regular Army as Battery B, 5th Regiment of Artillery. Organized 4 July 1861 at Fort Greble, Pennsylvania.

Reorganized and redesignated 13 February 1901 as the 50th Company, Coast Artillery, Artillery Corps. Redesignated 2 February 1907 as the 50th Company, Coast Artillery Corps. Redesignated in July 1916 as the 1st Company, Fort Levett [Maine]. Redesignated 31 August 1917 as the 9th Company, Coast Defenses of Portland. Redesignated 9 February 1921 as the 2d Company, Coast Defenses of Portland. Redesignated 1 June 1922 as the 50th Company, Coast Artillery Corps.

Redesignated 1 July 1924 as Battery B, 5th Coast Artillery, and inactivated in the Coast Defenses of Portland. Activated 15 January 1941 at Fort Wadsworth, New York. Inactivated 19 April 1944 at Camp Rucker, Alabama. Disbanded 26 June 1944. Reconstituted 28 June 1950 in the Regular Army.

Redesignated 12 August 1958 as Headquarters and Headquarters Battery, 3d Missile Battalion, 5th Artillery (organic elements concurrently constituted). Battalion activated 1 September 1958 at Bedford, Massachusetts. (Headquarters and Headquarters Battery, 3d Missile Battalion, 5th Artillery, consolidated 26 August 1960 with Battery A, 5th Field Artillery Battalion [organized in 1861], and consolidated unit designated as Headquarters and Headquarters Battery, 3d Missile Battalion, 5th Artillery.) Redesignated 20 December 1965 as the 3d Battalion, 5th Artillery.

Reorganized and redesignated (less former Battery A, 5th Field Artillery Battalion) 1 September 1971 as the 3d Battalion, 5th Air Defense Artillery (former Battery A, 5th Field Artillery Battalion, concurrently redesignated as the 3d Battalion, 5th Field Artillery—hereafter separate lineage). 3d Battalion, 5th Air Defense Artillery, inactivated 13 September 1972 at Coventry, Rhode Island.

Campaign Participation Credit

Civil War
  Peninsula
  Manassas
  Antietam
  Fredericksburg
  Chancellorsville
  Gettysburg
  Wilderness
  Spotsylvania
  Cold Harbor
  Petersburg
  *Shenandoah
  Appomattox
  Virginia 1862
  Virginia 1863
  *Virginia 1864

War With Spain
  *Puerto Rico

World War II
  Tunisia
  Sicily
  Naples-Foggia
  Anzio
  Rome-Arno
  Southern France (with arrowhead)
  Rhineland
  Ardennes-Alsace
  Central Europe

Korean War
  Second Korean winter
  Korea, summer–fall 1952
  Third Korean winter
  Korea, summer 1953

Decorations

None.

4th MISSILE BATTALION, 5th AIR DEFENSE ARTILLERY

RA
(inactive)

LINEAGE

Constituted 18 June 1861 in the Regular Army as Battery G, 5th Regiment of Artillery. Organized 4 July 1861 at Fort Greble, Pennsylvania.

Reorganized and redesignated 13 February 1901 as the 53d Company, Coast Artillery, Artillery Corps. Redesignated 2 February 1907 as the 53d Company, Coast Artillery Corps. Redesignated 30 June 1916 as the 1st Company, Fort Wadsworth [New York]. Redesignated 31 August 1917 as the 5th Company, Coast Defenses of Southern New York. Redesignated 1 June 1922 as the 53d Company, Coast Artillery Corps.

Redesignated 1 July 1924 as Battery G, 5th Coast Artillery, and inactivated in the Coast Defenses of Southern New York. Disbanded 26 June 1944.

Reconstituted 28 June 1950 in the Regular Army; concurrently consolidated with Battery C, 214th Antiaircraft Artillery Gun Battalion (*see* ANNEX), and consolidated unit redesignated as Battery C, 24th Antiaircraft Artillery Battalion. Redesignated 13 March 1952 as Battery C, 24th Antiaircraft Artillery Gun Battalion. Activated 16 April 1952 in Korea. Inactivated 20 December 1954 in Korea. Redesignated 23 May 1955 as Battery C, 24th Antiaircraft Artillery Missile Battalion. Activated 1 June 1955 at Fort Banks, Massachusetts. Redesignated 1 January 1956 as Battery B, 514th Antiaircraft Artillery Missile Battalion.

Reorganized and redesignated 1 September 1958 as Headquarters and Headquarters Battery, 4th Missile Battalion, 5th Artillery (organic elements constituted 12 August 1958 and activated 1 September 1958). Battalion inactivated 10 August 1960 at Laytonsville, Maryland. (Headquarters and Headquarters Battery, 4th Missile Battalion, 5th Artillery, consolidated 26 August 1960 with Battery C, 5th Field Artillery Battalion [organized in 1901], and consolidated unit designated as Headquarters and Headquarters Battery, 4th Missile Battalion, 5th Artillery.)

Redesignated (less former Battery C, 5th Field Artillery Battalion) 1 September 1971 as the 4th Missile Battalion, 5th Air Defense Artillery (former Battery C, 5th Field Artillery Battalion, concurrently redesignated as the 4th Missile Battalion, 5th Field Artillery—hereafter separate lineage).

ANNEX

Constituted 5 May 1942 in the Army of the United States as Battery C, 504th Coast Artillery. Activated 1 July 1942 at Camp Hulen, Texas.

Reorganized and redesignated 20 January 1943 as Battery C, 214th Coast Artillery Battalion. Redesignated 13 November 1943 as Battery C,

214th Antiaircraft Artillery Gun Battalion. Inactivated 12 February 1946 at Camp Kilmer, New Jersey.

CAMPAIGN PARTICIPATION CREDIT

Civil War
Peninsula
Manassas
Antietam
Fredericksburg
Chancellorsville
*Mississippi River
Gettysburg
Wilderness
Spotsylvania
Cold Harbor
*Petersburg
Shenandoah
*Appomattox
Virginia 1862
Virginia 1863
Virginia 1864
*Alabama 1864
*Louisiana 1864

World War II
Tunisia
*Sicily
*Naples-Foggia
Anzio
*Rome-Arno
*Southern France
*Rhineland
*Ardennes-Alsace
*Central Europe

Korean War
*Second Korean winter
*Korea, summer–fall 1952
*Third Korean winter
*Korea, summer 1953

DECORATIONS

*Republic of Korea Presidential Unit Citation, Streamer embroidered KOREA (24th Antiaircraft Artillery Gun Battalion cited; DA GO 24, 1954)
*Republic of Korea Presidential Unit Citation, Streamer embroidered DEFENSE OF KOREA (24th Antiaircraft Artillery Gun Battalion cited; DA GO 51, 1957)

5th BATTALION, 5th AIR DEFENSE ARTILLERY

AR
(inactive)

LINEAGE

Constituted 18 June 1861 in the Regular Army as Battery H, 5th Regiment of Artillery. Organized 4 July 1861 at Fort Greble, Pennsylvania.

Reorganized and redesignated 13 February 1901 as the 54th Company, Coast Artillery, Artillery Corps. Redesignated 2 February 1907 as the 54th Company, Coast Artillery Corps. Redesignated 3 July 1916 as the 2d Company, Fort Wadsworth [New York]. Redesignated 31 August 1917 as the 6th Company, Coast Defenses of Southern New York. Redesignated 1 June 1922 as the 54th Company, Coast Artillery Corps.

Redesignated 1 July 1924 as Battery E, 5th Coast Artillery, and inactivated in the Coast Defenses of Southern New York. Disbanded 26 June 1944.

Reconstituted 28 June 1950 in the Regular Army; concurrently consolidated with Battery A, 214th Antiaircraft Artillery Gun Battalion (*see* ANNEX), and consolidated unit redesignated as Battery A, 24th Antiaircraft Artillery Battalion. Redesignated 13 March 1952 as Battery A, 24th Antiaircraft Artillery Gun Battalion. Activated 16 April 1952 in Korea. Inactivated 20 December 1954 in Korea. Redesignated 23 May 1955 as Battery A, 24th Antiaircraft Artillery Missile Battalion. Activated 1 June 1955 at Fort Banks, Massachusetts. Redesignated 1 November 1956 as Battery C, 605th Antiaircraft Artillery Missile Battalion. Inactivated 1 September 1958 at Nahant, Massachusetts.

Redesignated 6 April 1959 as Headquarters and Headquarters Battery, 5th Rocket Howitzer Battalion, 5th Artillery; concurrently withdrawn from the Regular Army, allotted to the Army Reserve, and assigned to the 94th Infantry Division (organic elements concurrently constituted). Battalion activated 1 May 1959 with Headquarters at Boston, Massachusetts. (Headquarters and Headquarters Battery, 5th Rocket Howitzer Battalion, 5th Artillery, consolidated 26 August 1960 with Battery E, 5th Field Artillery [organized in 1898], and consolidated unit designated as Headquarters and Headquarters Battery, 5th Rocket Howitzer Battalion, 5th Artillery.) Reorganized and redesignated 7 January 1963 as the 5th Howitzer Battalion, 5th Artillery, relieved from assignment to the 94th Infantry Division, and assigned to the 187th Infantry Brigade; location of Headquarters concurrently changed to Roslindale, Massachusetts. Redesignated 31 January 1968 as the 5th Battalion, 5th Artillery.

Redesignated (less former Battery E, 5th Field Artillery) 1 September 1971 as the 5th Battalion, 5th Air Defense Artillery; concurrently inactivated at Roslindale, Massachusetts, and relieved from assignment to the 187th Infantry Brigade (former Battery E, 5th Field Artillery, concurrently reorganized and redesignated as the 5th Battalion, 5th Field Artillery—hereafter separate lineage).

ANNEX

Constituted 5 May 1942 in the Army of the United States as Battery A, 504th Coast Artillery. Activated 1 July 1942 at Camp Hulen, Texas.

Reorganized and redesignated 20 January 1943 as Battery A, 214th Coast Artillery Battalion. Redesignated 13 November 1943 as Battery A, 214th Antiaircraft Artillery Gun Battalion. Inactivated 12 February 1946 at Camp Kilmer, New Jersey.

CAMPAIGN PARTICIPATION CREDIT

Civil War
  Peninsula
  *Shiloh
  Manassas
  Antietam
  Fredericksburg
  *Murfreesborough
  Chancellorsville
  Gettysburg
  *Chickamauga
  *Chattanooga
  Wilderness
  Spotsylvania
  Cold Harbor
  Petersburg
  Shenandoah
  Appomattox
  *Kentucky 1862
  *Mississippi 1862
  *Tennessee 1862
  *Tennessee 1863

  *Tennessee 1864
  Virginia 1862
  Virginia 1863
  Virginia 1864

World War II
  Tunisia
  *Sicily
  *Naples-Foggia
  Anzio
  *Rome-Arno
  *Southern France
  *Rhineland
  *Ardennes-Alsace
  *Central Europe

Korean War
  *Second Korean winter
  *Korea, summer-fall 1952
  *Third Korean winter
  *Korea, summer 1953

DECORATIONS

*Republic of Korea Presidential Unit Citation, Streamer embroidered KOREA (24th Antiaircraft Artillery Gun Battalion cited; DA GO 24, 1954)

*Republic of Korea Presidential Unit Citation, Streamer embroidered DEFENSE OF KOREA (24th Antiaircraft Artillery Gun Battalion cited; DA GO 51, 1957)

6th BATTALION, 5th AIR DEFENSE ARTILLERY

AR
(inactive)

LINEAGE

Constituted 18 June 1861 in the Regular Army as Battery I, 5th Regiment of Artillery. Organized 4 July 1861 at Fort Greble, Pennsylvania.

Reorganized and redesignated 13 February 1901 as the 55th Company, Coast Artillery, Artillery Corps. Redesignated 2 February 1907 as the 55th Company, Coast Artillery Corps. Redesignated 18 July 1916 as the 2d Company, Fort DeRussey [Hawaii]. Redesignated 31 August 1917 as the 10th Company, Coast Defenses of Oahu. Redesignated 21 February 1921 as the 3d Company, Coast Defenses of Honolulu. Redesignated 1 June 1922 as the 55th Company, Coast Artillery Corps.

Redesignated 1 July 1924 as Battery F, 5th Coast Artillery, and inactivated in Hawaii. Disbanded 26 June 1944.

Reconstituted 28 June 1950 in the Regular Army; concurrently consolidated with Battery B, 214th Antiaircraft Artillery Gun Battalion (*see* ANNEX), and consolidated unit redesignated as Battery B, 24th Antiaircraft Artillery Battalion. Redesignated 13 March 1952 as Battery B, 24th Antiaircraft Artillery Gun Battalion. Activated 16 April 1952 in Korea. Inactivated 20 December 1954 in Korea. Redesignated 23 May 1955 as Battery B, 24th Antiaircraft Artillery Missile Battalion. Activated 1 June 1955 at Fort Banks, Massachusetts. Redesignated 1 November 1956 as Battery D, 605th Antiaircraft Artillery Missile Battalion. Inactivated 1 September 1958 at Reading, Pennsylvania.

Redesignated 7 April 1959 as Headquarters and Headquarters Battery, 6th Howitzer Battalion, 5th Artillery; concurrently withdrawn from the Regular Army, allotted to the Army Reserve, and assigned to the 77th Infantry Division (organic elements concurrently constituted). Battalion activated 1 May 1959 with Headquarters at Bronx, New York. (Headquarters and Headquarters Battery, 6th Howitzer Battalion, 5th Artillery, consolidated 26 August 1960 with Battery F, 5th Field Artillery [organized in 1901], and consolidated unit designated as Headquarters and Headquarters Battery, 6th Howitzer Battalion, 5th Artillery.) Redesignated 26 March 1963 as the 6th Battalion, 5th Artillery. Inactivated 30 December 1965 at Bronx, New York, and relieved from assignment to the 77th Infantry Division.

Redesignated (less former Battery F, 5th Field Artillery) 1 September 1971 as the 6th Battalion, 5th Air Defense Artillery (former Battery F, 5th Field Artillery, concurrently redesignated as the 6th Battalion, 5th Field Artillery—hereafter separate lineage).

ANNEX

Constituted 5 May 1942 in the Army of the United States as Battery B, 504th Coast Artillery. Activated 1 July 1942 at Camp Hulen, Texas.

Reorganized and redesignated 20 January 1943 as Battery B, 214th Coast Artillery Battalion. Redesignated 13 November 1943 as Battery B, 214th Antiaircraft Artillery Gun Battalion. Inactivated 12 February 1946 at Camp Kilmer, New Jersey.

CAMPAIGN PARTICIPATION CREDIT

Civil War
- *Peninsula
- *Manassas
- *Antietam
- *Fredericksburg
- *Chancellorsville
- *Gettysburg
- *Wilderness
- *Spotsylvania
- *Cold Harbor
- *Petersburg
- Shenandoah
- Appomattox
- *Virginia 1862
- Virginia 1863
- Virginia 1864

World War II
- Tunisia
- *Sicily
- *Naples-Foggia
- Anzio
- *Rome-Arno
- *Southern France
- *Rhineland
- *Ardennes-Alsace
- *Central Europe

Korean War
- *Second Korean winter
- *Korea, summer–fall 1952
- *Third Korean winter
- *Korea, summer 1953

DECORATIONS

*Republic of Korea Presidential Unit Citation, Streamer embroidered KOREA (24th Antiaircraft Artillery Gun Battalion cited; DA GO 24, 1954)

*Republic of Korea Presidential Unit Citation, Streamer embroidered, DEFENSE OF KOREA (24th Antiaircraft Artillery Gun Battalion cited; DA GO 51, 1957)

7th BATTALION, 5th AIR DEFENSE ARTILLERY

RA
(inactive)

LINEAGE

Constituted 18 June 1861 in the Regular Army as Battery C, 5th Regiment of Artillery. Organized 4 July 1861 at Fort Greble, Pennsylvania.

Reorganized and redesignated 13 February 1901 as the 51st Company, Coast Artillery, Artillery Corps. Redesignated 2 February 1901 as the 51st Company, Coast Artillery Corps. Redesignated 1 July 1916 as the 2d Company, Fort McKinley [Maine]. Redesignated 31 August 1917 as the 12th Company, Coast Defenses of Portland. Redesignated 1 December 1917 as Battery C, 54th Artillery (Coast Artillery Corps). Disbanded 1 March 1919 at Camp Devens, Massachusetts. Reconstituted 1 June 1922 in the Regular Army; concurrently consolidated with the 4th Company, Coast Defenses of Portland (organized in April 1918 and inactivated 1 November 1921), and consolidated unit redesignated as the 51st Company, Coast Artillery Corps.

Redesignated 1 July 1924 as Battery C, 5th Coast Artillery. Disbanded 26 June 1944. Reconstituted 28 June 1950 in the Regular Army.

Redesignated 26 August 1960 as Headquarters and Headquarters Battery, 7th Missile Battalion, 5th Artillery (organic elements concurrently constituted). Battalion activated 11 January 1962 at Fort Bliss, Texas. Redesignated 10 January 1966 as the 7th Battalion, 5th Artillery. Inactivated 21 June 1971 at Fort Lewis, Washington. Redesignated 1 September 1971 as the 7th Battalion, 5th Air Defense Artillery.

CAMPAIGN PARTICIPATION CREDIT

Civil War
*Peninsula
*Manassas
*Antietam
*Fredericksburg
*Chancellorsville
*Gettysburg
*Wilderness
*Spotsylvania
*Cold Harbor
*Petersburg
Shenandoah
Appomattox
Virginia 1862
*Virginia 1863
Virginia 1864

World War I
*Streamer without inscription

World War II
Tunisia
Sicily
Naples-Foggia
Anzio
Rome-Arno
Southern France (with arrowhead)
Rhineland
Ardennes-Alsace
Central Europe

Korean War
Second Korean winter
Korea, summer–fall 1952
Third Korean winter
Korea, summer 1953

DECORATIONS

None.

16th DETACHMENT, 5th AIR DEFENSE ARTILLERY

RA
(inactive)

LINEAGE

Constituted 1 September 1935 in the Regular Army as Battery I, 5th Coast Artillery. Disbanded 26 June 1944.

Reconstituted 5 August 1958 in the Regular Army and redesignated as the 16th Detachment, 5th Artillery. Activated 1 September 1958 at Fort Miles, Delaware. Inactivated 24 December 1965 at Fort George G. Meade, Maryland. Redesignated 1 September 1971 as the 16th Detachment, 5th Air Defense Artillery.

CAMPAIGN PARTICIPATION CREDIT

None.

DECORATIONS

None.

5TH AIR DEFENSE ARTILLERY BIBLIOGRAPHY

"Big Red One," 1st Infantry Division, Fort Riley, Kansas, 1963. Baton Rouge: Army and Navy Publishing Company, 1963. Contains information about the 1st Battalion, 5th Air Defense Artillery.

Bush, James C. *A Short History of the Fifth Regiment, U.S. Artillery.* Governor's Island, N.Y., 1895.

————. "The Fifth Regiment of Artillery." *The Army of the United States.* Edited by Theophilus F. Rodenbough and William L. Haskin, 376–98. New York: Maynard, Merrill and Company, 1896. Originally published in *Journal of the Military Service Institution of the United States* 17 (1895):213–34.

Dupuy, Richard Ernest. *With the 57th in France.* Brooklyn: Our Army, 1930. Contains information about the current 2d Battalion, 5th Air Defense Artillery.

Dyer, Frederick. "5th Regiment of Artillery." *A Compendium of the War of the Rebellion.* New York: Thomas Yoseloff, 1959.

Ginsburgh, A. R. "Rolling Along with Reilly." *Field Artillery Journal* 23 (1933): 21. Pertains to the former Battery F, 5th Regiment of Artillery.

Grace, James L. *A Brief History of the 2nd Battalion, 57th Artillery, C.A.C., 31st Brigade, Army Artillery, First Army, From July 20th, 1917, to January 15th, 1919.* N.p., 1919. Contains information about the current 2d Battalion, 5th Air Defense Artillery.

Hoadley, John Chipman. *Memorial of Henry Sanford Gansevoort, Captain, Fifth Artillery.* Boston: Rand Avery and Company, 1875.

MacCloskey, Monro. *Reilly's Battery.* New York: Richards Roset, 1969. Pertains to the former Battery F, 5th Regiment of Artillery.

McLaughlin, Joseph M. *Behind the Lines in France: Reminiscences of World*

War I. St. Cloud, Fla.: Double-D Publishing Company, 1970. Contains
   information about the current 7th Battalion, 5th Air Defense Artillery.
Ott, David Ewing. *Field Artillery, 1954–1973.* Vietnam Studies. Washington: Government Printing Office, 1975. Contains information
   about the 1st Battalion, 5th Air Defense Artillery.
Ott, Edward S. "Employment of Radar by XV Corps Artillery." *Field
   Artillery Journal* 36 (1946):462–67.

6th AIR DEFENSE ARTILLERY

HERALDIC ITEMS

COAT OF ARMS

Shield: Parti per pairle argent, gules and azure, in chief a mullet of five points of the second and in fess debased two fleurs-de-lis or.

Crest: On a wreath of the colors, argent and gules, a grizzly bear passant sable langued gules.

Motto: *Certo Dirigo Ictu* (I Aim With a Sure Blow).

Symbolism: The field of the shield, an adaptation of the flag of the Philippine insurgents, alludes to the regiment's service in the Philippine Insurrection. The scarlet star refers to artillery. The two fleurs-de-lis denote service in France during World War I by an element of the regiment.

The crest is taken from that of the Coast Defenses of San Francisco where the old regiment and the majority of its companies were stationed.

The motto is indicative of the character of the bear and is applicable to the personnel of the regiment in the performance of duty.

DISTINCTIVE INSIGNIA

The distinctive insignia is the crest and motto of the coat of arms.

LINEAGE AND HONORS

LINEAGE

Constituted 8 March 1898 in the Regular Army as the 6th Regiment of Artillery. Organized 23 March 1898 at Fort McHenry, Maryland. Regiment broken up 13 February 1901 and its elements reorganized and redesignated as separate numbered companies and batteries of Artillery Corps. Reconstituted 1 July 1924 in the Regular Army as the 6th Coast Artillery and partially organized with Headquarters at Fort Winfield Scott, California. (1st and 2d Battalions activated 1 July 1939 at Fort Winfield Scott, California; 3d Battalion activated 2 June 1941 at Fort Winfield Scott, California; 4th Battalion activated 15 June 1941 at Fort Funston, California.) Regiment broken up 18 October 1944 and its elements reorganized and redesignated as follows: Headquarters and Headquarters Battery disbanded at Fort Baker, California; 1st, 2d, 3d, and 4th Battalions reorganized and redesignated as the 6th, 172d, 173d, and 174th Coast Artillery Battalions, respectively.

Headquarters and Headquarters Battery, 6th Coast Artillery, reconstituted 28 June 1950 in the Regular Army; concurrently consolidated with Headquarters and Headquarters Battery, 6th Antiaircraft Artillery Group (*see* ANNEX 1), and consolidated unit designated as Headquarters and Headquarters Battery, 6th Antiaircraft Artillery Group. Activated 1 February 1952 at Fort Bliss, Texas. Redesignated 20 March 1958 as Headquarters and Headquarters Battery, 6th Artillery Group. Inactivated 1 September 1971 at Fort Bliss, Texas.

6th Coast Artillery Battalion disbanded 15 September 1945 in California. Reconstituted 28 June 1950 in the Regular Army and redesignated as the 6th Antiaircraft Artillery Battalion. Redesignated 4 October 1950 as the 6th Antiaircraft Artillery Automatic Weapons Battalion, assigned to the 6th Infantry Division, and activated at Fort Ord, California. Inactivated 3 April 1956 at Fort Ord, California, and relieved from assignment to the 6th Infantry Division.

172d Coast Artillery Battalion disbanded 15 September 1945 in California. Reconstituted 28 June 1950 in the Regular Army; concurrently consolidated with the 25th Antiaircraft Artillery Automatic Weapons Battalion (active) (*see* ANNEX 2), and consolidated unit designated as the 25th Antiaircraft Artillery Automatic Weapons Battalion, an element of the 25th Infantry Division. Inactivated 10 November 1951 in Korea and relieved from assignment to the 25th Infantry Division. Redesignated 19 November 1952 as the 25th Antiaircraft Artillery Gun Battalion. Activated 1 February 1953 in Germany. Redesignated 1 October 1953 as the 25th Antiaircraft Artillery Battalion. Redesignated 5 December 1957 as the 25th Antiaircraft Artillery Missile Battalion. Inactivated 1 September 1958 in Germany.

173d Coast Artillery Battalion disbanded 15 September 1945 at Fort Miley, California. Reconstituted 28 June 1950 in the Regular Army and redesignated as the 45th Antiaircraft Artillery Battalion. Redesignated 9 March 1951 as the 45th Antiaircraft Artillery Gun Battalion. Activated 19 March 1951 at Fort Bliss, Texas. Redesignated 1 October 1953 as the 45th Antiaircraft Artillery Battalion. Redesignated 1 November 1957 as the 45th Antiaircraft Artillery Missile Battalion. Inactivated 1 September 1958 in Germany.

174th Coast Artillery Battalion disbanded 15 September 1945 in California. Reconstituted 28 June 1950 in the Regular Army and redesignated as the 53d Antiaircraft Artillery Battalion. Redesignated 21 April 1952 as the 53d Antiaircraft Artillery Gun Battalion. Activated 5 May 1952 in Japan. Inactivated 24 June 1955 in Japan. Redesignated 6 October 1955 as the 53d Antiaircraft Artillery Battalion. Activated 15 November 1955 at Fort Bliss, Texas. Inactivated 25 March 1957 at Fort Bliss, Texas.

6th Antiaircraft Artillery Automatic Weapons Battalion, 25th and 45th Antiaircraft Artillery Missile Battalions, 53d Antiaircraft Artillery Battalion, and 6th Armored Field Artillery Battalion (organized in 1907) consolidated, reorganized, and redesignated 1 September 1963 as the 6th

Artillery, a parent regiment under the Combat Arms Regimental System.

6th Artillery (less former 6th Armored Field Artillery Battalion) consolidated 1 September 1971 with Headquarters and Headquarters Battery, 6th Artillery Group, and consolidated unit reorganized and redesignated as the 6th Air Defense Artillery, a parent regiment under the Combat Arms Regimental System (former 6th Armored Field Artillery Battalion concurrently reorganized and redesignated as the 6th Field Artillery—hereafter separate lineage).

ANNEX 1

Constituted 5 August 1942 in the Army of the United States as Headquarters and Headquarters Battery, 6th Antiaircraft Artillery Automatic Weapons Group. Activated 21 August 1942 at Camp Haan, California. Redesignated 26 May 1943 as Headquarters and Headquarters Battery, 6th Antiaircraft Artillery Group. Inactivated 10 December 1945 at Manila, Philippine Islands.

ANNEX 2

Constituted 8 February 1943 in the Army of the United States as the 778th Coast Artillery Battalion. Activated 10 March 1943 at Camp Haan, California. Redesignated 1 May 1943 as the 778th Antiaircraft Artillery Automatic Weapons Battalion. Inactivated 1 May 1946 at Camp Kilmer, New Jersey. Redesignated 13 October 1948 as the 25th Antiaircraft Artillery Automatic Weapons Battalion and allotted to the Regular Army. Assigned 20 March 1949 to the 25th Infantry Division and activated in Japan.

CAMPAIGN PARTICIPATION CREDIT

Philippine Insurrection
Streamer without inscription

World War II
Rhineland
Ardennes-Alsace
Central Europe
New Guinea
Bismarck Archipelago
Luzon

Vietnam
Defense

Counteroffensive
Counteroffensive, Phase II
Counteroffensive, Phase III
Tet Counteroffensive
Counteroffensive, Phase IV
Counteroffensive, Phase V
Counteroffensive, Phase VI
Tet 69/Counteroffensive
Summer–fall 1969
Winter–spring 1970

DECORATIONS

Meritorious Unit Commendation, Streamer embroidered VIETNAM 1966 (8th Battalion, 6th Artillery, cited; DA GO 17, 1968)

Meritorious United Commendation, Streamer embroidered VIETNAM 1967–1968 (8th Battalion, 6th Artillery, cited; DA GO 42, 1969)

Philippine Presidential Unit Citation, Streamer embroidered 17 OCTOBER 1944 TO 4 JULY 1945 (Headquarters and Headquarters Battery, 6th Antiaircraft Artillery Group, cited; DA GO 47, 1950)

1st BATTALION, 6th AIR DEFENSE ARTILLERY

LINEAGE

Constituted 8 March 1898 in the Regular Army as Battery L, 6th Regiment of Artillery. Organized 23 March 1898 at Fort McHenry, Maryland.

Reorganized and redesignated 13 February 1901 as the 68th Company, Coast Artillery, Artillery Corps. Redesignated 2 February 1907 as the 68th Company, Coast Artillery Corps. Redesignated 12 July 1916 as the 1st Company, Fort Kamehameha [Hawaii]. Redesignated 31 August 1917 as the 1st Company, Coast Defenses of Oahu. Redesignated 1 March 1921 as the 1st Company, Coast Defenses of Pearl Harbor. Redesignated 30 June 1922 as the 68th Company, Coast Artillery Corps.

Redesignated 1 July 1924 as Battery D, 6th Coast Artillery, and inactivated in Hawaii. Activated 15 January 1941 at Fort Barry, California.

Reorganized and redesignated 18 October 1944 as Battery C, 172d Coast Artillery Battalion. Redesignated 15 September 1945 as Battery D, Harbor Defenses of San Francisco. Inactivated 10 June 1946 at Fort Winfield Scott, California. Redesignated 28 June 1950 as Battery D, 6th Antiaircraft Artillery Battalion. Redesignated 4 October 1950 as Battery D, 6th Antiaircraft Artillery Automatic Weapons Battalion, an element of the 6th Infantry Division, and activated at Fort Ord, California. Inactivated 3 April 1956 at Fort Ord, California, and relieved from assignment to the 6th Infantry Division.

Consolidated 3 February 1962 with Headquarters and Headquarters Battery, 1st Battalion, 6th Artillery (active) (organized in 1798), and consolidated unit designated as Headquarters and Headquarters Battery, 1st Battalion, 6th Artillery, an element of the 1st Armored Division (organic elements constituted and activated 15 February 1957). Battalion relieved 5 May 1971 from assignment to the 1st Armored Division and assigned to the 1st Cavalry Division.

Redesignated (less former Headquarters and Headquarters Battery, 1st Battalion, 6th Artillery) 1 September 1971 as the 1st Battalion, 6th Air Defense Artillery; concurrently inactivated at Fort Hood, Texas, and relieved from assignment to the 1st Cavalry Division (former Headquarters and Headquarters Battery, 1st Battalion, 6th Artillery, concurrently reorganized and redesignated as the 1st Battalion, 6th Field Artillery—hereafter separate lineage).

CAMPAIGN PARTICIPATION CREDIT

Philippine Insurrection
  *Streamer without inscription

World War II
  Rhineland

Ardennes-Alsace
Central Europe
Bismarck Archipelago
Luzon

DECORATIONS

None.

2d BATTALION, 6th AIR DEFENSE ARTILLERY

RA
(inactive)

LINEAGE

Constituted 8 March 1898 in the Regular Army as Battery A, 6th Regiment of Artillery. Organized 23 March 1898 at Fort McHenry, Maryland.

Reorganized and redesignated 13 February 1901 as the 60th Company, Coast Artillery, Artillery Corps. Redesignated 2 February 1907 as the 60th Company, Coast Artillery Corps. Redesignated 20 July 1916 as the 2d Company, Fort Winfield Scott [California]. Redesignated 31 August 1917 as the 2d Company, Coast Defenses of San Francisco. Redesignated 16 September 1918 as Battery A, 50th Artillery (Coast Artillery Corps). Redesignated 2 December 1918 as the 2d Company, Coast Defenses of San Francisco. Redesignated 1 June 1922 as the 60th Company, Coast Artillery Corps.

Reorganized and redesignated 1 July 1924 as Battery A, 6th Coast Artillery.

Reorganized and redesignated 18 October 1944 as Battery A, 174th Coast Artillery Battalion. Disbanded 10 December 1945 at Fort Winfield Scott, California. Reconstituted 28 June 1950 in the Regular Army; concurrently redesignated as Battery A, 6th Antiaircraft Artillery Battalion. Redesignated 4 October 1950 as Battery A, 6th Antiaircraft Artillery Automatic Weapons Battalion, an element of the 6th Infantry Division, and activated at Fort Ord, California. Inactivated 3 April 1956 at Fort Ord, California, and relieved from assignment to the 6th Infantry Division.

Consolidated 1 September 1963 with Headquarters and Headquarters Battery, 2d Battalion, 6th Artillery (active) (organized in 1838), and consolidated unit designated as Headquarters and Headquarters Battery, 2d Battalion, 6th Artillery, an element of the 3d Armored Division (organic elements constituted 30 August 1957 and activated 1 October 1957).

Redesignated (less former Headquarters and Headquarters Battery, 2d Battalion, 6th Artillery) 1 September 1971 as the 2d Battalion, 6th Air Defense Artillery; concurrently inactivated in Germany, and relieved from assignment to the 3d Armored Division (former Headquarters and Headquarters Battery, 2d Battalion, 6th Artillery, concurrently reorganized and redesignated as the 2d Battalion, 6th Field Artillery—hereafter separate lineage).

CAMPAIGN PARTICIPATION CREDIT

Philippine Insurrection
    *Streamer without inscription

World War II
    Rhineland
    Ardennes-Alsace

Central Europe
New Guinea
Bismarck Archipelago
Luzon

DECORATIONS

None.

3d BATTALION, 6th AIR DEFENSE ARTILLERY

RA
(inactive)

LINEAGE

Constituted 8 March 1898 in the Regular Army as Battery B, 6th Regiment of Artillery. Organized 23 March 1898 at Fort McHenry, Maryland.

Reorganized and redesignated 13 February 1901 as the 61st Company, Coast Artillery, Artillery Corps. Redesignated 2 February 1907 as the 61st Company, Coast Artillery Corps. Redesignated 20 July 1916 as the 2d Company, Fort Baker [California]. Redesignated 31 August 1917 as the 11th Company, Coast Defenses of San Francisco. Redesignated in November 1917 as Battery C, 1st Antiaircraft Battalion. Redesignated 14 November 1918 as the 24th Antiaircraft Battery, 1st Antiaircraft Sector. Redesignated 29 March 1919 as the 11th Company, Coast Defenses of San Francisco. Redesignated 1 June 1922 as the 61st Company, Coast Artillery Corps.

Redesignated 1 July 1924 as Battery B, 6th Coast Artillery, and inactivated in the Coast Defenses of San Francisco. Activated 1 July 1939 at Fort Winfield Scott, California.

Reorganized and redesignated 18 October 1944 as Battery B, 6th Coast Artillery Battalion. Redesignated 15 September 1945 as Battery F, Harbor Defenses of San Francisco. Inactivated 10 June 1946 at Fort Winfield Scott, California. Redesignated 28 June 1950 as Battery B, 6th Antiaircraft Artillery Battalion. Redesignated 4 October 1950 as Battery B, 6th Antiaircraft Artillery Automatic Weapons Battalion, an element of the 6th Infantry Division, and activated at Fort Ord, California. Inactivated 3 April 1956 at Fort Ord, California, and relieved from assignment to the 6th Infantry Division.

Consolidated 1 September 1963 with Headquarters and Headquarters Battery, 3d Howitzer Battalion, 6th Artillery (active) (organized in 1901), and consolidated unit designated as Headquarters and Headquarters Battery, 3d Howitzer Battalion, 6th Artillery (organic elements constituted 2 June 1958 and activated 25 June 1958). Redesignated 1 April 1968 as the 3d Battalion, 6th Artillery. Inactivated 10 April 1970 at Fort Lewis, Washington.

Redesignated (less former Headquarters and Headquarters Battery, 3d Howitzer Battalion, 6th Artillery) 1 September 1971 as the 3d Battalion, 6th Air Defense Artillery (former Headquarters and Headquarters Battery, 3d Howitzer Battalion, 6th Artillery, concurrently redesignated as the 3d Battalion, 6th Field Artillery—hereafter separate lineage). 3d Battalion, 6th Air Defense Artillery, activated 13 September 1972 at Fort Bliss, Texas. Inactivated 21 December 1975 at Fort Bliss, Texas.

CAMPAIGN PARTICIPATION CREDIT

Philippine Insurrection
  *Streamer without inscription

World War I
  *Meuse-Argonne

World War II
  Rhineland
  Ardennes-Alsace
  Central Europe
  New Guinea
  Bismarck Archipelago
  Luzon

Vietnam
  *Counteroffensive
  *Counteroffensive, Phase II
  *Counteroffensive, Phase III
  *Tet Counteroffensive
  *Counteroffensive, Phase IV
  *Counteroffensive, Phase V
  *Counteroffensive, Phase VI
  *Tet 69/Counteroffensive
  *Summer–fall 1969
  *Winter–spring 1970

DECORATIONS

*Republic of Vietnam Cross of Gallantry with Palm, Streamer embroidered VIETNAM 1966–1970 (3d Battalion, 6th Artillery, cited; DA GO 54, 1974)

Battery A additionally entitled to Valorous Unit Award, Streamer embroidered DAK TO–BEN HET (Battery A, 3d Battalion, 6th Artillery, cited; DA GO 48, 1971)

4th BATTALION, 6th AIR DEFENSE ARTILLERY

RA
(inactive)

LINEAGE

Constituted 8 March 1898 in the Regular Army as Battery C, 6th Regiment of Artillery. Organized 23 March 1898 at Fort McHenry, Maryland.

Reorganized and redesignated 13 February 1901 as the 62d Company, Coast Artillery, Artillery Corps. Redesignated 2 February 1907 as the 62d Company, Coast Artillery Corps. Redesignated 15 July 1916 as the 2d Company, Fort Worden [Washington]. Redesignated 31 August 1917 as the 2d Company, Coast Defenses of Puget Sound. Redesignated 1 June 1922 as the 62d Company, Coast Artillery Corps. Inactivated 1 October 1922 in the Coast Defenses of Puget Sound.

Redesignated 1 July 1924 as Battery C, 6th Coast Artillery. Activated 1 July 1939 at Fort Winfield Scott, California.

Reorganized and redesignated 18 October 1944 as Battery A, 173d Coast Artillery Battalion. Disbanded 15 September 1945 at Fort Funston, California. Reconstituted 28 June 1950 in the Regular Army and redesignated as Battery C, 6th Antiaircraft Artillery Battalion. Redesignated 4 October 1950 as Battery C, 6th Antiaircraft Artillery Automatic Weapons Battalion, an element of the 6th Infantry Division, and activated at Fort Ord, California. Inactivated 3 April 1956 at Fort Ord, California, and relieved from assignment to the 6th Infantry Division.

Redesignated 12 August 1958 as Headquarters and Headquarters Battery, 4th Missile Battalion, 6th Artillery (organic elements concurrently constituted). Battalion activated 1 September 1958 in Germany. (Headquarters and Headquarters Battery, 4th Missile Battalion, 6th Artillery, consolidated 1 September 1963 with Battery C, 6th Armored Field Artillery Battalion [organized in 1901], and consolidated unit designated as Headquarters and Headquarters Battery, 4th Missile Battalion, 6th Artillery.) Redesignated 20 August 1965 as the 4th Battalion, 6th Artillery. Inactivated 26 March 1970 in Germany.

Redesignated (less former Battery C, 6th Armored Field Artillery Battalion), 1 September 1971 as the 4th Battalion, 6th Air Defense Artillery (former Battery C, 6th Armored Field Artillery Battalion, concurrently redesignated as the 4th Battalion, 6th Field Artillery—hereafter separate lineage).

CAMPAIGN PARTICIPATION CREDIT

Philippine Insurrection
    *Streamer without inscription

World War II
    Rhineland
    Ardennes-Alsace
    Central Europe
    New Guinea
    Bismarck Archipelago
    Luzon

DECORATIONS

None.

5th BATTALION, 6th AIR DEFENSE ARTILLERY

RA
(inactive)

LINEAGE

Constituted 8 March 1898 in the Regular Army as Battery E, 6th Regiment of Artillery. Organized 23 March 1898 at Fort McHenry, Maryland.

Reorganized and redesignated 13 February 1901 as the 63d Company, Coast Artillery, Artillery Corps. Redesignated 2 February 1907 as the 63d Company, Coast Artillery Corps. Redesignated 15 July 1916 as the 3d Company, Fort Worden [Washington]. Redesignated 31 August 1917 as the 3d Company, Coast Defenses of Puget Sound. Redesignated 1 June 1922 as the 63d Company, Coast Artillery Corps.

Reorganized and redesignated 1 July 1924 as Battery E, 6th Coast Artillery.

Reorganized and redesignated 18 October 1944 as Battery B, 173d Coast Artillery Battalion. Disbanded 15 September 1945 at Fort Cronkhite, California. Reconstituted 28 June 1950 in the Regular Army; concurrently consolidated with Battery A, 25th Antiaircraft Artillery Automatic Weapons Battalion (active) (*see* ANNEX), and consolidated unit designated as Battery A, 25th Antiaircraft Artillery Automatic Weapons Battalion, an element of the 25th Infantry Division. Inactivated 10 November 1951 in Korea and relieved from assignment to the 25th Infantry Division. Redesignated 19 November 1952 as Battery A, 25th Antiaircraft Artillery Gun Battalion. Activated 1 February 1953 in Germany. Redesignated 1 October 1953 as Battery A, 25th Antiaircraft Artillery Battalion. Redesignated 5 December 1957 as Battery A, 25th Antiaircraft Artillery Missile Battalion.

Reorganized and redesignated 1 September 1958 as Headquarters and Headquarters Battery, 5th Missile Battalion, 6th Artillery (organic elements constituted 12 August 1958 and activated 1 September 1958). (Headquarters and Headquarters Battery, 5th Missile Battalion, 6th Artillery, consolidated 1 September 1963 with Battery E, 6th Field Artillery [organized in 1901], and consolidated unit designated as Headquarters and Headquarters Battery, 5th Missile Battalion, 6th Artillery.) Redesignated 20 August 1965 as the 5th Battalion, 6th Artillery.

Reorganized and redesignated (less former Battery E, 6th Field Artillery) 1 September 1971 as the 5th Battalion, 6th Air Defense Artillery (former Battery E, 6th Field Artillery, concurrently redesignated as the 5th Battalion, 6th Field Artillery—hereafter separate lineage). 5th Battalion, 6th Air Defense Artillery, inactivated 30 June 1982 in Germany.

ANNEX

Constituted 8 February 1943 in the Army of the United States as Battery A, 778th Coast Artillery Battalion. Activated 10 March 1943 at

Camp Haan, California. Redesignated 1 May 1943 as Battery A, 778th Antiaircraft Artillery Automatic Weapons Battalion. Inactivated 1 May 1946 at Camp Kilmer, New Jersey. Redesignated 13 October 1948 as Battery A, 25th Antiaircraft Artillery Automatic Weapons Battalion, and allotted to the Regular Army. Activated 20 March 1949 in Japan as an element of the 25th Infantry Division.

CAMPAIGN PARTICIPATION CREDIT

Philippine Insurrection
  *Streamer without inscription

World War II
  *Rhineland
  *Ardennes-Alsace
  *Central Europe
  New Guinea
  Bismarck Archipelago
  Luzon

Korean War
  *UN defensive
  *UN offensive
  *CCF intervention
  *First UN counteroffensive
  *CCF spring offensive
  *UN summer–fall offensive

DECORATIONS

*Republic of Korea Presidential Unit Citation, Streamer embroidered MASAN-CHINJU (25th Antiaircraft Artillery Automatic Weapons Battalion cited; DA GO 35, 1951)

6th MISSILE BATTALION, 6th AIR DEFENSE ARTILLERY

RA
(inactive)

LINEAGE

Constituted 8 March 1898 in the Regular Army as Battery F, 6th Regiment of Artillery. Organized 23 March 1898 at Fort McHenry, Maryland.

Reorganized and redesignated 13 February 1901 as the 64th Company, Coast Artillery, Artillery Corps. Redesignated 2 February 1907 as the 64th Company, Coast Artillery Corps. Redesignated 20 July 1916 as the 8th Company, Fort Winfield Scott [California]. Redesignated 31 August 1917 as the 8th Company, Coast Defense of San Francisco. Redesignated 1 June 1922 as the 64th Company, Coast Artillery Corps.

Redesignated 1 July 1924 as Battery F, 6th Coast Artillery, and inactivated in the Coast Defenses of San Francisco. Activated 1 August 1940 at Fort Baker, California.

Reorganized and redesignated 18 October 1944 as Battery B, 174th Coast Artillery Battalion. Redesignated 15 September 1945 as Battery G, Harbor Defenses of San Francisco. Inactivated 10 June 1946 at Fort Baker, California. Consolidated 28 June 1950 with Battery B, 25th Antiaircraft Artillery Automatic Weapons Battalion (active) (*see* ANNEX), and consolidated unit designated as Battery B, 25th Antiaircraft Artillery Automatic Weapons Battalion, an element of the 25th Infantry Division. Inactivated 10 November 1951 in Korea and relieved from assignment to the 25th Infantry Division. Redesignated 19 November 1952 as Battery B, 25th Antiaircraft Artillery Gun Battalion. Activated 1 February 1953 in Germany. Redesignated 1 October 1953 as Battery B, 25th Antiaircraft Artillery Battalion. Redesignated 5 December 1957 as Battery B, 25th Antiaircraft Artillery Missile Battalion.

Reorganized and redesignated 1 September 1958 as Headquarters and Headquarters Battery, 6th Missile Battalion, 6th Artillery (organic elements constituted 12 August 1958 and activated 1 September 1958). Battalion inactivated 26 July 1960 at Finleyville, Pennsylvania. (Headquarters and Headquarters Battery, 6th Missile Battalion, 6th Artillery, consolidated 1 September 1963 with Battery F, 6th Field Artillery [organized in 1901], and consolidated unit designated as Headquarters and Headquarters Battery, 6th Missile Battalion, 6th Artillery.)

Redesignated (less former Battery F, 6th Field Artillery) 1 September 1971 as the 6th Missile Battalion, 6th Air Defense Artillery (former Battery F, 6th Field Artillery, concurrently redesignated as the 6th Missile Battalion, 6th Field Artillery—hereafter separate lineage).

ANNEX

Constituted 8 February 1943 in the Army of the United States as Battery B, 778th Coast Artillery Battalion. Activated 10 March 1943 at Camp Haan, California. Redesignated 1 May 1943 as Battery B, 778th Antiaircraft Artillery Automatic Weapons Battalion. Inactivated 1 May 1946 at Camp Kilmer, New Jersey. Redesignated 13 October 1948 as Battery B, 25th Antiaircraft Artillery Automatic Weapons Battalion, and allotted to the Regular Army. Activated 20 March 1949 in Japan as an element of the 25th Infantry Division.

CAMPAIGN PARTICIPATION CREDIT

Philippine Insurrection
  *Streamer without inscription

World War II
  *Northern France
  *Rhineland

*Ardennes-Alsace
*Central Europe
  New Guinea
  Bismarck Archipelago
  Luzon

DECORATIONS

None.

7th HOWITZER BATTALION, 6th AIR DEFENSE ARTILLERY

AR
(inactive)

LINEAGE

Constituted 8 March 1898 in the Regular Army as Battery M, 6th Regiment of Artillery. Organized 23 March 1898 at Fort McHenry, Maryland.

Reorganized and redesignated 13 February 1901 as the 69th Company, Coast Artillery, Artillery Corps. Redesignated 2 February 1907 as the 69th Company, Coast Artillery Corps. Redesignated 1 July 1916 as the 4th Company, Fort Monroe [Virginia]. Redesignated 31 August 1917 as the 4th Company, Coast Defenses of Chesapeake Bay. Consolidated 30 August 1919 with the 13th Company, Coast Defenses of Chesapeake Bay (organized 15 January 1918; consolidated in December 1918 with the 14th Company, Coast Defenses of Chesapeake Bay [organized in March 1918], and consolidated unit designated as the 13th Company, Coast Defenses of Chesapeake Bay), and consolidated unit designated as the 4th Company, Coast Defenses of Chesapeake Bay. Redesignated 1 June 1922 as the 69th Company, Coast Artillery Corps.

Redesignated 1 July 1924 as Battery G, 6th Coast Artillery, and inactivated in the Coast Defenses of Chesapeake Bay. Activated 1 July 1939 at Fort Winfield Scott, California.

Reorganized and redesignated 18 October 1944 as Battery A, 6th Coast Artillery Battalion. Redesignated 15 September 1945 as Battery E, Harbor Defenses of San Francisco. Inactivated 10 June 1946 at Fort Winfield Scott, California. Consolidated 28 June 1950 with Battery C, 25th Antiaircraft Artillery Automatic Weapons Battalion (active) (*see* ANNEX), and consolidated unit designated as Battery C, 25th Antiaircraft Artillery Automatic Weapons Battalion, an element of the 25th Infantry Division. Inactivated 10 November 1951 in Korea and relieved from assignment to the 25th Infantry Division. Redesignated 19 November 1952 as Battery C, 25th Antiaircraft Artillery Gun Battalion. Activated 1 February 1953 in Germany. Redesignated 1 October 1953 as Battery C, 25th Antiaircraft Artillery Battalion. Redesignated 5 December 1957 as Battery C, 25th Antiaircraft Artillery Missile Battalion. Inactivated 1 September 1958 in Germany.

Redesignated 17 March 1959 as Headquarters and Headquarters Battery, 7th Howitzer Battalion, 6th Artillery; concurrently withdrawn from the Regular Army, allotted to the Army Reserve, and assigned to the 79th Infantry Division (organic elements concurrently constituted). Battalion activated 20 April 1959 at Seaford, Delaware. Inactivated 28 February 1963 at Seaford, Delaware, and relieved from assignment to the 79th Infantry Division. (Headquarters and Headquarters Battery, 7th

Howitzer Battalion, 6th Artillery, consolidated 1 September 1963 with Battery G, 6th Field Artillery [constituted in 1940], and consolidated unit designated as Headquarters and Headquarters Battery, 7th Howitzer Battalion, 6th Artillery.)

Redesignated (less former Battery G, 6th Field Artillery) 1 September 1971 as the 7th Howitzer Battalion, 6th Air Defense Artillery (former Battery G, 6th Field Artillery, concurrently redesignated as the 7th Howitzer Battalion, 6th Field Artillery—hereafter separate lineage).

ANNEX

Constituted 8 February 1943 in the Army of the United States as Battery C, 778th Coast Artillery Battalion. Activated 10 March 1943 at Camp Haan, California. Redesignated 1 May 1943 as Battery C, 778th Antiaircraft Artillery Automatic Weapons Battalion. Inactivated 1 May 1946 at Camp Kilmer, New Jersey. Redesignated 13 October 1948 as Battery C, 25th Antiaircraft Artillery Automatic Weapons Battalion, and allotted to the Regular Army. Activated 20 March 1949 in Japan as an element of the 25th Infantry Division.

CAMPAIGN PARTICIPATION CREDIT

Philippine Insurrection
　　*Streamer without inscription

World War II
　　*Northern France
　　*Rhineland

*Ardennes-Alsace
*Central Europe
New Guinea
Bismarck Archipelago
Luzon

DECORATIONS

*Presidential Unit Citation (Army), Streamer embroidered LUXEM-BOURG (Battery C, 778th Antiaircraft Artillery Automatic Weapons Battalion, cited; WD GO 19, 1947, as amended by DA GO 74, 1948).

8th BATTALION, 6th AIR DEFENSE ARTILLERY

RA
(inactive)

LINEAGE

Constituted 8 March 1898 in the Regular Army as Battery H, 6th Regiment of Artillery. Organized 23 March 1898 at Fort McHenry, Maryland.

Reorganized and redesignated 13 February 1901 as the 65th Company, Coast Artillery, Artillery Corps. Redesignated 2 February 1907 as the 65th Company, Coast Artillery Corps. Redesignated 20 July 1916 as the 6th Company, Fort Winfield Scott [California]. Redesignated 31 August 1917 as the 6th Company, Coast Defenses of San Francisco. Redesignated 16 September 1918 as Battery C, 40th Artillery (Coast Artillery Corps). Redesignated 31 December 1918 as the 6th Company, Coast Defenses of San Francisco. Redesignated 1 June 1922 as the 65th Company, Coast Artillery Corps.

Redesignated 1 July 1924 as Battery H, 6th Coast Artillery, and inactivated in the Coast Defenses of San Francisco. Activated 2 June 1941 at Fort Baker, California.

Reorganized and redesignated 18 October 1944 as Battery A, 172d Coast Artillery Battalion. Redesignated 15 September 1945 as Battery B, Harbor Defenses of San Francisco. Inactivated 10 June 1946 at Fort Winfield Scott, California. Consolidated 28 June 1950 with Battery D, 25th Antiaircraft Artillery Automatic Weapons Battalion (active) (*see* ANNEX), and consolidated unit designated as Battery D, 25th Antiaircraft Artillery Automatic Weapons Battalion, an element of the 25th Infantry Division. Inactivated 10 November 1951 in Korea and relieved from assignment to the 25th Infantry Division. Redesignated 19 November 1952 as Battery D, 25th Antiaircraft Artillery Gun Battalion. Activated 1 February 1953 in Germany. Redesignated 1 October 1953 as Battery D, 25th Antiaircraft Artillery Battalion. Redesignated 5 December 1957 as Battery D, 25th Antiaircraft Artillery Missile Battalion. Inactivated 1 September 1958 in Germany.

Redesignated 4 April 1960 as Headquarters and Headquarters Battery, 8th Howitzer Battalion, 6th Artillery, and assigned to the 1st Infantry Division (organic elements concurrently constituted). Battalion activated 20 April 1960 at Fort Riley, Kansas. (Headquarters and Headquarters Battery, 8th Howitzer Battalion, 6th Artillery, consolidated 1 September 1963 with Battery H, 6th Field Artillery [constituted in 1940], and consolidated unit designated as Headquarters and Headquarters Battery, 8th Howitzer Battalion, 6th Artillery.) Redesignated 20 January 1964 as the 8th Battalion, 6th Artillery.

Redesignated (less former Battery H, 6th Field Artillery) 1 September 1971 as the 8th Battalion, 6th Air Defense Artillery; concurrently inactivated at Fort Riley, Kansas, and relieved from assignment to the 1st Infantry Division (former Battery H, 6th Field Artillery, concurrently reorganized and redesignated as the 8th Battalion, 6th Field Artillery—hereafter separate lineage).

ANNEX

Constituted 8 February 1943 in the Army of the United States as Battery D, 778th Coast Artillery Battalion. Activated 10 March 1943 at Camp Haan, California. Redesignated 1 May 1943 as Battery D, 778th Antiaircraft Artillery Automatic Weapons Battalion. Inactivated 1 May 1946 at Camp Kilmer, New Jersey. Redesignated 13 October 1948 as Battery D, 25th Antiaircraft Artillery Automatic Weapons Battalion, and allotted to the Regular Army. Activated 20 March 1949 in Japan as an element of the 25th Infantry Division.

CAMPAIGN PARTICIPATION CREDIT

Philippine Insurrection
  *Streamer without inscription

World War II
  *Rhineland
  *Ardennes-Alsace
  *Central Europe
  New Guinea
  Bismarck Archipelago
  Luzon

Vietnam
  *Defense
  *Counteroffensive
  *Counteroffensive, Phase II
  *Counteroffensive, Phase III
  *Tet Counteroffensive
  *Counteroffensive, Phase IV
  *Counteroffensive, Phase V
  *Counteroffensive, Phase VI
  *Tet 69/Counteroffensive
  *Summer–fall 1969
  *Winter–spring 1970

DECORATIONS

*Meritorious Unit Commendation, Streamer embroidered VIETNAM 1966 (8th Battalion, 6th Artillery, cited; DA GO 17, 1968)
    *Meritorious Unit Commendation, Streamer embroidered VIETNAM 1967–1968 (8th Battalion, 6th Artillery, cited; DA GO 42, 1969)
    *Republic of Vietnam Cross of Gallantry with Palm, Streamer embroidered VIETNAM 1965–1968 (8th Battalion, 6th Artillery, cited; DA GO 21, 1969)
    *Republic of Vietnam Civil Action Honor Medal, First Class, Streamer embroidered VIETNAM 1965–1970 (8th Battalion, 6th Artillery, cited; DA GO 53, 1970)

6TH AIR DEFENSE ARTILLERY BIBLIOGRAPHY

Baylis, C.D., ed. *Harbor Defenses of San Francisco, 1941*. Baton Rouge: Army and Navy Publishing Company, 1941.

"Big Red One," 1st Infantry Division, Fort Riley, Kansas, 1963. Baton Rouge: Army and Navy Publishing Company, 1963. Contains information about the 8th Battalion, 6th Air Defense Artillery.

Christmas of 1939, Battery "B," Sixth Coast Artillery. Fort Winfield Scott, 1939.

1st Armored Division, Fort Hood, Texas. Baton Rouge: Army and Navy
  Publishing Company, 1963. Contains information about the 1st Bat-
  talion, 6th Air Defense Artillery.
Lowry, Tom, ed. *778th AAA AW BN (SP) From Activation to Victory.* Munich:
  F. Bruckmann, 1945.
McMaster, R.K. "Bridgman's Bull Battery." *Field Artillery Journal* 42
  (July–August 1974): 21. Pertains to the former Battery G, 6th Regi-
  ment of Artillery.
Marquat, William F. "Automatic Artillery in Korea." *Antiaircraft Artillery
  Journal* 93 (November–December 1950):2–9; 94 (January–February
  1951):2–12; (March–April 1951):2–5; (May–June 1951):2–6;
  (July–August 1951):2–9; (September–October 1951):2–5; (Novem-
  ber–December 1951):2–6; 95 (January–February 1952):2–5;
  (March–April 1952):8–10; (May–June 1952):12–15.
Ott, David Ewing. *Field Artillery, 1954–1973.* Vietnam Studies. Washington: Government Printing Office, 1975. Contains information
  about the 8th Battalion, 6th Air Defense Artillery.
242nd AAA Group. London: Montgomery Publishing Company, 1953.

7th AIR DEFENSE ARTILLERY

HERALDIC ITEMS

COAT OF ARMS

Shield: Gules, a pile voided or crusilly fitchy of the like overall a railway gun in the act of firing argent, smoke proper.

Crest: On a wreath of the colors, or and gules, a panther passant guardant, incensed or, flames proper.

Motto: *Nullius Pavet Occursum* (He Fears No Encounter).

Symbolism: The shield is scarlet for artillery. The cross crosslets fitchy, from the arms of the Lords of Commercy, refer to the baptism of fire of a battery of the regiment at Royaumeix near Commercy, France, in World War I. The pile is from the coat of arms of the 53d Artillery (Coast Artillery Corps), elements of which were later consolidated with the 7th Coast Artillery. The railway gun commemorates the unique distinction of Battery E, 42d Artillery (Coast Artillery Corps) (which later became the 8th Battalion, 7th Air Defense Artillery), of firing one of the first shots by a coast artillery organization in World War I.

The panther in the crest is taken from the coat of arms of the Coast Defenses of Sandy Hook where the regiment was reorganized on 1 July 1924. The motto is "He [the panther] fears no encounter."

DISTINCTIVE INSIGNIA

The distinctive insignia is the crest and motto of the coat of arms.

LINEAGE AND HONORS

LINEAGE

Constituted 8 March 1898 in the Regular Army as the 7th Regiment of Artillery. Organized 29 March 1898 at Fort Slocum, New York. Regiment broken up 13 February 1901 and its elements reorganized and redesignated as separate numbered companies and batteries of Artillery Corps. Reconstituted 1 July 1924 in the Regular Army as the 7th Coast Artillery and organized with Headquarters at Fort Hancock, New Jersey. (2d Battalion inactivated 28 February 1930 at Fort Hancock, New Jersey; 1st Battalion inactivated 7 April 1930 at Fort Hancock, New Jersey; 1st and 2d Battalions activated 11 January 1941 at Fort Hancock, New Jersey.) Regiment (less 2d Battalion) inactivated 7 April 1944 at Fort Leonard Wood, Missouri. (2d Battalion inactivated 13 April 1944 at Camp

Chaffee, Arkansas.) Disbanded 14 June 1944.

Headquarters and Headquarters Battery, 7th Coast Artillery, reconstituted 28 June 1950 in the Regular Army; concurrently consolidated with Headquarters and Headquarters Battery, 7th Antiaircraft Artillery Group (*see* ANNEX 1), and consolidated unit designated as Headquarters and Headquarters Battery, 7th Antiaircraft Artillery Group. Activated 20 January 1952 at Fort Stewart, Georgia. Inactivated 15 January 1953 at Fort Stewart, Georgia. Activated 1 May 1954 in Korea. Inactivated 20 January 1955 in Korea. Activated 1 July 1955 in Greenland. Redesignated 20 March 1958 as Headquarters and Headquarters Battery, 7th Artillery Group. Inactivated 20 December 1965 at Fort Totten, New York.

1st Battalion, 7th Coast Artillery, reconstituted 28 June 1950 in the Regular Army; concurrently consolidated with the 126th Antiaircraft Artillery Gun Battalion (*see* ANNEX 2) and consolidated unit redesignated as the 7th Antiaircraft Artillery Battalion. Redesignated 13 December 1951 as the 7th Antiaircraft Artillery Automatic Weapons Battalion. Activated 20 December 1951 at Camp Edwards, Massachusetts. Redesignated 30 June 1955 as the 7th Antiaircraft Artillery Battalion. Inactivated 1 September 1958 in Germany.

2d Battalion, 7th Coast Artillery, reconstituted 28 June 1950 in the Regular Army; concurrently consolidated with the 26th Antiaircraft Artillery Automatic Weapons Battalion (active) (*see* ANNEX 3) and consolidated unit designated as the 26th Antiaircraft Artillery Automatic Weapons Battalion, an element of the 24th Infantry Division. Redesignated 1 January 1953 as the 26th Antiaircraft Artillery Battalion. Inactivated 15 October 1957 in Korea. Relieved 5 June 1958 from assignment to the 24th Infantry Division.

Headquarters and Headquarters Battery, 7th Artillery Group; 7th and 26th Antiaircraft Artillery Battalions; and 7th Field Artillery Battalion (organized in 1916) consolidated, reorganized, and redesignated 20 December 1965 as the 7th Artillery, a parent regiment under the Combat Arms Regimental System.

7th Artillery (less former 7th Field Artillery Battalion) reorganized and redesignated 1 September 1971 as the 7th Air Defense Artillery, a parent regiment under the Combat Arms Regimental System (former 7th Field Artillery Battalion concurrently reorganized and redesignated as the 7th Field Artillery—hereafter separate lineage).

ANNEX 1

Constituted 5 August 1942 in the Army of the United States as Headquarters and Headquarters Battery, 7th Antiaircraft Artillery Automatic Weapons Group. Activated 1 September 1942 at Camp Haan, California. Redesignated 26 May 1943 as Headquarters and Headquarters Battery, 7th Antiaircraft Artillery Group. Inactivated 17 February 1946 at Camp Kilmer, New Jersey.

ANNEX 2

Constituted 25 February 1943 in the Army of the United States as the 126th Coast Artillery Battalion. Activated 10 May 1943 at Camp Haan, California. Redesignated 28 June 1943 as the 126th Antiaircraft Artillery Gun Battalion. Inactivated 3 January 1946 at Camp Patrick Henry, Virginia.

ANNEX 3

Constituted 25 February 1943 in the Army of the United States as the 784th Coast Artillery Battalion. Activated 10 April 1943 at Fort Bliss, Texas. Redesignated 30 April 1943 as the 784th Antiaircraft Artillery Automatic Weapons Battalion. Inactivated 31 December 1945 in Germany. Redesignated 13 October 1948 as the 26th Antiaircraft Artillery Automatic Weapons Battalion and allotted to the Regular Army. Assigned 20 March 1949 to the 24th Infantry Division and activated in Japan.

CAMPAIGN PARTICIPATION CREDIT

World War II
    Normandy
    Northern France
    Rhineland
    Ardennes-Alsace
    Central Europe
    England 1944

Korean War
    UN defensive
    UN offensive
    CCF intervention
    First UN counteroffensive
    CCF spring offensive
    UN summer–fall offensive
    Second Korean winter
    Korea, summer 1953

Vietnam
    Defense
    Counteroffensive
    Counteroffensive, Phase II
    Counteroffensive, Phase III
    Tet Counteroffensive
    Counteroffensive, Phase IV
    Counteroffensive, Phase V
    Counteroffensive, Phase VI
    Tet 69/Counteroffensive
    Summer–fall 1969
    Winter–spring 1970

DECORATIONS

Presidential Unit Citation (Army), Streamer embroidered DEFENSE OF KOREA (24th Infantry Division cited; DA GO 45, 1950)

Meritorious Unit Commendation, Streamer embroidered VIETNAM 1966–1967 (1st Battalion, 7th Artillery, cited; DA GO 17, 1968)

Meritorious Unit Commendation, Streamer embroidered VIETNAM 1967–1968 (1st Battalion, 7th Artillery, cited; DA GO 17, 1969)

1st BATTALION, 7th AIR DEFENSE ARTILLERY

RA
(nondivisional)

LINEAGE

Constituted 8 March 1898 in the Regular Army as Battery A, 7th Regiment of Artillery. Organized 29 March 1898 at Fort Slocum, New York.

Reorganized and redesignated 13 February 1901 as the 72d Company, Coast Artillery, Artillery Corps. Redesignated 2 February 1907 as the 72d Company, Coast Artillery Corps. Redesignated in July 1916 as the 1st Company, Fort Screven [Georgia]. Redesignated 31 August 1917 as the 1st Company, Coast Defenses of Savannah. Redesignated 1 June 1922 as the 72d Company, Coast Artillery Corps.

Reorganized and redesignated 1 July 1924 as Battery A, 7th Coast Artillery. Inactivated 7 April 1930 at Fort Hancock, New Jersey. Activated 1 July 1939 at Fort Hancock, New Jersey. Inactivated 7 April 1944 at Fort Leonard Wood, Missouri. Disbanded 14 June 1944.

Reconstituted 28 June 1950 in the Regular Army; concurrently consolidated with Battery A, 126th Antiaircraft Artillery Gun Battalion (*see* ANNEX), and consolidated unit redesignated as Battery A, 7th Antiaircraft Artillery Battalion. Redesignated 13 December 1951 as Battery A, 7th Antiaircraft Artillery Automatic Weapons Battalion. Activated 20 December 1951 at Camp Edwards, Massachusetts. Redesignated 30 June 1955 as Battery A, 7th Antiaircraft Artillery Battalion.

Inactivated 1 September 1958 in Germany; concurrently consolidated with Headquarters and Headquarters Battery, 1st Howitzer Battalion, 7th Artillery (active) (organized in 1916), and consolidated unit designated as Headquarters and Headquarters Battery, 1st Howitzer Battalion, 7th Artillery, an element of the 1st Infantry Division (organic elements constituted 8 February 1957 and activated 15 February 1957). Redesignated 20 January 1964 as the 1st Battalion, 7th Artillery.

Redesignated (less former Headquarters and Headquarters Battery, 1st Howitzer Battalion, 7th Artillery) 1 September 1971 as the 1st Battalion, 7th Air Defense Artillery; concurrently inactivated at Fort Riley, Kansas, and relieved from assignment to the 1st Infantry Division (former Headquarters and Headquarters Battery, 1st Howitzer Battalion, 7th Artillery, concurrently reorganized and redesignated as the 1st Battalion, 7th Field Artillery—hereafter separate lineage). 1st Battalion, 7th Air Defense Artillery, activated 13 September 1972 at Fort Bliss, Texas.

ANNEX

Constituted 25 February 1943 in the Army of the United States as Battery A, 126th Coast Artillery Battalion. Activated 10 May 1943 at Camp Haan, California. Redesignated 28 June 1943 as Battery A, 126th Antiaircraft Artillery Gun Battalion. Inactivated 3 January 1946 at Camp Patrick Henry, Virginia.

Campaign Participation Credit

World War II
Normandy
Northern France
*Rhineland
*Ardennes-Alsace
*Central Europe
*England 1944

Korean War
UN defensive
UN offensive
CCF intervention
First UN counteroffensive
CCF spring offensive
UN summer–fall offensive

Second Korean winter
Korea, summer 1953

Vietnam
*Defense
*Counteroffensive
*Counteroffensive, Phase II
*Counteroffensive, Phase III
*Tet Counteroffensive
*Counteroffensive, Phase IV
*Counteroffensive, Phase V
*Counteroffensive, Phase VI
*Tet 69/Counteroffensive
*Summer–fall 1969
*Winter–spring 1970

Decorations

Presidential Unit Citation (Army), Streamer embroidered DEFENSE OF KOREA

*Meritorious Unit Commendation, Streamer embroidered VIETNAM 1966–1967 (1st Battalion, 7th Artillery, cited; DA GO 17, 1968)

*Meritorious Unit Commendation, Streamer embroidered VIETNAM 1967–1968 (1st Battalion, 7th Artillery, cited; DA GO 17, 1969)

*Belgian Fourragere 1940 (126th Antiaircraft Artillery Gun Battalion cited; DA GO 43, 1950)

*Cited in the Order of the Day of the Belgian Army for action at LIEGE (126th Antiaircraft Artillery Gun Battalion cited; DA GO 43, 1950)

*Cited in the Order of the Day of the Belgian Army for action in the ARDENNES (126th Antiaircraft Artillery Gun Battalion cited; DA GO 43, 1950)

*Republic of Vietnam Cross of Gallantry with Palm, Streamer embroidered VIETNAM 1965–1968 (1st Battalion, 7th Artillery, cited; DA GO 21, 1969)

*Republic of Vietnam Cross of Gallantry with Palm, Streamer embroidered VIETNAM 1969–1970 (1st Battalion, 7th Artillery, cited; DA GO 2, 1971)

*Republic of Vietnam Civil Action Honor Medal, First Class, Streamer embroidered VIETNAM 1965–1970 (1st Battalion, 7th Artillery, cited; DA GO 53, 1970)

2d BATTALION, 7th AIR DEFENSE ARTILLERY

RA
(inactive)

LINEAGE

Constituted 8 March 1898 in the Regular Army as Battery B, 7th Regiment of Artillery. Organized 31 March 1898 at Fort Slocum, New York.

Reorganized and redesignated 13 February 1901 as the 73d Company, Coast Artillery, Artillery Corps. Redesignated 2 February 1907 as the 73d Company, Coast Artillery Corps. Redesignated 1 July 1916 as the 6th Company, Fort Grant [Canal Zone]. Redesignated 31 August 1917 as the 6th Company, Coast Defenses of Balboa. Redesignated 30 June 1922 as the 73d Company, Coast Artillery Corps.

Reorganized and rededicated 1 July 1924 as Battery B, 7th Coast Artillery. Inactivated 28 February 1930 at Fort Hancock, New Jersey. Activated 1 July 1939 at Fort Hancock, New Jersey. Inactivated 7 April 1944 at Camp Leonard Wood, Missouri. Disbanded 14 June 1944.

Reconstituted 28 June 1950 in the Regular Army; concurrently consolidated with Battery B, 126th Antiaircraft Artillery Gun Battalion (*see* ANNEX), and consolidated unit redesignated as Battery B, 7th Antiaircraft Artillery Battalion. Redesignated 13 December 1951 as Battery B, 7th Antiaircraft Artillery Automatic Weapons Battalion. Activated 20 December 1951 at Camp Edwards, Massachusetts. Redesignated 30 June 1955 as Battery B, 7th Antiaircraft Artillery Battalion.

Inactivated 1 September 1958 in Germany; concurrently consolidated with Headquarters and Headquarters Battery, 2d Howitzer Battalion, 7th Artillery (organized in 1916), and consolidated unit designated as Headquarters and Headquarters Battery, 2d Howitzer Battalion, 7th Artillery (organic elements constituted 14 June 1957). Battalion assigned 1 April 1960 to the 24th Infantry Division and activated in Germany. Redesignated 1 February 1963 as the 2d Battalion, 7th Artillery. Inactivated 15 April 1970 in Germany and relieved from assignment to the 24th Infantry Division.

Redesignated (less former Headquarters and Headquarters Battery, 2d Howitzer Battalion, 7th Artillery) 1 September 1971 as the 2d Battalion, 7th Air Defense Artillery (former Headquarters and Headquarters Battery, 2d Howitzer Battalion, 7th Artillery, concurrently redesignated as the 2d Battalion, 7th Field Artillery—hereafter separate lineage).

ANNEX

Constituted 25 February 1943 in the Army of the United States as Battery B, 126th Coast Artillery Battalion. Activated 10 May 1943 at Camp Haan, California. Redesignated 28 June 1943 as Battery B, 126th Antiaircraft Artillery Gun Battalion. Inactivated 3 January 1946 at Camp Patrick Henry, Virginia.

Campaign Participation Credit

World War II
- Normandy
- Northern France
- *Rhineland
- *Ardennes-Alsace
- *Central Europe
- *England 1944

Korean War
- UN defensive
- UN offensive
- CCF intervention
- First UN counteroffensive
- CCF spring offensive
- UN summer–fall offensive
- Second Korean winter
- Korea, summer 1953

Decorations

Presidential Unit Citation (Army), Streamer embroidered DEFENSE OF KOREA

*Belgian Fourragere 1940 (126th Antiaircraft Artillery Gun Battalion cited; DA GO 43, 1950)

*Cited in the Order of the Day of the Belgian Army for action at LIEGE (126th Antiaircraft Artillery Gun Battalion cited; DA GO 43, 1950)

*Cited in the Order of the Day of the Belgian Army for action in the ARDENNES (126th Antiaircraft Artillery Gun Battalion cited; DA GO 43, 1950)

3d BATTALION, 7th AIR DEFENSE ARTILLERY

RA
(nondivisional)

LINEAGE

Constituted 8 March 1898 in the Regular Army as Battery I, 7th Regiment of Artillery. Organized 31 March 1898 at Fort Slocum, New York.

Reorganized and redesignated 13 February 1901 as the 79th Company, Coast Artillery, Artillery Corps. Redesignated 2 February 1907 as the 79th Company, Coast Artillery Corps. Redesignated in July 1916 as the 1st Company, Fort Michie [New York]. Redesignated 31 August 1917 as the 23d Company, Coast Defenses of Long Island Sound. Redesignated 15 April 1918 as the 18th Company, Coast Defenses of Long Island Sound. Redesignated 2 December 1918 as the 15th Company, Coast Defenses of Long Island Sound. Consolidated 30 September 1919 with the 6th Company, Coast Defenses of Long Island Sound (organized 1 January 1919), and consolidated unit designated as the 6th Company, Coast Defenses of Long Island Sound. Consolidated 7 March 1921 with the 7th, 8th, and 9th Companies, Coast Defenses of Long Island Sound, and consolidated unit designated as the 2d Company, Coast Defenses of Long Island Sound. Former 6th Company, Coast Defenses of Long Island Sound, withdrawn from the consolidation and reorganized 18 December 1921 at Fort H. G. Wright, New York (2d Company, Coast Defenses of Long Island Sound, concurrently redesignated as the 5th Company, Coast Defenses of Long Island Sound—hereafter separate lineage). Redesignated 1 June 1922 as the 79th Company, Coast Artillery Corps. Inactivated 20 November 1922 at Fort H. G. Wright, New York.

Redesignated 1 July 1924 as Battery C, 7th Coast Artillery. Activated 13 August 1940 at Fort Tilden, New York. Inactivated 7 April 1944 at Camp Leonard Wood, Missouri. Disbanded 14 June 1944.

Reconstituted 28 June 1950 in the Regular Army; concurrently consolidated with Battery C, 126th Antiaircraft Artillery Gun Battalion (*see* ANNEX), and consolidated unit redesignated as Battery C, 7th Antiaircraft Artillery Battalion. Redesignated 13 December 1951 as Battery C, 7th Antiaircraft Artillery Automatic Weapons Battalion. Activated 20 December 1951 at Camp Edwards, Massachusetts. Redesignated 30 June 1955 as Battery C, 7th Antiaircraft Artillery Battalion.

Consolidated 1 September 1958 with Battery C, 7th Field Artillery Battalion (organized in 1916), and consolidated unit reorganized and redesignated as Headquarters and Headquarters Battery, 3d Gun Battalion, 7th Artillery (organic elements constituted 12 August 1958 and activated 1 September 1958). Reorganized and redesignated 25 November 1960 as the 3d Missile Battalion, 7th Artillery. Redesignated 20 August 1965 as the 3d Battalion, 7th Artillery.

Reorganized and redesignated (less former Battery C, 7th Field Artillery Battalion) 1 September 1971 as the 3d Battalion, 7th Air Defense Artillery (former Battery C, 7th Field Artillery Battalion, concurrently redesignated as the 3d Battalion, 7th Field Artillery—hereafter separate lineage).

ANNEX

Constituted 25 February 1943 in the Army of the United States as Battery C, 126th Coast Artillery Battalion. Activated 10 May 1943 at Camp Haan, California. Redesignated 28 June 1943 as Battery C, 126th Antiaircraft Artillery Gun Battalion. Inactivated 3 January 1946 at Camp Patrick Henry, Virginia.

CAMPAIGN PARTICIPATION CREDIT

World War II	*Korean War*
Normandy	UN defensive
Northern France	UN offensive
*Rhineland	CCF intervention
*Ardennes-Alsace	First UN counteroffensive
*Central Europe	CCF spring offensive
*England 1944	UN summer-fall offensive
	Second Korean winter
	Korea, summer 1953

DECORATIONS

Presidential Unit Citation (Army), Streamer embroidered DEFENSE OF KOREA

*Belgian Fourragere 1940 (126th Antiaircraft Artillery Gun Battalion cited; DA GO 43, 1950)

*Cited in the Order of the Day of the Belgian Army for action at LIEGE (126th Antiaircraft Artillery Gun Battalion cited; DA GO 43, 1950)

*Cited in the Order of the Day of the Belgian Army for action in the ARDENNES (126th Antiaircraft Artillery Gun Battalion cited; DA GO 43, 1950)

4th MISSILE BATTALION, 7th AIR DEFENSE ARTILLERY

RA
(inactive)

LINEAGE

Constituted 8 March 1898 in the Regular Army as Battery D, 7th Regiment of Artillery. Organized 31 March 1898 at Fort Slocum, New York.

Reorganized and redesignated 13 February 1901 as the 74th Company, Coast Artillery, Artillery Corps. Redesignated 2 February 1907 as the 74th Company, Coast Artillery Corps. Redesignated 13 July 1916 as the 4th Company, Fort Screven [Georgia]. Redesignated 15 April 1917 as the 2d Company, Fort Screven [Georgia]. Redesignated 22 July 1917 as Battery M, 8th Provisional Regiment, Coast Artillery Corps. Redesignated 5 February 1918 as Battery M, 53d Artillery (Coast Artillery Corps). Redesignated 6 August 1918 as Battery F, 53d Artillery (Coast Artillery Corps). (Additionally designated 1 June 1922 as the 74th Company, Coast Artillery Corps; additional designation abolished 1 July 1924.)

Reorganized and redesignated 1 July 1924 as Battery D, 7th Coast Artillery. Inactivated 28 February 1930 at Fort Hancock, New Jersey. Activated 13 January 1941 at Fort Hancock, New Jersey. Inactivated 13 April 1944 at Camp Chaffee, Arkansas. Disbanded 14 June 1944.

Reconstituted 28 June 1950 in the Regular Army; concurrently consolidated with Battery D, 126th Antiaircraft Artillery Gun Battalion (*see* ANNEX), and consolidated unit redesignated as Battery D, 7th Antiaircraft Artillery Battalion. Redesignated 13 December 1951 as Battery D, 7th Antiaircraft Artillery Automatic Weapons Battalion. Activated 20 December 1951 at Camp Edwards, Massachusetts. Disbanded 30 June 1955 in Germany.

Reconstituted 12 August 1958 in the Regular Army; concurrently consolidated with Battery D, 7th Field Artillery (organized in 1916), and consolidated unit redesignated as Headquarters and Headquarters Battery, 4th Gun Battalion, 7th Artillery (organic elements concurrently constituted). Battalion activated 1 September 1958 at Savannah, Georgia. Inactivated 20 January 1960 at Savannah, Georgia. Redesignated 4 April 1960 as the 4th Missile Battalion, 7th Artillery. Activated 19 April 1960 at Bergstrom Air Force Base, Texas. Inactivated 25 June 1966 at Bergstrom Air Force Base, Texas.

Redesignated (less former Battery D, 7th Field Artillery) 1 September 1971 as the 4th Missile Battalion, 7th Air Defense Artillery (former Battery D, 7th Field Artillery, concurrently redesignated as the 4th Missile Battalion, 7th Field Artillery—hereafter separate lineage).

ANNEX

Constituted 25 February 1943 in the Army of the United States as Battery D, 126th Coast Artillery Battalion. Activated 10 May 1943 at Camp Haan, California. Redesignated 28 June 1943 as Battery D, 126th Antiaircraft Artillery Gun Battalion. Inactivated 3 January 1946 at Camp Patrick Henry, Virginia.

CAMPAIGN PARTICIPATION CREDIT

World War I
  *Champagne-Marne
  *St. Mihiel
  *Meuse-Argonne
  *Lorraine 1918
  *Champagne 1918

World War II
  Normandy
  Northern France
  *Rhineland
  *Ardennes-Alsace

*Central Europe
*England 1944

Korean War
  UN defensive
  UN offensive
  CCF intervention
  First UN counteroffensive
  CCF spring offensive
  UN summer–fall offensive
  Second Korean winter
  Korea, summer 1953

DECORATIONS

Presidential Unit Citation (Army), Streamer embroidered DEFENSE OF KOREA

*Belgian Fourragere 1940 (126th Antiaircraft Artillery Gun Battalion cited; DA GO 43, 1950)

*Cited in the Order of the Day of the Belgian Army for action at LIEGE (126th Antiaircraft Artillery Gun Battalion cited; DA GO 43, 1950)

*Cited in the Order of the day of the Belgian Army for action in the ARDENNES (126th Antiaircraft Artillery Gun Battalion cited; DA GO 43, 1950)

5th BATTALION, 7th AIR DEFENSE ARTILLERY

RA
(inactive)

LINEAGE

Constituted 8 March 1898 in the Regular Army as Battery E, 7th Regiment of Artillery. Organized 31 March 1898 at Fort Slocum, New York.

Reorganized and redesignated 13 February 1901 as the 75th Company, Coast Artillery, Artillery Corps. Redesignated 2 February 1907 as the 75th Company, Coast Artillery Corps. Redesignated 18 July 1916 as the 2d Company, Fort Kamehameha [Hawaii]. Redesignated 31 August 1917 as the 2d Company, Coast Defenses of Oahu. Redesignated in February 1921 as the 2d Company, Coast Defenses of Pearl Harbor. Redesignated 30 June 1922 as the 75th Company, Coast Artillery Corps.

Reorganized and redesignated 1 July 1924 as Battery E, 7th Coast Artillery. Inactivated 1 February 1940 at Fort Dupont, Delaware. Activated 13 February 1941 at Fort Hancock, New Jersey. Inactivated 13 April 1944 at Camp Chaffee, Arkansas. Disbanded 14 June 1944.

Reconstituted 28 June 1950 in the Regular Army; concurrently consolidated with Battery A, 26th Antiaircraft Artillery Automatic Weapons Battalion (active) (*see* ANNEX), and consolidated unit designated as Battery A, 26th Antiaircraft Artillery Automatic Weapons Battalion, an element of the 24th Infantry Division. Redesignated 1 January 1953 as Battery A, 26th Antiaircraft Artillery Battalion. Inactivated 15 October 1957 in Korea. (26th Antiaircraft Artillery Battalion relieved 5 June 1958 from assignment to the 24th Infantry Division.)

Consolidated 12 August 1958 with Battery E, 7th Field Artillery (organized in 1916), and consolidated unit redesignated as Headquarters and Headquarters Battery, 5th Missile Battalion, 7th Artillery (organic elements concurrently constituted). Battalion activated 1 September 1958 at Tappan, New York. Redesignated 20 December 1965 as the 5th Battalion, 7th Artillery. Inactivated 30 November 1968 at Tappan, New York.

Redesignated (less former Battery E, 7th Field Artillery) 1 September 1971 as the 5th Battalion, 7th Air Defense Artillery (former Battery E, 7th Field Artillery, concurrently redesignated as the 5th Battalion, 7th Field Artillery—hereafter separate lineage).

ANNEX

Constituted 25 February 1943 in the Army of the United States as Battery A, 784th Coast Artillery Battalion. Activated 10 April 1943 at Fort Bliss, Texas. Redesignated 30 April 1943 as Battery A, 784th Antiaircraft Artillery Automatic Weapons Battalion. Inactivated 31 December 1945 in Germany. Redesignated 13 October 1948 as Battery A, 26th Antiaircraft Artillery Automatic Weapons Battalion, and allotted to the Regular Army. Activated 20 March 1949 in Japan as an element of the 24th Infantry Division.

CAMPAIGN PARTICIPATION CREDIT

World War II
  *Normandy
  *Northern France
  *Rhineland
   Ardennes-Alsace
  *Central Europe
  *England 1944

Korean War
  *UN defensive
  *UN offensive
  *CCF intervention
  *First UN counteroffensive
  *CCF spring offensive
  *UN summer–fall offensive
  *Second Korean winter
  *Korea, summer 1953

DECORATIONS

*Presidential Unit Citation (Army), Streamer embroidered DEFENSE OF KOREA (24th Infantry Division cited; DA GO 45, 1950)

*Belgian Fourragere 1940 (784th Antiaircraft Artillery Automatic Weapons Battalion cited; DA GO 43, 1950)

*Cited in the Order of the Day of the Belgian Army for action at LIEGE (784th Antiaircraft Artillery Automatic Weapons Battalion cited; DA GO 43, 1950)

*Cited in the Order of the Day of the Belgian Army for action in the ARDENNES (784th Antiaircraft Artillery Automatic Weapons Battalion cited; DA GO 43, 1950)

*Republic of Korea Presidential Unit Citation, Streamer embroidered PYONGTAEK (26th Antiaircraft Artillery Automatic Weapons Battalion cited; DA GO 35, 1951)

*Republic of Korea Presidential Unit Citation, Streamer embroidered KOREA 1952–1953 (24th Infantry Division cited; DA GO 24, 1954)

6th BATTALION, 7th AIR DEFENSE ARTILLERY

AR
(inactive)

LINEAGE

Constituted 8 March 1898 in the Regular Army as Battery F, 7th Regiment of Artillery. Organized 31 March 1898 at Fort Slocum, New York.

Reorganized and redesignated 13 February 1901 as the 76th Company, Coast Artillery, Artillery Corps. Redesignated 2 February 1907 as the 76th Company, Coast Artillery Corps. Redesignated 3 July 1916 as the 2d Company, Fort Hancock [New Jersey]. Redesignated 31 August 1917 as the 2d Company, Coast Defenses of Sandy Hook. Redesignated 1 June 1922 as the 76th Company, Coast Artillery Corps.

Redesignated 1 July 1924 as Battery F, 7th Coast Artillery, and inactivated at Fort Hancock, New Jersey. Activated 13 January 1941 at Fort Hancock, New Jersey. Inactivated 13 April 1944 at Camp Chaffee, Arkansas. Disbanded 14 June 1944.

Reconstituted 28 June 1950 in the Regular Army; concurrently consolidated with Battery B, 26th Antiaircraft Artillery Automatic Weapons Battalion (active) (*see* ANNEX), and consolidated unit designated as Battery B, 26th Antiaircraft Artillery Automatic Weapons Battalion, an element of the 24th Infantry Division. Redesignated 1 January 1953 as Battery B, 26th Antiaircraft Artillery Battalion. Inactivated 15 October 1957 in Korea. (26th Antiaircraft Artillery Battalion relieved 5 June 1958 from assignment to the 24th Infantry Division.)

Consolidated 7 April 1959 with Battery F, 7th Field Artillery (organized in 1916), and consolidated unit redesignated as Headquarters and Headquarters Battery, 6th Howitzer Battalion, 7th Artillery; concurrently withdrawn from the Regular Army, allotted to the Army Reserve, and assigned to the 77th Infantry Division (organic elements concurrently constituted). Battalion activated 1 May 1959 with Headquarters at White Plains, New York. Redesignated 25 March 1963 as the 6th Battalion, 7th Artillery. Inactivated 30 December 1965 at White Plains, New York, and relieved from assignment to the 77th Infantry Division.

Redesignated (less former Battery F, 7th Field Artillery) 1 September 1971 as the 6th Battalion, 7th Air Defense Artillery (former Battery F, 7th Field Artillery, concurrently redesignated as the 6th Battalion, 7th Field Artillery—hereafter separate lineage).

ANNEX

Constituted 25 February 1943 in the Army of the United States as Battery B, 784th Coast Artillery Battalion. Activated 10 April 1943 at Fort Bliss, Texas. Redesignated 30 April 1943 as Battery B, 784th Antiaircraft Artillery Automatic Weapons Battalion. Inactivated 31 December 1945 in Germany. Redesignated 13 October 1948 as Battery B, 26th Antiaircraft

Artillery Automatic Weapons Battalion, and allotted to the Regular Army. Activated 20 March 1949 in Japan as an element of the 24th Infantry Division.

CAMPAIGN PARTICIPATION CREDIT

World War II
  *Normandy
  *Northern France
  *Rhineland
   Ardennes-Alsace
  *Central Europe
  *England 1944

Korean War
  *UN defensive
  *UN offensive
  *CCF intervention
  *First UN counteroffensive
  *CCF spring offensive
  *UN summer–fall offensive
  *Second Korean winter
  *Korea, summer 1953

DECORATIONS

*Presidential Unit Citation (Army), Streamer embroidered DEFENSE OF KOREA (24th Infantry Division cited; DA GO 45, 1950)

*Belgian Fourragere 1940 (784th Antiaircraft Artillery Automatic Weapons Battalion cited; DA GO 43, 1950)

*Cited in the Order of the Day of the Belgian Army for action at LIEGE (784th Antiaircraft Artillery Automatic Weapons Battalion cited; DA GO 43, 1950)

*Cited in the Order of the Day of the Belgian Army for action in the ARDENNES (784th Antiaircraft Artillery Automatic Weapons Battalion cited; DA GO 43, 1950)

*Republic of Korea Presidential Unit Citation, Streamer embroidered PYONGTAEK (26th Antiaircraft Artillery Automatic Weapons Battalion cited; DA GO 35, 1951)

*Republic of Korea Presidential Unit Citation, Streamer embroidered KOREA 1952–1953 (24th Infantry Division cited; DA GO 24, 1954)

7th HOWITZER BATTALION, 7th AIR DEFENSE ARTILLERY

AR
(inactive)

LINEAGE

Constituted 8 March 1898 in the Regular Army as Battery L, 7th Regiment of Artillery. Organized 31 March 1898 at Fort Slocum, New York.

Reorganized and redesignated 13 February 1901 as the 81st Company, Coast Artillery, Artillery Corps. Redesignated 2 February 1907 as the 81st Company, Coast Artillery Corps. Redesignated in July 1916 as the 1st Company, Fort Grant [Canal Zone]. Redesignated 31 August 1917 as the 1st Company, Coast Defenses of Balboa. Redesignated 30 June 1922 as the 81st Company, Coast Artillery Corps.

Redesignated 1 July 1924 as Battery G, 7th Coast Artillery, and inactivated in the Canal Zone. Activated 1 June 1941 at Fort Tilden, New York. Inactivated 20 March 1944 at Fort Jackson, South Carolina. Disbanded 14 June 1944.

Reconstituted 28 June 1950 in the Regular Army; concurrently consolidated with Battery C, 26th Antiaircraft Artillery Automatic Weapons Battalion (active) (*see* ANNEX), and consolidated unit designated as Battery C, 26th Antiaircraft Artillery Automatic Weapons Battalion, an element of the 24th Infantry Division. Redesignated 1 January 1953 as Battery C, 26th Antiaircraft Artillery Battalion. Inactivated 15 October 1957 in Korea. (26th Antiaircraft Artillery Battalion relieved 5 June 1958 from assignment to the 24th Infantry Division.)

Consolidated 6 April 1959 with Battery G, 7th Field Artillery (organized in 1940), and consolidated unit redesignated as Headquarters and Headquarters Battery, 7th Howitzer Battalion, 7th Artillery; concurrently withdrawn from the Regular Army, allotted to the Army Reserve, and assigned to the 94th Infantry Division (organic elements concurrently constituted). Battalion activated 1 May 1959 at Worcester, Massachusetts. Inactivated 1 March 1963 at Worcester, Massachusetts, and relieved from assignment to the 94th Infantry Division.

Redesignated (less former Battery G, 7th Field Artillery) 1 September 1971 as the 7th Howitzer Battalion, 7th Air Defense Artillery (former Battery G, 7th Field Artillery, concurrently redesignated as the 7th Howitzer Battalion, 7th Field Artillery—hereafter separate lineage).

ANNEX

Constituted 25 February 1943 in the Army of the United States as Battery C, 784th Coast Artillery Battalion. Activated 10 April 1943 at Fort Bliss, Texas. Redesignated 30 April 1943 as Battery C, 784th Antiaircraft Artillery Automatic Weapons Battalion, and allotted to the Regular Army. Activated 20 March 1949 in Japan as an element of the 24th Infantry Division.

CAMPAIGN PARTICIPATION CREDIT

World War II
- *Normandy
- *Northern France
- *Rhineland
- Ardennes-Alsace
- *Central Europe
- *England 1944

Korean War
- *UN defensive
- *UN offensive
- *CCF intervention
- *First UN counteroffensive
- *CCF spring offensive
- *UN summer-fall offensive
- *Second Korean winter
- *Korea, summer 1953

DECORATIONS

*Presidential Unit Citation (Army), Streamer embroidered DEFENSE OF KOREA (24th Infantry Division cited; DA GO 45, 1950)

*Belgian Fourragere 1940 (784th Antiaircraft Artillery Automatic Weapons Battalion cited; DA GO 43, 1950)

*Cited in the Order of the Day of the Belgian Army for action at LIEGE (784th Antiaircraft Artillery Automatic Weapons Battalion cited; DA GO 43, 1950)

*Cited in the Order of the Day of the Belgian Army for action in the ARDENNES (784th Antiaircraft Artillery Automatic Weapons Battalion cited; DA GO 43, 1950)

*Republic of Korea Presidential Unit Citation, Streamer embroidered PYONGTAEK (26th Antiaircraft Artillery Automatic Weapons Battalion cited; DA GO 35, 1951)

*Republic of Korea Presidential Unit Citation, Streamer embroidered KOREA 1952 (Battery C, 26th Antiaircraft Artillery Automatic Weapons Battalion, cited; DA GO 50, 1954)

*Republic of Korea Presidential Unit Citation, Streamer embroidered KOREA 1952–1953 (24th Infantry Division cited; DA GO 24, 1954)

8th BATTALION, 7th AIR DEFENSE ARTILLERY

RA
(inactive)

LINEAGE

Constituted 8 March 1898 in the Regular Army as Battery H, 7th Regiment of Artillery. Organized 31 March 1898 at Fort Slocum, New York.

Reorganized and redesignated 13 February 1901 as the 78th Company, Coast Artillery, Artillery Corps. Redesignated 2 February 1907 as the 78th Company, Coast Artillery Corps. Redesignated 1 July 1916 as the 2d Company, Fort Moultrie [South Carolina]. Redesignated 22 July 1917 as Battery H, 8th Provisional Regiment, Coast Artillery Corps. Redesignated 5 February 1918 as Battery H, 53d Artillery (Coast Artillery Corps). Redesignated 7 August 1918 as Battery E, 42d Artillery (Coast Artillery Corps). (Additionally designated 1 June 1922 as the 78th Company, Coast Artillery Corps; additional designation abolished 1 July 1924.)

Reorganized and redesignated 1 July 1924 as Headquarters Battery, 7th Coast Artillery. Inactivated 7 April 1944 at Fort Leonard Wood, Missouri. Disbanded 14 June 1944.

Reconstituted 28 June 1950 in the Regular Army; concurrently consolidated with Headquarters Battery, 7th Antiaircraft Artillery Group (see ANNEX), and consolidated unit designated as Headquarters Battery, 7th Antiaircraft Artillery Group. Activated 20 January 1952 at Camp Stewart, Georgia. Inactivated 15 January 1953 at Camp Stewart, Georgia. Activated 1 May 1954 in Korea. Inactivated 20 January 1955 in Korea. Activated 1 July 1955 in Greenland. Redesignated 20 March 1958 as Headquarters Battery, 7th Artillery Group.

Inactivated 20 December 1965 at Fort Totten, New York; concurrently consolidated with Headquarters and Headquarters Battery, 8th Battalion, 7th Artillery (active) (organized in 1916), and consolidated unit designated as Headquarters and Headquarters Battery, 8th Battalion, 7th Artillery (organic elements constituted 18 January 1962 and activated 9 April 1962).

Reorganized and redesignated (less former Headquarters and Headquarters Battery, 8th Battalion, 7th Artillery) 1 September 1971 as the 8th Battalion, 7th Air Defense Artillery (former Headquarters and Headquarters Battery, 8th Battalion, 7th Artillery, concurrently redesignated as the 8th Battalion, 7th Field Artillery—hereafter separate lineage). 8th Battalion, 7th Air Defense Artillery, inactivated 13 September 1972 at Fort Bliss, Texas.

ANNEX

Constituted 5 August 1942 in the Army of the United States as Headquarters Battery, 7th Antiaircraft Artillery Automatic Weapons Group. Activated 1 September 1942 at Camp Haan, California. Redesignated

26 May 1943 as Headquarters Battery, 7th Antiaircraft Artillery Group. Inactivated 17 February 1946 at Camp Kilmer, New Jersey.

CAMPAIGN PARTICIPATION CREDIT

World War I
    *Champagne-Marne
    *Champagne 1918

World War II
    Normandy
    *Northern France
    *Rhineland
    *Ardennes-Alsace
    *Central Europe
    England 1944

Korean War
    UN defensive
    UN offensive
    CCF intervention
    First UN counteroffensive
    CCF spring offensive
    UN summer–fall offensive
    Second Korean winter
    Korea, summer 1953

DECORATIONS

Presidential Unit Citation (Army), Streamer embroidered DEFENSE OF KOREA

*French Croix de Guerre with Palm, World War I, Streamer embroidered CHAMPAGNE (Battery H, 53d Artillery [Coast Artillery Corps], cited; WD GO 11, 1924)

7TH AIR DEFENSE ARTILLERY BIBLIOGRAPHY

Aaron, John S. "24th Division Antiaircraft Artillery." *Antiaircraft Artillery Journal* 95 (January–February 1952): 18–20. Contains information about the 26th Antiaircraft Artillery Battalion.

Alf, William L. "The Guns of Battery 'O'." *Field Artillery Journal* 27 (November 1937): 439–42.

"Big Red One," 1st Infantry Division, Fort Riley, Kansas, 1963. Baton Rouge: Army and Navy Publishing Company, 1963. Contains information about the 1st Battalion, 7th Air Defense Artillery.

Harvey, Lynn C. *24th Infantry Division (Mechanized), 1963. ROAD Reorganization Day.* Germany, 1963. Contains information about the 2d Battalion, 7th Air Defense Artillery.

Marquat, William F. "Automatic Artillery in Korea." *Antiaircraft Artillery Journal* 93 (November–December 1950):2–9; 94 (January–February 1951):2–12; (March–April 1951):2–5; (May–June 1951):2–6; (July–August 1951):2–9; (September–October 1951):2–5; (November–December 1951):2–6; 95 (January–February 1952):2–5; (March–April 1952):8–10; (May–June 1952):12–15. Contains information about the 26th Antiaircraft Artillery Battalion.

Ott, David Ewing. *Field Artillery, 1954–1973.* Vietnam Studies. Washington: Government Printing Office, 1975. Contains information about the 1st Battalion, 7th Air Defense Artillery.

7th Antiaircraft Artillery Automatic Weapons Battalion (Mbl), Camp Stewart, 1952. Baton Rouge: Army and Navy Publishing Company, 1952.

Swindell, Archie C. *24th Infantry Division: Follow Me. Special Taro Leaf Historical Edition. Re–Activation Day, 1960.* Germany, 1960. Contains information about the 2d Battalion, 7th Air Defense Artillery.

24th Infantry Division, A Brief History: The Story of the 24th Infantry Division's Actions in the Korean Conflict. Tokyo: Japan News, 1954. Contains information about the 26th Antiaircraft Artillery Battalion.

Weise, Carl, ed. *9th Infantry Division, Fort Carson, Colorado.* Dallas: Miller Publishing Company, 1956. Contains information about the 42d Anti-aircraft Artillery Battalion.

43d AIR DEFENSE ARTILLERY

COAT OF ARMS

Shield: Gules, on a bend or three oozlefinches vert.

Crest: On a wreath of the colors, or and gules, an épi or around and behind a French locomotive affronté gules.

Motto: *Sustinemus* (We Support).

Symbolism: The shield is red for artillery. The bend is taken from the arms of Lorraine, which is gold with three golden alerions on a red bend, with the colors reversed; the three oozlefinches are used instead of the alerions. The green oozlefinch was the device on the shoulder patch worn by the railway artillery reserve in France of which this regiment was a unit.

The locomotive and épi show the character of the regiment.

The motto "Sustinemus" alludes to the mission of the railway artillery.

DISTINCTIVE INSIGNIA

The distinctive insignia is the shield, crest, and motto of the coat of arms.

LINEAGE AND HONORS

LINEAGE

Constituted 29 June 1918 in the Regular Army as the 43d Artillery (Coast Artillery Corps). Organized 7 August 1918 at Haussimont, France, from existing Regular Army units and one New York National Guard company. (National Guard company demobilized in February 1919; regiment continued on active status.) Inactivated 17 August 1921 at Camp Eustis, Virginia. Redesignated 20 February 1924 as the 43d Coast Artillery. Disbanded 14 June 1944.

Headquarters and Headquarters Battery, 43d Coast Artillery, reconstituted 28 June 1950 in the Regular Army and redesignated as Headquarters and Headquarters Battery, 43d Field Artillery Group.

1st Battalion, 43d Coast Artillery, reconstituted 28 June 1950 in the Regular Army; concurrently consolidated with the 43d Field Artillery Battalion (*see* ANNEX 1), and consolidated unit designated as the 43d Field Artillery Battalion, an element of the 8th Infantry Division. Activated 17 August 1950 at Fort Jackson, South Carolina. Inactivated 1 August 1957 in Germany and relieved from assignment to the 8th Infantry Division.

2d Battalion, 43d Coast Artillery, reconstituted 28 June 1950 in the Regular Army; concurrently consolidated with the 61st Field Artillery Battalion (active) (*see* ANNEX 2), and consolidated unit designated as the 61st Field Artillery Battalion, an element of the 1st Cavalry Division. Inactivated 15 October 1957 in Japan and relieved from assignment to the 1st Cavalry Division.

3d Battalion, 43d Coast Artillery, reconstituted 28 June 1950 in the Regular Army; concurrently consolidated with the 64th Field Artillery Battalion (active) (*see* ANNEX 3), and consolidated unit designated as the 64th Field Artillery Battalion, an element of the 25th Infantry Division. Inactivated 1 February 1957 in Hawaii and relieved from assignment to the 25th Infantry Division.

Headquarters and Headquarters Battery, 43d Field Artillery Group, and 43d, 61st, and 64th Field Artillery Battalions consolidated, reorganized, and redesignated August 1958–July 1959 as the 43d Artillery, a parent regiment under the Combat Arms Regimental System. Redesignated 1 September 1971 as the 43d Air Defense Artillery.

ANNEX 1

Constituted 1 October 1933 in the Regular Army as the 43d Field Artillery. Redesignated 13 January 1941 as the 43d Field Artillery Battalion. Assigned 1 June 1941 to the 8th Division (later redesignated as the 8th Infantry Division) and activated at Fort Jackson, South Carolina. Inactivated 20 October 1945 at Fort Leonard Wood, Missouri.

ANNEX 2

Constituted 16 December 1940 in the Regular Army as the 61st Field Artillery Battalion. Assigned 3 January 1941 to the 1st Cavalry Division and activated at Fort Bliss, Texas.

ANNEX 3

Constituted 26 August 1941 in the Regular Army as the 64th Field Artillery Battalion and assigned to the 25th Infantry Division. Activated 1 October 1941 in Hawaii.

CAMPAIGN PARTICIPATION CREDIT

World War I
  St. Mihiel
  Meuse-Argonne
  Lorraine 1918

World War II
  Normandy
  Northern France
  Rhineland
  Central Europe
  Central Pacific
  Guadalcanal
  Northern Solomons
  New Guinea
  Bismarck Archipelago

  Leyte (with arrowhead)
  Luzon

Korean War
  UN defensive
  UN offensive
  CCF intervention
  First UN counteroffensive
  CCF spring offensive
  UN summer–fall offensive
  Second Korean winter
  Korea, summer–fall 1952
  Third Korean winter
  Korea, summer 1953

DECORATIONS

Presidential Unit Citation (Army), Streamer embroidered GUADALCANAL (64th Field Artillery Battalion cited; DA GO 36, 1951)

Presidential Unit Citation (Army), Streamer embroidered NAM RIVER (64th Field Artillery Battalion cited; DA GO 49, 1951)

Presidential Unit Citation (Army), Streamer embroidered PAKCHON, KOREA (61st Field Artillery Battalion cited; DA GO 33, 1952)

Presidential Unit Citation (Navy), Streamer embroidered WONJU-HWACHON (64th Field Artillery Battalion cited; DA GO 38, 1957)

Navy Unit Commendation, Streamer embroidered PANMUNJOM (64th Field Artillery Battalion cited; DA GO 38, 1957)

Air Force Outstanding Unit Award, Streamer embroidered ALASKA (1st Battalion, 43d Air Defense Artillery, cited; DA GO 23, 1979)

1st BATTALION, 43d AIR DEFENSE ARTILLERY

RA
(nondivisional)

LINEAGE

Constituted 14 August 1901 in the Regular Army as the 107th Company, Coast Artillery, Artillery Corps. Organized 19 August 1901 at Fort Preble, Maine. Redesignated 2 February 1907 as the 107th Company, Coast Artillery Corps. Redesignated in July 1916 as the 1st Company, Fort Preble [Maine].

Reorganized and redesignated 21 July 1917 as Battery E, 6th Provisional Regiment, Coast Artillery Corps. Redesignated 5 February 1918 as Battery E, 51st Artillery (Coast Artillery Corps).

Redesignated 7 August 1918 as Battery E, 43d Artillery (Coast Artillery Corps). Inactivated 17 August 1921 at Camp Eustis, Virginia. (Additionally designated 1 June 1922 as the 107th Company, Coast Artillery Corps; additional designation abolished 20 February 1924.) Redesignated 20 February 1924 as Battery E, 43d Coast Artillery. Disbanded 14 June 1944.

Reconstituted 28 June 1950 in the Regular Army; concurrently consolidated with Battery A, 64th Field Artillery Battalion (active) (*see* ANNEX), and consolidated unit designated as Battery A, 64th Field Artillery Battalion, an element of the 25th Infantry Division. Inactivated 1 February 1957 in Hawaii and relieved from assignment to the 25th Infantry Division.

Redesignated 12 August 1958 as Headquarters and Headquarters Battery, 1st Missile Battalion, 43d Artillery (organic elements concurrently constituted). Battalion activated 1 September 1958 at Fairchild Air Force Base, Washington. Inactivated 25 March 1966 at Fairchild Air Force Base, Washington. Redesignated 1 September 1971 as the 1st Missile Battalion, 43d Air Defense Artillery. Redesignated 13 September 1972 as the 1st Battalion, 43d Air Defense Artillery, and activated at Fort Richardson, Alaska. Inactivated 31 July 1979 at Fort Richardson, Alaska. Activated 1 May 1982 at Fort Bliss, Texas.

ANNEX

Constituted 26 August 1941 in the Regular Army as Battery A, 64th Field Artillery Battalion, an element of the 25th Infantry Division. Activated 1 October 1941 in Hawaii.

CAMPAIGN PARTICIPATION CREDIT

World War I
  *St. Mihiel
  *Meuse-Argonne
  Lorraine 1918

World War II
  Normandy
  Northern France
  Rhineland
  Central Europe
  *Central Pacific
  *Guadalcanal
  *Northern Solomons
  New Guinea
  Bismarck Archipelago
  Leyte (with arrowhead)
  *Luzon

Korean War
  *UN defensive
  *UN offensive
  *CCF intervention
  *First UN counteroffensive
  *CCF spring offensive
  *UN summer-fall offensive
  *Second Korean winter
  *Korea, summer-fall 1952
  *Third Korean winter
  *Korea, summer 1953

DECORATIONS

*Presidential Unit Citation (Army), Streamer embroidered GUADAL-CANAL (64th Field Artillery Battalion cited; DA GO 36, 1951)

*Presidential Unit Citation (Army), Streamer embroidered NAM RIVER (64th Field Artillery Battalion cited; DA GO 49, 1951)

Presidential Unit Citation (Army), Streamer embroidered PAKCHON, KOREA

*Presidential Unit Citation (Navy), Streamer embroidered WONJU-HWACHON (64th Field Artillery Battalion cited; DA GO 38, 1957)

*Navy Unit Commendation, Streamer embroidered PANMUNJOM (64th Field Artillery Battalion cited; DA GO 38, 1957)

*Air Force Outstanding Unit Award, Streamer embroidered ALASKA (1st Battalion, 43d Air Defense Artillery, cited; DA GO 23, 1979)

*Philippine Presidential Unit Citation, Streamer embroidered 17 OCTOBER 1944 TO 4 JULY 1945 (64th Field Artillery Battalion cited; DA GO 47, 1950)

*Republic of Korea Presidential Unit Citation, Streamer embroidered MASAN-CHINJU (64th Field Artillery Battalion cited; DA GO 35, 1951)

*Republic of Korea Presidential Unit Citation, Streamer embroidered MUNSAN-NI (64th Field Artillery Battalion cited; DA GO 19, 1955)

2d MISSILE BATTALION, 43d AIR DEFENSE ARTILLERY

RA
(inactive)

LINEAGE

Constituted 10 July 1907 in the Regular Army as the 138th Company, Coast Artillery Corps. Organized in August 1907 at Fort Mott, New Jersey. Redesignated in August 1916 as the 1st Company, Fort Mills [Philippine Islands]. Redesignated 31 August 1917 as the 1st Company, Coast Defenses of Manila and Subic Bays. Redesignated 30 June 1922 as the 138th Company, Coast Artillery Corps. Inactivated 18 December 1922 at Fort Mills, Philippine Islands.

Redesignated 20 February 1924 as Battery C, 43d Coast Artillery. Disbanded 14 June 1944.

Reconstituted 28 June 1950 in the Regular Army; concurrently consolidated with Battery A, 61st Field Artillery Battalion (active) (*see* ANNEX), and consolidated unit designated as Battery A, 61st Field Artillery Battalion, an element of the 1st Cavalry Division. Inactivated 15 October 1957 in Japan and relieved from assignment to the 1st Cavalry Division.

Redesignated 12 August 1958 as Headquarters and Headquarters Battery, 2d Missile Battalion, 43d Artillery (organic elements concurrently constituted). Battalion activated 1 September 1958 at Redmond, Washington. Inactivated 25 March 1966 at Turner Air Force Base, Georgia. Redesignated 1 September 1971 as the 2d Missile Battalion, 43d Air Defense Artillery.

ANNEX

Constituted 16 December 1940 in the Regular Army as Battery A, 61st Field Artillery Battalion, an element of the 1st Cavalry Division. Activated 3 January 1941 at Fort Bliss, Texas.

CAMPAIGN PARTICIPATION CREDIT

World War I
  St. Mihiel
  Meuse-Argonne
  Lorraine 1918

World War II
  Normandy
  Northern France
  Rhineland
  Central Europe
  Central Pacific
  Guadalcanal
  Northern Solomons
  *New Guinea
  *Bismarck Archipelago
  *Leyte (with arrowhead)
  *Luzon

Korean War
  *UN defensive
  *UN offensive
  *CCF intervention
  *First UN counteroffensive
  *CCF spring offensive
  *UN summer-fall offensive
  *Second Korean winter
   Korea, summer-fall 1952
  *Third Korean winter
   Korea, summer 1953

DECORATIONS

Presidential Unit Citation (Army), Streamer embroidered GUADALCANAL

Presidential Unit Citation (Army), Streamer embroidered NAM RIVER

*Presidential Unit Citation (Army), Streamer embroidered PAKCHON, KOREA (61st Field Artillery Battalion cited; DA GO 33, 1952)

Presidential Unit Citation (Navy), Streamer embroidered WONJU-HWACHON

Navy Unit Commendation, Streamer embroidered PANMUNJOM

*Philippine Presidential Unit Citation, Streamer embroidered 17 OCTOBER 1944 TO 4 JULY 1945 (61st Field Artillery Battalion cited; DA GO 47, 1950)

*Republic of Korea Presidential Unit Citation, Streamer embroidered WAEGWAN-TAEGU (61st Field Artillery Battalion cited; DA GO 35, 1951)

*Chryssoun Aristion Andrias (Bravery Gold Medal of Greece), Streamer embroidered KOREA (61st Field Artillery Battalion cited; DA GO 2, 1956)

3d BATTALION, 43d AIR DEFENSE ARTILLERY

RA
(inactive)

LINEAGE

Organized 5 August 1916 in the Regular Army at Fort Mills, Philippine Islands, as the Fort Command Company, Fort Mills. Redesignated in December 1916 as the 17th Company, Fort Mills [Philippine Islands]. Redesignated 31 August 1917 as the 17th Company, Coast Defenses of Manila and Subic Bays. Redesignated 30 June 1922 as the 187th Company, Coast Artillery Corps. Inactivated 18 December 1922 at Fort Mills, Philippine Islands.

Redesignated 20 February 1924 as Battery F, 43d Coast Artillery. Disbanded 14 June 1944.

Reconstituted 28 June 1950 in the Regular Army; concurrently consolidated with Battery B, 64th Field Artillery Battalion (active) (*see* ANNEX), and consolidated unit designated as Battery B, 64th Field Artillery Battalion, an element of the 25th Infantry Division. Inactivated 1 February 1957 in Hawaii and relieved from assignment to the 25th Infantry Division.

Redesignated 12 August 1958 as Headquarters and Headquarters Battery, 3d Missile Battalion, 43d Artillery (organic elements concurrently constituted). Battalion activated 1 September 1958 at Lumberton, New Jersey. Redesignated 20 December 1965 as the 3d Battalion, 43d Artillery. Redesignated 1 September 1971 as the 3d Battalion, 43d Air Defense Artillery. Inactivated 30 October 1974 at Pedricktown, New Jersey.

ANNEX

Constituted 26 August 1941 in the Regular Army as Battery B, 64th Field Artillery Battalion, an element of the 25th Infantry Division. Activated 1 October 1941 in Hawaii.

CAMPAIGN PARTICIPATION CREDIT

World War I
  St. Mihiel
  Meuse-Argonne
  Lorraine 1918

World War II
  Normandy
  Northern France
  Rhineland
  Central Europe
  *Central Pacific
  *Guadalcanal
  *Northern Solomons
  New Guinea
  Bismarck Archipelago

  Leyte (with arrowhead)
  *Luzon

Korean War
  *UN defensive
  *UN offensive
  *CCF intervention
  *First UN counteroffensive
  *CCF spring offensive
  *UN summer-fall offensive
  *Second Korean winter
  *Korea, summer–fall 1952
  *Third Korean winter
  *Korea, summer 1953

Decorations

*Presidential Unit Citation (Army), Streamer embroidered GUA-DALCANAL (64th Field Artillery Battalion cited; DA GO 36, 1951)

*Presidential Unit Citation (Army), Streamer embroidered NAM RIVER (64th Field Artillery Battalion cited; DA GO 49, 1951)

Presidential Unit Citation (Army), Streamer embroidered PAKCHON, KOREA

*Presidential Unit Citation (Navy), Streamer embroidered WONJU-HWACHON (64th Field Artillery Battalion cited; DA GO 38, 1957)

*Navy Unit Commendation, Streamer embroidered PANMUNJOM (64th Field Artillery Battalion cited; DA GO 38, 1957)

*Philippine Presidential Unit Citation, Streamer embroidered 17 OCTOBER 1944 TO 4 JULY 1945 (64th Field Artillery Battalion cited; DA GO 47, 1950)

*Republic of Korea Presidential Unit Citation, Streamer embroidered MASAN-CHINJU (64th Field Artillery Battalion cited; DA GO 35, 1951)

*Republic of Korea Presidential Unit Citation, Streamer embroidered MUNSAN-NI (64th Field Artillery Battalion cited; DA GO 19, 1955)

4th BATTALION, 43d AIR DEFENSE ARTILLERY

RA
(inactive)

LINEAGE

Constituted 1 November 1917 in the Regular Army as Battery C, 57th Artillery (Coast Artillery Corps). Organized 11 January 1918 at Fort Hancock, New Jersey.

Redesignated 7 August 1918 as Battery A, 43d Artillery (Coast Artillery Corps). Inactivated 17 August 1921 at Camp Eustis, Virginia. (Additionally designated 1 June 1922 as the 206th Company, Coast Artillery Corps; additional designation abolished 20 February 1924.) Redesignated 20 February 1924 as Battery A, 43d Coast Artillery. Disbanded 14 June 1944.

Reconstituted 28 June 1950 in the Regular Army; concurrently consolidated with Battery A, 43d Field Artillery Battalion (*see* ANNEX), and consolidated unit designated as Battery A, 43d Field Artillery Battalion, an element of the 8th Infantry Division. Activated 17 August 1950 at Fort Jackson, South Carolina. Inactivated 1 August 1957 in Germany and relieved from assignment to the 8th Infantry Division.

Redesignated 5 August 1958 as Headquarters and Headquarters Battery, 4th Gun Battalion, 43d Artillery (organic elements concurrently constituted). Battalion activated 15 September 1958 at Fort Richardson, Alaska. Reorganized and redesignated 1 March 1959 as the 4th Missile Battalion, 43d Artillery. Redesignated 15 February 1969 as the 4th Battalion, 43d Artillery. Redesignated 1 September 1971 as the 4th Battalion, 43d Air Defense Artillery. Inactivated 13 September 1972 at Fort Richardson, Alaska.

ANNEX

Constituted 1 October 1933 in the Regular Army as Battery A, 43d Field Artillery. Redesignated 13 January 1941 as Battery A, 43d Field Artillery Battalion. Activated 1 June 1941 at Fort Jackson, South Carolina, as an element of the 8th Division (later redesignated as the 8th Infantry Division). Inactivated 20 October 1945 at Fort Leonard Wood, Missouri.

Campaign Participation Credit

World War I
  *St. Mihiel
  *Meuse-Argonne
  *Lorraine 1918

World War II
  *Normandy
  *Northern France
  *Rhineland
  *Central Europe
  Central Pacific
  Guadalcanal
  Northern Solomons
  New Guinea

Bismarck Archipelago
Leyte (with arrowhead)
Luzon

Korean War
  UN defensive
  UN offensive
  CCF intervention
  First UN counteroffensive
  CCF spring offensive
  UN summer-fall offensive
  Second Korean winter
  Korea, summer–fall 1952
  Third Korean winter
  Korea, summer 1953

Decorations

Presidential Unit Citation (Army), Streamer embroidered GUA-DALCANAL

Presidential Unit Citation (Army), Streamer embroidered NAM RIVER

Presidential Unit Citation (Army), Streamer embroidered PAKCHON, KOREA

Presidential Unit Citation (Navy), Streamer embroidered WONJU-HWACHON

Navy Unit Commendation, Streamer embroidered PANMUNJOM

*Luxembourg Croix de Guerre, Streamer embroidered LUXEMBOURG (8th Infantry Division cited; DA GO 59, 1969)

Battery A additionally entitled to Meritorious Unit Commendation, Streamer embroidered ALASKA (Battery A, 4th Missile Battalion, 43d Artillery, cited; DA GO 27, 1964)

5th BATTALION, 43d AIR DEFENSE ARTILLERY

AR
(inactive)

LINEAGE

Organized in February 1919 in the Regular Army at Fort Winfield Scott, California, as Battery B, 43d Artillery (Coast Artillery Corps). Inactivated 17 August 1921 at Camp Eustis, Virginia. (Additionally designated 1 June 1922 as the 207th Company, Coast Artillery Corps; additional designation abolished 20 February 1924.) Redesignated 20 February 1924 as Battery B, 43d Coast Artillery. Disbanded 14 June 1944.

Reconstituted 28 June 1950 in the Regular Army; concurrently consolidated with Battery B, 43d Field Artillery Battalion (*see* ANNEX), and consolidated unit designated as Battery B, 43d Field Artillery Battalion, an element of the 8th Infantry Division. Activated 17 August 1950 at Fort Jackson, South Carolina. Inactivated 1 August 1957 in Germany and relieved from assignment to the 8th Infantry Division.

Redesignated 30 April 1959 as Headquarters and Headquarters Battery, 5th Automatic Weapons Battalion, 43d Artillery; concurrently withdrawn from the Regular Army, allotted to the Army Reserve, and assigned to the Second United States Army (organic elements concurrently constituted). Battalion activated 1 June 1959 with Headquarters at Glassmere, Pennsylvania. Reorganized and redesignated 1 April 1960 as the 5th Howitzer Battalion, 43d Artillery; location of Headquarters concurrently changed to New Kensington, Pennsylvania. Ordered into active military service 6 October 1961 at New Kensington, Pennsylvania; released 15 August 1962 from active military service and reverted to reserve status. Relieved 1 January 1966 from assignment to the Second United States Army and assigned to the First United States Army. Redesignated 15 July 1966 as the 5th Battalion, 43d Artillery. Inactivated 31 January 1968 at New Kensington, Pennsylvania. Redesignated 1 September 1971 as the 5th Battalion, 43d Air Defense Artillery.

ANNEX

Constituted 1 October 1933 in the Regular Army as Battery B, 43d Field Artillery. Redesignated 13 January 1941 as Battery B, 43d Field Artillery Battalion. Activated 1 June 1941 at Fort Jackson, South Carolina, as an element of the 8th Division (later redesignated as the 8th Infantry Division). Inactivated 20 October 1945 at Fort Leonard Wood, Missouri.

CAMPAIGN PARTICIPATION CREDIT

World War I
St. Mihiel
Meuse-Argonne
Lorraine 1918

World War II
*Normandy
*Northern France
*Rhineland
*Central Europe
Central Pacific
Guadalcanal
Northern Solomons
New Guinea
Bismarck Archipelago

Leyte (with arrowhead)
Luzon

Korean War
UN defensive
UN offensive
CCF intervention
First UN counteroffensive
CCF spring offensive
UN summer-fall offensive
Second Korean winter
Korea, summer–fall 1952
Third Korean winter
Korea, summer 1953

DECORATIONS

Presidential Unit Citation (Army), Streamer embroidered GUA-DALCANAL

Presidential Unit Citation (Army), Streamer embroidered NAM RIVER

Presidential Unit Citation (Army), Streamer embroidered PAKCHON, KOREA

Presidential Unit Citation (Navy), Streamer embroidered WONJU-HWACHON

Navy Unit Commendation, Streamer embroidered PANMUNJOM

*Luxembourg Croix de Guerre, Streamer embroidered LUXEMBOURG (8th Infantry Division cited; DA GO 59, 1969)

6th MISSILE BATTALION, 43d AIR DEFENSE ARTILLERY

RA
(inactive)

LINEAGE

Organized 14 April 1917 in the Regular Army at Fort McKinley, Maine, as the 5th Company, Fort McKinley [Maine].

Reorganized and redesignated 21 July 1917 as Battery D, 6th Provisional Regiment, Coast Artillery Corps. Redesignated 5 February 1918 as Battery D, 51st Artillery (Coast Artillery Corps).

Redesignated 7 August 1918 as Battery D, 43d Artillery (Coast Artillery Corps). Inactivated 17 August 1921 at Camp Eustis, Virginia. (Additionally designated 1 June 1922 as the 208th Company, Coast Artillery Corps; additional designation abolished 20 February 1924.) Redesignated 20 February 1924 as Battery D, 43d Coast Artillery. Disbanded 14 June 1944.

Reconstituted 28 June 1950 in the Regular Army; concurrently consolidated with Battery B, 61st Field Artillery Battalion (active) (*see* ANNEX), and consolidated unit designated as Battery B, 61st Field Artillery Battalion, an element of the 1st Cavalry Division. Inactivated 15 October 1957 in Japan and relieved from assignment to the 1st Cavalry Division.

Redesignated 31 July 1959 as Headquarters and Headquarters Battery, 6th Battalion, 43d Artillery. Redesignated 26 April 1960 as Headquarters and Headquarters Battery, 6th Missile Battalion, 43d Artillery (organic elements concurrently constituted). Battalion activated 24 June 1960 at Omaha Air Force Base, Nebraska. Inactivated 25 June 1966 at Omaha Air Force Base, Nebraska. Redesignated 1 September 1971 as the 6th Missile Battalion, 43d Air Defense Artillery.

ANNEX

Constituted 16 December 1940 in the Regular Army as Battery B, 61st Field Artillery Battalion, an element of the 1st Cavalry Division. Activated 3 January 1941 at Fort Bliss, Texas.

Campaign Participation Credit

World War I
St. Mihiel
Meuse-Argonne
*Lorraine 1918

World War II
Normandy
Northern France
Rhineland
Central Europe
Central Pacific
Guadalcanal
Northern Solomons
*New Guinea
*Bismarck Archipelago

*Leyte (with arrowhead)
*Luzon

Korean War
*UN defensive
*UN offensive
*CCF intervention
*First UN counteroffensive
*CCF spring offensive
*UN summer-fall offensive
*Second Korean winter
Korea, summer–fall 1952
*Third Korean winter
Korea, summer 1953

Decorations

*Presidential Unit Citation (Army), Streamer embroidered LUZON (Battery B, 61st Field Artillery Battalion, cited; WD GO 38, 1946)

Presidential Unit Citation (Army), Streamer embroidered GUADALCANAL

Presidential Unit Citation (Army), Streamer embroidered NAM RIVER

*Presidential Unit Citation (Army), Streamer embroidered PAKCHON, KOREA (61st Field Artillery Battalion cited; DA GO 33, 1952)

Presidential Unit Citation (Navy), Streamer embroidered WONJU-HWACHON

Navy Unit Commendation, Streamer embroidered PANMUNJOM

*Philippine Presidential Unit Citation, Streamer embroidered 17 OCTOBER 1944 TO 4 JULY 1945 (61st Field Artillery Battalion cited; DA GO 47, 1950)

*Republic of Korea Presidential Unit Citation, Streamer embroidered WAEGWAN-TAEGU (61st Field Artillery Battalion cited; DA GO 35, 1951)

*Chryssoun Aristion Andrias (Bravery Gold Medal of Greece), Streamer embroidered KOREA (61st Field Artillery Battalion cited; DA GO 2, 1956)

16th DETACHMENT, 43d AIR DEFENSE ARTILLERY

RA
(inactive)

LINEAGE

Constituted 5 August 1958 in the Regular Army as the 16th Detachment, 43d Artillery. Activated 1 September 1958 at Fort Lewis, Washington. Inactivated 2 July 1962 at Fort Lewis, Washington. Redesignated 1 September 1971 as the 16th Detachment, 43d Air Defense Artillery.

CAMPAIGN PARTICIPATION CREDIT

None.

DECORATIONS

None.

43D AIR DEFENSE ARTILLERY BIBLIOGRAPHY

Appleman, Roy E. *South to the Naktong, North to the Yalu.* United States Army in the Korean War. Washington: Government Printing Office, 1961. Contains information about the 61st and 64th Field Artillery Battalions.

Brigham, Eugene V. "The Artilleryman is the Thing!" *Armor* 51 (November 1952): 39. Pertains to the 61st Field Artillery Battalion.

Cannon, M. Hamlin. *Leyte: The Return to the Philippines.* United States Army in World War II. Washington: Government Printing Office, 1954. Contains information about the 61st Field Artillery Battalion.

Chandler, Rex E. "First Cavalry Division Combat Operations." *Armored Cavalry Journal* 56 (May 1947): 20–23. Contains information about the 61st Field Artillery Battalion.

Dall'Acqua, Robert. "Artillery Repulses Chinese Attack." *Antiaircraft Artillery Journal* 94 (March 1951): 12. Pertains to the 61st Field Artillery Battalion.

The Dixie-Golden Arrow Yearbook, Fort Carson, Colorado, 1954. Marceline: Walsworth Brothers, 1954. Contains information about the 43d Field Artillery Battalion.

Dupuy, Richard Ernest. *With the 57th in France.* Brooklyn: Our Army, 1930. Contains information about the current 4th Battalion, 43d Air Defense Artillery.

Eighth Infantry Division, A Combat History by Regiments and Special Units. Baton Rouge: Army and Navy Publishing Company, 1946. Contains information about the 43d Field Artillery Battalion.

Eighth Infantry Division, Fort Jackson, South Carolina. Baton Rouge: Army and Navy Publishing Company, 1953. Contains information about the 43d Field Artillery Battalion.

Grace, James L. *A Brief History of the 2nd Battalion, 57th Artillery, C.A.C., 31st Brigade, Army Artillery, First Army, From July 20th, 1917, to January 15th,*

1919. N.p., 1919. Contains information about the current 4th Battalion, 43d Air Defense Artillery.

Gugeler, Russell A. *Combat Actions in Korea.* Washington: Combat Forces Press, 1954. Rev. ed. Washington: Government Printing Office, 1970. Contains information about the 64th Field Artillery Battalion.

————. "The Defense of a Battery Position." *Combat Forces Journal,* 4 (June 1954): 34–37. Pertains to the 64th Field Artillery Battalion.

Headquarters Battery, 8th Motorized Division Artillery, Fort Jackson, South Carolina, 1942. Baton Rouge: Army and Navy Publishing Company, 1942. Contains information about the 43d Field Artillery Battalion.

Hermes, Walter G. *Truce Tent and Fighting Front.* United States Army in the Korean War. Washington: Government Printing Office, 1966. Contains information about the 61st and 64th Field Artillery Battalions.

Historical Division, War Department. *The Admiralties: Operations of the 1st Cavalry Division (29 February–18 May 1944).* American Forces in Action. Washington: Government Printing Office, 1945. Contains information about the 61st Field Artillery Battalion.

Jackson, Miles H., ed. *8th Infantry Golden Arrow Division, Fort Carson, Colorado, October 1955.* Dallas: Miller Publishing Company, 1955. Contains information about the 43d Field Artillery Battalion.

Marshall, S.L.A. *The River and the Gauntlet.* New York: William Morrow and Company, 1953. Contains information about the 61st and 64th Field Artillery Battalions.

Miller, John, jr. *Guadalcanal: The First Offensive.* United States Army in World War II. Washington: Government Printing Office, 1949. Contains information about the 64th Field Artillery Battalion.

————. *CARTWHEEL: The Reduction of Rabaul.* United States Army in World War II. Washington: Government Printing Office, 1959. Contains information about the 61st and 64th Field Artillery Battalions.

Pullen, Richard T., ed. *25th Infantry Division, Tropic Lightning in Korea.* Atlanta: Albert Love Enterprises, 1954. Contains information about the 64th Field Artillery Battalion.

Wiese, Carl, ed. *8th Infantry Division, Gyroscope 1956.* Dallas: Miller Publishing Company, 1956. Contains information about the 43d Field Artillery Battalion.

44th AIR DEFENSE ARTILLERY

HERALDIC ITEMS

COAT OF ARMS

Shield: Gules, a bend double cottised potenté counterpotenté or.

Crest: On a wreath of the colors, or and gules, a double quatrefoil or charged with a chameleon displayed paleways barry of four gules and vert.

Motto: *Per Ardua* (Through Difficulties).

Symbolism: The shield is red for artillery with a gold bend cottised potenté counterpotenté alluding to the arms of Lorraine and Champagne.

The elements of this regiment changed several times between 1917 and 1918, and the variegated chameleon alludes to this fact. The double quatrefoil with the chameleon is an anagram of the figure "44".

DISTINCTIVE INSIGNIA

The distinctive insignia is the shield, crest, and motto of the coat of arms.

LINEAGE AND HONORS

LINEAGE

Organized 26 March 1918 in the Regular Army in France from existing units as the Howitzer Regiment, 30th Brigade, Coast Artillery Corps. Redesignated 7 August 1918 as the 44th Artillery (Coast Artillery Corps). Inactivated 31 August 1921 at Camp Jackson, South Carolina. Redesignated 20 February 1924 as the 44th Coast Artillery. Redesignated 13 January 1941 as the 54th Coast Artillery. Activated 10 February 1941 at Camp Wallace, Texas. Regiment broken up 28 February–5 June 1944 and its elements reorganized and redesignated as follows: Headquarters and Headquarters Battery on 5 June 1944 as Headquarters and Headquarters Battery, 152d Coast Artillery Group; 1st Battalion on 5 June 1944 as the 606th Coast Artillery Battalion; 2d Battalion on 28 February 1944 as the 49th Coast Artillery Battalion; 3d Battalion on 5 June 1944 as the 607th Coast Artillery Battalion.

Headquarters and Headquarters Battery, 152d Coast Artillery Group, disbanded 3 August 1944 at Camp Livingston, Louisiana. Reconstituted 28 June 1950 in the Regular Army and redesignated as Headquarters and Headquarters Battery, 54th Field Artillery Group. Activated 17 January 1955 at Fort Bragg, North Carolina. Redesignated 21 June 1958 as Headquarters and Headquarters Battery, 54th Artillery Group. Inactivated

7 November 1969 in Vietnam.

606th Coast Artillery Battalion disbanded 3 August 1944 at Camp Livingston, Louisiana. Reconstituted 28 June 1950 in the Regular Army; concurrently consolidated with the 54th Armored Field Artillery Battalion (active) (*see* ANNEX 1), and consolidated unit designated as the 54th Armored Field Artillery Battalion, an element of the 3d Armored Division. Inactivated 1 October 1957 in Germany and relieved from assignment to the 3d Armored Division.

49th Coast Artillery Battalion inactivated 20 January 1946 in Zambales, Philippine Islands. Consolidated 28 June 1950 with the 49th Field Artillery Battalion (active) (*see* ANNEX 2), and consolidated unit designated as the 49th Field Artillery Battalion, an element of the 7th Infantry Division. Inactivated 1 July 1957 in Korea and relieved from assignment to the 7th Infantry Division.

607th Coast Artillery Battalion disbanded 31 July 1944 at Camp Rucker, Alabama. Reconstituted 28 June 1950 in the Regular Army; concurrently consolidated with the 44th Field Artillery Battalion (active) (*see* ANNEX 3), and consolidated unit designated as the 44th Field Artillery Battalion, an element of the 4th Infantry Division. Inactivated 1 April 1957 at Fort Lewis, Washington, and relieved from assignment to the 4th Infantry Division.

Headquarters and Headquarters Battery, 54th Artillery Group; 54th Armored Field Artillery Battalion; and 49th and 44th Field Artillery Battalions consolidated, reorganized, and redesignated 7 November 1969 as the 44th Artillery, a parent regiment under the Combat Arms Regimental System. Redesignated 1 September 1971 as the 44th Air Defense Artillery.

ANNEX 1

Constituted 1 October 1933 in the Regular Army as the 54th Field Artillery. Redesignated 13 January 1941 as the 54th Field Artillery Battalion and assigned to the 3d Armored Division. Activated 15 April 1941 at Camp Beauregard, Louisiana. Reorganized and redesignated 1 January 1942 as the 54th Armored Field Artillery Battalion. Inactivated 10 November 1945 in Germany. Activated 15 July 1947 at Fort Knox, Kentucky.

ANNEX 2

Constituted 1 October 1933 in the Regular Army as the 49th Field Artillery. Redesignated 1 June 1941 as the 49th Field Artillery Battalion, assigned to the 7th Division (later redesignated as the 7th Infantry Division), and activated at Fort Ord, California. Inactivated 20 July 1947 in Korea. Activated 20 March 1949 in Japan.

ANNEX 3

Constituted 1 October 1933 in the Regular Army as the 2d Battalion, 47th Field Artillery. Activated 1 June 1941 at Fort Bragg, North Carolina.

Reorganized and redesignated 17 December 1941 as the 44th Field Artillery Battalion and assigned to the 4th Motorized Division (later redesignated as the 4th Infantry Division). Inactivated 18 February 1946 at Camp Butner, North Carolina. Activated 15 July 1947 at Fort Ord, California.

CAMPAIGN PARTICIPATION CREDIT

World War I
Champagne-Marne
St. Mihiel
Lorraine 1918
Alsace 1918
Champagne 1918

World War II
Normandy (with arrowhead)
Northern France
Rhineland
Ardennes-Alsace
Central Europe
Aleutian Islands (with arrowhead)
Northern Solomons
Eastern Mandates
Leyte
Ryukyus

Korean War
UN defensive
UN offensive
CCF intervention

First UN counteroffensive
CCF spring offensive
UN summer-fall offensive
Second Korean winter
Korea, summer–fall 1952
Third Korean winter
Korea, summer 1953

Vietnam
Counteroffensive, Phase II
Counteroffensive, Phase III
Tet Counteroffensive
Counteroffensive, Phase IV
Counteroffensive, Phase V
Counteroffensive, Phase VI
Tet 69/Counteroffensive
Summer–fall 1969
Winter–spring 1970
Sanctuary Counteroffensive
Counteroffensive, Phase VII
Consolidation I
Consolidation II

DECORATIONS

Presidential Unit Citation (Army), Streamer embroidered BEACHES OF NORMANDY (44th Field Artillery Battalion cited; WD GO 86, 1946)

Presidential Unit Citation (Army), Streamer embroidered ST. LO (44th Field Artillery Battalion cited; WD GO 97, 1946)

Presidential Unit Citation (Navy), Streamer embroidered VIETNAM 1966–1967 (1st Battalion, 44th Artillery, cited; DA GO 32, 1973)

Valorous Unit Award, Streamer embroidered QUANG TRI–THUA THIEN (1st Battalion, 44th Artillery, cited; DA GO 48, 1968)

Meritorious Unit Commendation, Streamer embroidered VIETNAM 1966–1967 (Headquarters and Headquarters Battery, 54th Artillery Group, cited; DA GO 17, 1968)

Meritorious Unit Commendation, Streamer embroidered VIETNAM 1968–1969 (Headquarters and Headquarters Battery, 54th Artillery Group, cited; DA GO 39, 1970)

Air Force Outstanding Unit Award, Streamer embroidered KOREA 1978–1980 (1st Battalion, 44th Air Defense Artillery, cited; DA GO 8, 1982)

Republic of Vietnam Civil Action Honor Medal, First Class, Streamer embroidered VIETNAM 1966–1969 (Headquarters and Headquarters Battery, 54th Artillery Group, cited; DA GO 51, 1971)

1st BATTALION, 44th AIR DEFENSE ARTILLERY

RA
(inactive)

LINEAGE

Constituted 2 March 1899 in the Regular Army as Battery O, 1st Regiment of Artillery. Organized in 1899 at Jackson Barracks, New Orleans, Louisiana.

Reorganized and redesignated 13 February 1901 as the 12th Company, Coast Artillery, Artillery Corps. Redesignated 2 February 1907 as the 12th Company, Coast Artillery Corps. Redesignated 3 July 1916 as the 2d Company, Fort H.G. Wright [New York]. Redesignated 22 July 1917 as Battery E, 7th Provisional Regiment, Coast Artillery Corps. Redesignated 5 February 1918 as Battery E, 52d Artillery (Coast Artillery Corps).

Redesignated 26 March 1918 as the 1st Battery, Howitzer Regiment, 30th Brigade, Coast Artillery Corps. Redesignated 7 August 1918 as Battery E, 44th Artillery (Coast Artillery Corps). Inactivated 31 August 1921 at Camp Jackson, South Carolina. (Additionally designated 1 June 1922 as the 12th Company, Coast Artillery Corps; additional designation abolished 20 February 1924.) Redesignated 20 February 1924 as Battery E, 44th Coast Artillery. Redesignated 13 January 1941 as Battery E, 54th Coast Artillery. Activated 10 February 1941 at Camp Wallace, Texas.

Reorganized and redesignated 5 June 1944 as Battery A, 607th Coast Artillery Battalion. Disbanded 31 July 1944 at Camp Rucker, Alabama. Reconstituted 28 June 1950 in the Regular Army; concurrently consolidated with Battery A, 44th Field Artillery Battalion (active) (*see* ANNEX), and consolidated unit designated as Battery A, 44th Field Artillery Battalion, an element of the 4th Infantry Division. Inactivated 1 April 1957 at Fort Lewis, Washington, and relieved from assignment to the 4th Infantry Division.

Redesignated 12 August 1958 as Headquarters and Headquarters Battery, 1st Automatic Weapons Battalion, 44th Artillery (organic elements concurrently constituted). Battalion activated 1 September 1958 in Germany. Inactivated 10 August 1960 in Germany. Redesignated 30 December 1965 as the 1st Battalion, 44th Artillery. Activated 1 March 1966 at Fort Bliss, Texas. Redesignated 1 September 1971 as the 1st Battalion, 44th Air Defense Artillery. Inactivated 30 June 1980 in Korea.

ANNEX

Constituted 1 October 1933 in the Regular Army as Battery D, 47th Field Artillery. Activated 1 June 1941 at Fort Bragg, North Carolina.

Reorganized and redesignated 17 December 1941 as Battery A, 44th Field Artillery Battalion, an element of the 4th Motorized Division (later redesignated as the 4th Infantry Division). Inactivated 18 February 1946 at Camp Butner, North Carolina. Activated 15 July 1947 at Fort Ord, California.

CAMPAIGN PARTICIPATION CREDIT

World War I
*Champagne-Marne
*St. Mihiel
*Lorraine 1918
 Alsace 1918
*Champagne 1918

World War II
*Normandy (with arrowhead)
*Northern France
*Rhineland
*Ardennes-Alsace
*Central Europe
 Aleutian Islands (with arrowhead)
 Northern Solomons
 Eastern Mandates
 Leyte
 Ryukyus

Korean War
 UN defensive
 UN offensive
 CCF intervention

First UN counteroffensive
CCF spring offensive
UN summer-fall offensive
Second Korean winter
Korea, summer–fall 1952
Third Korean winter
Korea, summer 1953

Vietnam
*Counteroffensive, Phase II
*Counteroffensive, Phase III
*Tet Counteroffensive
*Counteroffensive, Phase IV
*Counteroffensive, Phase V
*Counteroffensive, Phase VI
*Tet 69/Counteroffensive
*Summer–fall 1969
*Winter–spring 1970
*Sanctuary Counteroffensive
*Counteroffensive, Phase VII
*Consolidation I
*Consolidation II

DECORATIONS

*Presidential Unit Citation (Army), Streamer embroidered BEACHES OF NORMANDY (44th Field Artillery Battalion cited; WD GO 86, 1946)

*Presidential Unit Citation (Army), Streamer embroidered ST. LO (44th Field Artillery Battalion cited; WD GO 97, 1946)

*Presidential Unit Citation (Navy), Streamer embroidered VIETNAM 1966–1967 (1st Battalion, 44th Artillery, cited; DA GO 32, 1973)

*Valorous Unit Award, Streamer embroidered QUANG TRI–THUA THIEN (1st Battalion, 44th Artillery, cited; DA GO 48, 1968)

*Air Force Outstanding Unit Award, Streamer embroidered KOREA 1978–1980 (1st Battalion, 44th Air Defense Artillery, cited; DA GO 8, 1982)

*Belgian Fourragere 1940 (44th Field Artillery Battalion cited; DA GO 43, 1950)

*Cited in the Order of the Day of the Belgian Army for action in BELGIUM (44th Field Artillery Battalion cited; DA GO 43, 1950)

*Cited in the Order of the Day of the Belgian Army for action in the ARDENNES (44th Field Artillery Battalion cited; DA GO 43, 1950)

*Republic of Vietnam Cross of Gallentry with Palm, Streamer embroidered VIETNAM 1971 (1st Battalion, 44th Artillery, cited; DA GO 6, 1974)

Battery A additionally entitled to Navy Unit Commendation, Streamer embroidered VIETNAM 1968 (Battery A, 1st Battalion, 44th Artillery, cited; DA GO 32, 1973)

2d BATTALION, 44th AIR DEFENSE ARTILLERY

RA
(inactive)

LINEAGE

Constituted 2 August 1901 in the Regular Army as the 101st Company, Coast Artillery, Artillery Corps. Organized in 1901 at Fort Totten, New York. Redesignated 2 February 1907 as the 101st Company, Coast Artillery Corps. Redesignated 30 June 1916 as the 2d Company, Fort Totten [New York]. Redesignated 22 July 1917 as Battery G, 7th Provisional Regiment, Coast Artillery Corps. Redesignated 5 February 1918 as Battery G, 52d Artillery (Coast Artillery Corps).

Redesignated 26 March 1918 as the 3d Battery, Howitzer Regiment, 30th Brigade, Coast Artillery Corps. Redesignated 7 August 1918 as Battery A, 44th Artillery (Coast Artillery Corps). Inactivated 31 August 1921 at Camp Jackson, South Carolina. (Additionally designated 1 June 1922 as the 101st Company, Coast Artillery Corps; additional designation abolished 20 February 1924.) Redesignated 20 February 1924 as Battery A, 44th Coast Artillery. Redesignated 13 January 1941 as Battery A, 54th Coast Artillery. Activated 10 February 1941 at Camp Wallace, Texas.

Reorganized and redesignated 5 June 1944 as Battery A, 606th Coast Artillery Battalion. Disbanded 3 August 1944 at Camp Livingston, Louisiana. Reconstituted 28 June 1950 in the Regular Army; concurrently consolidated with Battery A, 54th Armored Field Artillery Battalion (active) (*see* ANNEX), and consolidated unit designated as Battery A, 54th Armored Field Artillery Battalion, an element of the 3d Armored Division. Inactivated 1 October 1957 in Germany and relieved from assignment to the 3d Armored Division.

Redesignated 31 March 1958 as Headquarters and Headquarters Battery, 2d Automatic Weapons Battalion, 44th Artillery, and activated at Fort Lewis, Washington (organic elements concurrently constituted and activated). Battalion inactivated 26 July 1960 at Fort Lewis, Washington. Redesignated 30 March 1962 as the 2d Battalion, 44th Artillery. Activated 22 June 1962 at Fort Sill, Oklahoma. Inactivated 1 September 1971 at Fort Sill, Oklahoma; concurrently redesignated as the 2d Battalion, 44th Air Defense Artillery. Activated 13 September 1972 in Korea. Inactivated 30 September 1977 in Korea.

ANNEX

Constituted 1 October 1933 in the Regular Army as Battery A, 54th Field Artillery. Redesignated 13 January 1941 as Battery A, 54th Field Artillery Battalion, an element of the 3d Armored Division. Activated 15 April 1941 at Camp Beauregard, Louisiana. Reorganized and redesignated 1 January 1942 as Battery A, 54th Armored Field Artillery Battalion. Inactivated 10 November 1945 in Germany. Activated 15 July 1947 at Fort Knox, Kentucky.

CAMPAIGN PARTICIPATION CREDIT

World War I
  *Champagne-Marne
  *St. Mihiel
  *Lorraine 1918
   Alsace 1918
  *Champagne 1918

World War II
  *Normandy
  *Northern France
  *Rhineland
  *Ardennes-Alsace
  *Central Europe
   Aleutian Islands (with arrowhead)
   Northern Solomons

Eastern Mandates
Leyte
Ryukyus

Korean War
  UN defensive
  UN offensive
  CCF intervention
  First UN counteroffensive
  CCF spring offensive
  UN summer-fall offensive
  Second Korean winter
  Korea, summer–fall 1952
  Third Korean winter
  Korea, summer 1953

DECORATIONS

Presidential Unit Citation (Army), Streamer embroidered BEACHES OF NORMANDY

Presidential Unit Citation (Army), Streamer embroidered ST. LO

*Belgian Fourragere 1940 (54th Armored Field Artillery Battalion cited; DA GO 43, 1950)

*Cited in the Order of the Day of the Belgian Army for action in BELGIUM (54th Armored Field Artillery Battalion cited; DA GO 43, 1950)

*Cited in the Order of the Day of the Belgian Army for action in the ARDENNES (54th Armored Field Artillery Battalion cited; DA GO 43, 1950)

3d MISSILE BATTALION, 44th AIR DEFENSE ARTILLERY

RA
(inactive)

LINEAGE

Constituted 10 July 1907 in the Regular Army as the 151st Company, Coast Artillery Corps. Organized 5 August 1907 at Fort Revere, Massachusetts. Redesignated in July 1916 as the 2d Company, Fort Andrews [Massachusetts]. Redesignated 21 July 1917 as Battery I, 6th Provisional Regiment, Coast Artillery Corps. Redesignated 5 February 1918 as Battery I, 51st Artillery (Coast Artillery Corps).

Redesignated 26 March 1918 as the 5th Battery, Howitzer Regiment, 30th Brigade, Coast Artillery Corps. Redesignated 7 August 1918 as Battery C, 44th Artillery (Coast Artillery Corps). Inactivated 31 August 1921 at Camp Jackson, South Carolina. (Additionally designated 1 June 1922 as the 151st Company, Coast Artillery Corps; additional designation abolished 20 February 1924.) Redesignated 20 February 1924 as Battery C, 44th Coast Artillery. Redesignated 13 January 1941 as Battery C, 54th Coast Artillery. Activated 10 February 1941 at Camp Wallace, Texas.

Reorganized and redesignated 28 February 1944 as Battery A, 49th Coast Artillery Battalion. Inactivated 20 January 1946 in the Philippine Islands. Consolidated 28 June 1950 with Battery A, 49th Field Artillery Battalion (active) (*see* ANNEX), and consolidated unit designated as Battery A, 49th Field Artillery Battalion, an element of the 7th Infantry Division. Inactivated 1 July 1957 in Korea and relieved from assignment to the 7th Infantry Division.

Redesignated 12 August 1958 as Headquarters and Headquarters Battery, 3d Missile Battalion, 44th Artillery (organic elements concurrently constituted). Battalion activated 1 September 1958 at Fairfield, Connecticut. Inactivated 25 March 1961 at Fairfield, Connecticut. Redesignated 1 September 1971 as the 3d Missile Battalion, 44th Air Defense Artillery.

ANNEX

Constituted 1 October 1933 in the Regular Army as Battery A, 49th Field Artillery. Redesignated 1 June 1941 as Battery A, 49th Field Artillery Battalion, and activated at Fort Ord, California, as an element of the 7th Division (later redesignated as the 7th Infantry Division). Inactivated 20 July 1947 in Korea. Activated 20 March 1949 in Japan.

CAMPAIGN PARTICIPATION CREDIT

World War I
Champagne-Marne
*St. Mihiel
*Lorraine 1918
*Alsace 1918
Champagne 1918

World War II
Normandy (with arrowhead)
Northern France
Rhineland
Ardennes-Alsace
Central Europe
*Aleutian Islands (with arrowhead)
*Northern Solomons

*Eastern Mandates
*Leyte
*Ryukyus

Korean War
*UN defensive
*UN offensive
*CCF intervention
*First UN counteroffensive
*CCF spring offensive
*UN summer-fall offensive
*Second Korean winter
*Korea, summer–fall 1952
*Third Korean winter
*Korea, summer 1953

DECORATIONS

Presidential Unit Citation (Army), Streamer embroidered BEACHES OF NORMANDY

Presidential Unit Citation (Army), Streamer embroidered ST. LO

*Philippine Presidential Unit Citation, Streamer embroidered 17 OCTOBER 1944 TO 4 JULY 1945 (49th Field Artillery Battalion cited; DA GO 47, 1950)

*Republic of Korea Presidential Unit Citation, Streamer embroidered INCHON (49th Field Artillery Battalion cited; DA GO 35, 1951)

*Republic of Korea Presidential Unit Citation, Streamer embroidered KOREA 1950–1953 (49th Field Artillery Battalion cited; DA GO 22, 1956)

*Republic of Korea Presidential Unit Citation, Streamer embroidered KOREA 1945–1947, 1953–1957 (7th Infantry Division cited; DA GO 50, 1971)

4th BATTALION, 44th AIR DEFENSE ARTILLERY

RA
(inactive)

LINEAGE

Organized 12 April 1917 in the Regular Army at Fort Totten, New York, as the 6th Company, Fort Totten [New York]. Redesignated 22 July 1917 as Battery H, 7th Provisional Regiment, Coast Artillery Corps. Redesignated 5 February 1918 as Battery H, 52d Artillery (Coast Artillery Corps).

Redesignated 26 March 1918 as the 4th Battery, Howitzer Regiment, 30th Brigade, Coast Artillery Corps. Redesignated 7 August 1918 as Battery B, 44th Artillery (Coast Artillery Corps). Inactivated 31 August 1921 at Camp Jackson, South Carolina. (Additionally designated 1 June 1922 as the 214th Company, Coast Artillery Corps; additional designation abolished 20 February 1924.) Redesignated 20 February 1924 as Battery B, 44th Coast Artillery. Redesignated 13 January 1941 as Battery B, 54th Coast Artillery. Activated 10 February 1941 at Camp Wallace, Texas.

Reorganized and redesignated 5 June 1944 as Battery B, 606th Coast Artillery Battalion. Disbanded 3 August 1944 at Camp Livingston, Louisiana. Reconstituted 28 June 1950 in the Regular Army; concurrently consolidated with Battery B, 54th Armored Field Artillery Battalion (active) (*see* ANNEX), and consolidated unit designated as Battery B, 54th Armored Field Artillery Battalion, an element of the 3d Armored Division. Inactivated 1 October 1957 in Germany and relieved from assignment to the 3d Armored Division.

Redesignated 12 August 1958 as Headquarters and Headquarters Battery, 4th Missile Battalion, 44th Artillery (organic elements concurrently constituted). Battalion activated 1 September 1958 at Fort Bliss, Texas. Redesignated 10 January 1966 as the 4th Battalion, 44th Artillery. Redesignated 1 September 1971 as the 4th Battalion, 44th Air Defense Artillery. Inactivated 13 September 1972 in Korea.

ANNEX

Constituted 1 October 1933 in the Regular Army as Battery B, 54th Field Artillery. Redesignated 13 January 1941 as Battery B, 54th Field Artillery Battalion, an element of the 3d Armored Division. Activated 15 April 1941 at Camp Beauregard, Louisiana. Reorganized and redesignated 1 January 1942 as Battery B, 54th Armored Field Artillery Battalion. Inactivated 10 November 1945 in Germany. Activated 15 July 1947 at Fort Knox, Kentucky.

Campaign Participation Credit

World War I
- *Champagne-Marne
- *St. Mihiel
- *Lorraine 1918
- Alsace 1918
- *Champagne 1918

World War II
- *Normandy
- *Northern France
- *Rhineland
- *Ardennes–Alsace
- *Central Europe
- Aleutian Islands (with arrowhead)
- Northern Solomons

Eastern Mandates
Leyte
Ryukyus
Korean War
- UN defensive
- UN offensive
- CCF intervention
- First UN counteroffensive
- CCF spring offensive
- UN summer–fall offensive
- Second Korean winter
- Korea, summer–fall 1952
- Third Korean winter
- Korea, summer 1953

Decorations

Presidential Unit Citation (Army), Streamer embroidered BEACHES OF NORMANDY

Presidential Unit Citation (Army), Streamer embroidered ST. LO

*Belgian Fourragere 1940 (54th Armored Field Artillery Battalion cited; DA GO 43, 1950)

*Cited in the Order of the Day of the Belgian Army for action in BELGIUM (54th Armored Field Artillery Battalion cited; DA GO 43, 1950)

*Cited in the Order of the Day of the Belgian Army for action in the ARDENNES (54th Armored Field Artillery Battalion cited; DA GO 43, 1950)

5th MISSILE BATTALION, 44th AIR DEFENSE ARTILLERY

RA
(inactive)

LINEAGE

Organized 5 July 1917 in the Regular Army at Fort Mills, Philippine Islands, as the 21st Company, Fort Mills [Philippine Islands]. Redesignated 31 August 1917 as the 21st Company, Coast Defenses of Manila and Subic Bays. Redesignated 30 June 1922 as the 191st Company, Coast Artillery Corps.

Redesignated 20 February 1924 as Battery D, 44th Coast Artillery, and inactivated in the Philippine Islands. Redesignated 13 January 1941 as Battery D, 54th Coast Artillery. Activated 10 February 1941 at Camp Wallace, Texas.

Reorganized and redesignated 28 February 1944 as Battery B, 49th Coast Artillery Battalion. Inactivated 20 January 1946 in the Philippine Islands. Consolidated 28 June 1950 with Battery B, 49th Field Artillery Battalion (active) (*see* ANNEX), and consolidated unit designated as Battery B, 49th Field Artillery Battalion, an element of the 7th Infantry Division. Inactivated 1 July 1957 in Korea and relieved from assignment to the 7th Infantry Division.

Redesignated 4 April 1960 as Headquarters and Headquarters Battery, 5th Missile Battalion, 44th Artillery (organic elements concurrently constituted). Battalion activated 18 April 1960 at Schilling Air Force Base, Kansas. Inactivated 26 June 1960 at Schilling Air Force Base, Kansas. Redesignated 1 September 1971 as the 5th Missile Battalion, 44th Air Defense Artillery.

ANNEX

Constituted 1 October 1933 in the Regular Army as Battery B, 49th Field Artillery. Redesignated 1 June 1941 as Battery B, 49th Field Artillery Battalion, and activated at Fort Ord, California, as an element of the 7th Division (later redesignated as the 7th Infantry Division). Inactivated 20 July 1947 in Korea. Activated 20 March 1949 in Japan.

Campaign Participation Credit

World War I
Champagne-Marne
St. Mihiel
Lorraine 1918
Alsace 1918
Champagne 1918

World War II
Normandy (with arrowhead)
Northern France
Rhineland
Ardennes-Alsace
Central Europe
*Aleutian Islands (with arrowhead)
*Northern Solomons

*Eastern Mandates
*Leyte
*Ryukyus

Korean War
*UN defensive
*UN offensive
*CCF intervention
*First UN counteroffensive
*CCF spring offensive
*UN summer-fall offensive
*Second Korean winter
*Korea, summer–fall 1952
*Third Korean winter
*Korea, summer 1953

Decorations

Presidential Unit Citation (Army), Streamer embroidered BEACHES OF NORMANDY

Presidential Unit Citation (Army), Streamer embroidered ST. LO

*Philippine Presidential Unit Citation, Streamer embroidered 17 OCTOBER 1944 TO 4 JULY 1945 (49th Field Artillery Battalion cited; DA GO 47, 1950)

*Republic of Korea Presidential Unit Citation, Streamer embroidered INCHON (49th Field Artillery Battalion cited; DA GO 35, 1951)

*Republic of Korea Presidential Unit Citation, Streamer embroidered KOREA 1950–1953 (49th Field Artillery Battalion cited; DA GO 22, 1956)

*Republic of Korea Presidential Unit Citation, Streamer embroidered KOREA 1945–1947, 1953–1957 (7th Infantry Division cited; DA GO 50, 1971)

6th BATTALION, 44th AIR DEFENSE ARTILLERY

RA
(inactive)

LINEAGE

Organized 8 June 1917 in the Regular Army at Fort Schuyler, New York, as the 2d Company, Fort Schuyler [New York]. Redesignated 22 July 1917 as Battery F, 7th Provisional Regiment, Coast Artillery Corps. Redesignated 5 February 1918 as Battery F, 52d Artillery (Coast Artillery Corps).

Redesignated 26 March 1918 as the 2d Battery, Howitzer Regiment, 30th Brigade, Coast Artillery Corps. Redesignated 7 August 1918 as Battery F, 44th Artillery (Coast Artillery Corps). Inactivated 31 August 1921 at Camp Jackson, South Carolina. (Additionally designated 1 June 1922 as the 215th Company, Coast Artillery Corps; additional designation abolished 20 February 1924.) Redesignated 20 February 1924 as Battery F, 44th Coast Artillery. Redesignated 13 January 1941 as Battery F, 54th Coast Artillery. Activated 10 February 1941 at Camp Wallace, Texas.

Reorganized and redesignated 5 June 1944 as Battery B, 607th Coast Artillery Battalion. Disbanded 31 July 1944 at Camp Rucker, Alabama. Reconstituted 28 June 1950 in the Regular Army; concurrently consolidated with Battery B, 44th Field Artillery Battalion (active) (*see* ANNEX), and consolidated unit designated as Battery B, 44th Field Artillery Battalion, an element of the 4th Infantry Division. Inactivated 1 April 1957 at Fort Lewis, Washington, and relieved from assignment to the 4th Infantry Division.

Redesignated 30 March 1962 as Headquarters and Headquarters Battery, 6th Missile Battalion, 44th Artillery (organic elements concurrently constituted). Battalion activated 1 July 1962 at Fort Bliss, Texas. Redesignated 10 January 1966 as the 6th Battalion, 44th Artillery. Redesignated 1 September 1971 as the 6th Battalion, 44th Air Defense Artillery. Inactivated 13 September 1972 in Korea.

ANNEX

Constituted 1 October 1933 in the Regular Army as Battery E, 47th Field Artillery. Activated 1 June 1941 at Fort Bragg, North Carolina.

Reorganized and redesignated 17 December 1941 as Battery B, 44th Field Artillery Battalion, an element of the 4th Motorized Division (later redesignated as the 4th Infantry Division). Inactivated 18 February 1946 at Camp Butner, North Carolina. Activated 15 July 1947 at Fort Ord, California.

Campaign Participation Credit

World War I
  *Champagne-Marne
  *St. Mihiel
  *Lorraine 1918
   Alsace 1918
  *Champagne 1918

World War II
  *Normandy (with arrowhead)
  *Northern France
  *Rhineland
  *Ardennes-Alsace
  *Central Europe
   Aleutian Islands (with arrowhead)
   Northern Solomons

Eastern Mandates
Leyte
Ryukyus
Korean War
  UN defensive
  UN offensive
  CCF intervention
  First UN counteroffensive
  CCF spring offensive
  UN summer-fall offensive
  Second Korean winter
  Korea, summer–fall 1952
  Third Korean winter
  Korea, summer 1953

Decorations

*Presidential Unit Citation (Army), Streamer embroidered BEACHES OF NORMANDY (44th Field Artillery Battalion cited; WD GO 86, 1946)

*Presidential Unit Citation (Army), Streamer embroidered ST. LO (44th Field Artillery Battalion cited; WD GO 97, 1946)

*Belgian Fourragere 1940 (44th Field Artillery Battalion cited; DA GO 43, 1950)

  *Cited in the Order of the Day of the Belgian Army for action in BELGIUM (44th Field Artillery Battalion cited; DA GO 43, 1950)

  *Cited in the Order of the Day of the Belgian Army for action in the ARDENNES (44th Field Artillery Battalion cited; DA GO 43, 1950)

12th DETACHMENT, 44th AIR DEFENSE ARTILLERY

AR
(inactive)

LINEAGE

Constituted 1 October 1933 in the Regular Army as Battery C, 54th Field Artillery. Redesignated 13 January 1941 as Battery C, 54th Field Artillery Battalion, an element of the 3d Armored Division. Activated 15 April 1941 at Camp Beauregard, Louisiana. Reorganized and redesignated 1 January 1942 as Battery C, 54th Armored Field Artillery Battalion. Inactivated 10 November 1945 in Germany. Activated 15 July 1947 at Fort Knox, Kentucky. Inactivated 1 October 1957 in Germany and relieved from assignment to the 3d Armored Division.

Redesignated 13 December 1959 as the 12th Detachment, 44th Artillery; concurrently withdrawn from the Regular Army, allotted to the Army Reserve, and assigned to the First United States Army. Activated 1 February 1960 at Waterbury, Connecticut. Inactivated 1 March 1963 at Waterbury, Connecticut. Redesignated 1 September 1971 as the 12th Detachment, 44th Air Defense Artillery.

CAMPAIGN PARTICIPATION CREDIT

World War II–EAME
Normandy
Northern France
Rhineland
Ardennes-Alsace
Central Europe

DECORATIONS

Belgian Fourragere 1940 (54th Armored Field Artillery Battalion cited; DA GO 43, 1950)
Cited in the Order of the Day of the Belgian Army for action in BELGIUM (54th Armored Field Artillery Battalion cited; DA GO 43, 1950)
Cited in the Order of the Day of the Belgian Army for action in the ARDENNES (54th Armored Field Artillery Battalion cited; DA GO 43, 1950)

16th DETACHMENT, 44th AIR DEFENSE ARTILLERY

RA
(inactive)

LINEAGE

Constituted 5 August 1958 in the Regular Army as the 16th Detachment, 44th Artillery. Activated 1 September 1958 at Fort Bliss, Texas. Inactivated 12 February 1959 at Fort Bliss, Texas. Redesignated 1 September 1971 as the 16th Detachment, 44th Air Defense Artillery.

CAMPAIGN PARTICIPATION CREDIT

None.

DECORATIONS

None.

44TH AIR DEFENSE ARTILLERY BIBLIOGRAPHY

Appleman, Roy E. *South to the Naktong, North to the Yalu.* United States Army in the Korean War. Washington: Government Printing Office, 1961. Contains information about the 44th Field Artillery Battalion.

Berry, Edward S. "From the Seine to the Siegfried Line." *Armored Cavalry Journal* 59 (January 1950): 35–41. Contains information about the 54th Armored Field Artillery Battalion.

Blumenson, Martin. *Breakout and Pursuit.* United States Army in World War II. Washington: Government Printing Office, 1961. Contains information about the 44th Field Artillery Battalion and the 54th Armored Field Artillery Battalion.

Cannon, M. Hamlin. *Leyte: The Return to the Philippines.* United States Army in World War II. Washington: Government Printing Office, 1954. Contains information about the 49th Field Artillery Battalion.

The Capture of Attu. Washington: Infantry Journal Press, 1944. Contains information about the 49th Field Artillery Battalion.

Crowl, Philip A., and Edmund G. Love. *Seizure of the Gilberts and Marshalls.* United States Army in World War II. Washington: Government Printing Office, 1955. Contains information about the 49th Field Artillery Battalion.

Dupuy, Richard Ernest. "Parker's Crossroads." *Infantry Journal* 62 (April 1948): 14–16. Pertains to the 54th Armored Field Artillery Battalion.

Falls, Bruce F., et al. *The Seventh Division in Korea.* Tokyo: FEC Printing Plant, 1948. Contains information about the 44th Field Artillery Battalion.

54th Armored Field Artillery Battalion. Baton Rouge: Army and Navy Publishing Company, 1950.

4th Division Artillery. Baton Rouge: Army and Navy Publishing Company, 1946. Contains information about the 44th Field Artillery Battalion.

Harrison, Gordon A. *Cross-Channel Attack*. United States Army in World War II. Washington: Government Printing Office, 1951. Contains information about the 44th Field Artillery Battalion.

Historical Division, War Department. *Utah Beach to Cherbourg (6 June–27 June 1944)*. American Forces in Action. Washington: Government Printing Office, 1947. Contains information about the 44th Field Artillery Battalion.

Hurlbut, H. *The Saga of Battery "B," 54th Armored Field Artillery Battalion*. N.p. 1945.

Kimmel, Irving, ed. *3rd Armored Division, "Spearhead," Fort Knox, Kentucky*. Dallas: Miller Publishing Company, 1956. Contains information about the 54th Armored Field Artillery Battalion.

Powers, Patrick W. "Every Pershing in the Pickle Barrel." *Army Information Digest* 19 (February 1964): 1–13. Pertains to the 2d Battalion, 44th Air Defense Artillery.

Public Information Office, 7th Infantry Division. *The Bayonet, the History of the 7th Infantry Division in Korea*. Tokyo: Dai Nippon Printing Company, 1953. Contains information about the 49th Field Artillery Battalion.

7th Infantry Division in Korea. Atlanta: Albert Love Enterprises, 1954. Contains information about the 49th Field Artillery Battalion.

67th Armored FA Bn, 54th Armored FA Bn, 391st Armored FA Bn, Camp Polk, 1942. Baton Rouge: Army and Navy Publishing Company, 1942.

Third Armored Division, Basic Training. Baton Rouge: Army and Navy Publishing Company, 1950. Contains information about the 54th Armored Field Artillery Battalion.

Third Armored Division, Fort Knox, Kentucky, 1948. Baton Rouge: Army and Navy Publishing Company, 1948. Contains information about the 54th Armored Field Artillery Battalion.

Waring, Paul C., ed. *History of the 7th Infantry (Bayonet) Division*. Tokyo: Dai Nippon Printing Company, 1967. Contains information about the 49th Field Artillery Battalion.

51st AIR DEFENSE ARTILLERY

HERALDIC ITEMS

COAT OF ARMS

Shield: Per saltire or and gules a caterpillar bendwise passant vert.

Crest: On a wreath of the colors, or and gules, a lion's face gules jessant-de-lis or.

Motto: Fire for Effect.

Symbolism: The colors, red and yellow, are for artillery. The shield is taken from the arms of the former 51st Field Artillery Battalion; the caterpillar and crest are from the coat of arms of the 51st Coast Artillery Battalion. They represent descent from those organizations. The caterpillar is symbolic of the tractor.

The lion's face on the crest represents the initial war service of an element of the regiment—the War of 1812—and the fleur-de-lis is for service in France.

DISTINCTIVE INSIGNIA

The distinctive insignia is the shield and motto of the coat of arms.

LINEAGE AND HONORS

LINEAGE

Constituted 6 July 1917 in the Regular Army as the 6th Provisional Regiment, Coast Artillery Corps. Organized 21 July 1917 at Fort Adams, Rhode Island. Redesignated 5 February 1918 as the 51st Artillery (Coast Artillery Corps). (2d Battalion inactivated 1 August 1922 at Camp Eustis, Virginia.) Redesignated 20 February 1924 as the 51st Coast Artillery. Inactivated 11 March 1930 at Fort Eustis, Virginia. Activated 16 March 1942 at San Juan, Puerto Rico. Regiment broken up 1 June 1944 and its elements reorganized and redesignated as follows: Headquarters and Headquarters Battery as Headquarters and Headquarters Battery, 145th Coast Artillery Group; 1st and 2d Battalions as the 51st and 52d Coast Artillery Battalions, respectively.

Headquarters and Headquarters Battery, 145th Coast Artillery Group, disbanded 28 February 1946 at Port of Spain, Trinidad. Reconstituted 28 June 1950 in the Regular Army and redesignated as Headquarters and Headquarters Battery, 51st Field Artillery Group. Activated 17 January 1952 at Fort Bragg, North Carolina. Inactivated 22 August 1955 at Fort Bragg, North Carolina.

51st Coast Artillery Battalion disbanded 28 February 1946 at Port of Spain, Trinidad. Reconstituted 28 June 1950 in the Regular Army; concurrently consolidated with the 51st Field Artillery Battalion (*see* AN-NEX 1), and consolidated unit designated as the 51st Field Artillery Battalion, an element of the 6th Infantry Division. Activated 4 October 1950 at Fort Ord, California. Inactivated 3 April 1956 at Ford Ord, California, and relieved from assignment to the 6th Infantry Division.

52d Coast Artillery Battalion disbanded 28 February 1946 at Port of Spain, Trinidad. Reconstituted 28 June 1950 in the Regular Army; concurrently consolidated with the 47th Armored Field Artillery Battalion (*see* ANNEX 2), and consolidated unit designated as the 47th Armored Field Artillery Battalion, an element of the 5th Armored Division. Activated 1 September 1950 at Camp Chaffee, Arkansas. Inactivated 16 March 1956 at Camp Chaffee, Arkansas, and relieved from assignment to the 5th Armored Division.

Headquarters and Headquarters Battery, 51st Field Artillery Group; 51st Field Artillery Battalion; and 47th Armored Field Artillery Battalion consolidated, reorganized, and redesignated 31 July 1959 as the 51st Artillery, a parent regiment under the Combat Arms Regimental System. Redesignated 1 September 1971 as the 51st Air Defense Artillery.

ANNEX 1

Constituted 1 October 1933 in the Regular Army as the 51st Field Artillery. Redesignated 1 October 1940 as the 51st Field Artillery Battalion, assigned to the 6th Division (later redesignated as the 6th Infantry Division), and activated at Fort Sill, Oklahoma. Inactivated 20 July 1947 in Korea.

ANNEX 2

Constituted 1 October 1933 in the Regular Army as the 47th Field Artillery. Activated 1 June 1941 at Fort Bragg, North Carolina.

Reorganized and redesignated (less 2d Battalion) 1 September 1942 as the 47th Armored Field Artillery Battalion and assigned to the 5th Armored Division (2d Battalion concurrently reorganized and redesignated as the 44th Field Artillery Battalion—hereafter separate lineage). Inactivated 9 October 1945 at Camp Myles Standish, Massachusetts. Activated 6 July 1948 at Camp Chaffee, Arkansas. Inactivated 1 January 1950 at Camp Chaffee, Arkansas.

CAMPAIGN PARTICIPATION CREDIT

World War I
St. Mihiel
Meuse-Argonne
Lorraine 1918

World War II
American Theater, Streamer
without inscription

Normandy
Northern France
Rhineland
Ardennes–Alsace
Central Europe
Luzon (with arrowhead)

DECORATIONS

None.

1st BATTALION, 51st AIR DEFENSE ARTILLERY

RA
(7th Infantry Division)

LINEAGE

Constituted 12 April 1808 in the Regular Army as a company in the Regiment of Light Artillery. Organized in 1808 at Fort Preble, Maine, as Capt. Joseph Chandler's Company of Light Artillery, Regiment of Light Artillery. Redesignated 20 April 1809 as Capt. Thomas Pitts' Company of Light Artillery, Regiment of Light Artillery. Redesignated in 1813 as Capt. Benjamin Branch's Company of Light Artillery, Regiment of Light Artillery. Redesignated in 1815 as Capt. John N. McIntosh's Company of Light Artillery, Regiment of Light Artillery. Redesignated in April 1815 as Capt. Andrew McDowell's Company of Light Artillery, Regiment of Light Artillery. Redesignated 22 May 1816 as Company A, Regiment of Light Artillery. Redesignated 1 June 1821 as Company A, 1st Regiment of Artillery.

Reorganized and redesignated 13 February 1901 as the 1st Company, Coast Artillery, Artillery Corps. Redesignated 2 February 1907 as the 1st Company, Coast Artillery Corps. Redesignated in 1916 as the 1st Company, Fort McKinley [Maine].

Reorganized and redesignated 21 July 1917 as Battery A, 6th Provisional Regiment, Coast Artillery Corps. Redesignated 5 February 1918 as Battery A, 51st Artillery (Coast Artillery Corps). (Additionally designated 1 June 1922 as the 1st Company, Coast Artillery Corps; additional designation abolished 20 February 1924.) Redesignated 20 February 1924 as Battery A, 51st Coast Artillery. Inactivated 11 March 1930 at Fort Eustis, Virginia. Activated 16 March 1942 in Puerto Rico.

Reorganized and redesignated 1 June 1944 as Battery A, 51st Coast Artillery Battalion. Disbanded 28 February 1946 at Port of Spain, Trinidad. Reconstituted 28 June 1950 in the Regular Army; concurrently consolidated with Battery A, 51st Field Artillery Battalion (*see* ANNEX), and consolidated unit designated as Battery A, 51st Field Artillery Battalion, an element of the 6th Infantry Division. Activated 4 October 1950 at Fort Ord, California. Inactivated 3 April 1956 at Fort Ord, California, and relieved from assignment to the 6th Infantry Division.

Redesignated 12 August 1958 as Headquarters and Headquarters Battery, 1st Missile Battalion, 51st Artillery (organic elements concurrently constituted). Battalion activated 1 September 1958 at Plainville, Connecticut. Inactivated 25 March 1961 at Plainville, Connecticut. Redesignated 1 September 1971 as the 1st Missile Battalion, 51st Air Defense Artillery. Redesignated 13 September 1972 as the 1st Battalion, 51st Air Defense Artillery, and activated at Highlands, New Jersey. Inactivated 4 June 1973 at Highlands, New Jersey. Assigned 21 December 1975 to the 7th Infantry Division and activated at Fort Ord, California.

ANNEX

Constituted 1 October 1933 in the Regular Army as Battery A, 51st Field Artillery. Redesignated 1 October 1940 as Battery A, 51st Field Artillery Battalion, and activated at Fort Sill, Oklahoma, as an element of the 6th Division (later redesignated as the 6th Infantry Division). Inactivated 20 July 1947 in Korea.

CAMPAIGN PARTICIPATION CREDIT

War of 1812
  *Canada

Indian Wars
  *Seminoles

Civil War
  *Mississippi River
  *Florida 1861
  *Florida 1862
  *Louisiana 1864

World War I
  *St. Mihiel
  Meuse-Argonne
  *Lorraine 1918

World War II
  *American Theater, Streamer
    without inscription
  Normandy
  Northern France
  Rhineland
  Ardennes-Alsace
  Central Europe
  *Luzon (with arrowhead)

DECORATIONS

*Philippine Presidential Unit Citation, Streamer embroidered 17 OCTOBER 1944 TO 4 JULY 1945 (6th Infantry Division cited; DA GO 47, 1950)

2d BATTALION, 51st AIR DEFENSE ARTILLERY

RA
(nondivisional)

LINEAGE

Constituted 14 August 1901 in the Regular Army as the 109th Company, Coast Artillery, Artillery Corps. Organized 3 September 1901 at Fort Greble, Rhode Island. Redesignated 2 February 1907 as the 109th Company, Coast Artillery Corps. Redesignated in July 1916 as the 2d Company, Fort Greble [Rhode Island].

Reorganized and redesignated 21 July 1917 as Battery B, 6th Provisional Regiment, Coast Artillery Corps. Redesignated 5 February 1918 as Battery B, 51st Artillery (Coast Artillery Corps). (Additionally designated 1 June 1922 as the 109th Company, Coast Artillery Corps; additional designation abolished 20 February 1924.) Redesignated 20 February 1924 as Battery B, 51st Coast Artillery. Inactivated 11 March 1930 at Fort Eustis, Virginia. Activated 16 March 1942 in Puerto Rico.

Reorganized and redesignated 1 June 1944 as Battery B, 51st Coast Artillery Battalion. Disbanded 28 February 1946 at Port of Spain, Trinidad. Reconstituted 28 June 1950 in the Regular Army; concurrently consolidated with Battery B, 51st Field Artillery Battalion (*see* ANNEX), and consolidated unit designated as Battery B, 51st Field Artillery Battalion, an element of the 6th Infantry Division. Activated 4 October 1950 at Fort Ord, California. Inactivated 3 April 1956 at Fort Ord, California, and relieved from assignment to the 6th Infantry Division.

Redesignated 12 August 1958 as Headquarters and Headquarters Battery, 2d Missile Battalion, 51st Artillery (organic elements concurrently constituted). Battalion activated 1 September 1958 at San Francisco, California. Redesignated 20 December 1965 as the 2d Battalion, 51st Artillery. Inactivated 30 June 1971 at Fort Baker, California. Redesignated 1 September 1971 as the 2d Battalion, 51st Air Defense Artillery. Activated 1 September 1978 at Fort Riley, Kansas.

ANNEX

Constituted 1 October 1933 in the Regular Army as Battery B, 51st Field Artillery. Redesignated 1 October 1940 as Battery B, 51st Field Artillery Battalion, and activated at Fort Sill, Oklahoma, as an element of the 6th Division (later redesignated as the 6th Infantry Division). Inactivated 20 July 1947 in Korea.

CAMPAIGN PARTICIPATION CREDIT

World War I
  *St. Mihiel
   Meuse-Argonne
  *Lorraine 1918

World War II
  *American Theater, Streamer
   without inscription

Normandy
Northern France
Rhineland
Ardennes-Alsace
Central Europe
*Luzon (with arrowhead)

DECORATIONS

*Philippine Presidential Unit Citation, Streamer embroidered 17 OCTOBER 1944 TO 4 JULY 1945 (6th Infantry Division cited; DA GO 47, 1950)

3d BATTALION, 51st AIR DEFENSE ARTILLERY

RA
(inactive)

LINEAGE

Constituted 14 August 1901 in the Regular Army as the 114th Company, Coast Artillery, Artillery Corps. Organized 22 August 1901 at Fort Slocum, New York. Redesignated 2 February 1907 as the 114th Company, Coast Artillery Corps. Redesignated in July 1916 as the 3d Company, Fort Wadsworth [New York]. Redesignated 22 July 1917 as Battery E, 8th Provisional Regiment, Coast Artillery Corps. Redesignated 5 February 1918 as Battery E, 53d Artillery (Coast Artillery Corps). Redesignated 26 March 1918 as the 7th Battery, Howitzer Regiment, 30th Brigade, Coast Artillery Corps.

Reorganized and redesignated 6 August 1918 as Battery E, 51st Artillery (Coast Artillery Corps). (Additionally designated 1 June 1922 as the 114th Company, Coast Artillery Corps; additional designation abolished 20 February 1924.) Inactivated 1 August 1922 at Camp Eustis, Virginia. Redesignated 20 February 1924 as Battery E, 51st Coast Artillery.

Consolidated 12 August 1958 with Battery C, 51st Field Artillery Battalion (*see* ANNEX), and consolidated unit redesignated as Headquarters and Headquarters Battery, 3d Missile Battalion, 51st Artillery (organic elements concurrently constituted). Battalion activated 1 September 1958 at Fort Tilden, New York. Redesignated 20 December 1965 as the 3d Battalion, 51st Artillery. Redesignated 1 September 1971 as the 3d Battalion, 51st Air Defense Artillery. Inactivated 13 September 1972 at Highlands, New Jersey.

ANNEX

Constituted 1 October 1933 in the Regular Army as Battery C, 51st Field Artillery. Redesignated 1 October 1940 as Battery C, 51st Field Artillery Battalion, and activated at Fort Sill, Oklahoma, as an element of the 6th Division (later redesignated as the 6th Infantry Division). Inactivated 20 July 1947 in Korea. Activated 4 October 1950 at Fort Ord, California. Inactivated 3 April 1956 at Fort Ord, California, and relieved from assignment to the 6th Infantry Division.

CAMPAIGN PARTICIPATION CREDIT

World War I
  *St. Mihiel
  *Meuse-Argonne
  Lorraine 1918

World War II
  American Theater, Streamer
    without inscription

Normandy
Northern France
Rhineland
Ardennes-Alsace
Central Europe
*Luzon (with arrowhead)

DECORATIONS

*Philippine Presidential Unit Citation, Streamer embroidered 17 OCTOBER 1944 TO 4 JULY 1945 (6th Infantry Division cited; DA GO 47, 1950)

4th MISSILE BATTALION, 51st AIR DEFENSE ARTILLERY

RA
(inactive)

LINEAGE

Constituted 10 July 1907 in the Regular Army as the 153d Company, Coast Artillery Corps. Organized in 1907 at Fort Andrews, Massachusetts. Redesignated 30 June 1916 as the 3d Company, Fort Andrews [Massachusetts].

Reorganized and redesignated 21 July 1917 as Battery L, 6th Provisional Regiment, Coast Artillery Corps. Redesignated 5 February 1918 as Battery L, 51st Artillery (Coast Artillery Corps). Redesignated 6 August 1918 as Battery C, 51st Artillery (Coast Artillery Corps). (Additionally designated 1 June 1922 as the 153d Company, Coast Artillery Corps; additional designation abolished 20 February 1924.) Redesignated 20 February 1924 as Battery C, 51st Coast Artillery. Inactivated 11 March 1930 at Fort Eustis, Virginia. Activated 16 March 1942 in Puerto Rico.

Reorganized and redesignated 1 June 1944 as Battery A, 52d Coast Artillery Battalion. Disbanded 28 February 1946 at Port of Spain, Trinidad. Reconstituted 28 June 1950 in the Regular Army; concurrently consolidated with Battery A, 47th Armored Field Artillery Battalion (*see* ANNEX), and consolidated unit designated as Battery A, 47th Armored Field Artillery Battalion, an element of the 5th Armored Division. Activated 1 September 1950 at Camp Chaffee, Arkansas. Inactivated 16 March 1956 at Camp Chaffee, Arkansas, and relieved from assignment to the 5th Armored Division.

Redesignated 12 August 1958 as Headquarters and Headquarters Battery, 4th Missile Battalion, 51st Artillery (organic elements concurrently constituted). Battalion activated 1 September 1958 at Fort Monroe, Virginia. Inactivated 26 July 1960 at Fort Monroe, Virginia. Redesignated 1 September 1971 as the 4th Missile Battalion, 51st Air Defense Artillery.

ANNEX

Constituted 1 October 1933 in the Regular Army as Battery A, 47th Field Artillery. Activated 1 June 1941 at Fort Bragg, North Carolina.

Reorganized and redesignated 1 September 1942 as Battery A, 47th Armored Field Artillery Battalion, an element of the 5th Armored Division. Inactivated 9 October 1945 at Camp Myles Standish, Massachusetts. Activated 6 July 1948 at Camp Chaffee, Arkansas. Inactivated 1 January 1950 at Camp Chaffee, Arkansas.

Campaign Participation Credit

World War I
  *St. Mihiel
  Meuse-Argonne
  *Lorraine 1918

World War II
  *American Theater, Streamer
    without inscription

*Normandy
*Northern France
*Rhineland
*Ardennes-Alsace
*Central Europe
  Luzon

Decorations

*Luxembourg Croix de Guerre, Streamer embroidered LUXEMBOURG
(47th Armored Field Artillery Battalion cited; DA GO 44, 1951)

5th BATTALION, 51st AIR DEFENSE ARTILLERY

AR
(inactive)

LINEAGE

Organized 31 October 1916 in the Regular Army at Fort Andrews, Massachusetts, as the 4th Company, Fort Andrews [Massachusetts].

Reorganized and redesignated 21 July 1917 as Battery M, 6th Provisional Regiment, Coast Artillery Corps. Redesignated 5 February 1918 as Battery M, 51st Artillery (Coast Artillery Corps). Redesignated 6 August 1918 as Battery D, 51st Artillery (Coast Artillery Corps). (Additionally designated 1 June 1922 as the 221st Company, Coast Artillery Corps; additional designation abolished 20 February 1924.) Inactivated 1 August 1922 at Fort Eustis, Virginia. Redesignated 20 February 1924 as Battery D, 51st Coast Artillery. Activated 1 May 1942 at Borinquen Field, Puerto Rico.

Reorganized and redesignated 1 June 1944 as Battery B, 52d Coast Artillery Battalion. Disbanded 28 February 1946 at Port of Spain, Trinidad. Reconstituted 28 June 1950 in the Regular Army; concurrently consolidated with Battery B, 47th Armored Field Artillery Battalion (*see* ANNEX), and consolidated unit designated as Battery B, 47th Armored Field Artillery Battalion, an element of the 5th Armored Division. Activated 1 September 1950 at Camp Chaffee, Arkansas. Inactivated 16 March 1956 at Camp Chaffee, Arkansas, and relieved from assignment to the 5th Armored Division.

Redesignated 30 June 1959 as Headquarters and Headquarters Battery, 5th Automatic Weapons Battalion, 51st Artillery; concurrently withdrawn from the Regular Army, allotted to the Army Reserve, and assigned to the First United States Army (organic elements concurrently constituted). Battalion activated 8 August 1959 with Headquarters at Fort Tilden, New York. Reorganized and redesignated 15 August 1960 as the 5th Howitzer Battalion, 51st Artillery. Redesignated 1 May 1964 as the 5th Battalion, 51st Artillery. Inactivated 1 September 1971 at Fort Tilden, New York; concurrently redesignated as the 5th Battalion, 51st Air Defense Artillery.

ANNEX

Constituted 1 October 1933 in the Regular Army as Battery B, 47th Field Artillery. Activated 1 June 1941 at Fort Bragg, North Carolina.

Reorganized and redesignated 1 September 1942 as Battery B, 47th Armored Field Artillery Battalion, an element of the 5th Armored Division. Inactivated 9 October 1945 at Camp Myles Standish, Massachusetts. Activated 6 July 1948 at Camp Chaffee, Arkansas. Inactivated 1 January 1950 at Camp Chaffee, Arkansas.

CAMPAIGN PARTICIPATION CREDIT

World War I
  *St. Mihiel
  Meuse-Argonne
  *Lorraine 1918

World War II
  *American Theater, Streamer
    without inscription

*Normandy
*Northern France
*Rhineland
*Ardennes-Alsace
*Central Europe
Luzon

DECORATIONS

*Luxembourg Croix de Guerre, Streamer embroidered LUXEMBOURG (47th Armored Field Artillery Battalion cited; DA GO 44, 1951)

51ST AIR DEFENSE ARTILLERY BIBLIOGRAPHY

Britton, Ray D., ed. *Camp Chaffee, Arkansas, Home of the Fifth Armored Division.* Dallas: Taylor Publishing Company, 1952. Contains information about the 47th Armored Field Artillery Battalion.

Carlson, Raymond. "Howitzer Firing with Kentucky Windage" [battle of Munoz, Philippine Islands]. *Field Artillery Journal* 35 (October 1945): 609–13. Contains information about the 51st Field Artillery Battalion.

Division Artillery, 5th Armored Division, Camp Chaffee, Arkansas. Baton Rouge: Army and Navy Publishing Company, 1951. Contains information about the 47th Armored Field Artillery Battalion.

Dyer, Frederick. "1st Regiment of Artillery." *A Compendium of the War of the War of the Rebellion.* New York: Thomas Yoseloff, 1959. Contains information about the present 1st Battalion, 51st Air Defense Artillery.

Haskin, William Lawrence. "The First Regiment of Artillery, 1821–1876." *The Army of the United States.* Edited by Theophilus F. Rodenbough and William L. Haskin, 301–11. New York: Maynard, Merrill and Company, 1896. Originally published in *Journal of the Military Service Institution of the United States* 15 (1894): 1321–31. Contains information about the current 1st Battalion, 51st Air Defense Artillery.

———. *The History of the First Regiment of Artillery; From Organization in 1821 to January 1st, 1876.* Portland, Maine: B. Thurston and Company, 1879. Contains information about the current 1st Battalion, 51st Air Defense Artillery.

Smith, Robert Ross. *The Approach to the Philippines.* United States Army in World War II. Washington: Government Printing Office, 1953. Contains information about the 51st Field Artillery Battalion.

Sprague, John T. *The Origin, Progress, and Conclusion of the Florida War.* New York: D. Appleton and Company, 1848. Reprint. Gainesville, Fla.: University of Florida Press, 1964. Contains information about the current 1st Battalion, 51st Air Defense Artillery.

The Victory in Training. Baton Rouge: Army and Navy Publishing Company, 1949. Contains information about the 47th Armored Field Artillery Battalion.

52d AIR DEFENSE ARTILLERY

HERALDIC ITEMS

COAT OF ARMS

Shield: Gules, a bend potenté or.

Crest: On a wreath of the colors, or and gules, a locomotive affronté gules, charged with the number "52" or.

Motto: *Semper Paratus* (Always Prepared).

Symbolism: The shield is red for artillery. The gold potenté bend is an adaptation of the cottised bend on the arms of Champagne.

The crest alludes to service in France during World War I.

DISTINCTIVE INSIGNIA

The distinctive insignia is the shield and motto of the coat of arms.

LINEAGE AND HONORS

LINEAGE

Organized 22 July 1917 in the Regular Army at Fort Adams, Rhode Island, as the 7th Provisional Regiment, Coast Artillery Corps. Redesignated 5 February 1918 as the 52d Artillery (Coast Artillery Corps). (3d Battalion inactivated 16 May 1921 at Fort Eustis, Virginia; activated 18 August 1921 at Fort Eustis, Virginia. 1st Battalion inactivated 1 August 1922 at Fort Eustis, Virginia.) Redesignated 20 February 1924 as the 52d Coast Artillery. (Battery D inactivated 1 November 1938 at Fort Monroe, Virginia. Battery F inactivated 1 February 1940 at Fort Monroe, Virginia. Batteries D and F activated 8 January 1941 at Fort Hancock, New Jersey. 1st Battalion activated 1 June 1941 at Fort Hancock, New Jersey.) Regiment broken up 1 May 1943 and its elements reorganized and redesignated as follows: Headquarters and Headquarters Battery disbanded at Fort Hancock, New Jersey; 1st, 2d, and 3d Battalions as the 286th, 287th, and 288th Coast Artillery Battalions, respectively (Headquarters and Headquarters Battery, 288th Coast Artillery Battalion, concurrently inactivated at Fort Hancock, New Jersey).

Headquarters and Headquarters Battery, 52d Coast Artillery, reconstituted 28 June 1950 in the Regular Army and redesignated as Headquarters and Headquarters Battery, 52d Field Artillery Group. Activated 18 January 1952 at Fort Sill, Oklahoma. Redesignated 25 June 1958 as Headquarters and Headquarters Battery, 52d Artillery Group. Inactivated 30 June 1971 at Fort Sill, Oklahoma.

286th Coast Artillery Battalion reorganized and redesignated 30 August 1944 as the 538th Field Artillery Battalion. Inactivated 14 December 1945 at Camp Myles Standish, Massachusetts. Activated

31 December 1946 on Luzon, Philippine Islands. Inactivated 30 May 1947 on Luzon, Philippine Islands. Activated 22 March 1951 at Camp Carson, Colorado. Inactivated 1 June 1958 in Germany.

287th Coast Artillery Battalion converted and redesignated 30 August 1944 as the 539th Field Artillery Battalion. Inactivated 28 December 1945 at Camp Myles Standish, Massachusetts. Activated 31 December 1946 on Luzon, Philippine Islands. Inactivated 30 May 1947 on Luzon, Philippine Islands. Activated 18 March 1955 in Japan. Inactivated 25 March 1956 in Japan.

288th Coast Artillery Battalion inactivated 18 April 1944 at Camp Shelby, Mississippi. Disbanded 14 June 1944. Reconstituted 28 June 1950 in the Regular Army; concurrently consolidated with the 52d Field Artillery Battalion (active) (*see* ANNEX), and consolidated unit designated as the 52d Field Artillery Battalion, an element of the 24th Infantry Division. Inactivated 5 June 1958 and relieved from assignment to the 24th Infantry Division.

Headquarters and Headquarters Battery, 52d Artillery Group, and 538th, 539th, and 52d Field Artillery Battalions consolidated, reorganized, and redesignated 30 June 1971 as the 52d Artillery, a parent regiment under the Combat Arms Regimental System. Redesignated 1 September 1971 as the 52d Air Defense Artillery.

ANNEX

Constituted 1 October 1933 in the Regular Army as the 52d Field Artillery. Redesignated 26 August 1941 as the 52d Field Artillery Battalion and assigned to the 24th Infantry Division. Activated 1 October 1941 at Schofield Barracks, Hawaii.

CAMPAIGN PARTICIPATION CREDIT

World War I
    Champagne-Marne
    St. Mihiel
    Meuse-Argonne
    Champagne 1918
    Lorraine 1918

World War II
    Central Europe
    Central Pacific
    New Guinea (with arrowhead)
    Leyte
    Luzon
    Southern Philippines (with arrowhead)

Korean War
    UN defensive
    UN offensive
    CCF intervention
    First UN counteroffensive

    CCF spring offensive
    UN summer–fall offensive
    Second Korean winter
    Korea, summer 1953

Vietnam
    Counteroffensive
    Counteroffensive, Phase II
    Counteroffensive, Phase III
    Tet Counteroffensive
    Counteroffensive, Phase IV
    Counteroffensive, Phase V
    Counteroffensive, Phase VI
    Tet 69/Counteroffensive
    Summer–fall 1969
    Winter–spring 1970
    Sanctuary Counteroffensive
    Counteroffensive, Phase VII

DECORATIONS

Presidential Unit Citation (Army), Streamer embroidered DEFENSE OF KOREA (24th Infantry Division cited; DA GO 45, 1950)

Valorous Unit Award, Streamer embroidered DAK TO–BEN HET (Headquarters and Headquarters Battery, 52d Artillery Group, cited; DA GO 48, 1971)

Meritorious Unit Commendation, Streamer embroidered FLORIDA 1962–1963 (2d Missile Battalion [less Battery B], 52d Artillery, cited; DA GO 33, 1963)

Meritorious Unit Commendation, Streamer embroidered VIETNAM 1966–1969 (Headquarters and Headquarters Battery, 52d Artillery Group, cited; DA GO 36, 1970)

1st MISSILE BATTALION, 52d AIR DEFENSE ARTILLERY

RA
(inactive)

LINEAGE

Constituted 10 July 1907 in the Regular Army as the 134th Company, Coast Artillery Corps. Organized in 1907 at Fort Michie, New York. Redesignated in July 1916 as the 1st Company, Fort H. G. Wright [New York].

Reorganized and redesignated 22 July 1917 as Battery A, 7th Provisional Regiment, Coast Artillery Corps. Redesignated 5 February 1918 as Battery A, 52d Artillery (Coast Artillery Corps). (Additionally designated 1 June 1922 as the 134th Company, Coast Artillery Corps; additional designation abolished 20 February 1924.) Inactivated 1 August 1922 at Fort Eustis, Virginia. Redesignated 20 February 1924 as Battery A, 52d Coast Artillery. Activated 1 June 1941 at Fort Hancock, New Jersey.

Reorganized and redesignated 1 May 1943 as Battery A, 286th Coast Artillery Battalion. Converted and redesignated 30 August 1944 as Battery A, 538th Field Artillery Battalion. Inactivated 14 December 1945 at Camp Myles Standish, Massachusetts. Activated 31 December 1946 on Luzon, Philippine Islands. Inactivated 30 May 1947 on Luzon, Philippine Islands. Activated 22 March 1951 at Camp Carson, Colorado. Inactivated 1 June 1958 in Germany.

Redesignated 12 August 1958 as Headquarters and Headquarters Battery, 1st Missile Battalion, 52d Artillery (organic elements concurrently constituted). Battalion activated 1 September 1958 at Camp Hanford, Washington. Inactivated 23 December 1960 at Camp Hanford, Washington. Redesignated 1 September 1971 as the 1st Missile Battalion, 52d Air Defense Artillery.

CAMPAIGN PARTICIPATION CREDIT

World War I
  Champagne-Marne
  *St. Mihiel
  Meuse-Argonne
  Champagne 1918
  Lorraine 1918

World War II
  *Central Europe
  Central Pacific
  New Guinea (with arrowhead)
  Leyte
  Luzon

Southern Philippines (with arrowhead)

Korean War
  UN defensive
  UN offensive
  CCF intervention
  First UN counteroffensive
  CCF spring offensive
  UN summer–fall offensive
  Second Korean winter
  Korea, summer 1953

DECORATIONS

Presidential Unit Citation (Army), Streamer embroidered DEFENSE OF KOREA

2d BATTALION, 52d AIR DEFENSE ARTILLERY

RA
(nondivisional)

LINEAGE

Organized 1 April 1917 in the Regular Army at Fort Terry, New York, as the 6th Company, Fort Terry [New York].

Reorganized and redesignated 22 July 1917 as Battery B, 7th Provisional Regiment, Coast Artillery Corps. Redesignated 5 February 1918 as Battery B, 52d Artillery (Coast Artillery Corps). (Additionally designated 1 June 1922 as the 225th Company, Coast Artillery Corps; additional designation abolished 20 February 1924.) Inactivated 1 August 1922 at Fort Eustis, Virginia. Redesignated 20 February 1924 as Battery B, 52d Coast Artillery. Activated 1 June 1941 at Fort Hancock, New Jersey.

Reorganized and redesignated 1 May 1943 as Battery B, 286th Coast Artillery Battalion. Converted and redesignated 30 August 1944 as Battery B, 538th Field Artillery Battalion. Inactivated 14 December 1945 at Camp Myles Standish, Massachusetts. Activated 31 December 1946 on Luzon, Philippine Islands. Inactivated 30 May 1947 on Luzon, Philippine Islands. Activated 22 March 1951 at Camp Carson, Colorado. Inactivated 1 June 1958 in Germany.

Redesignated 26 February 1959 as Headquarters and Headquarters Battery, 2d Missile Battalion, 52d Artillery (organic elements concurrently constituted). Battalion activated 15 April 1959 at Fort Bliss, Texas. Redesignated 20 December 1965 as the 2d Battalion, 52d Artillery. Redesignated 1 September 1971 as the 2d Battalion, 52d Air Defense Artillery.

CAMPAIGN PARTICIPATION CREDIT

World War I
  Champagne-Marne
  *St. Mihiel
  Meuse-Argonne
  Champagne 1918
  Lorraine 1918

World War II
  *Central Europe
  Central Pacific
  New Guinea (with arrowhead)
  Leyte
  Luzon

Southern Philippines (with arrowhead)

Korean War
  UN defensive
  UN offensive
  CCF intervention
  First UN counteroffensive
  CCF spring offensive
  UN summer–fall offensive
  Second Korean winter
  Korea, summer 1953

DECORATIONS

Presidential Unit Citation (Army), Streamer embroidered DEFENSE OF KOREA

*Meritorious Unit Commendation, Streamer embroidered FLORIDA 1962–1963 (2d Missile Battalion [less Battery B], 52d Artillery, cited; DA GO 33, 1963)

3d MISSILE BATTALION, 52d AIR DEFENSE ARTILLERY

RA
(inactive)

LINEAGE

Constituted 28 February 1901 in the Regular Army as the 88th Company, Coast Artillery, Artillery Corps. Organized in 1901 at Fort Trumball, Connecticut. Redesignated 2 February 1907 as the 88th Company, Coast Artillery Corps. Redesignated in July 1916 as the 2d Company, Fort Terry [New York].

Reorganized and redesignated 22 July 1917 as Battery C, 7th Provisional Regiment, Coast Artillery Corps. Redesignated 5 February 1918 as Battery C, 52d Artillery (Coast Artillery Corps). (Additionally designated 1 June 1922 as the 88th Company, Coast Artillery Corps; additional designation abolished 20 February 1924.) Redesignated 20 February 1924 as Battery C, 52d Coast Artillery.

Reorganized and redesignated 1 May 1943 as Battery A, 287th Coast Artillery Battalion. Converted and redesignated 30 August 1944 as Battery A, 539th Field Artillery Battalion. Inactivated 28 December 1945 at Camp Myles Standish, Massachusetts. Activated 31 December 1946 on Luzon, Philippine Islands. Inactivated 30 March 1947 on Luzon, Philippine Islands. Activated 18 March 1955 in Japan. Inactivated 25 March 1956 in Japan.

Redesignated 12 August 1958 as Headquarters and Headquarters Battery, 3d Missile Battalion, 52d Artillery (organic elements concurrently constituted). Battalion activated 1 September 1958 at Squantam, Massachusetts. Inactivated 15 December 1961 at Quincy, Massachusetts. Redesignated 1 September 1971 as the 3d Missile Battalion, 52d Air Defense Artillery.

CAMPAIGN PARTICIPATION CREDIT

World War I
    Champagne-Marne
    *St. Mihiel
    *Meuse-Argonne
    Champagne 1918
    Lorraine 1918

World War II
    Central Europe
    Central Pacific
    New Guinea (with arrowhead)
    Leyte

Luzon
Southern Philippines (with arrowhead)

Korean War
    UN defensive
    UN offensive
    CCF intervention
    First UN counteroffensive
    CCF spring offensive
    UN summer–fall offensive
    Second Korean winter
    Korea, summer 1953

DECORATIONS

Presidential Unit Citation (Army), Streamer embroidered DEFENSE OF KOREA

4th MISSILE BATTALION, 52d AIR DEFENSE ARTILLERY

RA
(inactive)

LINEAGE

Organized 1 April 1917 in the Regular Army at Fort H. G. Wright, New York, as the 6th Company, Fort H. G. Wright [New York].

Reorganized and redesignated 22 July 1917 as Battery D, 7th Provisional Regiment, Coast Artillery Corps. Redesignated 5 February 1918 as Battery D, 52d Artillery (Coast Artillery Corps). (Additionally designated 1 June 1922 as the 226th Company, Coast Artillery Corps; additional designation abolished 20 February 1924.) Redesignated 20 February 1924 as Battery D, 52d Coast Artillery. Inactivated 1 November 1938 at Fort Monroe, Virginia. Activated 8 January 1941 at Fort Hancock, New Jersey.

Reorganized and redesignated 1 May 1943 as Battery B, 287th Coast Artillery Battalion. Converted and redesignated 30 August 1944 as Battery B, 539th Field Artillery Battalion. Inactivated 28 December 1945 at Camp Myles Standish, Massachusetts. Activated 31 December 1946 on Luzon, Philippine Islands. Inactivated 30 March 1947 on Luzon, Philippine Islands. Activated 18 March 1955 in Japan. Inactivated 25 March 1956 in Japan.

Redesignated 12 August 1958 as Headquarters and Headquarters Battery, 4th Missile Battalion, 52d Artillery (organic elements concurrently constituted). Battalion activated 1 September 1958 at Chicago, Illinois. Inactivated 24 June 1960 at Chicago, Illinois. Redesignated 1 September 1971 as the 4th Missile Battalion, 52d Air Defense Artillery.

CAMPAIGN PARTICIPATION CREDIT

World War I
  Champagne-Marne
  *St. Mihiel
  *Meuse-Argonne
  Champagne 1918
  Lorraine 1918

World War II
  Central Europe
  Central Pacific
  New Guinea (with arrowhead)
  Leyte
  Luzon

Southern Philippines (with arrowhead)

Korean War
  UN defensive
  UN offensive
  CCF intervention
  First UN counteroffensive
  CCF spring offensive
  UN summer–fall offensive
  Second Korean winter
  Korea, summer 1953

DECORATIONS

Presidential Unit Citation (Army), Streamer embroidered DEFENSE OF KOREA

5th BATTALION, 52d AIR DEFENSE ARTILLERY

RA
(24th Infantry Division)

LINEAGE

Organized 6 July 1916 in the Regular Army at Fort Washington, Maryland, as the 1st Company, Fort Washington [Maryland].

Reorganized and redesignated 6 July 1917 as Battery I, 8th Provisional Regiment, Coast Artillery Corps. Redesignated 5 February 1918 as Battery I, 53d Artillery (Coast Artillery Corps). Redesignated 15 July 1918 as Battery E, 52d Artillery (Coast Artillery Corps). Inactivated 16 May 1921 at Fort Eustis, Virginia. Activated 18 August 1921 at Fort Eustis, Virginia. (Additionally designated 1 June 1922 as the 227th Company, Coast Artillery Corps; additional designation abolished 20 February 1924.) Redesignated 20 February 1924 as Battery E, 52d Coast Artillery.

Reorganized and redesignated 1 May 1943 as Battery A, 285th Coast Artillery Battalion. Inactivated 5 May 1944 at Camp Breckinridge, Kentucky. Disbanded 14 June 1944. Reconstituted 28 June 1950 in the Regular Army; concurrently consolidated with Battery A, 52d Field Artillery Battalion (active) (*see* ANNEX), and consolidated unit designated as Battery A, 52d Field Artillery Battalion, an element of the 24th Infantry Division. Inactivated 5 June 1958 and relieved from assignment to the 24th Infantry Division.

Redesignated 18 May 1959 as Headquarters and Headquarters Battery, 5th Automatic Weapons Battalion, 52d Artillery; concurrently withdrawn from the Regular Army and allotted to the Army Reserve (organic elements concurrently constituted). Redesignated 1 September 1971 as the 5th Automatic Weapons Battalion, 52d Air Defense Artillery. Redesignated 21 December 1975 as the 5th Battalion, 52d Air Defense Artillery; concurrently withdrawn from the Army Reserve, allotted to the Regular Army, assigned to the 24th Infantry Division, and activated at Fort Stewart, Georgia.

ANNEX

Constituted 1 October 1933 in the Regular Army as Battery A, 52d Field Artillery. Redesignated 26 August 1941 as Battery A, 52d Field Artillery Battalion, an element of the 24th Infantry Division. Activated 1 October 1941 at Schofield Barracks, Hawaii.

CAMPAIGN PARTICIPATION CREDIT

World War I
  *Champagne-Marne
  St. Mihiel
  *Meuse-Argonne
  *Champagne 1918
  *Lorraine 1918

World War II
  Central Europe
  *Central Pacific
  *New Guinea (with arrowhead)
  *Leyte

  *Luzon
  *Southern Philippines (with arrowhead)

Korean War
  *UN defensive
  *UN offensive
  *CCF intervention
  *First UN counteroffensive
  *CCF spring offensive
  *UN summer–fall offensive
  *Second Korean winter
  *Korea, summer 1953

DECORATIONS

*Presidential Unit Citation (Army), Streamer embroidered DEFENSE OF KOREA (24th Infantry Division cited; DA GO 45, 1950)

*Philippine Presidential Unit Citation, Streamer embroidered 17 OCTOBER 1944 TO 4 JULY 1945 (52d Field Artillery Battalion cited; DA GO 47, 1950)

*Republic of Korea Presidential Unit Citation, Streamer embroidered PYONGTAEK (52d Field Artillery Battalion cited; DA GO 35, 1951)

*Republic of Korea Presidential Unit Citation, Streamer embroidered KOREA 1952–1953 (52d Field Artillery Battalion cited; DA GO 24, 1954)

6th BATTALION, 52d AIR DEFENSE ARTILLERY

RA
(nondivisional)

LINEAGE

Organized 1 June 1917 in the Regular Army at Fort Washington, Maryland, as the 3d Company, Fort Washington [Maryland].

Reorganized and redesignated 17 July 1917 as Battery K, 8th Provisional Regiment, Coast Artillery Corps. Redesignated 5 February 1918 as Battery K, 53d Artillery (Coast Artillery Corps). Redesignated 15 July 1918 as Battery F, 52d Artillery (Coast Artillery Corps). Inactivated 16 May 1921 at Fort Eustis, Virginia. Activated 18 August 1921 at Fort Eustis, Virginia. (Additionally designated 1 June 1922 as the 229th Company, Coast Artillery Corps; additional designation abolished 20 February 1924.) Redesignated 20 February 1924 as Battery F, 52d Coast Artillery. Inactivated 1 February 1940 at Fort Monroe, Virginia. Activated 8 January 1941 at Fort Hancock, New Jersey.

Reorganized and redesignated 1 May 1943 as Battery A, 288th Coast Artillery Battalion. Inactivated 18 April 1944 at Camp Shelby, Mississippi. Disbanded 14 June 1944. Reconstituted 28 June 1950 in the Regular Army; concurrently consolidated with Battery B, 52d Field Artillery Battalion (active) (*see* ANNEX), and consolidated unit designated as Battery B, 52d Field Artillery Battalion, an element of the 24th Infantry Division. Inactivated 5 June 1958 and relieved from assignment to the 24th Infantry Division.

Redesignated 1 November 1960 as Headquarters and Headquarters Battery, 6th Missile Battalion, 52d Artillery (organic elements concurrently constituted). Battalion activated 17 November 1960 at Fort Bliss, Texas. Redesignated 20 August 1965 as the 6th Battalion, 52d Artillery. Redesignated 1 September 1971 as the 6th Battalion, 52d Air Defense Artillery.

ANNEX

Constituted 1 October 1933 in the Regular Army as Battery B, 52d Field Artillery. Redesignated 26 August 1941 as Battery B, 52d Field Artillery Battalion, an element of the 24th Infantry Division. Activated 1 October 1941 at Schofield Barracks, Hawaii.

CAMPAIGN PARTICIPATION CREDIT

World War I
  *Champagne-Marne
  St. Mihiel
  *Meuse-Argonne
  *Champagne 1918
  *Lorraine 1918

World War II
  Central Europe
  *Central Pacific
  *New Guinea (with arrowhead)
  *Leyte

*Luzon
*Southern Philippines (with arrowhead)

Korean War
  *UN defensive
  *UN offensive
  *CCF intervention
  *First UN counteroffensive
  *CCF spring offensive
  *UN summer–fall offensive
  *Second Korean winter
  *Korea, summer 1953

Decorations

*Presidential Unit Citation (Army), Streamer embroidered DEFENSE OF KOREA (24th Infantry Division cited; DA GO 45, 1950)

*Philippine Presidential Unit Citation, Streamer embroidered 17 OCTOBER 1944 TO 4 JULY 1945 (52d Field Artillery Battalion cited; DA GO 47, 1950)

*Republic of Korea Presidential Unit Citation, Streamer embroidered PYONGTAEK (52d Field Artillery Battalion cited; DA GO 35, 1951)

*Republic of Korea Presidential Unit Citation, Streamer embroidered KOREA 1952–1953 (52d Field Artillery Battalion cited; DA GO 24, 1954)

52D AIR DEFENSE ARTILLERY BIBLIOGRAPHY

Appleman, Roy E. *South to the Naktong, North to the Yalu.* United States Army in the Korean War. Washington: Government Printing Office, 1961. Contains information about the 52d Field Artillery Battalion.

Barth, George B. "The First Days in Korea." *Combat Forces Journal* 2 (March 1952):21–24. Contains information about the 52d Field Artillery Battalion.

Cannon, M. Hamlin. *Leyte: The Return to the Philippines.* United States Army in World War II. Washington: Government Printing Office, 1961. Contains information about the 52d Field Artillery Battalion.

Ott, David Ewing. *Field Artillery, 1954–1973.* Vietnam Studies. Washington: Government Printing Office, 1975. Contains information about the 52d Artillery Group.

Smith, Robert Ross. *The Approach to the Philippines.* United States Army in World War II. Washington: Government Printing Office, 1953. Contains information about the 52d Field Artillery Battalion.

Turtle, Lewis. "Field Training of the 52d Coast Artillery (Railway)." *Coast Artillery Journal* 75 (1932):325–31.

24th Infantry Division, A Brief History: The Story of the 24th Infantry Division's Actions in the Korean Conflict. Tokyo: Japan News, 1954. Contains information about the 52d Field Artillery Battalion.

55th AIR DEFENSE ARTILLERY

HERALDIC ITEMS

COAT OF ARMS

Shield: Gules, on a pile wavy or, a pine tree eradicated azure, in base two fire arrows point up of the second enflamed proper.

Crest: On a wreath of the colors, or and gules, an isosceles triangle of the first, bordure of the second bearing between a pellet from which issues an arrow with double barbs palewise sable and the arabic numerals "55" gules, a caterpillar fesswise of the last, all conjoined.

Motto: *Vigilantia* (Vigilance).

Symbolism: Red and yellow are the colors of the artillery branch. The wavy pile alludes to the unit's origin as coast artillery and further suggests service across two oceans, noting that the 55th Air Defense Artillery campaigned in both the European and Pacific theaters. The fire arrow, a highly effective artillery weapon of pre-gunpowder days, is an allusion to the firepower of present day artillery; the two of them represent participation in both world wars. The blue pine tree denotes award of the Presidential Unit Citation (Army) to the regiment for the Ardennes campaign of World War II.

DISTINCTIVE INSIGNIA

The distinctive insignia is the crest and motto of the coat of arms.

LINEAGE AND HONORS

LINEAGE

Constituted 1 December 1917 in the Regular Army as the 55th Artillery (Coast Artillery Corps) and organized at Boston, Massachusetts, from existing Regular Army companies and National Guard companies from Massachusetts and Rhode Island. (National Guard companies demobilized in February 1919 at Camp Winfield Scott, California; regiment continued on active status.) (3d Battalion organized 7 January 1922 at Fort Kamehameha, Hawaii; inactivated 31 October 1925 at Fort Kamehameha, Hawaii.) Redesignated 20 February 1924 as the 55th Coast Artillery. (3d Battalion activated 22 May 1943 in Hawaii.) Inactivated 31 May 1944 at Fort Ruger, Hawaii. Disbanded 14 June 1944.

Headquarters and Headquarters Battery 55th Coast Artillery, reconstituted 28 June 1950 in the Regular Army and redesignated as Headquarters and Headquarters Battery, 55th Field Artillery Group.

1st Battalion, 55th Coast Artillery, reconstituted 28 June 1950 in the Regular Army; concurrently consolidated with the 55th Field Artillery Battalion (*see* ANNEX 1), and consolidated unit designated as the 55th Field Artillery Battalion. Activated 19 January 1952 at Camp McCoy, Wisconsin. Inactivated 25 June 1958 in Germany.

2d Battalion, 55th Coast Artillery, reconstituted 28 June 1950 in the Regular Army; concurrently consolidated with the 50th Field Artillery Battalion (*see* ANNEX 2), and consolidated unit designated as the 50th Field Artillery Battalion, an element of the 5th Infantry Division. Activated 1 March 1951 at Indiantown Gap Military Reservation, Pennsylvania. Inactivated 1 September 1953 at Indiantown Gap Military Reservation, Pennsylvania. Activated 25 March 1954 in Germany. Inactivated 1 June 1957 at Fort Ord, California, and relieved from assignment to the 5th Infantry Division.

3d Battalion, 55th Coast Artillery, reconstituted 28 June 1950 in the Regular Army; concurrently consolidated with the 66th Armored Field Artillery Battalion (*see* ANNEX 3), and consolidated unit designated as the 66th Armored Field Artillery Battalion. Assigned 25 February 1953 to the 4th Armored Division. Activated 15 June 1954 at Fort Hood, Texas. Inactivated 1 April 1957 at Ford Hood, Texas, and relieved from assignment to the 4th Armored Division.

Headquarters and Headquarters Battery, 55th Field Artillery Group; 55th and 50th Field Artillery Battalions; and 66th Armored Field Artillery Battalion consolidated, reorganized, and redesignated 31 July 1959 as the 55th Artillery, a parent regiment under the Combat Arms Regimental System. Redesignated 1 September 1971 as the 55th Air Defense Artillery.

ANNEX 1

Constituted 16 December 1940 in the Regular Army as the 55th Field Artillery Battalion. (Battery C activated 3 January 1941 at Fort Myer, Virginia.) Activated (less Battery C) 18 June 1943 at Fort Bragg, North Carolina. Inactivated 15 April 1946 at Manila, Philippine Islands.

ANNEX 2

Constituted 1 October 1933 in the Regular Army as the 50th Field Artillery. Redesignated 1 October 1940 as the 50th Field Artillery Battalion, assigned to the 5th Division (later redesignated as the 5th Infantry Division), and activated at Fort Sheridan, Illinois. Inactivated 20 September 1946 at Camp Campbell, Kentucky. Activated 15 July 1947 at Fort Jackson, South Carolina. Inactivated 30 April 1950 at Fort Jackson, South Carolina.

ANNEX 3

Constituted 16 December 1940 in the Regular Army as the 66th Field Artillery and assigned to the 4th Armored Division. Activated 15 April 1941 at Pine Camp, New York.

Reorganized and redesignated 1 January 1942 as the 66th Armored Field Artillery Battalion. Relieved 1 May 1946 from assignment to the 4th Armored Division; concurrently converted and redesignated as the 66th Constabulary Squadron and assigned to the 2d Constabulary Regiment. Inactivated 20 December 1948 in Germany and relieved from assignment to the 2d Constabulary Regiment; concurrently converted as the 66th Armored Field Artillery Battalion.

CAMPAIGN PARTICIPATION CREDIT

World War I
Aisne-Marne
Oise-Aisne
Meuse-Argonne
Champagne 1918

World War II
Normandy
Northern France
Rhineland
Ardennes-Alsace
Central Europe
Central Pacific
New Guinea
Luzon

Vietnam
Tet Counteroffensive
Counteroffensive, Phase IV
Counteroffensive, Phase V
Counteroffensive, Phase VI
Tet 69/Counteroffensive
Summer–fall 1969
Winter–spring 1970
Sanctuary Counteroffensive
Counteroffensive, Phase VII
Consolidation I

DECORATIONS

Presidential Unit Citation (Army), Streamer embroidered ARDENNES (4th Armored Division cited; WD GO 54, 1945)

1st BATTALION, 55th AIR DEFENSE ARTILLERY

RA
(5th Infantry Division)

LINEAGE

Constituted 28 February 1901 in the Regular Army as the 83d Company, Coast Artillery, Artillery Corps. Organized 6 April 1901 at Fort Hamilton, New York. Redesignated 2 February 1907 as the 83d Company, Coast Artillery Corps. Redesignated 30 June 1916 as the 4th Company, Fort Strong [Massachusetts]. Redesignated 31 August 1917 as the 8th Company, Coast Defenses of Boston.

Reorganized and redesignated 1 December 1917 as Battery C, 55th Artillery (Coast Artillery Corps). (Additionally designated 30 June 1922 as the 83d Company, Coast Artillery Corps; additional designation abolished 20 February 1924.) Redesignated 20 February 1924 as Battery C, 55th Coast Artillery. Inactivated 31 May 1944 at Fort Ruger, Hawaii. Disbanded 14 June 1944.

Reconstituted 28 June 1950 in the Regular Army; concurrently consolidated with Battery A, 50th Field Artillery Battalion (*see* ANNEX), and consolidated unit designated as Battery A, 50th Field Artillery Battalion, an element of the 5th Infantry Division. Activated 1 March 1951 at Indiantown Gap Military Reservation, Pennsylvania. Inactivated 1 September 1953 at Indiantown Gap Military Reservation, Pennsylvania. Activated 25 March 1954 in Germany. Inactivated 1 June 1957 at Fort Ord, California, and relieved from assignment to the 5th Infantry Division.

Redesignated 12 August 1958 as Headquarters and Headquarters Battery, 1st Missile Battalion, 55th Artillery (organic elements concurrently constituted). Battalion activated 1 September 1958 at Fort Totten, New York. Inactivated 26 July 1960 at Fort Totten, New York. Redesignated 1 September 1971 as the 1st Missile Battalion, 55th Air Defense Artillery. Redesignated 21 December 1975 as the 1st Battalion, 55th Air Defense Artillery, assigned to the 5th Infantry Division, and activated at Fort Bliss, Texas.

ANNEX

Constituted 1 October 1933 in the Regular Army as Battery A, 50th Field Artillery. Redesignated 1 October 1940 as Battery A, 50th Field Artillery Battalion, and activated at Fort Sheridan, Illinois, as an element of the 5th Division (later redesignated as the 5th Infantry Division). Inactivated 20 September 1946 at Camp Campbell, Kentucky. Activated 15 July 1947 at Fort Jackson, South Carolina. Inactivated 30 April 1950 at Fort Jackson, South Carolina.

CAMPAIGN PARTICIPATION CREDIT

World War I
*Aisne-Marne
*Oise-Aisne
*Meuse-Argonne
*Champagne 1918

World War II
*Normandy
*Northern France
*Rhineland
*Ardennes-Alsace
*Central Europe
*Central Pacific
New Guinea
Luzon

DECORATIONS

Presidential Unit Citation (Army), Streamer embroidered ARDENNES

2d BATTALION, 55th AIR DEFENSE ARTILLERY

RA
(nondivisional)

LINEAGE

Constituted 6 June 1901 in the Regular Army as the 96th Company, Coast Artillery, Artillery Corps. Organized 13 June 1901 at Fort Warren, Massachusetts. Redesignated 2 February 1907 as the 96th Company, Coast Artillery Corps. Redesignated 30 June 1916 as the 1st Company, Fort Revere [Massachusetts]. Redesignated 31 August 1917 as the 1st Company, Coast Defenses of Boston.

Reorganized and redesignated 1 December 1917 as Battery A, 55th Artillery (Coast Artillery Corps). (Additionally designated 30 June 1922 as the 96th Company, Coast Artillery Corps; additional designation abolished 20 February 1924.) Redesignated 20 February 1924 as Battery A, 55th Coast Artillery. Inactivated 31 May 1944 at Fort Ruger, Hawaii. Disbanded 14 June 1944.

Reconstituted 28 June 1950 in the Regular Army; concurrently consolidated with Battery A, 55th Field Artillery Battalion (*see* ANNEX), and consolidated unit designated as Battery A, 55th Field Artillery Battalion. Activated 19 January 1952 at Camp McCoy, Wisconsin. Inactivated 25 June 1958 in Germany.

Redesignated 12 August 1958 as Headquarters and Headquarters Battery, 2d Missile Battalion, 55th Artillery (organic elements concurrently constituted). Battalion activated 1 September 1958 at Manchester, Connecticut. Inactivated 24 December 1964 at New Britain, Connecticut. Redesignated 1 September 1971 as the 2d Missile Battalion, 55th Air Defense Artillery. Redesignated 13 September 1972 as the 2d Battalion, 55th Air Defense Artillery, and activated at Fort Bliss, Texas.

ANNEX

Constituted 16 December 1940 in the Regular Army as Battery A, 55th Field Artillery Battalion. Activated 18 June 1943 at Fort Bragg, North Carolina. Inactivated 15 April 1946 at Manila, Philippine Islands.

CAMPAIGN PARTICIPATION CREDIT

World War I	*World War II*
*Aisne-Marne	Normandy
*Oise-Aisne	Northern France
*Meuse-Argonne	Rhineland
*Champagne 1918	Ardennes-Alsace
	Central Europe
	*Central Pacific
	*New Guinea
	*Luzon

DECORATIONS

Presidential Unit Citation (Army), Streamer embroidered ARDENNES
*Philippine Presidential Unit Citation, Streamer embroidered 17 OCTOBER 1944 TO 4 JULY 1945 (55th Field Artillery Battalion cited; DA GO 47, 1950)

3d MISSILE BATTALION, 55th AIR DEFENSE ARTILLERY

RA
(inactive)

LINEAGE

Organized in February 1919 in the Regular Army at Fort Winfield Scott, California, as Battery B, 55th Artillery (Coast Artillery Corps). (Additionally designated 30 June 1922 as the 239th Company, Coast Artillery Corps; additional designation abolished 20 February 1924.) Redesignated 20 February 1924 as Battery B, 55th Coast Artillery. Inactivated 31 May 1944 at Fort Ruger, Hawaii. Disbanded 14 June 1944.

Reconstituted 28 June 1950 in the Regular Army; concurrently consolidated with Battery B, 55th Field Artillery Battalion (*see* ANNEX), and consolidated unit designated as Battery B, 55th Field Artillery Battalion. Activated 19 January 1952 at Camp McCoy, Wisconsin. Inactivated 25 June 1958 in Germany.

Redesignated 12 August 1958 as Headquarters and Headquarters Battery, 3d Missile Battalion, 55th Artillery (organic elements concurrently constituted). Battalion activated 1 September 1958 at Fort Wayne, Michigan. Inactivated 23 December 1960 at Kercheval, Michigan. Redesignated 1 September 1971 as the 3d Missile Battalion, 55th Air Defense Artillery.

ANNEX

Constituted 16 December 1940 in the Regular Army as Battery B, 55th Field Artillery Battalion. Activated 18 June 1943 at Fort Bragg, North Carolina. Inactivated 15 April 1946 at Manila, Philippine Islands.

CAMPAIGN PARTICIPATION CREDIT

World War I
  Aisne-Marne
  Oise-Aisne
  Meuse-Argonne
  Champagne 1918

World War II
  Normandy

Northern France
Rhineland
Ardennes-Alsace
Central Europe
*Central Pacific
*New Guinea
*Luzon

DECORATIONS

Presidential Unit Citation (Army), Streamer embroidered ARDENNES
  *Philippine Presidential Unit Citation, Streamer embroidered 17 OCTOBER 1944 TO 4 JULY 1945 (55th Field Artillery Battalion cited; DA GO 47, 1950)

4th MISSILE BATTALION, 55th AIR DEFENSE ARTILLERY

RA
(inactive)

LINEAGE

Organized in February 1919 in the Regular Army at Fort Winfield Scott, California, as Battery D, 55th Artillery (Coast Artillery Corps). (Additionally designated 30 June 1922 as the 240th Company, Coast Artillery Corps; additional designation abolished 20 February 1924.) Redesignated 20 February 1924 as Battery D, 55th Coast Artillery. Inactivated 31 May 1944 at Fort Ruger, Hawaii. Disbanded 14 June 1944.

Reconstituted 28 June 1950 in the Regular Army; concurrently consolidated with Battery B, 50th Field Artillery Battalion (*see* ANNEX), and consolidated unit designated as Battery B, 50th Field Artillery Battalion, an element of the 5th Infantry Division. Activated 1 March 1951 at Indiantown Gap Military Reservation, Pennsylvania. Inactivated 1 September 1953 in Indiantown Gap Military Reservation, Pennsylvania. Activated 25 March 1954 in Germany. Inactivated 1 June 1957 at Fort Ord, California, and relieved from assignment to the 5th Infantry Division.

Redesignated 12 August 1958 as Headquarters and Headquarters Battery, 4th Missile Battalion, 55th Artillery (organic elements concurrently constituted). Battalion activated 1 September 1958 in Greenland. Inactivated 20 December 1960 at Fort Totten, New York. Redesignated 1 September 1971 as the 4th Missile Battalion, 55th Air Defense Artillery.

ANNEX

Constituted 1 October 1933 in the Regular Army as Battery B, 50th Field Artillery. Redesignated 1 October 1940 as Battery B, 50th Field Artillery Battalion, and activated at Fort Sheridan, Illinois, as an element of the 5th Division (later redesignated as the 5th Infantry Division). Inactivated 20 September 1946 at Camp Campbell, Kentucky. Activated 15 July 1947 at Fort Jackson, South Carolina. Inactivated 30 April 1950 at Fort Jackson, South Carolina.

CAMPAIGN PARTICIPATION CREDIT

World War I
Aisne-Marne
Oise-Aisne
Meuse-Argonne
Champagne 1918

World War II
*Normandy
*Northern France

*Rhineland
*Ardennes-Alsace
*Central Europe
*Central Pacific
New Guinea
Luzon

DECORATIONS

Presidential Unit Citation (Army), Streamer embroidered ARDENNES

5th BATTALION, 55th AIR DEFENSE ARTILLERY

RA
(inactive)

LINEAGE

Organized in February 1919 in the Regular Army at Fort Winfield Scott, California, as Battery E, 55th Artillery (Coast Artillery Corps). (Additionally designated 30 June 1922 as the 241st Company, Coast Artillery Corps; additional designation abolished 20 February 1924.) Redesignated 20 February 1924 as Battery E, 55th Coast Artillery. Inactivated 31 May 1944 at Fort Ruger, Hawaii. Disbanded 14 June 1944.

Reconstituted 28 June 1950 in the Regular Army; concurrently consolidated with Battery A, 66th Armored Field Artillery Battalion (*see* ANNEX), and consolidated unit designated as Battery A, 66th Armored Field Artillery Battalion. (66th Armored Field Artillery Battalion assigned 25 February 1953 to the 4th Armored Division.) Activated 15 June 1954 at Fort Hood, Texas. Inactivated 1 April 1957 at Fort Hood, Texas, and relieved from assignment to the 4th Armored Division.

Redesignated 1 May 1959 as Headquarters and Headquarters Battery, 5th Missile Battalion, 55th Artillery (organic elements concurrently constituted). Battalion activated 1 June 1959 at Kansas City, Missouri. Redesignated 20 December 1965 as the 5th Battalion, 55th Artillery. Inactivated 10 February 1969 at Olathe Naval Air Station, Kansas. Redesignated 1 September 1971 as the 5th Battalion, 55th Air Defense Artillery.

ANNEX

Constituted 16 December 1940 in the Regular Army as Battery A, 66th Field Artillery, an element of the 4th Armored Division. Activated 15 April 1941 at Pine Camp, New York.

Reorganized and redesignated 1 January 1942 as Battery A, 66th Armored Field Artillery Battalion. Converted and redesignated 1 May 1946 as Troop A, 66th Constabulary Squadron, an element of the 2d Constabulary Regiment. Inactivated 20 December 1948 in Germany and relieved from assignment to the 2d Constabulary Regiment; concurrently converted and redesignated as Battery A, 66th Armored Field Artillery Battalion.

CAMPAIGN PARTICIPATION CREDIT

World War I
  Aisne-Marne
  Oise-Aisne
  Meuse-Argonne
  Champagne 1918

World War II
  *Normandy

*Northern France
*Rhineland
*Ardennes-Alsace
*Central Europe
*Central Pacific
  New Guinea
  Luzon

DECORATIONS

*Presidential Unit Citation (Army), Streamer embroidered ARDENNES (4th Armored Division cited; WD GO 54, 1945)

*French Croix de Guerre with Palm, World War II, Streamer embroidered NORMANDY (66th Armored Field Artillery Battalion cited; DA GO 43, 1950)

*French Croix de Guerre with Palm, World War II, Streamer embroidered MOSELLE RIVER (66th Armored Field Artillery Battalion cited; DA GO 43, 1950)

*French Croix de Guerre, World War II, Fourragere (66th Armored Field Artillery Battalion cited; DA GO 43, 1950)

BATTERY F, 55th AIR DEFENSE ARTILLERY

RA
(inactive)

LINEAGE

Organized in February 1919 in the Regular Army at Fort Winfield Scott, California, as Battery F, 55th Artillery (Coast Artillery Corps). (Additionally designated 30 June 1922 as the 242d Company, Coast Artillery Corps; additional designation abolished 20 February 1924.) Redesignated 20 February 1924 as Battery F, 55th Coast Artillery. Inactivated 31 May 1944 at Fort Ruger, Hawaii. Disbanded 14 June 1944.

Reconstituted 28 June 1950 in the Regular Army; concurrently consolidated with Battery B, 66th Armored Field Artillery Battalion (*see* ANNEX), and consolidated unit designated as Battery B, 66th Armored Field Artillery Battalion. (66th Armored Field Artillery Battalion assigned 25 February 1953 to the 4th Armored Division.) Activated 15 June 1954 at Fort Hood, Texas. Inactivated 1 April 1957 at Fort Hood, Texas, and relieved from assignment to the 4th Armored Division.

Redesignated 31 July 1959 as Headquarters and Headquarters Battery, 6th Battalion, 55th Artillery. Redesignated 5 April 1960 as Battery F, 55th Artillery. Activated 22 April 1960 at Fort Bliss, Texas. Inactivated 10 September 1960 at Fort Amador, Canal Zone. Redesignated 1 September 1971 as Battery F, 55th Air Defense Artillery.

ANNEX

Constituted 16 December 1940 in the Regular Army as Battery B, 66th Field Artillery, an element of the 4th Armored Division. Activated 15 April 1941 at Pine Camp, New York.

Reorganized and redesignated 1 January 1942 as Battery B, 66th Armored Field Artillery Battalion. Converted and redesignated 1 May 1946 as Troop B, 66th Constabulary Squadron, an element of the 2d Constabulary Regiment. Inactivated 20 December 1948 in Germany and relieved from assignment to the 2d Constabulary Regiment; concurrently converted and redesignated as Battery B, 66th Armored Field Artillery Battalion.

CAMPAIGN PARTICIPATION CREDIT

World War II–EAME
    Normandy
    Northern France
    Rhineland
    Ardennes-Alsace
    Central Europe

World War II–AP
    Central Pacific

DECORATIONS

Presidential Unit Citation (Army), Streamer embroidered ARDENNES (4th Armored Division cited; WD GO 54, 1945)

French Croix de Guerre with Palm, World War II, Streamer embroidered NORMANDY (66th Armored Field Artillery Battalion cited; DA GO 43, 1950)

French Croix de Guerre with Palm, World War II, Streamer embroidered MOSELLE RIVER (66th Armored Field Artillery Battalion cited; DA GO 43, 1950)

French Croix de Guerre, World War II, Fourragere (66th Armored Field Artillery cited; DA GO 43, 1950)

BATTERY G, 55th AIR DEFENSE ARTILLERY

RA
(inactive)

LINEAGE

Organized 7 January 1922 in the Regular Army at Fort Kamehameha, Hawaii, as Battery G, 55th Artillery (Coast Artillery Corps). (Additionally designated 30 June 1922 as the 243d Company, Coast Artillery Corps; additional designation abolished 20 February 1924.) Redesignated 20 February 1924 as Battery G, 55th Coast Artillery. Inactivated 31 October 1925 at Fort Kamehameha, Hawaii. Activated 22 May 1943 at Fort Ruger, Hawaii. Inactivated 31 May 1944 at Fort Ruger, Hawaii. Disbanded 14 June 1944. Reconstituted 28 June 1950 in the Regular Army.

Consolidated 31 July 1959 with Battery C, 55th Field Artillery Battalion (*see* ANNEX), and consolidated unit redesignated as Headquarters and Headquarters Battery, 7th Battalion, 55th Artillery. Redesignated 17 May 1966 as Battery G, 55th Artillery. Activated 14 October 1966 at Fort Bliss, Texas. Inactivated 20 January 1967 at Fort Bliss, Texas. Activated 1 August 1967 at Fort Bliss, Texas. Inactivated 31 July 1971 in Vietnam. Redesignated 1 September 1971 as Battery G, 55th Air Defense Artillery.

ANNEX

Constituted 16 December 1940 in the Regular Army as Battery C, 55th Field Artillery Battalion. Activated 3 January 1941 at Fort Myer, Virginia. Inactivated 15 April 1946 at Manila, Philippine Islands.

CAMPAIGN PARTICIPATION CREDIT

World War II–AP
  Central Pacific
  New Guinea
  Luzon

Vietnam
  Tet Counteroffensive
  Counteroffensive, Phase IV
  Counteroffensive, Phase V

Counteroffensive, Phase VI
Tet 69/Counteroffensive
Summer–fall 1969
Winter–spring 1970
Sanctuary Counteroffensive
Counteroffensive, Phase VII
Consolidation I

DECORATIONS

Philippine Presidential Unit Citation, Streamer embroidered 17 OCTOBER 1944 TO 4 JULY 1945 (55th Field Artillery Battalion cited; DA GO 47, 1950)

Republic of Vietnam Cross of Gallantry with Palm, Streamer embroidered VIETNAM 1969–1970 (Battery G, 55th Artillery, cited; DA GO 42, 1972)

Republic of Vietnam Cross of Gallantry with Palm, Streamer embroidered VIETNAM 1971 (Battery G, 55th Artillery, cited; DA GO 6, 1974)

12th PLATOON, 55th AIR DEFENSE ARTILLERY

RA
(inactive)

LINEAGE

Constituted 16 December 1940 in the Regular Army as Headquarters and Headquarters Battery, 66th Field Artillery, an element of the 4th Armored Division. Activated 15 April 1941 at Pine Camp, New York.

Reorganized and redesignated 1 January 1942 as Headquarters and Headquarters Battery, 66th Armored Field Artillery Battalion. Converted and redesignated 1 May 1946 as Headquarters and Headquarters Troop, 66th Constabulary Squadron, an element of the 2d Constabulary Regiment. Inactivated 20 December 1948 in Germany and relieved from assignment to the 2d Constabulary Regiment; concurrently converted and redesignated as Headquarters and Headquarters Battery, 66th Armored Field Artillery Battalion. (66th Armored Field Artillery Battalion assigned 25 February 1953 to the 4th Armored Division.) Activated 15 June 1954 at Fort Hood, Texas. Inactivated 1 April 1957 at Fort Hood, Texas, and relieved from assignment to the 4th Armored Division.

Redesignated 6 June 1958 as the 12th Platoon, 55th Artillery. Activated 20 June 1958 at Fort Benning, Georgia. Inactivated 23 September 1960 at Fort Benning, Georgia. Redesignated 1 September 1971 as the 12th Platoon, 55th Air Defense Artillery.

CAMPAIGN PARTICIPATION CREDIT

World War II–EAME
   Normandy
   Northern France

Rhineland
Ardennes-Alsace
Central Europe

DECORATIONS

Presidential Unit Citation (Army), Streamer embroidered ARDENNES (4th Armored Division cited; WD GO 54, 1945)

French Croix de Guerre with Palm, World War II, Streamer embroidered NORMANDY (66th Armored Field Artillery Battalion cited; DA GO 43, 1950)

French Croix de Guerre with Palm, World War II, Streamer embroidered MOSELLE RIVER (66th Armored Field Artillery Battalion cited; DA GO 43, 1950)

French Croix de Guerre, World War II, Fourragere (66th Armored Field Artillery Battalion cited; DA GO 43, 1950)

16th DETACHMENT, 55th AIR DEFENSE ARTILLERY

RA
(inactive)

LINEAGE

Constituted 5 August 1958 in the Regular Army as the 16th Detachment, 55th Artillery. Activated 1 September 1958 at Fort Stewart, Georgia. Inactivated 12 November 1963 at Fort Stewart, Georgia. Redesignated 1 September 1971 as the 16th Detachment, 55th Air Defense Artillery.

CAMPAIGN PARTICIPATION CREDIT

None.

DECORATIONS

None.

55TH AIR DEFENSE ARTILLERY BIBLIOGRAPHY

Crowl, Philip A. *Campaign in the Marianas.* United States Army in World War II. Washington: Government Printing Office, 1960. Contains a reference to the 55th Coast Artillery.

Cutler, Frederick Morse. *The 55th Artillery (C.A.C.) in the American Expeditionary Forces. France, 1918.* Worcester, Mass.: Commonwealth Press, 1920.

————. *The Old First Massachusetts Coast Artillery in War and Peace.* Boston: Pilgrim Press, 1917. Pertains to the Massachusetts National Guard companies that were in the 55th Artillery (CAC) during World War I.

Davis, Harold S. "Artillery in Defense Along the Moselle." *Field Artillery Journal* 35 (October 1945):620–23. Pertains to the 66th Armored Field Artillery Battalion.

Division Artillery, 5th Division. Philadelphia: Dorville Corporation, 1956. Contains information about the 50th Field Artillery Battalion.

Historical and Pictorial Review, 5th Infantry Division, United States Army, Fort Custer, Michigan, 1941. Baton Rouge: Army and Navy Publishing Company, 1941. Contains information about the 50th Field Artillery Battalion.

Letes, Leroy. "Long Range Firings in Hawaii." *Coast Artillery Journal* 75 (1932):405–12.

56th AIR DEFENSE ARTILLERY

HERALDIC ITEMS

COAT OF ARMS

Shield: Gules, four searchlight beams radiant from middle base or; on a chief sable a winged projectile of the second.

Crest: On a wreath of the colors, or and gules, on a mound vert a hurst of five trees proper, the holes interlaced with an arrow fesswise or and issuant in base a trident of the first surmounting and interlacing a torii sable.

Motto: Night Hides Not.

Symbolism: The shield is red for artillery. The searchlight beams and winged projectile denote the character of the 506th Coast Artillery, while the winged projectile on the black chief alludes to the motto, "Night Hides Not," signifying that the night does not hide the enemy from the regiment's artillery fire.

The hurst of trees and the arrow commemorate action in World War II at Hurtgen Forest by an element of the regiment for which the Distinguished Unit Citation (now Presidential Unit Citation) (Army) was awarded. The trident and torii allude to the Presidential Unit Citation (Navy), awarded to an element of the regiment for action at Inchon during the Korean War.

DISTINCTIVE INSIGNIA

The distinctive insignia is the shield and motto of the coat of arms.

LINEAGE AND HONORS

LINEAGE

Constituted 29 July 1921 in the Organized Reserves as the 506th Artillery (Antiaircraft). Organized in August 1922 with Headquarters at LaCrosse, Wisconsin. Redesignated 20 February 1924 as the 506th Coast Artillery. Inactivated 1 October 1933; concurrently withdrawn from the Organized Reserves and allotted to the Regular Army. Redesignated 16 December 1940 as the 56th Coast Artillery. Activated 2 June 1941 at Fort Cronkhite, California. Regiment broken up 22 January–11 February 1944 and its elements reorganized and redesignated as follows: Headquarters and Headquarters Battery disbanded 11 February 1944 at Camp Cooke, California; 1st Battalion (less Battery A) on 22 January 1944 as the 44th Coast Artillery Battalion; Battery A on 22 January 1944 as the

722d Coast Artillery Battery; 2d Battalion on 22 January 1944 as the 45th Coast Artillery Battalion; 3d Battalion on 22 January 1944 as the 48th Coast Artillery Battalion.

Headquarters and Headquarters Battery, 56th Coast Artillery, reconstituted 28 June 1950 in the Regular Army and redesignated as Headquarters and Headquarters Battery, 56th Field Artillery Group. Activated 19 January 1952 at Camp Carson, Colorado. Redesignated 21 June 1958 as Headquarters and Headquarters Battery, 56th Artillery Group. Inactivated 18 September 1970 in Germany.

44th Coast Artillery Battalion inactivated 11 December 1945 on Iwo Jima. Consolidated 28 June 1950 with the 56th Field Artillery Battalion (*see* ANNEX 1), and consolidated unit designated as the 56th Field Artillery Battalion, an element of the 8th Infantry Division. Activated 17 August 1950 at Fort Jackson, South Carolina. Inactivated 1 August 1957 in Germany and relieved from assignment to the 8th Infantry Division.

722d Coast Artillery Battery disbanded 31 July 1944 at Adak, Alaska. Reconstituted 1 August 1957 in the Regular Army and consolidated with Battery A, 56th Field Artillery Battalion (see above).

45th Coast Artillery Battalion disbanded 2 December 1945 on Leyte, Philippine Islands. Reconstituted 28 June 1950 in the Regular Army; concurrently consolidated with the 45th Field Artillery Battalion (*see* ANNEX 2), and consolidated unit designated as the 45th Field Artillery Battalion, an element of the 8th Infantry Division. Activated 1 August 1950 at Fort Jackson, South Carolina. Inactivated 1 August 1957 in Germany and relieved from assignment to the 8th Infantry Division.

48th Coast Artillery Battalion inactivated 2 November 1945 in Hawaii. Consolidated 28 June 1950 with the 48th Field Artillery Battalion (active) (*see* ANNEX 3), and consolidated unit designated as the 48th Field Artillery Battalion, an element of the 7th Infantry Division. Inactivated 1 July 1957 in Korea and relieved from assignment to the 7th Infantry Division.

Headquarters and Headquarters Battery, 56th Artillery Group, and 56th, 45th, and 48th Field Artillery Battalions consolidated, reorganized, and redesignated 18 September 1970 as the 56th Artillery, a parent regiment under the Combat Arms Regimental System. Redesignated 1 September 1971 as the 56th Air Defense Artillery.

ANNEX 1

Constituted 13 January 1941 in the Regular Army as the 56th Field Artillery Battalion. Assigned 1 June 1941 to the 8th Division (later redesignated as the 8th Infantry Division) and activated at Fort Jackson, South Carolina. Inactivated 20 October 1945 at Fort Leonard Wood, Missouri.

ANNEX 2

Constituted 1 October 1933 in the Regular Army as the 45th Field Artillery. Redesignated 13 January 1941 as the 45th Field Artillery Battalion. Assigned 1 June 1941 to the 8th Division (later redesignated as the

8th Infantry Division) and activated at Fort Jackson, South Carolina. Inactivated 20 October 1945 at Fort Leonard Wood, Missouri.

ANNEX 3

Constituted 1 October 1933 in the Regular Army as the 48th Field Artillery. Redesignated 13 January 1941 as the 48th Field Artillery Battalion. Assigned 1 June 1941 to the 7th Division (later redesignated as the 7th Infantry Division) and activated at Fort Ord, California.

CAMPAIGN PARTICIPATION CREDIT

World War II
  Normandy
  Northern France
  Rhineland
  Central Europe
  Air offensive, Japan
  Aleutian Islands (with arrowhead)
  Eastern Mandates
  Western Pacific
  Leyte
  Ryukyus (with arrowhead)

Korean War
  UN defensive
  UN offensive
  CCF intervention
  First UN counteroffensive
  CCF spring offensive

UN summer–fall offensive
Second Korean winter
Korea, summer–fall 1952
Third Korean winter
Korea, summer 1953

Vietnam
  Defense
  Counteroffensive
  Counteroffensive, Phase II
  Counteroffensive, Phase III
  Tet Counteroffensive
  Counteroffensive, Phase IV
  Counteroffensive, Phase V
  Counteroffensive, Phase VI
  Tet 69/Counteroffensive
  Summer–fall 1969

DECORATIONS

Presidential Unit Citation (Army), Streamer embroidered HURTGEN FOREST (56th Field Artillery Battalion cited; WD GO 21, 1947)

Presidential Unit Citation (Navy), Streamer embroidered INCHON (32d Regimental Combat Team cited; DA GO 63, 1952)

Meritorious Unit Commendation, Streamer embroidered VIETNAM 1965–1966 (6th Battalion, 56th Artillery, cited; DA GO 17, 1968)

1st BATTALION, 56th AIR DEFENSE ARTILLERY

RA
(inactive)

LINEAGE

Constituted 29 July 1921 in the Organized Reserves as Battery A, 506th Artillery (Antiaircraft). Organized in August 1922 in Wisconsin. Redesignated 20 February 1924 as Battery A, 506th Coast Artillery. Inactivated 1 October 1933; concurrently withdrawn from the Organized Reserves and allotted to the Regular Army. Redesignated 16 December 1940 as Battery A, 56th Coast Artillery. Activated 2 June 1941 at Fort Cronkhite, California.

Reorganized and redesignated 22 January 1944 as the 722d Coast Artillery Battery. Disbanded 31 July 1944 at Adak, Alaska. Reconstituted 1 August 1957 in the Regular Army; concurrently consolidated with Battery A, 56th Field Artillery Battalion (*see* ANNEX), and consolidated unit designated as Battery A, 56th Field Artillery Battalion.

Redesignated 12 August 1958 as Headquarters and Headquarters Battery, 1st Missile Battalion, 56th Artillery (organic elements concurrently constituted). Battalion activated 1 September 1958 at Pasadena, California. Redesignated 20 December 1965 as the 1st Battalion, 56th Artillery. Inactivated 12 December 1968 at Saugus, California. Redesignated 1 September 1971 as the 1st Battalion, 56th Air Defense Artillery.

ANNEX

Constituted 13 January 1941 in the Regular Army as Battery A, 56th Field Artillery Battalion. Activated 1 June 1941 at Fort Jackson, South Carolina, as an element of the 8th Division (later redesignated as the 8th Infantry Division). Inactivated 20 October 1945 at Fort Leonard Wood, Missouri. Activated 17 August 1950 at Fort Jackson, South Carolina. Inactivated 1 August 1957 in Germany and relieved from assignment to the 8th Infantry Division.

CAMPAIGN PARTICIPATION CREDIT

World War II	*Korean War*
*Normandy	UN defensive
*Northern France	UN offensive
*Rhineland	CCF intervention
*Central Europe	First UN counteroffensive
Air offensive, Japan	CCF spring offensive
*Aleutian Islands	UN summer–fall offensive
Eastern Mandates	Second Korean winter
Western Pacific	Korea, summer–fall 1952
Leyte	Third Korean winter
Ryukyus (with arrowhead)	Korea, summer 1953

DECORATIONS

*Presidential Unit Citation (Army), Streamer embroidered HURTGEN FOREST (56th Field Artillery Battalion cited; WD GO 21, 1947)

Presidential Unit Citation (Navy), Streamer embroidered INCHON
*Luxembourg Croix de Guerre, Streamer embroidered LUXEMBOURG
(8th Infantry Division cited; DA GO 59, 1969)

2d BATTALION, 56th AIR DEFENSE ARTILLERY

RA
(nondivisional)

LINEAGE

Constituted 29 July 1921 in the Organized Reserves as Battery B, 506th Artillery (Antiaircraft). Organized in August 1922 in Wisconsin. Redesignated 20 February 1924 as Battery B, 506th Coast Artillery. Inactivated 1 October 1933; concurrently withdrawn from the Organized Reserves and allotted to the Regular Army. Redesignated 16 December 1940 as Battery B, 56th Coast Artillery. Activated 2 June 1941 at Fort Cronkhite, California.

Reorganized and redesignated 22 January 1944 as Battery B, 44th Coast Artillery Battalion. Inactivated 11 December 1945 on Iwo Jima. Consolidated 28 June 1950 with Battery B, 56th Field Artillery Battalion (see ANNEX), and consolidated unit designated as Battery B, 56th Field Artillery Battalion, an element of the 8th Infantry Division. Activated 17 August 1950 at Fort Jackson, California. Inactivated 1 August 1957 in Germany and relieved from assignment to the 8th Infantry Division.

Redesignated 12 August 1958 as Headquarters and Headquarters Battery, 2d Missile Battalion, 56th Artillery (organic elements concurrently constituted). Battalion activated 1 September 1958 in Germany. Redesignated 20 December 1965 as the 2d Battalion, 56th Artillery. Redesignated 1 September 1971 as the 2d Battalion, 56th Air Defense Artillery.

ANNEX

Constituted 13 January 1941 in the Regular Army as Battery B, 56th Field Artillery Battalion. Activated 1 June 1941 at Fort Jackson, South Carolina, as an element of the 8th Division (later redesignated as the 8th Infantry Division). Inactivated 20 October 1945 at Fort Leonard Wood, Missouri.

CAMPAIGN PARTICIPATION CREDIT

World War II	Korean War
*Normandy	UN defensive
*Northern France	UN offensive
*Rhineland	CCF intervention
*Central Europe	First UN counteroffensive
*Air offensive, Japan	CCF spring offensive
Aleutian Islands (with arrowhead)	UN summer–fall offensive
Eastern Mandates	Second Korean winter
*Western Pacific	Korea, summer–fall 1952
Leyte	Third Korean winter
Ryukyus (with arrowhead)	Korea, summer 1953

DECORATIONS

*Presidential Unit Citation (Army), Streamer embroidered HURTGEN FOREST (56th Field Artillery Battalion cited; WD GO 21, 1947)

Presidential Unit Citation (Navy), Streamer embroidered INCHON
*Luxembourg Croix de Guerre, Streamer embroidered LUXEMBOURG
(8th Infantry Division cited; DA GO 59, 1969)

BATTERY C, 56th AIR DEFENSE ARTILLERY

RA
(inactive)

LINEAGE

Constituted 29 July 1921 in the Organized Reserves as Battery C, 506th Artillery (Antiaircraft). Organized in August 1922 in Wisconsin. Redesignated 20 February 1924 as Battery C, 506th Coast Artillery. Inactivated 1 October 1933; concurrently withdrawn from the Organized Reserves and allotted to the Regular Army. Redesignated 16 December 1940 as Battery C, 56th Coast Artillery. Activated 2 June 1941 at Fort Cronkhite, California.

Reorganized and redesignated 22 January 1944 as Battery A, 45th Coast Artillery Battalion. Disbanded 2 January 1945 on Leyte, Philippine Islands. Reconstituted 28 June 1950 in the Regular Army; concurrently consolidated with Battery A, 45th Field Artillery Battalion (see ANNEX), and consolidated unit designated as Battery A, 45th Field Artillery Battalion, an element of the 8th Infantry Division. Activated 17 August 1950 at Fort Jackson, South Carolina. Inactivated 1 August 1957 in Germany and relieved from assignment to the 8th Infantry Division.

Redesignated 12 August 1958 as Headquarters and Headquarters Battery, 3d Missile Battalion, 56th Artillery (organic elements concurrently constituted). Battalion activated 1 September 1958 at West Haven, Connecticut. Inactivated 1 September 1961 at West Haven, Connecticut. Redesignated 17 May 1966 as the 3d Battalion, 56th Artillery. Activated 1 August 1966 at Fort Bliss, Texas. Inactivated 20 January 1967 at Fort Bliss, Texas. Headquarters and Headquarters Battery, 3d Battalion, 56th Artillery, redesignated 30 June 1971 as Battery C, 56th Artillery, and activated at Fort Bliss, Texas. Redesignated 1 September 1971 as Battery C, 56th Air Defense Artillery. Inactivated 27 December 1971 at Fort Bliss, Texas.

ANNEX

Constituted 1 October 1933 in the Regular Army as Battery A, 45th Field Artillery Battalion. Redesignated 13 January 1941 as Battery A, 45th Field Artillery Battalion. Activated 1 June 1941 at Fort Jackson, South Carolina, as an element of the 8th Division (later redesignated as the 8th Infantry Division). Inactivated 20 October 1945 at Fort Leonard Wood, Missouri.

CAMPAIGN PARTICIPATION CREDIT

World War II–EAME
  Normandy
  Northern France
  Rhineland
  Central Europe

World War II–AP
  Western Pacific
  Leyte

Decorations

Luxembourg Croix de Guerre, Streamer embroidered LUXEMBOURG (8th Infantry Division cited; DA GO 59, 1969)

Philippine Presidential Unit Citation, Streamer embroidered 17 OCTOBER 1944 TO 4 JULY 1945 (45th Coast Artillery Battalion cited; DA GO 47, 1950)

4th BATTALION, 56th AIR DEFENSE ARTILLERY

RA
(inactive)

LINEAGE

Constituted 29 July 1921 in the Organized Reserves as Battery D, 506th Artillery (Antiaircraft). Organized in August 1922 in Wisconsin. Redesignated 20 February 1924 as Battery D, 506th Coast Artillery. Inactivated 1 October 1933; concurrently withdrawn from the Organized Reserves and allotted to the Regular Army. Redesignated 16 December 1940 as Battery D, 56th Coast Artillery. Activated 2 June 1941 at Fort Cronkhite, California.

Reorganized and redesignated 22 January 1944 as Battery B, 45th Coast Artillery Battalion. Disbanded 2 December 1945 on Leyte, Philippine Islands. Reconstituted 28 June 1950 in the Regular Army; concurrently consolidated with Battery B, 45th Field Artillery Battalion (see ANNEX), and consolidated unit designated as Battery B, 45th Field Artillery Battalion, an element of the 8th Infantry Division. Activated 17 August 1950 at Fort Jackson, South Carolina. Inactivated 1 August 1957 in Germany and relieved from assignment to the 8th Infantry Division.

Redesignated 12 August 1958 as Headquarters and Headquarters Battery, 4th Missile Battalion, 56th Artillery (organic elements concurrently constituted). Battalion activated 1 September 1958 at Bristol, Rhode Island. Inactivated 26 August 1963 at Rehoboth, Massachusetts. Redesignated 2 March 1967 as the 4th Battalion, 56th Artillery. Activated 20 May 1967 at Fort Bliss, Texas. Inactivated 31 March 1970 at Fort Bliss, Texas. Redesignated 1 September 1971 as the 4th Battalion, 56th Air Defense Artillery.

ANNEX

Constituted 1 October 1933 in the Regular Army as Battery B, 45th Field Artillery. Redesignated 13 January 1941 as Battery B, 45th Field Artillery Battalion. Activated 1 June 1941 at Fort Jackson, South Carolina, as an element of the 8th Division (later redesignated as the 8th Infantry Division). Inactivated 20 October 1945 at Fort Leonard Wood, Missouri.

CAMPAIGN PARTICIPATION CREDIT

World War II	Korean War
*Normandy	UN defensive
*Northern France	UN offensive
*Rhineland	CCF intervention
*Central Europe	First UN counteroffensive
Air offensive, Japan	CCF spring offensive
Aleutian Islands (with arrowhead)	UN summer–fall offensive
Eastern Mandates	Second Korean winter
*Western Pacific	Korea, summer–fall 1952
*Leyte	Third Korean winter
Ryukyus (with arrowhead)	Korea, summer 1953

DECORATIONS

Presidential Unit Citation (Army), Streamer embroidered HURTGEN FOREST

Presidential Unit Citation (Navy), Streamer embroidered INCHON

*Luxembourg Croix de Guerre, Streamer embroidered LUXEMBOURG (8th Infantry Division cited; DA GO 59, 1969)

*Philippine Presidential Unit Citation, Streamer embroidered 17 OCTOBER 1944 TO 4 JULY 1945 (45th Coast Artillery Battalion cited; DA GO 47, 1950)

5th BATTALION, 56th AIR DEFENSE ARTILLERY

RA
(inactive)

LINEAGE

Constituted 29 July 1921 in the Organized Reserves as Battery E, 506th Artillery (Antiaircraft). Organized in August 1922 in Wisconsin. Redesignated 20 February 1924 as Battery E, 506th Coast Artillery. Inactivated 1 October 1933; concurrently withdrawn from the Organized Reserves and allotted to the Regular Army. Redesignated 16 December 1940 as Battery E, 56th Coast Artillery. Activated 2 June 1941 at Fort Cronkhite, California.

Reorganized and redesignated 22 January 1944 as Battery A, 48th Coast Artillery Battalion. Inactivated 2 November 1945 in Hawaii. Consolidated 28 June 1950 with Battery A, 48th Field Artillery Battalion (active) (*see* ANNEX), and consolidated unit designated as Battery A, 48th Field Artillery Battalion, an element of the 7th Infantry Division. Inactivated 1 July 1957 in Korea and relieved from assignment to the 7th Infantry Division.

Redesignated 1 May 1959 as Headquarters and Headquarters Battery, 5th Missile Battalion, 56th Artillery (organic elements concurrently constituted). Battalion activated 15 June 1959 at Cincinnati, Ohio. Redesignated 20 December 1965 as the 5th Battalion, 56th Artillery. Inactivated 31 March 1970 at Wilmington, Ohio. Redesignated 1 September 1971 as the 5th Battalion, 56th Air Defense Artillery.

ANNEX

Constituted 1 October 1933 in the Regular Army as Battery A, 48th Field Artillery. Redesignated 13 January 1941 as Battery A, 48th Field Artillery Battalion. Activated 1 June 1941 at Fort Ord, California, as an element of the 7th Division (later redesignated as the 7th Infantry Division).

CAMPAIGN PARTICIPATION CREDIT

World War II	*Korean War*
Normandy	*UN defensive
Northern France	*UN offensive
Rhineland	*CCF intervention
Central Europe	*First UN counteroffensive
Air offensive, Japan	*CCF spring offensive
*Aleutian Islands (with arrowhead)	*UN summer–fall offensive
*Eastern Mandates	*Second Korean winter
*Western Pacific	*Korea, summer–fall 1952
*Leyte	*Third Korean winter
*Ryukyus (with arrowhead)	*Korea, summer 1953

DECORATIONS

Presidential Unit Citation (Army), Streamer embroidered HURTGEN FOREST

*Presidential Unit Citation (Navy), Streamer embroidered INCHON (32d Regimental Combat Team cited; DA GO 63, 1952)

*Philippine Presidential Unit Citation, Streamer embroidered 17 OCTOBER 1944 TO 4 JULY 1945 (48th Field Artillery Battalion cited; DA GO 47, 1950)

*Republic of Korea Presidential Unit Citation, Streamer embroidered INCHON (48th Field Artillery Battalion cited; DA GO 35, 1951)

*Republic of Korea Presidential Unit Citation, Streamer embroidered KOREA 1950–1953 (48th Field Artillery Battalion cited; DA GO 22, 1956)

*Republic of Korea Presidential Unit Citation, Streamer embroidered KOREA 1945–1948, 1953–1957 (7th Infantry Division cited; DA GO 50, 1971)

6th BATTALION, 56th AIR DEFENSE ARTILLERY

RA
(nondivisional)

LINEAGE

Constituted 29 July 1921 in the Organized Reserves as Battery F, 506th Artillery (Antiaircraft). Organized in August 1922 in Wisconsin. Redesignated 20 February 1924 as Battery F, 506th Coast Artillery. Inactivated 1 October 1933; concurrently withdrawn from the Organized Reserves and allotted to the Regular Army. Redesignated 16 December 1940 as Battery F, 56th Coast Artillery. Activated 2 June 1941 at Fort Cronkhite, California.

Reorganized and redesignated 22 January 1944 as Battery B, 48th Coast Artillery Battalion. Inactivated 2 November 1945 in Hawaii. Consolidated 28 June 1950 with Battery B, 48th Field Artillery Battalion (active) (*see* ANNEX), and consolidated unit designated as Battery B, 48th Field Artillery Battalion, an element of the 7th Infantry Division. Inactivated 1 July 1957 in Korea and relieved from assignment to the 7th Infantry Division.

Redesignated 30 March 1962 as Headquarters and Headquarters Battery, 6th Missile Battalion, 56th Artillery (organic elements concurrently constituted). Battalion activated 25 July 1962 at Fort Bliss, Texas. Redesignated 14 June 1965 as the 6th Battalion, 56th Artillery. (Battery C inactivated 5 June 1969 in Vietnam.) Inactivated (less Battery C) 15 August 1969 at Fort Bliss, Texas. Redesignated 1 September 1971 as the 6th Battalion, 56th Air Defense Artillery. Activated 13 September 1972 in Germany.

ANNEX

Constituted 1 October 1933 in the Regular Army as Battery B, 48th Field Artillery. Redesignated 13 January 1941 as Battery B, 48th Field Artillery Battalion. Activated 1 June 1941 at Fort Ord, California, as an element of the 7th Division (later redesignated as the 7th Infantry Division).

Campaign Participation Credit

World War II
  Normandy
  Northern France
  Rhineland
  Central Europe
  Air offensive, Japan
  *Aleutian Islands (with arrowhead)
  *Eastern Mandates
  *Western Pacific
  *Leyte
  *Ryukyus (with arrowhead)

Korean War
  *UN defensive
  *UN offensive
  *CCF intervention
  *First UN counteroffensive
  *CCF spring offensive

*UN summer–fall offensive
*Second Korean winter
*Korea, summer–fall 1952
*Third Korean winter
*Korea, summer 1953

Vietnam
  *Defense
  *Counteroffensive
  *Counteroffensive, Phase II
  *Counteroffensive, Phase III
  *Tet Counteroffensive
  *Counteroffensive, Phase IV
  *Counteroffensive, Phase V
  *Counteroffensive, Phase VI
  *Tet 69/Counteroffensive
  *Summer–fall 1969

Decorations

Presidential Unit Citation (Army), Streamer embroidered HURTGEN FOREST

*Presidential Unit Citation (Navy), Streamer embroidered INCHON (32d Regimental Combat Team cited; DA GO 63, 1952)

*Meritorious Unit Commendation, Streamer embroidered VIETNAM 1965–1966 (6th Battalion, 56th Artillery, cited; DA GO 17, 1968)

*Philippine Presidential Unit Citation, Streamer embroidered 17 OCTOBER 1944 TO 4 JULY 1945 (48th Field Artillery Battalion cited; DA GO 47, 1950)

*Republic of Korea Presidential Unit Citation, Streamer embroidered INCHON (48th Field Artillery Battalion cited; DA GO 35, 1951)

*Republic of Korea Presidential Unit Citation, Streamer embroidered KOREA 1950–1953 (48th Field Artillery Battalion cited; DA GO 22, 1956)

*Republic of Korea Presidential Unit Citation, Streamer embroidered KOREA 1945–1948, 1953–1957 (7th Infantry Division cited; DA GO 50, 1971)

16th DETACHMENT, 56th AIR DEFENSE ARTILLERY

RA
(inactive)

LINEAGE

Constituted 5 August 1958 in the Regular Army as the 16th Detachment, 56th Artillery. Activated 1 September 1958 at Camp Wellfleet, Massachusetts. Inactivated 25 June 1961 at Camp Wellfleet, Massachusetts. Redesignated 1 September 1971 as the 16th Detachment, 56th Air Defense Artillery.

CAMPAIGN PARTICIPATION CREDIT
None.

DECORATIONS
None.

56TH AIR DEFENSE ARTILLERY BIBLIOGRAPHY

Appleman, Roy E. *South to the Naktong, North to the Yalu.* United States Army in the Korean War. Washington: Government Printing Office, 1961. Contains information about the 48th Field Artillery Battalion.

The Capture of Attu. Washington: Infantry Journal Press, 1944. Contains information about the 48th Field Artillery Battalion.

Conn, Stetson, and Byron Fairchild. *The Framework of Hemisphere Defense.* United States Army in World War II. Washington: Government Printing Office, 1960. Contains information about the 56th Coast Artillery.

Crowl, Philip A., and Edmund G. Love. *Seizure of the Gilberts and Marshalls.* United States Army in World War II. Washington: Government Printing Office, 1955. Contains information about the 48th Field Artillery Battalion.

The Dixie–Golden Arrow Yearbook, Fort Carson, Colorado, 1954. Marceline: Walsworth Brothers, 1954. Contains information about the 45th and 56th Field Artillery Battalions.

Eighth Infantry Division Artillery. Baton Rouge: Army and Navy Publishing Company, 1946. Contains information about the 45th and 56th Field Artillery Battalions.

Eighth Infantry Division, Fort Jackson, South Carolina. Baton Rouge: Army and Navy Publishing Company, 1953. Contains information about the 45th and 56th Field Artillery Battalions.

Falls, Bruce F., et al. *The Seventh Division in Korea.* Tokyo: FEC Printing Plant, 1948. Contains information about the 48th Field Artillery Battalion.

Jackson, Miles H., ed. *8th Infantry Golden Arrow Division, Fort Carson, Colorado, October 1955.* Dallas: Miller Publishing Company, 1955. Contains information about the 45th Field Artillery Battalion.

Marshall, S.L.A. *Pork Chop Hill.* New York: William Morrow, 1956. Contains information about the 48th Field Artillery Battalion.

Public Information Office, 7th Infantry Division. *The Bayonet, The History of the 7th Infantry Division in Korea.* Tokyo: Dai Nippon Printing Company, 1953. Contains information about the 48th Field Artillery Battalion.

7th Infantry Division in Korea. Atlanta: Albert Love Enterprises, 1954. Contains information about the 48th Field Artillery Battalion.

Waring, Paul C., ed. *History of the 7th Infantry (Bayonet) Division.* Tokyo: Dai Nippon Printing Company, 1967. Contains information about the 48th Field Artillery Battalion.

Wiese, Carl, ed. *8th Infantry Division, Gyroscope, 1956.* Dallas: Miller Publishing Company, 1956. Contains information about the 45th and 56th Field Artillery Battalions.

57th AIR DEFENSE ARTILLERY

HERALDIC ITEMS

COAT OF ARMS

Shield: Or, a lion rampant gules, armed and langued azure, in chief a bar gemel rompu sable engouled on dexter by the head of a boar couped at the ears and issuant from edge of shield, on sinister by the same of a lion, both of the last and armed of the second.

Crest: On a wreath of the colors, or and gules, a dragon's head erased argent, langued triparté and keeled vert, enfiled with a castle turret with broken chain all azure, the turret charged with a bezant.

Motto: *Veto* (I Forbid).

Symbolism: The outstanding feat of this regiment's service in France was the cutting of the railway line between Montmedy and Sedan, November 6, 1918, from positions near Stenay. This is shown by the shield. The arms of Montmedy bear a black lion, those of Sedan a black boar, those of Stenay a gold lion rampant. The two broken bars represent the broken railroad line between the black lion (Montmedy) and the black boar (Sedan); the position of the regiment at Stenay being shown by the rampant lion in red for artillery. The shield is gold, the same as the shield of Lorraine where this engagement took place.

In heraldry, one of the symbols for a staunch defender is the dragon. The three-pronged tongue represents the participation of elements of the regiment in World Wars I and II and the Korean War. It also alludes to the 3d Armored Division to which elements of the organization were assigned during World War II and the three German trains disabled by the 67th Armored Field Artillery Battalion at Braisne and Soissons during World War II. The castle turret and broken chain are used to symbolize Mons and the Falaise Pocket campaign where the resistance of the enemy was completely broken and the cities were liberated. The bezant refers to the Philippine sun and denotes the action of the 57th Field Artillery Battalion, 7th Infantry Division, in that area during World War II.

DISTINCTIVE INSIGNIA

The distinctive insignia is the shield and motto of the coat of arms.

Lineage and Honors

Lineage

Constituted 1 November 1917 in the Regular Army as the 57th Artillery (Coast Artillery Corps). Organized 11 January 1918 at Fort Hancock, New Jersey, from new and existing Regular Army and New York National Guard companies. (New York National Guard companies demobilized in January 1919 at Camp Merritt, New Jersey; regiment continued on active status.) Demobilized 30 June 1921 at Camp Lewis, Washington. Reconstituted 22 January 1926 in the Regular Army as the 57th Coast Artillery. (1st Battalion activated 1 June 1940 at Fort Monroe, Virginia.) Regiment (less 1st and 3d Battalions) activated 3 January 1941 at Fort Monroe, Virginia. (3d Battalion activated 15 June 1941 at Camp Pendleton, Virginia.) Inactivated 31 May 1944 in Hawaii. Disbanded 14 June 1944.

Headquarters and Headquarters Battery, 57th Coast Artillery, reconstituted 28 June 1950 in the Regular Army and redesignated as Headquarters and Headquarters Battery, 57th Field Artillery Group. Activated 21 January 1952 at Fort Lewis, Washington. Inactivated 10 October 1954 at Fort Lewis, Washington. Redesignated 14 February 1957 as Headquarters and Headquarters Battery, 57th Field Artillery Missile Group. Activated 1 March 1957 at Fort Hood, Texas. Redesignated 2 June 1958 as Headquarters and Headquarters Battery, 57th Artillery Group. Inactivated 19 February 1962 at Fort Carson, Colorado.

1st Battalion, 57th Coast Artillery, reconstituted 28 June 1950 in the Regular Army; concurrently consolidated with the 57th Field Artillery Battalion (active) (see ANNEX 1), and consolidated unit designated as the 57th Field Artillery Battalion, an element of the 7th Infantry Division. Inactivated 1 July 1957 in Korea and relieved from assignment to the 7th Infantry Division.

2d Battalion, 57th Coast Artillery, reconstituted 28 June 1950 in the Regular Army; concurrently consolidated with the 46th Field Artillery Battalion (see ANNEX 2), and consolidated unit designated as the 46th Field Artillery Battalion, an element of the 5th Infantry Division. Activated 1 March 1951 at Indiantown Gap Military Reservation, Pennsylvania. Inactivated 1 September 1953 at Indiantown Gap Military Reservation, Pennsylvania. Activated 25 May 1954 in Germany. Inactivated 1 June 1957 at Fort Ord, California, and relieved from assignment to the 5th Infantry Division.

3d Battalion, 57th Coast Artillery, reconstituted 28 June 1950 in the Regular Army; concurrently consolidated with the 67th Armored Field Artillery Battalion (active) (see ANNEX 3), and consolidated unit designated as the 67th Armored Field Artillery Battalion, an element of the 3d Armored Division. Inactivated 1 October 1957 in Germany and relieved from assignment to the 3d Armored Division.

Headquarters and Headquarters Battery, 57th Artillery Group; 57th and 46th Field Artillery Battalions; and 67th Armored Field Artillery Battalion consolidated, reorganized, and redesignated 19 February 1962 as the 57th Artillery, a parent regiment under the Combat Arms Regimental System. Redesignated 1 September 1971 as the 57th Air Defense Artillery.

ANNEX 1

Constituted 1 October 1933 in the Regular Army as the 57th Field Artillery. Redesignated 13 January 1941 as the 57th Field Artillery Battalion. Assigned 1 June 1941 to the 7th Division (later redesignated as the 7th Infantry Division) and activated at Fort Ord, California.

ANNEX 2

Constituted 1 October 1933 in the Regular Army as the 46th Field Artillery. Redesignated 1 October 1940 as the 46th Field Artillery Battalion, assigned to the 5th Division (later redesignated as the 5th Infantry Division), and activated at Fort Knox, Kentucky. Inactivated 20 September 1946 at Camp Campbell, Kentucky. Activated 15 July 1947 at Fort Jackson, South Carolina. Inactivated 30 April 1950 at Fort Jackson, South Carolina.

ANNEX 3

Constituted 1 October 1933 in the Regular Army as the 67th Field Artillery. Assigned 13 January 1941 to the 3d Armored Division. Activated 15 April 1941 at Camp Beauregard, Louisiana.

Reorganized and redesignated 1 January 1942 as the 67th Armored Field Artillery Battalion. Inactivated 10 November 1945 in Germany. Activated 15 July 1947 at Fort Knox, Kentucky.

CAMPAIGN PARTICIPATION CREDIT

World War I
   St. Mihiel
   Meuse-Argonne
   Lorraine 1918

World War II
   Normandy
   Northern France
   Rhineland
   Ardennes-Alsace
   Central Europe
   Aleutian Islands
   Eastern Mandates

   Leyte
   Ryukyus (with arrowhead)

Korean War
   UN defensive
   UN offensive
   CCF intervention
   First UN counteroffensive
   CCF spring offensive
   UN summer–fall offensive
   Second Korean winter
   Korea, summer–fall 1952
   Third Korean winter
   Korea, summer 1953

DECORATIONS

Presidential Unit Citation (Navy), Streamer embroidered CHOSIN RESERVOIR (Provisional Battalion cited; DA GO 86, 1953)

1st BATTALION, 57th AIR DEFENSE ARTILLERY

RA
(inactive)

LINEAGE

Constituted 1 November 1917 in the Regular Army as Battery A, 57th Artillery (Coast Artillery Corps). Organized 11 January 1918 at Fort Hancock, New Jersey. Demobilized 30 June 1921 at Camp Lewis, Washington. Reconstituted 22 January 1926 in the Regular Army and redesignated as Battery A, 57th Coast Artillery. Activated 1 June 1940 at Fort Monroe, Virginia. Inactivated 31 May 1944 in Hawaii. Disbanded 14 June 1944.

Reconstituted 28 June 1950 in the Regular Army; concurrently consolidated with Battery A, 57th Field Artillery Battalion (active) (*see* ANNEX), and consolidated unit designated as Battery A, 57th Field Artillery Battalion, an element of the 7th Infantry Division. Inactivated 1 July 1957 in Korea and relieved from assignment to the 7th Infantry Division.

Redesignated 12 August 1958 as Headquarters and Headquarters Battery, 1st Missile Battalion, 57th Artillery (organic elements concurrently constituted). Battalion activated 1 September 1958 at Boston, Massachusetts. Inactivated 25 June 1960 at Nahant, Massachusetts. Activated 24 March 1961 at Fort Sill, Oklahoma. Inactivated 1 December 1968 on Okinawa. Redesignated 16 August 1971 as the 1st Battalion, 57th Artillery, and activated at Fort Bliss, Texas. Redesignated 1 September 1971 as the 1st Battalion, 57th Air Defense Artillery. Inactivated 19 March 1973 at Fort Bliss, Texas.

ANNEX

Constituted 1 October 1933 in the Regular Army as Battery A, 57th Field Artillery. Redesignated 13 January 1941 as Battery A, 57th Field Artillery Battalion. Activated 1 June 1941 at Fort Ord, California, as an element of the 7th Division (later redesignated as the 7th Infantry Division).

CAMPAIGN PARTICIPATION CREDIT

World War I
  *St. Mihiel
  *Meuse-Argonne
  Lorraine 1918

World War II
  Normandy
  Northern France
  Rhineland
  Ardennes-Alsace
  Central Europe
  *Central Pacific
  *Aleutian Islands
  *Eastern Mandates

  *Leyte
  *Ryukyus (with arrowhead)

Korean War
  *UN defensive
  *UN offensive
  *CCF intervention
  *First UN counteroffensive
  *CCF spring offensive
  *UN summer–fall offensive
  *Second Korean winter
  *Korea, summer-fall 1952
  *Third Korean winter
  *Korea, summer 1953

DECORATIONS

*Presidential Unit Citation (Navy), Streamer embroidered CHOSIN RESERVOIR (Provisional Battalion cited; DA GO 86, 1953)

*Philippine Presidential Unit Citation, Streamer embroidered 17 OCTOBER 1944 TO 4 JULY 1945 (57th Field Artillery Battalion cited; DA GO 47, 1950)

*Republic of Korea Presidential Unit Citation, Streamer embroidered INCHON (57th Field Artillery Battalion cited; DA GO 35, 1951)

*Republic of Korea Presidential Unit Citation, Streamer embroidered KOREA 1950–1953 (57th Field Artillery Battalion cited; DA GO 22, 1956)

*Republic of Korea Presidential Unit Citation, Streamer embroidered KOREA 1945–1948, 1953–1957 (7th Infantry Division cited; DA GO 50, 1971)

2d BATTALION, 57th AIR DEFENSE ARTILLERY

RA
(nondivisional)

LINEAGE

Organized in February 1919 in the Regular Army at Fort Winfield Scott, California, as Battery B, 57th Artillery (Coast Artillery Corps). Demobilized 30 June 1921 at Camp Lewis, Washington. Reconstituted 22 January 1926 in the Regular Army and redesignated as Battery B, 57th Coast Artillery. Activated 1 June 1940 at Fort Monroe, Virginia. Inactivated 31 May 1944 in Hawaii. Disbanded 14 June 1944.

Reconstituted 28 June 1950 in the Regular Army; concurrently consolidated with Battery B, 57th Field Artillery Battalion (active) (*see* ANNEX), and consolidated unit designated as Battery B, 57th Field Artillery Battalion, an element of the 7th Infantry Division. Inactivated 1 July 1957 in Korea and relieved from assignment to the 7th Infantry Division.

Redesignated 12 August 1958 as Headquarters and Headquarters Battery, 2d Missile Battalion, 57th Artillery (organic elements concurrently constituted). Battalion activated 1 September 1958 at Chicago, Illinois. Inactivated 23 August 1963 at Chicago, Illinois. Redesignated 1 September 1971 as the 2d Missile Battalion, 57th Air Defense Artillery. Redesignated 13 September 1972 as the 2d Battalion, 57th Air Defense Artillery, and activated in Germany.

ANNEX

Constituted 1 October 1933 in the Regular Army as Battery B, 57th Field Artillery. Redesignated 13 January 1941 as Battery B, 57th Field Artillery Battalion. Activated 1 June 1941 at Fort Ord, California, as an element of the 7th Division (later redesignated as the 7th Infantry Division).

CAMPAIGN PARTICIPATION CREDIT

World War I
  St. Mihiel
  Meuse-Argonne
  Lorraine 1918

World War II
  Normandy
  Northern France
  Rhineland
  Ardennes-Alsace
  Central Europe
  *Aleutian Islands
  *Eastern Mandates

*Leyte
*Ryukyus (with arrowhead)

Korean War
  *UN defensive
  *UN offensive
  *CCF intervention
  *First UN counteroffensive
  *CCF spring offensive
  *UN summer–fall offensive
  *Second Korean winter
  *Korea, summer-fall 1952
  *Third Korean winter
  *Korea, summer 1953

DECORATIONS

*Presidential Unit Citation (Navy), Streamer embroidered CHOSIN RESERVOIR (Provisional Battalion cited; DA GO 86, 1953)

*Philippine Presidential Unit Citation, Streamer embroidered 17 OCTOBER 1944 TO 4 JULY 1945 (57th Field Artillery Battalion cited; DA GO 47, 1950)

*Republic of Korea Presidential Unit Citation, Streamer embroidered INCHON (57th Field Artillery Battalion cited; DA GO 35, 1951)

*Republic of Korea Presidential Unit Citation, Streamer embroidered KOREA 1950–1953 (57th Field Artillery Battalion cited; DA GO 22, 1956)

*Republic of Korea Presidential Unit Citation, Streamer embroidered KOREA 1945–1948, 1953–1957 (7th Infantry Division cited; DA GO 50, 1971)

3d MISSILE BATTALION, 57th AIR DEFENSE ARTILLERY

RA
(inactive)

LINEAGE

Constituted 22 January 1926 in the Regular Army as Battery C, 57th Coast Artillery. Activated 3 January 1941 at Fort Monroe, Virginia. Inactivated 31 May 1944 in Hawaii. Disbanded 14 June 1944.

Reconstituted 28 June 1950 in the Regular Army; concurrently consolidated with Battery A, 46th Field Artillery Battalion (*see* ANNEX), and consolidated unit designated as Battery A, 46th Field Artillery Battalion, an element of the 5th Infantry Division. Activated 1 March 1951 at Indiantown Gap Military Reservation, Pennsylvania. Inactivated 1 September 1953 at Indiantown Gap Military Reservation, Pennsylvania. Activated 25 May 1954 in Germany. Inactivated 1 June 1957 at Fort Ord, California, and relieved from assignment to the 5th Infantry Division.

Redesignated 12 August 1958 as Headquarters and Headquarters Battery, 3d Missile Battalion, 57th Artillery (organic elements concurrently constituted). Battalion activated 1 September 1958 at Los Angeles, California. Inactivated 23 April 1964 at Fort MacArthur, California. Redesignated 1 September 1971 as the 3d Missile Battalion, 57th Air Defense Artillery.

ANNEX

Constituted 1 October 1933 in the Regular Army as Battery A, 46th Field Artillery. Redesignated 1 October 1940 as Battery A, 46th Field Artillery Battalion, and activated at Fort Knox, Kentucky, as an element of the 5th Division (later redesignated as the 5th Infantry Division). Inactivated 20 September 1946 at Camp Campbell, Kentucky. Activated 15 July 1947 at Fort Jackson, South Carolina. Inactivated 30 April 1950 at Fort Jackson, South Carolina.

CAMPAIGN PARTICIPATION CREDIT

World War I
  St. Mihiel
  Meuse-Argonne
  Lorraine 1918

World War II
  *Normandy
  *Northern France
  *Rhineland
  *Ardennes-Alsace
  *Central Europe
  Aleutian Islands
  Eastern Mandates

Leyte
Ryukyus (with arrowhead)

Korean War
  UN defensive
  UN offensive
  CCF intervention
  First UN counteroffensive
  CCF spring offensive
  UN summer–fall offensive
  Second Korean winter
  Korea, summer–fall 1952
  Third Korean winter
  Korea, summer 1953

DECORATIONS

Presidential Unit Citation (Navy), Streamer embroidered CHOSIN RESERVOIR

4th BATTALION, 57th AIR DEFENSE ARTILLERY

RA
(inactive)

LINEAGE

Constituted 22 January 1926 in the Regular Army as Battery D, 57th Coast Artillery. Activated 3 January 1941 at Fort Monroe, Virginia. Inactivated 31 May 1944 in Hawaii. Disbanded 14 June 1944.

Reconstituted 28 June 1950 in the Regular Army; concurrently consolidated with Battery B, 46th Field Artillery Battalion (*see* ANNEX), and consolidated unit designated as Battery B, 46th Field Artillery Battalion, an element of the 5th Infantry Division. Activated 1 March 1951 at Indiantown Gap Military Reservation, Pennsylvania. Inactivated 1 September 1953 at Indiantown Gap Military Reservation, Pennsylvania. Activated 25 May 1954 in Germany. Inactivated 1 June 1957 at Fort Ord, California, and relieved from assignment to the 5th Infantry Division.

Redesignated 12 August 1958 as Headquarters and Headquarters Battery, 4th Gun Battalion, 57th Artillery (organic elements concurrently constituted). Battalion activated 1 September 1958 in Germany. Reorganized and redesignated 25 November 1960 as the 4th Missile Battalion, 57th Artillery. Redesignated 20 August 1965 as the 4th Battalion, 57th Artillery. Redesignated 1 September 1971 as the 4th Battalion, 57th Air Defense Artillery. Inactivated 13 September 1972 in Germany.

ANNEX

Constituted 1 October 1933 in the Regular Army as Battery B, 46th Field Artillery. Redesignated 1 October 1940 as Battery B, 46th Field Artillery Battalion, and activated at Fort Knox, Kentucky, as an element of the 5th Division (later redesignated as the 5th Infantry Division). Inactivated 20 September 1946 at Camp Campbell, Kentucky. Activated 15 July 1947 at Fort Jackson, South Carolina. Inactivated 30 April 1950 at Fort Jackson, South Carolina.

CAMPAIGN PARTICIPATION CREDIT

World War I
  St. Mihiel
  Meuse-Argonne
  Lorraine 1918

World War II
  *Normandy
  *Northern France
  *Rhineland
  *Ardennes-Alsace
  *Central Europe
  *Central Pacific
  Aleutian Islands
  Eastern Mandates

Leyte
Ryukyus (with arrowhead)

Korean War
  UN defensive
  UN offensive
  CCF intervention
  First UN counteroffensive
  CCF spring offensive
  UN summer–fall offensive
  Second Korean winter
  Korea, summer–fall 1952
  Third Korean winter
  Korea, summer 1953

DECORATIONS

Presidential Unit Citation (Navy), Streamer embroidered CHOSIN RESERVOIR

5th BATTALION, 57th AIR DEFENSE ARTILLERY

RA
(nondivisional)

LINEAGE

Organized in February 1919 in the Regular Army at Fort Winfield Scott, California, as Battery E, 57th Artillery (Coast Artillery Corps). Demobilized 30 June 1921 at Camp Lewis, Washington. Reconstituted 22 January 1926 in the Regular Army as Battery E, 57th Coast Artillery. Activated 15 June 1941 at Camp Pendleton, Virginia. Inactivated 31 May 1944 in Hawaii. Disbanded 14 June 1944.

Reconstituted 28 June 1950 in the Regular Army; concurrently consolidated with Battery A, 67th Armored Field Artillery Battalion (active) (*see* ANNEX), and consolidated unit designated as Battery A, 67th Armored Field Artillery Battalion, an element of the 3d Armored Division. Inactivated 1 October 1957 in Germany and relieved from assignment to the 3d Armored Division.

Redesignated 27 April 1959 as Headquarters and Headquarters Battery, 5th Missile Battalion, 57th Artillery (organic elements concurrently constituted). Battalion activated 15 June 1959 at Fort Bliss, Texas. Redesignated 14 June 1965 as the 5th Battalion, 57th Artillery. Redesignated 1 September 1971 as the 5th Battalion, 57th Air Defense Artillery.

ANNEX

Constituted 1 October 1933 in the Regular Army as Battery A, 67th Field Artillery. (67th Field Artillery assigned 13 January 1941 to the 3d Armored Division.) Activated 15 April 1941 at Camp Beauregard, Louisiana.

Reorganized and redesignated 1 January 1942 as Battery A, 67th Armored Field Artillery Battalion. Inactivated 10 November 1945 in Germany. Activated 15 July 1947 at Fort Knox, Kentucky.

CAMPAIGN PARTICIPATION CREDIT

World War I
St. Mihiel
Meuse-Argonne
Lorraine 1918

World War II
*Normandy
*Northern France
*Rhineland
*Ardennes-Alsace
*Central Europe
Aleutian Islands
Eastern Mandates
Leyte
Ryukyus (with arrowhead)

Korean War
UN defensive
UN offensive
CCF intervention
First UN counteroffensive
CCF spring offensive
UN summer–fall offensive
Second Korean winter
Korea, summer–fall 1952
Third Korean winter
Korea, summer 1953

DECORATIONS

Presidential Unit Citation (Navy) Streamer embroidered CHOSIN RESERVOIR

*Belgian Fourragere 1940 (67th Armored Field Artillery Battalion cited; DA GO 43, 1950)

*Cited in the Order of the Day of the Belgian Army for action in BELGIUM (67th Armored Field Artillery Battalion cited; DA GO 43, 1950)

*Cited in the Order of the Day of the Belgian Army for action in the ARDENNES (67th Armored Field Artillery Battalion cited; DA GO 43, 1950)

6th BATTALION, 57th AIR DEFENSE ARTILLERY

RA
(inactive)

LINEAGE

Organized in February 1919 in the Regular Army at Fort Winfield Scott, California, as Battery F, 57th Artillery (Coast Artillery Corps). Demobilized 30 June 1921 at Camp Lewis, Washington. Reconstituted 22 January 1926 in the Regular Army and redesignated as Battery F, 57th Coast Artillery. Activated 15 June 1941 at Camp Pendleton, Virginia. Inactivated 31 May 1944 in Hawaii. Disbanded 14 June 1944.

Reconstituted 28 June 1950 in the Regular Army; concurrently consolidated with Battery B, 67th Armored Field Artillery Battalion (active) (*see* ANNEX), and consolidated unit designated as Battery B, 67th Armored Field Artillery Battalion, an element of the 3d Armored Division.

Inactivated 1 October 1957 in Germany and relieved from assignment to the 3d Armored Division; concurrently redesignated as Headquarters and Headquarters Battery, 6th Battalion, 57th Artillery (organic elements constituted 12 July 1967). Battalion activated 25 October 1967 at Fort Bliss, Texas. Inactivated 25 July 1968 at Fort Bliss, Texas. Redesignated 1 September 1971 as the 6th Battalion, 57th Air Defense Artillery.

ANNEX

Constituted 1 October 1933 in the Regular Army as Battery B, 67th Field Artillery. (67th Field Artillery assigned 13 January 1941 to the 3d Armored Division.) Activated 15 April 1941 at Camp Beauregard, Louisiana.

Reorganized and redesignated 1 January 1942 as Battery B, 67th Armored Field Artillery Battalion. Inactivated 10 November 1945 in Germany. Activated 15 July 1947 at Fort Knox, Kentucky.

CAMPAIGN PARTICIPATION CREDIT

World War I
  St. Mihiel
  Meuse-Argonne
  Lorraine 1918

World War II
  *Normandy
  *Northern France
  *Rhineland
  *Ardennes-Alsace
  *Central Europe
  Aleutian Islands
  Eastern Mandates

Leyte
Ryukyus (with arrowhead)

Korean War
  UN defensive
  UN offensive
  CCF intervention
  First UN counteroffensive
  CCF spring offensive
  UN summer–fall offensive
  Second Korean winter
  Korea, summer–fall 1952
  Third Korean winter
  Korea, summer 1953

DECORATIONS

Presidential Unit Citation (Navy), Streamer embroidered CHOSIN RESERVOIR

*Belgian Fourragere 1940 (67th Armored Field Artillery Battalion cited; DA GO 43, 1950)

*Cited in the Order of the Day of the Belgian Army for action in BELGIUM (67th Armored Field Artillery Battalion cited; DA GO 43, 1950)

*Cited in the Order of the Day of the Belgian Army for action in the ARDENNES (67th Armored Field Artillery Battalion cited; DA GO 43, 1950)

57TH AIR DEFENSE ARTILLERY BIBLIOGRAPHY

Appleman, Roy E. *South to the Naktong, North to the Yalu.* United States Army in the Korean War. Washington: Government Printing Office, 1961. Contains information about the 57th Field Artillery Battalion.

Berry, Edward S. "From the Seine to the Siegfried Line." *Armored Cavalry Journal* 59 (January 1950):35–41. Contains information about the 67th Armored Field Artillery Battalion.

Cannon, M. Hamlin. *Leyte: The Return to the Philippines.* United States Army in World War II. Washington: Government Printing Office, 1954. Contains information about the 57th Field Artillery Battalion.

Crowl, Philip A., and Edmund G. Love. *Seizure of the Gilberts and Marshalls.* United States Army in World War II. Washington: Government Printing Office, 1955. Contains information about the 57th Field Artillery Battalion.

Division Artillery, 5th Division. Philadelphia: Dorville Corporation, 1956. Contains information about the 46th Field Artillery Battalion.

Dupuy, Richard Ernest. *With the 57th in France.* Brooklyn: Our Army, Inc., 1930. Originally published by installments in *Our Army* (July 1929–February 1930).

Falls, Bruce F., et al. *The Seventh Division in Korea.* Tokyo: FEC Printing Plant, 1948. Contains information about the 57th Field Artillery Battalion.

First Battalion, 57th Artillery, C.A.C. in the World War. Brooklyn: Eagle Press, 1919?

Grace, James L. *A Brief History of the 2nd Battalion, 57th Artillery, C.A.C., 31st Brigade, Army Artillery, First Army From July 20th, 1917 to January 15th, 1919.* N.p., 1919.

Gugeler, Russell A. *Combat Actions in Korea.* Washington: Combat Forces Journal Press, 1954. Rev. ed. Washington: Government Printing Office, 1970. Contains information about the 57th Field Artillery Battalion.

Hermes, Walter G. *Truce Tent and Fighting Front.* United States Army in the Korean War. Washington: Government Printing Office, 1966. Contains information about the 57th Field Artillery Battalion.

Howe, George F. *Northwest Africa: Seizing the Initiative in the West.* United States Army in World War II. Washington: Government Printing Office, 1957. Contains information about the 67th Armored Field Artillery Battalion.

Kimmel, Irving, ed. *3d Armored Division, "Spearhead," Fort Knox, Kentucky*. Dallas: Miller Publishing Company, 1956. Contains information about the 67th Armored Field Artillery Battalion.

MacDonald, Charles B., and Sidney T. Mathews. *Three Battles: Arnaville, Altuzzo, and Schmidt*. United States Army in World War II. Washington: Government Printing Office, 1952. Contains information about the 46th Field Artillery Battalion.

Public Information Office, 7th Infantry Division. *The Bayonet, the History of the 7th Infantry Division in Korea*. Tokyo: Dai Nippon Printing Company, 1953. Contains information about the 57th Field Artillery Battalion.

7th Infantry Division in Korea. Atlanta: Albert Love Enterprises, 1954. Contains information about the 57th Field Artillery Battalion.

67th Armored FA, Bn, 54th Armored FA Bn, 391st Armored FA Bn, Camp Polk, 1942. Baton Rouge: Army and Navy Publishing Company, 1942.

Third Armored Division, Basic Training. Baton Rouge: Army and Navy Publishing Company, 1950. Contains information about the 67th Armored Field Artillery Battalion.

Third Armored Division, Fort Knox, Kentucky, 1948. Baton Rouge: Army and Navy Publishing Company, 1948. Contains information about the 67th Armored Field Artillery Battalion.

Waring, Paul C., ed. *History of the 7th Infantry (Bayonet) Division*. Tokyo: Dai Nippon Printing Company, 1967. Contains information about the 57th Field Artillery Battalion.

59th AIR DEFENSE ARTILLERY

COAT OF ARMS

Shield: Per fess vair and argent, in base a thistle proper.

Crest: On a wreath of the colors, argent and azure, a demi-lion rampant gules armed and langued azure grasping in dexter claw a sword or.

Motto: *Defendimus* (We Defend).

Symbolism: The vair on the shield is from the arms of the Coast Defenses of New York; the thistle is one of the emblems of Lorraine and is borne on the arms of Nancy not far from St. Mihiel.

The lion, from the arms of St. Menehould, is red for artillery.

DISTINCTIVE INSIGNIA

The distinctive insignia is the shield, crest, and motto of the coat of arms.

LINEAGE AND HONORS

LINEAGE

Constituted 1 December 1917 in the Regular Army as the 59th Artillery (Coast Artillery Corps). Organized 1 January 1918 at Fort Hamilton, New York, from existing Regular Army companies and New York National Guard companies. (National Guard companies demobilized January–February 1919 at Camp Upton, New York; regiment continued on active status.) (Service Battery; Headquarters Detachment and Combat Train, 1st Battalion; and the 2d and 3d Battalions inactivated 30 September 1922 at Fort Mills, Philippine Islands. Batteries G and H organized 11 October 1922 at Fort Mills, Philippine Islands.) Redesignated 20 February 1924 as the 59th Coast Artillery (Batteries C, D, E, and F concurrently activated at Fort Mills, Philippine Islands). Remainder of regiment activated 30 May 1941 at Fort Mills, Philippine Islands. Surrendered 6 May 1942 to the Japanese forces on Corregidor Island, Philippine Islands. Inactivated 2 April 1946 at Fort Mills, Philippine Islands.

Redesignated 26 December 1947 as the 59th Antiaircraft Artillery Automatic Weapons Battalion. Activated 1 January 1948 at Fort Bliss,

Texas. Redesignated 24 February 1953 as the 59th Antiaircraft Artillery Battalion. Inactivated 1 September 1958 at Fort Bliss, Texas.

Reorganized and redesignated 31 July 1959 as the 59th Artillery, a parent regiment under the Combat Arms Regimental System. Redesignated 1 September 1971 as the 59th Air Defense Artillery.

CAMPAIGN PARTICIPATION CREDIT

World War I	*World War II*
St. Mihiel	Philippine Islands
Meuse-Argonne	
Lorraine 1918	

DECORATIONS

Presidential Unit Citation (Army), Streamer embroidered BATAAN (Harbor Defenses of Manila and Subic Bays, United States Army in the Far East, cited; WD GO 14, 1942)

Presidential Unit Citation (Army), Streamer embroidered MANILA AND SUBIC BAYS (59th Coast Artillery cited; WD GO 21, 1942)

Presidential Unit Citation (Army), Streamer embroidered DEFENSE OF THE PHILIPPINES (Military and naval forces of the United States engaged in the defense of the Philippines cited; WD GO 22, 1942, as amended by DA GO 46, 1948)

Philippine Presidential Unit Citation, Streamer embroidered 7 DECEMBER 1941 TO 10 MAY 1942 (59th Coast Artillery cited; DA GO 47, 1950)

1st BATTALION, 59th AIR DEFENSE ARTILLERY

RA
(8th Infantry Division)

LINEAGE

Organized 15 June 1917 in the Regular Army at Fort Hamilton, New York, as the 7th Company, Fort Hamilton [New York]. Redesignated 31 August 1917 as the 4th Company, Coast Defenses of Southern New York.

Reorganized and redesignated 1 January 1918 as Battery A, 59th Artillery (Coast Artillery Corps). (Additionally designated 30 June 1922 as the 176th Company, Coast Artillery Corps; additional designation abolished 20 February 1924.) Redesignated 20 February 1924 as Battery A, 59th Coast Artillery. Surrendered 6 May 1942 to the Japanese forces on Corregidor Island, Philippine Islands. Inactivated 2 April 1946 at Fort Mills, Philippine Islands.

Redesignated 26 December 1947 as Battery A, 59th Antiaircraft Artillery Automatic Weapons Battalion. Activated 1 January 1948 at Fort Bliss, Texas. Redesignated 24 February 1953 as Battery A, 59th Antiaircraft Artillery Battalion.

Reorganized and redesignated 1 September 1958 as Headquarters and Headquarters Battery, 1st Gun Battalion, 59th Artillery (organic elements constituted 12 August 1958 and activated 1 September 1958). Battalion (less Battery B) inactivated 25 May 1960 at Fort Bliss, Texas. (Battery B inactivated 26 March 1963 at Fort Bliss, Texas.) Redesignated 5 May 1969 as the 1st Battalion, 59th Artillery, and activated at Fort Bliss, Texas. Assigned 4 November 1969 to the 8th Infantry Division. Redesignated 1 September 1971 as the 1st Battalion, 59th Air Defense Artillery.

CAMPAIGN PARTICIPATION CREDIT

World War I
  *St. Mihiel
  *Meuse-Argonne
  *Lorraine 1918

World War II
  *Philippine Islands

DECORATIONS

*Presidential Unit Citation (Army), Streamer embroidered BATAAN (Harbor Defenses of Manila and Subic Bays, United States Army in the Far East, cited; WD GO 14, 1942)

*Presidential Unit Citation (Army), Streamer embroidered MANILA AND SUBIC BAYS (59th Coast Artillery cited; WD GO 21, 1942)

*Presidential Unit Citation (Army), Streamer embroidered DEFENSE OF THE PHILIPPINES (Military and naval forces of the United States engaged in the defense of the Philippines cited; WD GO 22, 1942, as amended by DA GO 46, 1948)

*Philippine Presidential Unit Citation, Streamer embroidered

7 DECEMBER 1941 TO 10 MAY 1942 (59th Coast Artillery cited; DA GO 47, 1950)

Battery B additionally entitled to Meritorious Unit Commendation, Streamer embroidered FLORIDA 1962–1963 (Battery B, 1st Gun Battalion, 59th Artillery, cited; DA GO 33, 1963)

2d BATTALION, 59th AIR DEFENSE ARTILLERY

RA
(1st Armored Division)

LINEAGE

Organized in February 1919 in the Regular Army at Fort Winfield Scott, California, as Battery B, 59th Artillery (Coast Artillery Corps). (Additionally designated 30 June 1922 as the 252d Company, Coast Artillery Corps; additional designation abolished 20 February 1924.) Redesignated 20 February 1924 as Battery B, 59th Coast Artillery. Surrendered 6 May 1942 to the Japanese forces on Corregidor Island, Philippine Islands. Inactivated 2 April 1946 at Fort Mills, Philippine Islands.

Redesignated 26 December 1947 as Battery B, 59th Antiaircraft Artillery Automatic Weapons Battalion. Activated 1 January 1948 at Fort Bliss, Texas. Redesignated 24 February 1953 as Battery B, 59th Antiaircraft Artillery Battalion.

Reorganized and redesignated 1 September 1958 as Headquarters and Headquarters Battery, 2d Missile Battalion, 59th Artillery (organic elements constituted 12 August 1958 and activated 1 September 1958). Battalion inactivated 9 October 1964 at Edgemont, Pennsylvania. Redesignated 1 May 1970 as the 2d Battalion, 59th Artillery, and activated at Fort Bliss, Texas. Assigned 4 November 1970 to the 4th Armored Division. Relieved 10 May 1971 from the 4th Armored Division and assigned to the 1st Armored Division. Redesignated 1 September 1971 as the 2d Battalion, 59th Air Defense Artillery.

CAMPAIGN PARTICIPATION CREDIT

World War I
St. Mihiel
Meuse-Argonne
Lorraine 1918

World War II
*Philippine Islands

DECORATIONS

*Presidential Unit Citation (Army), Streamer embroidered BATAAN (Harbor Defenses of Manila and Subic Bays, United States Army in the Far East, cited; WD GO 14, 1942)

*Presidential Unit Citation (Army), Streamer embroidered MANILA AND SUBIC BAYS (59th Coast Artillery cited; WD GO 21, 1942)

*Presidential Unit Citation (Army), Streamer embroidered DEFENSE OF THE PHILIPPINES (Military and naval forces of the United States engaged in the defense of the Philippines cited; WD GO 22, 1942, as amended by DA GO 46, 1948)

*Philippine Presidential Unit Citation, Streamer embroidered 7 DECEMBER 1941 TO 10 MAY 1942 (59th Coast Artillery cited; DA GO 47, 1950)

3d BATTALION, 59th AIR DEFENSE ARTILLERY

RA
(nondivisional)

LINEAGE

Organized 13 January 1919 in the Regular Army at Fort Wadsworth, New York, as the 2d Company, Coast Defenses of Southern New York. Redesignated 1 June 1922 as the 253d Company, Coast Artillery Corps.

Reorganized and redesignated 20 February 1924 as Battery C, 59th Coast Artillery. Surrendered 6 May 1942 to the Japanese forces on Corregidor Island, Philippine Islands. Inactivated 2 April 1946 at Fort Mills, Philippine Islands.

Redesignated 26 December 1947 as Battery C, 59th Antiaircraft Artillery Automatic Weapons Battalion. Activated 1 January 1948 at Fort Bliss, Texas. Redesignated 24 February 1953 as Battery C, 59th Antiaircraft Artillery Battalion.

Reorganized and redesignated 1 September 1958 as Headquarters and Headquarters Battery, 3d Missile Battalion, 59th Artillery (organic elements constituted 12 August 1958 and activated 1 September 1958). Redesignated 20 December 1965 as the 3d Battalion, 59th Artillery. Inactivated 30 June 1971 at Milwaukee, Wisconsin. Redesignated 1 September 1971 as the 3d Battalion, 59th Air Defense Artillery. Activated 13 September 1972 in Germany.

CAMPAIGN PARTICIPATION CREDIT

World War I
  St. Mihiel
  Meuse-Argonne
  Lorraine 1918

World War II
  *Philippine Islands

DECORATIONS

*Presidential Unit Citation (Army), Streamer embroidered BATAAN (Harbor Defenses of Manila and Subic Bays, United States Army in the Far East, cited; WD GO 14, 1942)

*Presidential Unit Citation (Army), Streamer embroidered MANILA AND SUBIC BAYS (59th Coast Artillery cited; WD GO 21, 1942)

*Presidential Unit Citation (Army), Streamer embroidered DEFENSE OF THE PHILIPPINES (Military and naval forces of the United States engaged in the defense of the Philippines cited; WD GO 22, 1942, as amended by DA GO 46, 1948)

*Philippine Presidential Unit Citation, Streamer embroidered 7 DECEMBER 1941 TO 10 MAY 1942 (59th Coast Artillery cited; DA GO 47, 1950)

4th BATTALION, 59th AIR DEFENSE ARTILLERY

RA
(inactive)

LINEAGE

Organized in February 1919 in the Regular Army at Fort Winfield Scott, California, as Battery D, 59th Artillery (Coast Artillery Corps). (Additionally designated 30 June 1922 as the 254th Company, Coast Artillery Corps; additional designation abolished 20 February 1924.) Inactivated 30 September 1922 at Fort Mills, Philippine Islands. Redesignated 20 February 1924 as Battery D, 59th Coast Artillery, and activated at Fort Mills, Philippine Islands. Surrendered 6 May 1942 to the Japanese forces on Corregidor Island, Philippine Islands. Inactivated 2 April 1946 at Fort Mills, Philippine Islands.

Redesignated 26 December 1947 as Battery D, 59th Antiaircraft Artillery Automatic Weapons Battalion. Activated 1 January 1948 at Fort Bliss, Texas. Redesignated 24 February 1953 as Battery D, 59th Antiaircraft Artillery Battalion.

Reorganized and redesignated 1 September 1958 as Headquarters and Headquarters Battery, 4th Missile Battalion, 59th Artillery (organic elements constituted 12 August 1958 and activated 1 September 1958). Redesignated 20 December 1965 as the 4th Battalion, 59th Artillery. (Batteries A, B, and C inactivated 31 March 1970 at Norfolk, Virginia.) Inactivated (less Batteries A, B, and C) 30 June 1971 at Norfolk, Virginia. Redesignated 1 September 1971 as the 4th Battalion, 59th Air Defense Artillery.

CAMPAIGN PARTICIPATION CREDIT

World War I
St. Mihiel
Meuse-Argonne
Lorraine 1918

World War II
*Philippine Islands

DECORATIONS

*Presidential Unit Citation (Army), Streamer embroidered BATAAN (Harbor Defenses of Manila and Subic Bays, United States Army in the Far East, cited; WD GO 14, 1942)

*Presidential Unit Citation (Army), Streamer embroidered MANILA AND SUBIC BAYS (59th Coast Artillery cited; WD GO 21, 1942)

*Presidential Unit Citation (Army), Streamer embroidered DEFENSE OF THE PHILIPPINES (Military and naval forces of the United States engaged in the defense of the Philippines cited; WD GO 22, 1942, as amended by DA GO 46, 1948)

*Philippine Presidential Unit Citation, Streamer embroidered 7 DECEMBER 1941 TO 10 MAY 1942 (59th Coast Artillery cited; DA GO 47, 1950)

5th BATTALION, 59th AIR DEFENSE ARTILLERY

RA
(inactive)

LINEAGE

Constituted 2 August 1901 in the Regular Army as the 98th Company, Coast Artillery, Artillery Corps. Organized in 1901 at Fort Hamilton, New York. Redesignated 2 February 1907 as the 98th Company, Coast Artillery Corps. Redesignated 31 August 1917 as the 9th Company, Coast Defenses of Southern New York. Disbanded 1 June 1921 at Fort Hamilton, New York.

Reconstituted 30 June 1922 in the Regular Army; concurrently consolidated with Headquarters Battery, 59th Artillery (Coast Artillery Corps) (active) (*see* ANNEX), and consolidated unit designated as Headquarters Battery, 59th Artillery (Coast Artillery Corps) (additionally designated as the 98th Company, Coast Artillery Corps; additional designation abolished 20 February 1924). Redesignated 20 February 1924 as Headquarters Battery, 59th Coast Artillery. Surrendered 6 May 1942 to the Japanese forces on Corregidor Island, Philippine Islands. Inactivated 2 April 1946 at Fort Mills, Philippine Islands.

Redesignated 26 December 1947 as Headquarters Battery, 59th Antiaircraft Artillery Automatic Weapons Battalion. Activated 1 January 1948 at Fort Bliss, Texas. Redesignated 24 February 1953 as Headquarters Battery, 59th Antiaircraft Artillery Battalion. Inactivated 1 September 1958 at Fort Bliss, Texas.

Redesignated 31 July 1959 as Headquarters and Headquarters Battery, 5th Battalion, 59th Artillery. Activated 11 January 1971 at Fort Bliss, Texas (organic elements concurrently constituted and activated). Redesignated 1 September 1971 as the 5th Battalion, 59th Air Defense Artillery. Inactivated 30 September 1974 at Fort Bliss, Texas.

ANNEX

Organized 30 June 1916 in the Regular Army at Fort Hamilton, New York, as the 1st Company, Fort Hamilton [New York]. Redesignated 31 August 1917 as the 1st Company, Coast Defenses of Southern New York.

Reorganized and redesignated 1 January 1918 as Headquarters Company, 59th Artillery (Coast Artillery Corps). Redesignated in 1921 as Headquarters Battery, 59th Artillery (Coast Artillery Corps).

CAMPAIGN PARTICIPATION CREDIT

World War I
    *St. Mihiel
    *Meuse-Argonne
    *Lorraine 1918

World War II
    *Philippine Islands

DECORATIONS

*Presidential Unit Citation (Army), Streamer embroidered BATAAN (Harbor Defenses of Manila and Subic Bays, United States Army in the Far East, cited; WD GO 14, 1942)

*Presidential Unit Citation (Army), Streamer embroidered MANILA AND SUBIC BAYS (59th Coast Artillery cited; WD GO 21, 1942)

*Presidential Unit Citation (Army), Streamer embroidered DEFENSE OF THE PHILIPPINES (Military and naval forces of the United States engaged in the defense of the Philippines cited; WD GO 22, 1942, as amended by DA GO 46, 1948)

*Philippine Presidential Unit Citation, Streamer embroidered 7 DECEMBER 1941 TO 10 MAY 1942 (59th Coast Artillery cited; DA GO 47, 1950)

6th BATTALION, 59th AIR DEFENSE ARTILLERY

RA
(inactive)

LINEAGE

Organized in February 1919 in the Regular Army at Fort Winfield Scott, California, as Battery E, 59th Artillery (Coast Artillery Corps). (Additionally designated 30 June 1922 as the 255th Company, Coast Artillery Corps; additional designation abolished 20 February 1924.) Inactivated 30 September 1922 at Fort Mills, Philippine Islands. Redesignated 20 February 1924 as Battery E, 59th Coast Artillery, and activated at Fort Mills, Philippine Islands. Surrendered 6 May 1942 to the Japanese forces on Corregidor Island, Philippine Islands. Inactivated 2 April 1946 at Fort Mills, Philippine Islands. Disbanded 24 December 1947.

Reconstituted 31 July 1959 in the Regular Army and redesignated as Headquarters and Headquarters Battery, 6th Battalion, 59th Artillery. Redesignated 1 November 1960 as Headquarters and Headquarters Battery, 6th Missile Battalion, 59th Artillery (organic elements concurrently constituted). Battalion activated 17 November 1960 at Fort Bliss, Texas. Redesignated 20 August 1965 as the 6th Battalion, 59th Artillery. Redesignated 1 September 1971 as the 6th Battalion, 59th Air Defense Artillery. Inactivated 13 September 1972 in Germany.

CAMPAIGN PARTICIPATION CREDIT

World War I	*World War II*
St. Mihiel	*Philippine Islands
Meuse-Argonne	
Lorraine 1918	

DECORATIONS

*Presidential Unit Citation (Army), Streamer embroidered BATAAN (Harbor Defenses of Manila and Subic Bays, United States Army in the Far East, cited; WD GO 14, 1942)

*Presidential Unit Citation (Army), Streamer embroidered MANILA AND SUBIC BAYS (59th Coast Artillery cited; WD GO 21, 1942)

*Presidential Unit Citation (Army), Streamer embroidered DEFENSE OF THE PHILIPPINES (Military and naval forces of the United States engaged in the defense of the Philippines cited; WD GO 22, 1942, as amended by DA GO 46, 1948)

*Philippine Presidential Unit Citation, Streamer embroidered 7 DECEMBER 1941 TO 10 MAY 1942 (59th Coast Artillery cited; DA GO 47, 1950)

12th PLATOON, 59th AIR DEFENSE ARTILLERY

RA
(inactive)

LINEAGE

Organized 1 August 1921 in the Regular Army on board the U.S.A.T. *Sherman* as Headquarters Detachment and Combat Train, 1st Battalion, 59th Artillery (Coast Artillery Corps). (Additionally designated 30 June 1922 as the 248th Company, Coast Artillery Corps; additional designation abolished 20 February 1924.) Inactivated 30 September 1922 at Fort Mills, Philippine Islands. Redesignated 20 February 1924 as Headquarters Battery and Combat Train, 1st Battalion, 59th Coast Artillery. Activated 30 May 1941 at Fort Mills, Philippine Islands. Surrendered 6 May 1942 to the Japanese forces on Corregidor Island, Philippine Islands. Disbanded 24 December 1947.

Reconstituted 6 June 1958 in the Regular Army and redesignated as the 12th Platoon, 59th Artillery. Activated 24 June 1958 at Fort Sill, Oklahoma. Inactivated 12 September 1960 at Fort Sill, Oklahoma. Redesignated 1 September 1971 as the 12th Platoon, 59th Air Defense Artillery.

CAMPAIGN PARTICIPATION CREDIT

World War II–AP
   Philippine Islands

DECORATIONS

Presidential Unit Citation (Army), Streamer embroidered BATAAN (Harbor Defenses of Manila and Subic Bays, United States Army in the Far East, cited; WD GO 14, 1942)

Presidential Unit Citation (Army), Streamer embroidered MANILA AND SUBIC BAYS (59th Coast Artillery cited; WD GO 21, 1942)

Presidential Unit Citation (Army), Streamer embroidered DEFENSE OF THE PHILIPPINES (Military and naval forces of the United States engaged in the defense of the Philippines cited; WD GO 22, 1942, as amended by DA GO 46, 1948)

Philippine Presidential Unit Citation, Streamer embroidered 7 DECEMBER 1941 TO 10 MAY 1942 (59th Coast Artillery cited; DA GO 47, 1950)

16th DETACHMENT, 59th AIR DEFENSE ARTILLERY

RA
(inactive)

LINEAGE

Organized 30 May 1941 in the Regular Army at Fort Mills, Philippine Islands, as Battery K, 59th Coast Artillery. Surrendered 6 May 1942 to the Japanese forces on Corregidor Island, Philippine Islands. Inactivated 2 April 1946 at Fort Mills, Philippine Islands. Disbanded 24 December 1947.

Reconstituted 5 August 1958 in the Regular Army and redesignated as the 16th Detachment, 59th Artillery. Activated 1 September 1958 at Fort Bliss, Texas. Inactivated 17 September 1962 at Fort Bliss, Texas. Redesignated 1 September 1971 as the 16th Detachment, 59th Air Defense Artillery.

CAMPAIGN PARTICIPATION CREDIT

World War II–AP
   Philippine Islands

DECORATIONS

Presidential Unit Citation (Army), Streamer embroidered BATAAN (Harbor Defenses of Manila and Subic Bays, United States Army in the Far East, cited; WD GO 14, 1942)

Presidential Unit Citation (Army), Streamer embroidered MANILA AND SUBIC BAYS (59th Coast Artillery cited; WD GO 21, 1942)

Presidential Unit Citation (Army), Streamer embroidered DEFENSE OF THE PHILIPPINES (Military and naval forces of the United States engaged in the defense of the Philippines cited; WD GO 22, 1942, as amended by DA GO 46, 1948)

Philippine Presidential Unit Citation, Streamer embroidered 7 DECEMBER 1941 TO 10 MAY 1942 (59th Coast Artillery cited; DA GO 47, 1950)

59TH AIR DEFENSE ARTILLERY BIBLIOGRAPHY

Belote, James H., and William M. *Corregidor. The Saga of a Fortress.* New York: Harper and Row Publishers, 1967.

59th AAA, AW Battalion (SP), Fort Bliss, Texas, 1949. Baton Rouge: Army and Navy Publishing Company, 1949.

Morton, Louis. *The Fall of the Philippines.* United States Army in World War II. Washington: Government Printing Office, 1953.

60th AIR DEFENSE ARTILLERY

HERALDIC ITEMS

COAT OF ARMS

Shield: Per fess embattled sable and gules fimbriated or a pile in bend of the third the lower portion obscured by the second tincture, in sinister chief a mullet of the third.

Crest: On a wreath of the colors, or and sable, a carabao skull sable horned or.

Motto: *Coelis Imperamus* (We Rule the Heavens).

Symbolism: The shield is divided horizontally, the dividing line embattled to represent defense. The lower half of the shield is red for artillery; the upper half black and gold significant of service in the Orient. A searchlight beam symbolizes the never-ending vigilance the organization exercises in searching for enemy aircraft. The star has a double significance. It is symbolic of Texas, the Lone Star State, where the unit was reorganized after World War I, and its battleground in the sky.

The carabao horns are symbolic of service in the Philippine Islands.

DISTINCTIVE INSIGNIA

The distinctive insignia is the shield and motto of the coat of arms.

LINEAGE AND HONORS

LINEAGE

Constituted 23 December 1917 in the Regular Army as the 60th Artillery (Coast Artillery Corps) and organized at Fort Monroe, Virginia, from existing Regular Army companies and National Guard companies from Virginia and the District of Columbia. Demobilized 24 February 1919 at Fort Washington, Maryland. Reconstituted 26 October 1922 in the Regular Army as the 60th Artillery Battalion (Antiaircraft) and organized at Fort Crockett, Texas. Expanded, reorganized, and redesignated 1 July 1924 as the 60th Coast Artillery, with 1st Battalion organized at Fort William McKinley, Philippine Islands. Headquarters activated 31 August 1925 at Fort William McKinley, Philippine Islands (1st Battalion [less Batteries A and B] concurrently inactivated and Battery E activated at Fort William McKinley, Philippine Islands). (1st Battalion and Battery F activated 1 April 1929 at Fort Mills, Philippine Islands.) Remainder of regiment activated 30 May 1941 at Fort Mills, Philippine Islands.

Surrendered 6 May 1942 to the Japanese forces on Corregidor Island, Philippine Islands. Inactivated 2 April 1946 at Fort Mills, Philippine Islands.

Redesignated 1 August 1946 as the 60th Antiaircraft Artillery Automatic Weapons Battalion and activated at Fort Bliss, Texas. Redesignated 7 December 1949 as the 60th Antiaircraft Artillery Automatic Weapons Battalion, Mobile. Redesignated 27 July 1950 as the 60th Antiaircraft Artillery Battalion. Inactivated 17 June 1957 at Southampton, England.

Reorganized and redesignated 31 July 1959 as the 60th Artillery, a parent regiment under the Combat Arms Regimental System. Redesignated 1 September 1971 as the 60th Air Defense Artillery.

CAMPAIGN PARTICIPATION CREDIT

World War I
St. Mihiel
Meuse-Argonne

World War II
Philippine Islands

Vietnam
Counteroffensive, Phase II
Counteroffensive, Phase III
Tet Counteroffensive

Counteroffensive, Phase IV
Counteroffensive, Phase V
Counteroffensive, Phase VI
Tet Counteroffensive
Summer–fall 1969
Winter–spring 1970
Sanctuary Counteroffensive
Counteroffensive, Phase VII
Consolidation I
Consolidation II

DECORATIONS

Presidential Unit Citation (Army), Streamer embroidered BATAAN (Harbor Defenses of Manila and Subic Bays, United States Army in the Far East, cited; WD GO 14, 1942)

Presidential Unit Citation (Army), Streamer embroidered MANILA AND SUBIC BAYS (60th Coast Artillery cited; WD GO 21, 1942)

Presidential Unit Citation (Army), Streamer embroidered DEFENSE OF THE PHILIPPINES (Military and naval forces of the United States engaged in the defense of the Philippines cited; WD GO 22, 1942, as amended by DA GO 46, 1948)

Meritorious Unit Commendation, Streamer embroidered VIETNAM 1967–1968 (4th Battalion, 60th Artillery, cited; DA GO 1, 1969)

Meritorious Unit Commendation, Streamer embroidered VIETNAM 1968–1969 (4th Battalion, 60th Artillery, cited; DA GO 39, 1970)

Philippine Presidential Unit Citation, Streamer embroidered 7 DECEMBER 1941 TO 10 MAY 1942 (60th Coast Artillery cited; DA GO 47, 1950)

1st BATTALION, 60th AIR DEFENSE ARTILLERY

RA
(inactive)

LINEAGE

Constituted 8 March 1898 in the Regular Army as Battery G, 7th Regiment of Artillery. Organized 29 March 1898 at Fort Slocum, New York.

Reorganized and redesignated 13 February 1901 as the 77th Company, Coast Artillery, Artillery Corps. Redesignated 2 February 1907 as the 77th Company, Coast Artillery Corps. Redesignated 6 July 1916 as the 3d Company, Fort Barrancas [Florida]. Redesignated 31 August 1917 as the 3d Company, Coast Defenses of Pensacola. Disbanded 30 November 1919 at Pensacola, Florida. Reconstituted 1 June 1922 in the Regular Army; concurrently consolidated with the 3d Company, Coast Defenses of Key West (active) (organized 9 August 1921 in the Regular Army at Key West, Florida), and consolidated unit redesignated as the 77th Company, Coast Artillery Corps.

Reorganized and redesignated 26 October 1922 as Battery B, 60th Artillery Battalion (Antiaircraft). Redesignated 1 July 1924 as Battery B, 60th Coast Artillery. Surrendered 6 May 1942 to the Japanese forces on Corregidor Island, Philippine Islands. Inactivated 2 April 1946 at Fort Mills, Philippine Islands.

Redesignated 1 August 1946 as Battery B, 60th Antiaircraft Artillery Automatic Weapons Battalion, and activated at Fort Bliss, Texas. Redesignated 7 December 1949 as Battery B, 60th Antiaircraft Artillery Automatic Weapons Battalion, Mobile. Redesignated 27 July 1950 as Battery B, 60th Antiaircraft Artillery Battalion. Inactivated 17 June 1957 at Southampton, England.

Redesignated 12 August 1958 as Headquarters and Headquarters Battery, 1st Missile Battalion, 60th Artillery (organic elements concurrently constituted). Battalion activated 1 September 1958 at Gary, Indiana. Redesignated 20 December 1965 as the 1st Battalion, 60th Artillery. Redesignated 1 September 1971 as the 1st Battalion, 60th Air Defense Artillery. Inactivated 30 September 1974 at Munster, Indiana.

CAMPAIGN PARTICIPATION CREDIT

World War I	*World War II*
St. Mihiel	*Philippine Islands
Meuse-Argonne	

DECORATIONS

*Presidential Unit Citation (Army), Streamer embroidered BATAAN (Harbor Defenses of Manila and Subic Bays, United States Army in the Far East, cited; WD GO 14, 1942)

*Presidential Unit Citation (Army), Streamer embroidered MANILA AND SUBIC BAYS (60th Coast Artillery cited; WD GO 21, 1942)

*Presidential Unit Citation (Army), Streamer embroidered DEFENSE OF THE PHILIPPINES (Military and naval forces of the United States engaged in the defense of the Philippines cited; WD GO 22, 1942, as amended by DA GO 46, 1948)

*Philippine Presidential Unit Citation, Streamer embroidered 7 DECEMBER 1941 TO 10 MAY 1942 (60th Coast Artillery cited; DA GO 47, 1950)

2d BATTALION, 60th AIR DEFENSE ARTILLERY

RA
(nondivisional)

LINEAGE

Constituted 8 March 1898 in the Regular Army as Battery K, 7th Regiment of Artillery. Organized 29 March 1898 at Fort Slocum, New York.

Reorganized and redesignated 13 February 1901 as the 80th Company, Coast Artillery, Artillery Corps. Redesignated 2 February 1907 as the 80th Company, Coast Artillery Corps. Redesignated 6 July 1916 as the 1st Company, Key West Barracks [Florida]. Redesignated 31 August 1917 as the 1st Company, Coast Defenses of Key West. Redesignated 1 June 1922 as the 80th Company, Coast Artillery Corps.

Consolidated 26 October 1922 with Battery C, 60th Artillery (Coast Artillery Corps) (see ANNEX), and consolidated unit reorganized and redesignated as Battery C, 60th Artillery Battalion (Antiaircraft). Redesignated 1 July 1924 as Battery C, 60th Coast Artillery. Inactivated 31 August 1925 at Fort William McKinley, Philippine Islands. Activated 1 April 1929 at Fort Mills, Philippine Islands. Surrendered 6 May 1942 to the Japanese forces on Corregidor Island, Philippine Islands. Inactivated 2 April 1946 at Fort Mills, Philippine Islands.

Redesignated 1 August 1946 as Battery C, 60th Antiaircraft Artillery Automatic Weapons Battalion, and activated at Fort Bliss, Texas. Redesignated 7 December 1949 as Battery C, 60th Antiaircraft Artillery Automatic Weapons Battalion, Mobile. Redesignated 27 July 1950 as Battery C, 60th Antiaircraft Artillery Battalion. Inactivated 17 June 1957 at Southampton, England.

Redesignated 12 August 1958 as Headquarters and Headquarters Battery, 2d Missile Battalion, 60th Artillery (organic elements concurrently constituted). Battalion activated 1 September 1958 at Orland Park, Illinois. Inactivated 15 December 1961 at Orland Park, Illinois. Redesignated 12 January 1970 as the 2d Battalion, 60th Artillery, and activated at Fort Bliss, Texas. Redesignated 1 September 1971 as the 2d Battalion, 60th Air Defense Artillery.

ANNEX

Constituted 23 December 1917 in the Regular Army as Battery C, 60th Artillery (Coast Artillery Corps), and organized at Fort Monroe, Virginia. Demobilized 24 February 1919 at Fort Washington, Maryland. Reconstituted 26 October 1922 in the Regular Army.

CAMPAIGN PARTICIPATION CREDIT

World War I	World War II
*St. Mihiel	*Philippine Islands
*Meuse-Argonne	

Decorations

*Presidential Unit Citation (Army), Streamer embroidered BATAAN (Harbor Defenses of Manila and Subic Bays, United States Army in the Far East, cited; WD GO 14, 1942)

*Presidential Unit Citation (Army), Streamer embroidered MANILA AND SUBIC BAYS (60th Coast Artillery cited; WD GO 21, 1942)

*Presidential Unit Citation (Army), Streamer embroidered DEFENSE OF THE PHILIPPINES (Military and naval forces of the United States engaged in defense of the Philippines cited; WD GO 22, 1942, as amended by DA GO 46, 1948)

*Philippine Presidential Unit Citation, Streamer embroidered 7 DECEMBER 1941 TO 10 MAY 1942 (60th Coast Artillery cited; DA GO 47, 1950)

3d BATTALION, 60th AIR DEFENSE ARTILLERY

RA
(nondivisional)

LINEAGE

Constituted 7 June 1907 in the Regular Army as the 128th Company, Coast Artillery Corps. Organized in 1907 at Fort McHenry, Maryland. Redesignated in July 1916 as the 1st Company, Fort Crockett [Texas]. Redesignated 31 August 1917 as the 1st Company, Coast Defenses of Galveston. Redesignated 1 June 1922 as the 128th Company, Coast Artillery Corps.

Reorganized and redesignated 26 October 1922 as Battery A, 60th Artillery Battalion (Antiaircraft). Redesignated 1 July 1924 as Battery A, 60th Coast Artillery. Surrendered 6 May 1942 to the Japanese forces on Corregidor Island, Philippine Islands. Inactivated 2 April 1946 at Fort Mills, Philippine Islands.

Redesignated 1 August 1946 as Battery A, 60th Antiaircraft Artillery Automatic Weapons Battalion, and activated at Fort Bliss, Texas. Redesignated 7 December 1949 as Battery A, 60th Antiaircraft Artillery Automatic Weapons Battalion, Mobile. Redesignated 27 July 1950 as Battery A, 60th Antiaircraft Artillery Battalion. Inactivated 17 June 1957 at Southampton, England.

Redesignated 12 August 1958 as Headquarters and Headquarters Battery, 3d Missile Battalion, 60th Artillery (organic elements concurrently constituted). Battalion activated 1 September 1958 at Eureka, Pennsylvania. Inactivated 1 September 1961 in Pennsylvania. Redesignated 1 September 1971 as the 3d Missile Battalion, 60th Air Defense Artillery. Redesignated 13 September 1972 as the 3d Battalion, 60th Air Defense Artillery, and activated in Germany.

CAMPAIGN PARTICIPATION CREDIT

World War I
St. Mihiel
Meuse-Argonne

World War II
*Philippine Islands

DECORATIONS

*Presidential Unit Citation (Army), Streamer embroidered BATAAN (Harbor Defenses of Manila and Subic Bays, United States Army in the Far East, cited; WD GO 14, 1942)

*Presidential Unit Citation (Army), Streamer embroidered MANILA AND SUBIC BAYS (60th Coast Artillery cited; WD GO 21, 1942)

*Presidential Unit Citation (Army), Streamer embroidered DEFENSE OF THE PHILIPPINES (Military and naval forces of the United States engaged in the defense of the Philippines cited; WD GO 22, 1942, as amended by DA GO 46, 1948)

*Philippine Presidential Unit Citation, Streamer embroidered 7 DECEMBER 1941 TO 10 MAY 1942 (60th Coast Artillery cited; DA GO 47, 1950)

4th BATTALION, 60th AIR DEFENSE ARTILLERY

RA
(inactive)

LINEAGE

Constituted 1 July 1924 in the Regular Army as Battery F, 60th Coast Artillery. Activated 1 April 1929 at Fort Mills, Philippine Islands. Surrendered 6 May 1942 to the Japanese forces on Corregidor Island, Philippine Islands. Inactivated 2 April 1946 at Fort Mills, Philippine Islands.

Absorbed 1 August 1946 by Battery B, 60th Antiaircraft Artillery Automatic Weapons Battalion. (Battery B, 60th Coast Artillery, redesignated 1 August 1946 as Battery B, 60th Antiaircraft Artillery Automatic Weapons Battalion, and activated at Fort Bliss, Texas; redesignated 7 December 1949 as Battery B, 60th Antiaircraft Artillery Automatic Weapons Battalion, Mobile; redesignated 27 July 1950 as Battery B, 60th Antiaircraft Artillery Battalion; inactivated 17 June 1957 at Southampton, England.)

Former Battery F, 60th Coast Artillery, reconstituted 12 August 1958 in the Regular Army and redesignated as Headquarters and Headquarters Battery, 4th Missile Battalion, 60th Artillery (organic elements concurrently constituted). Battalion activated 1 September 1958 at Midway, Washington. Inactivated 15 December 1961 at Redmond, Washington. Redesignated 25 April 1966 as the 4th Battalion, 60th Artillery. Activated 25 June 1966 at Fort Bliss, Texas. Redesignated 1 September 1971 as the 4th Battalion, 60th Air Defense Artillery. Inactivated 31 July 1972 at Fort Lewis, Washington.

CAMPAIGN PARTICIPATION CREDIT

World War I
   St. Mihiel
   Meuse-Argonne

World War II
   *Philippine Islands

Vietnam
   *Counteroffensive, Phase II
   *Counteroffensive, Phase III
   *Tet Counteroffensive

*Counteroffensive, Phase IV
*Counteroffensive, Phase V
*Counteroffensive, Phase VI
*Tet 69/Counteroffensive
*Summer–fall 1969
*Winter–spring 1970
*Sanctuary Counteroffensive
*Counteroffensive, Phase VII
*Consolidation I
*Consolidation II

DECORATIONS

*Presidential Unit Citation (Army), Streamer embroidered BATAAN (Harbor Defenses of Manila and Subic Bays, United States Army in the Far East, cited; WD GO 14, 1942)

*Presidential Unit Citation (Army), Streamer embroidered MANILA AND SUBIC BAYS (60th Coast Artillery cited; WD GO 21, 1942)

*Presidential Unit Citation (Army), Streamer embroidered DEFENSE OF THE PHILIPPINES (Military and naval forces of the United States engaged in the defense of the Philippines cited; WD GO 22, 1942, as amended by DA GO 46, 1948)

*Meritorious Unit Commendation, Streamer embroidered VIETNAM 1967–1968 (4th Battalion, 60th Artillery, cited; DA GO 1, 1969)

*Meritorious Unit Commendation, Streamer embroidered VIETNAM 1968–1969 (4th Battalion, 60th Artillery, cited; DA GO 39, 1970)

*Philippine Presidential Unit Citation, Streamer embroidered 7 DECEMBER 1941 TO 10 MAY 1942 (60th Coast Artillery cited; DA GO 47, 1950)

*Republic of Vietnam Cross of Gallantry with Palm, Streamer embroidered VIETNAM 1967–1972 (4th Battalion, 60th Artillery, cited; DA GO 54, 1974)

Battery A additionally entitled to Presidential Unit Citation (Army), Streamer embroidered BINH THUAN PROVINCE (Battery A, 4th Battalion, 60th Artillery, cited; DA GO 2, 1973)

Battery D additionally entitled to Republic of Vietnam Civil Action Honor Medal, First Class, Streamer embroidered VIETNAM 1967–1969 (Battery D, 4th Battalion, 60th Artillery, cited; DA GO 53, 1970)

5th BATTALION, 60th AIR DEFENSE ARTILLERY

AR
(inactive)

LINEAGE

Constituted 2 February 1907 in the Regular Army as the 127th Company, Coast Artillery Corps. Organized in 1907 at Fort Fremont, South Carolina. Redesignated in July 1916 as the 2d Company, Fort Crockett [Texas]. Redesignated 31 August 1917 as the 2d Company, Coast Defenses of Galveston. Redesignated 1 June 1922 as the 127th Company, Coast Artillery Corps.

Reorganized and redesignated 26 October 1922 as Headquarters Detachment and Combat Train, 60th Artillery Battalion (Antiaircraft). Redesignated 1 July 1924 as Headquarters Battery, 60th Coast Artillery, and inactivated at Fort William McKinley, Philippine Islands. Activated 31 August 1925 at Fort William McKinley, Philippine Islands. Surrendered 6 May 1942 to the Japanese forces on Corregidor Island, Philippine Islands. Inactivated 2 April 1946 at Fort Mills, Philippine Islands.

Redesignated 1 August 1946 as Headquarters Battery, 60th Antiaircraft Artillery Automatic Weapons Battalion, and activated at Fort Bliss, Texas. Redesignated 7 December 1949 as Headquarters Battery, 60th Antiaircraft Artillery Automatic Weapons Battalion, Mobile. Redesignated 27 July 1950 as Headquarters Battery, 60th Antiaircraft Artillery Battalion. Inactivated 17 June 1957 at Southampton, England. Consolidated 12 August 1958 with Headquarters and Headquarters Battery, 1st Battalion, 60th Coast Artillery (*see* ANNEX), and consolidated unit designated as Headquarters and Headquarters Battery, 1st Battalion, 60th Coast Artillery.

Redesignated 31 July 1959 as Headquarters and Headquarters Battery, 5th Automatic Weapons Battalion, 60th Artillery. Relieved 3 August 1959 from allotment to the Regular Army, allotted to the Army Reserve, and assigned to the Fifth United States Army (organic elements concurrently constituted). Battalion activated 1 September 1959 at South Bend, Indiana. Reorganized and redesignated 1 October 1960 as the 5th Howitzer Battalion, 60th Artillery. Redesignated 23 June 1966 as the 5th Battalion, 60th Artillery. Inactivated 1 September 1971 at South Bend, Indiana; concurrently redesignated as the 5th Battalion, 60th Air Defense Artillery.

ANNEX

Constituted 23 December 1917 in the Regular Army as Headquarters, 1st Battalion, 60th Artillery (Coast Artillery Corps), and organized at Fort Monroe, Virginia. Demobilized 24 February 1919 at Fort Washington, Maryland. Reconstituted 1 July 1924 in the Regular Army as Headquarters Battery and Combat Train, 1st Battalion, 60th Coast Artillery, and activated at Fort William McKinley, Philippine Islands. Inactivated

31 August 1925 at Fort William McKinley, Philippine Islands. Redesignated 17 March 1930 as Headquarters and Headquarters Battery, 1st Battalion, 60th Coast Artillery. Activated 30 May 1941 at Fort Mills, Philippine Islands. Surrendered 6 May 1942 to the Japanese forces on Corregidor Island, Philippine Islands. Inactivated 2 April 1946 at Fort Mills, Philippine Islands.

Absorbed 1 August 1946 by Headquarters and Headquarters Battery, 60th Antiaircraft Artillery Automatic Weapons Battalion. (Headquarters and Headquarters Battery, 60th Coast Artillery, redesignated 1 August 1946 as Headquarters and Headquarters Battery, 60th Antiaircraft Artillery Automatic Weapons Battalion, and activated at Fort Bliss, Texas; redesignated 7 December 1949 as Headquarters and Headquarters Battery, 60th Antiaircraft Artillery Automatic Weapons Battalion, Mobile; redesignated 27 July 1950 as Headquarters and Headquarters Battery, 60th Antiaircraft Artillery Battalion; inactivated 17 June 1957 at Southampton, England.) Former Headquarters and Headquarters Battery, 1st Battalion, 60th Coast Artillery, reconstituted 12 August 1958 in the Regular Army.

CAMPAIGN PARTICIPATION CREDIT

World War I
  *St. Mihiel
  *Meuse-Argonne

World War II
  *Philippine Islands

DECORATIONS

*Presidential Unit Citation (Army), Streamer embroidered BATAAN (Harbor Defenses of Manila and Subic Bays, United States Army in the Far East, cited; WD GO 14, 1942)

*Presidential Unit Citation (Army), Streamer embroidered MANILA AND SUBIC BAYS (60th Coast Artillery cited; WD GO 21, 1942)

*Presidential Unit Citation (Army), Streamer embroidered DEFENSE OF THE PHILIPPINES (Military and naval forces of the United States engaged in the defense of the Philippines cited; WD GO 22, 1942, as amended by DA GO 46, 1948)

*Philippine Presidential Unit Citation, Streamer embroidered 7 DECEMBER 1941 TO 10 MAY 1942 (60th Coast Artillery cited; DA GO 47, 1950)

6th BATTALION, 60th AIR DEFENSE ARTILLERY

RA
(inactive)

LINEAGE

Constituted 23 December 1917 in the Regular Army as Headquarters, 2d Battalion, 60th Artillery (Coast Artillery Corps), and organized at Fort Monroe, Virginia. Demobilized 24 February 1919 at Fort Washington, Maryland. Reconstituted 1 July 1924 in the Regular Army and redesignated as Headquarters, 2d Battalion, 60th Coast Artillery. Redesignated 17 March 1930 as Headquarters and Headquarters Battery, 2d Battalion, 60th Coast Artillery. Activated 30 May 1941 at Fort Mills, Philippine Islands. Surrendered 6 May 1942 to the Japanese forces on Corregidor Island, Philippine Islands.

Absorbed 1 August 1946 by Headquarters and Headquarters Battery, 60th Antiaircraft Artillery Automatic Weapons Battalion. (Headquarters and Headquarters Battery, 60th Coast Artillery, redesignated 1 August 1946 as Headquarters and Headquarters Battery, 60th Antiaircraft Artillery Automatic Weapons Battalion, and activated at Fort Bliss, Texas; redesignated 7 December 1949 as Headquarters and Headquarters Battery, 60th Antiaircraft Artillery Automatic Weapons Battalion, Mobile; redesignated 27 July 1950 as Headquarters and Headquarters Battery, 60th Antiaircraft Artillery Battalion; inactivated 17 June 1957 at Southampton, England.) Former Headquarters and Headquarters Battery, 2d Battalion, 60th Coast Artillery, reconstituted 12 August 1958 in the Regular Army.

Redesignated 31 July 1959 as Headquarters and Headquarters Battery, 6th Battalion, 60th Artillery. Redesignated 16 February 1961 as Headquarters and Headquarters Battery, 6th Missile Battalion, 60th Artillery (organic elements concurrently constituted). Battalion activated 25 March 1961 at Fort Bliss, Texas. Redesignated 20 August 1965 as the 6th Battalion, 60th Artillery. Redesignated 1 September 1971 as the 6th Battalion, 60th Air Defense Artillery. Inactivated 13 September 1972 in Germany.

CAMPAIGN PARTICIPATION CREDIT

World War I
  *St. Mihiel
  *Meuse-Argonne

World War II
  *Philippine Islands

DECORATIONS

*Presidential Unit Citation (Army), Streamer embroidered BATAAN (Harbor Defenses of Manila and Subic Bays, United States Army in the Far East, cited; WD GO 14, 1942)

*Presidential Unit Citation (Army), Streamer embroidered MANILA AND SUBIC BAYS (60th Coast Artillery cited; WD GO 21, 1942)

*Presidential Unit Citation (Army), Streamer embroidered DEFENSE OF THE PHILIPPINES (Military and naval forces of the United States engaged in the defense of the Philippines cited; WD GO 22, 1942, as amended by DA GO 46, 1948)

*Philippine Presidential Unit Citation, Streamer embroidered 7 DECEMBER 1941 TO 10 MAY 1942 (60th Coast Artillery cited; DA GO 47, 1950)

7th BATTALION, 60th AIR DEFENSE ARTILLERY

RA
(inactive)

LINEAGE

Constituted 1 July 1924 in the Regular Army as Battery D, 60th Coast Artillery. Activated 1 April 1929 at Fort Mills, Philippine Islands. Surrendered 6 May 1942 to the Japanese forces on Corregidor Island, Philippine Islands. Inactivated 2 April 1946 at Fort Mills, Philippine Islands.

Redesignated 1 August 1946 as Battery D, 60th Antiaircraft Artillery Automatic Weapons Battalion, and activated at Fort Bliss, Texas. Redesignated 7 December 1949 as Battery D, 60th Antiaircraft Artillery Automatic Weapons Battalion, Mobile. Redesignated 27 July 1950 as Battery D, 60th Antiaircraft Artillery Battalion. Disbanded 15 November 1954 at Southampton, England. Reconstituted 12 July 1958 in the Regular Army.

Redesignated 31 July 1959 as Headquarters and Headquarters Battery, 7th Battalion, 60th Artillery. Redesignated 18 June 1966 as Battery G, 60th Artillery. Redesignated 29 June 1970 as Headquarters and Headquarters Battery, 7th Battalion, 60th Artillery, and activated at Fort Bliss, Texas (organic elements concurrently constituted and activated). Battalion assigned 11 December 1970 to the 82d Airborne Division. Redesignated 1 September 1971 as the 7th Battalion, 60th Air Defense Artillery. Inactivated 13 September 1972 at Fort Bragg, North Carolina, and relieved from assignment to the 82d Airborne Division.

CAMPAIGN PARTICIPATION CREDIT

World War I	*World War II*
St. Mihiel	*Philippine Islands
Meuse-Argonne	

DECORATIONS

*Presidential Unit Citation (Army), Streamer embroidered BATAAN (Harbor Defenses of Manila and Subic Bays, United States Army in the Far East, cited; WD GO 14, 1942)

*Presidential Unit Citation (Army), Streamer embroidered MANILA AND SUBIC BAYS (60th Coast Artillery cited; WD GO 21, 1942)

*Presidential Unit Citation (Army), Streamer embroidered DEFENSE OF THE PHILIPPINES (Military and naval forces of the United States engaged in the defense of the Philippines cited; WD GO 22, 1942, as amended by DA GO 46, 1948)

*Philippine Presidential Unit Citation, Streamer embroidered 7 DECEMBER 1941 TO 10 MAY 1942 (60th Coast Artillery cited; DA GO 47, 1950)

8th BATTALION, 60th AIR DEFENSE ARTILLERY

RA
(inactive)

LINEAGE

Constituted 1 July 1924 in the Regular Army as Battery E, 60th Coast Artillery. Activated 1 April 1929 at Fort Mills, Philippine Islands. Surrendered 6 May 1942 to the Japanese forces on Corregidor Island, Philippine Islands. Inactivated 2 April 1946 at Fort Mills, Philippine Islands.

Absorbed 1 August 1946 by Battery A, 60th Antiaircraft Artillery Automatic Weapons Battalion. (Battery A, 60th Coast Artillery, redesignated 1 August 1946 as Battery A, 60th Antiaircraft Artillery Automatic Weapons Battalion, and activated at Fort Bliss, Texas; redesignated 7 December 1949 as Battery A, 60th Antiaircraft Artillery Automatic Weapons Battalion, Mobile; redesignated 27 July 1950 as Battery A, 60th Antiaircraft Artillery Battalion; inactivated 17 June 1957 at Southampton, England.) Former Battery E, 60th Coast Artillery, reconstituted 12 August 1958 in the Regular Army.

Redesignated 31 July 1959 as Headquarters and Headquarters Battery, 8th Battalion, 60th Artillery. Activated 7 November 1970 at Fort Bliss, Texas (organic elements concurrently constituted and activated). Battalion assigned 20 May 1971 to the 2d Armored Division. Redesignated 1 September 1971 as the 8th Battalion, 60th Air Defense Artillery. Inactivated 13 September 1972 at Fort Hood, Texas, and relieved from assignment to the 2d Armored Division.

CAMPAIGN PARTICIPATION CREDIT

World War I
    St. Mihiel
    Meuse-Argonne

World War II
    *Philippine Islands

DECORATIONS

*Presidential Unit Citation (Army), Streamer embroidered BATAAN (Harbor Defenses of Manila and Subic Bays, United States Army in the Far East, cited; WD GO 14, 1942)

*Presidential Unit Citation (Army), Streamer embroidered MANILA AND SUBIC BAYS (60th Coast Artillery cited; WD GO 21, 1942)

*Presidential Unit Citation (Army), Streamer embroidered DEFENSE OF THE PHILIPPINES (Military and naval forces of the United States engaged in the defense of the Philippines cited; WD GO 22, 1942, as amended by DA GO 46, 1948)

*Philippine Presidential Unit Citation, Streamer embroidered 7 DECEMBER 1941 TO 10 MAY 1942 (60th Coast Artillery cited; DA GO 47, 1950)

12th DETACHMENT, 60th AIR DEFENSE ARTLLLERY

RA
(inactive)

LINEAGE

Constituted 30 May 1941 in the Regular Army as Battery I, 60th Coast Artillery, and activated at Fort Mills, Philippine Islands. Surrendered 6 May 1942 to the Japanese forces on Corregidor Island, Philippine Islands. Inactivated 2 April 1946 at Fort Mills, Philippine Islands.

Absorbed 1 August 1946 by Battery A, 60th Antiaircraft Artillery Automatic Weapons Battalion. (Battery A, 60th Coast Artillery, redesignated 1 August 1946 as Battery A, 60th Antiaircraft Artillery Automatic Weapons Battalion, and activated at Fort Bliss, Texas; redesignated 7 December 1949 as Battery A, 60th Antiaircraft Artillery Automatic Weapons Battalion, Mobile; redesignated 27 July 1950 as Battery A, 60th Antiaircraft Artillery Battalion; inactivated 17 June 1957 at Southampton, England.)

Former Battery I, 60th Coast Artillery, reconstituted 5 August 1958 in the Regular Army and redesignated as the 12th Detachment, 60th Artillery. Activated 15 September 1958 at Ladd Air Force Base, Alaska. Inactivated 15 September 1960 at Ladd Air Force Base, Alaska. Redesignated 1 September 1971 as the 12th Detachment, 60th Air Defense Artillery.

CAMPAIGN PARTICIPATION CREDIT

World War II—AP
    Philippine Islands

DECORATIONS

Presidential Unit Citation (Army), Streamer embroidered BATAAN (Harbor Defenses of Manila and Subic Bays, United States Army in the Far East, cited; WD GO 14, 1942)

Presidential Unit Citation (Army), Streamer embroidered HARBOR DEFENSES OF MANILA AND SUBIC BAYS (60th Coast Artillery cited; WD GO 21, 1942)

Presidential Unit Citation (Army), Streamer embroidered DEFENSE OF THE PHILIPPINES (Military and naval forces of the United States engaged in the defense of the Philippines cited; WD GO 22, 1942, as amended by DA GO 46, 1948)

Philippine Presidential Unit Citation, Streamer embroidered 7 DECEMBER 1941 TO 10 MAY 1942 (60th Coast Artillery cited; DA GO 47, 1950)

16th DETACHMENT, 60th AIR DEFENSE ARTILLERY

RA
(inactive)

LINEAGE

Constituted 30 May 1941 in the Regular Army as Battery K, 60th Coast Artillery, and activated at Fort Mills, Philippine Islands. Surrendered 6 May 1942 to the Japanese forces on Corregidor Island, Philippine Islands. Inactivated 2 April 1946 at Fort Mills, Philippine Islands.

Absorbed 1 August 1946 by Battery B, 60th Antiaircraft Artillery Automatic Weapons Battalion. (Battery B, 60th Coast Artillery, redesignated 1 August 1946 as Battery B, 60th Antiaircraft Artillery Automatic Weapons Battalion, and activated at Fort Bliss, Texas; redesignated 7 December 1949 as Battery B, 60th Antiaircraft Artillery Automatic Weapons Battalion, Mobile; redesignated 27 July 1950 as Battery B, 60th Antiaircraft Artillery Battalion; inactivated 17 June 1957 at Southampton, England.)

Former Battery K, 60th Coast Artillery, reconstituted 5 August 1958 in the Regular Army and redesignated as the 16th Detachment, 60th Artillery. Activated 1 September 1958 at Fort Stewart, Georgia. Inactivated 1 July 1962 at Fort Stewart, Georgia. Redesignated 1 September 1971 as the 16th Detachment, 60th Air Defense Artillery.

CAMPAIGN PARTICIPATION CREDIT

World War II–AP
   Philippine Islands

DECORATIONS

Presidential Unit Citation (Army), Streamer embroidered BATAAN (Harbor Defenses of Manila and Subic Bays, United States Army in the Far East, cited; WD GO 14, 1942)

Presidential Unit Citation (Army), Streamer embroidered HARBOR DEFENSES OF MANILA AND SUBIC BAYS (60th Coast Artillery cited; WD GO 21, 1942)

Presidential Unit Citation (Army), Streamer embroidered DEFENSE OF THE PHILIPPINES (Military and naval forces of the United States engaged in the defense of the Philippines cited; WD GO 22, 1942, as amended by DA GO 46, 1948)

Philippine Presidential Unit Citation, Streamer embroidered 7 DECEMBER 1941 TO 10 MAY 1942 (60th Coast Artillery cited; DA GO 47, 1950)

60TH AIR DEFENSE ARTILLERY BIBLIOGRAPHY

Belote, James H., and William M. *Corregidor. The Saga of a Fortress.* New York: Harper and Row Publishers, 1967.

Coleman, J.D. *1st Air Cavalry Division, Memoirs of the First Team, Vietnam, August 1965–December 1969.* Tokyo: Dai Nippon Printing Company, 1970. Contains information about the 4th Battalion, 60th Air Defense Artillery.

The District of Columbia Coast Artillery National Guard, 1915–1919. Menasha, Wis.: George Banta Publishing Company, 1921. Contains information about Battery D, 60th Artillery (Coast Artillery Corps) in World War I.

"History of Battery F, Sixtieth Regiment, Coast Artillery Corps (Formerly Ninth Company, Virginia Coast Artillery)." *Virginia Military Organizations in the World War.* Richmond: Virginia War History Commission, 1927, pp. 351–54.

Milton, Marshall M. "History of Battery B, Sixtieth Regiment, Coast Artillery Corps (Formerly Fifth Company, Virginia Coast Artillery)." *Virginia Military Organizations in the World War.* Richmond: Virginia War History Commission, 1927, pp. 340–49.

Morton, Louis. *The Fall of the Philippines.* United States Army in World War II. Washington: Government Printing Office, 1953.

60th AAA, AW Battalion (M), Fort Bliss, Texas, 1949. Baton Rouge: Army and Navy Publishing Company, 1949.

61st AIR DEFENSE ARTILLERY

HERALDIC ITEMS

COAT OF ARMS

Shield: Per fess dancetté argent and sable, a thunderbolt bendwise proper penetrating the chariot wheel of Helios winged with two dexter wings inverted forming a saltire with the first charge all counterchanged and upon the wheel the sun in splendor of the third.

Crest: On a wreath of the colors, argent and sable, an eagle's head erased or.

Motto: *Non Est ad Astra Mollis e Terris Via* (The Way to the Stars Is Not Easy).

Symbolism: The purpose of the regiment is depicted in Greek mythology by the winged chariot of Helios brought to earth by a lightning bolt thrown by Zeus, as follows: Helios, the sun, drove across the heavens from east to west daily, in a winged chariot drawn by the celestial horses. Phaeton, his son, obtained permission from his father to take his place in the chariot for one day. He had scarcely taken the reins when the horses, despising their weak driver, turned out of their path and set everything on fire. When the chariot came so near the earth that the Ethiopians were blackened by the near approach of the sun, Zeus, with a well-aimed lightning bolt, wrecked the chariot and sent it plunging into the river Po. This is the first pictorial record of a hit being scored against an aerial target.

The shield is divided by the sawtooth line taken from Lord Delaware's arms, the basis of the coat of arms for the Coast Defenses of the Chesapeake. The colors white and black, dividing the shield, stand for day and night.

The crest is from the arms of James Monroe with the colors reversed, a red eagle's head on a gold shield.

DISTINCTIVE INSIGNIA

The distinctive insignia is the shield of the coat of arms.

LINEAGE AND HONORS

LINEAGE

Constituted 9 March 1918 in the Regular Army as the 61st Artillery (Coast Artillery Corps) and organized at Fort Moultrie, South Carolina,

297

from existing Regular Army companies and National Guard companies from Georgia and South Carolina. Demobilized 28 February 1919 at Camp Upton, New York. Reconstituted 1 July 1921 in the Regular Army as the 1st Antiaircraft Battalion and organized at Fort Monroe, Virginia, from existing Regular Army units. Redesignated 1 June 1922 as the 61st Artillery Battalion (Antiaircraft). Expanded, reorganized, and redesignated 1 July 1924 as the 61st Coast Artillery with Batteries A, B, and E and Headquarters organized at Fort Monroe, Virginia. (1st Battalion [less Batteries A and B] activated 18 November 1939 at Fort Sheridan, Illinois; 2d Battalion [less Battery E] activated 28 November 1939 at Fort Sheridan, Illinois; 3d Battalion constituted 9 October 1942 in the Regular Army and activated 8 January 1943 at Reykjavik, Iceland.)

Regiment inactivated 10 August 1943 at Honiton, England, and personnel concurrently transferred to the following units, which were constituted 25 February 1943 in the Army of the United States and activated 10 August 1943 at Honiton, England: Headquarters and Headquarters Battery to Headquarters and Headquarters Battery, 92d Antiaircraft Artillery Group; 1st Battalion to the 184th Antiaircraft Artillery Gun Battalion; 2d Battalion to the 634th Antiaircraft Artillery Automatic Weapons Battalion; and 3d Battalion to the 635th Antiaircraft Artillery Automatic Weapons Battalion.

Headquarters and Headquarters Battery, 92d Antiaircraft Artillery Group, inactivated 30 October 1945 in Germany. Consolidated 28 June 1950 with Headquarters and Headquarters Battery, 61st Coast Artillery (disbanded 14 June 1944 and reconstituted 28 June 1950 in the Regular Army), and consolidated unit redesignated as Headquarters and Headquarters Battery, 61st Antiaircraft Artillery Group. Activated 1 April 1955 at Camp Stewart, Georgia. Redesignated 1 April 1958 as Headquarters and Headquarters Battery, 61st Artillery Group. Inactivated 25 August 1961 at Milwaukee, Wisconsin.

184th Antiaircraft Artillery Gun Battalion inactivated 4 December 1945 at Camp Myles Standish, Massachusetts. Consolidated 28 June 1950 with the 1st Battalion, 61st Coast Artillery (disbanded 14 June 1944 and reconstituted 28 June 1950 in the Regular Army), and consolidated unit redesignated as the 61st Antiaircraft Artillery Battalion. Redesignated 21 August 1950 as the 61st Antiaircraft Artillery Automatic Weapons Battalion and assigned to the 6th Armored Division. Activated 5 September 1950 at Fort Leonard Wood, Missouri. Inactivated 16 March 1956 at Fort Leonard Wood, Missouri, and relieved from assignment to the 6th Armored Division.

634th Antiaircraft Artillery Automatic Weapons Battalion inactivated 6 October 1945 at Camp Kilmer, New Jersey. Consolidated 28 June 1950 with the 2d Battalion, 61st Coast Artillery (disbanded 14 June 1944 and reconstituted 28 June 1950 in the Regular Army), and the 39th Antiaircraft Artillery Automatic Weapons Battalion, Mobile (active) (*see* ANNEX), and consolidated unit designated as the 39th Antiaircraft Artillery Automatic Weapons Battalion, Mobile. Redesignated 31 July 1950 as the 39th Antiaircraft Artillery Battalion. Inactivated 17 June 1957 in England.

635th Antiaircraft Artillery Automatic Weapons Battalion inactivated 27 March 1946 at Camp Kilmer, New Jersey. Consolidated 28 June 1950 with the 3d Battalion, 61st Coast Artillery (disbanded 14 June 1944 and reconstituted 28 June 1950 in the Regular Army), and consolidated unit redesignated as the 52d Antiaircraft Artillery Battalion. Redesignated 20 October 1950 as the 52d Antiaircraft Artillery Automatic Weapons Battalion and activated at Fort Lewis, Washington. Inactivated 10 November 1951 in Korea. Redesignated 19 November 1952 as the 52d Antiaircraft Artillery Automatic Weapons Battalion, Mobile. Activated 26 November 1952 at Camp Roberts, California. Redesignated 31 March 1953 as the 52d Antiaircraft Artillery Battalion. Inactivated 15 June 1957 at Castle Air Force Base, California.

Headquarters and Headquarters Battery, 61st Artillery Group; 61st Antiaircraft Artillery Automatic Weapons Battalion; and 39th and 52d Antiaircraft Artillery Battalions consolidated, reorganized, and redesignated 25 August 1961 as the 61st Artillery, a parent regiment under the Combat Arms Regimental System. Redesignated 1 September 1971 as the 61st Air Defense Artillery.

ANNEX

Constituted 25 February 1943 in the Army of the United States as the 788th Coast Artillery Battalion. Activated 20 April 1943 at Camp Hulen, Texas. Redesignated 30 April 1943 as the 788th Antiaircraft Artillery Automatic Weapons Battalion. Inactivated 29 June 1946 in France. Redesignated 13 October 1948 as the 39th Antiaircraft Artillery Automatic Weapons Battalion, Mobile, and allotted to the Regular Army. Activated 15 January 1949 at Fort Bliss, Texas.

CAMPAIGN PARTICIPATION CREDIT

World War I	Central Europe
Streamer without inscription	Iceland 1942
World War II	England 1944
Normandy	*Korean War*
Northern France	CCF intervention
Rhineland	First UN counteroffensive
Ardennes-Alsace	CCF spring offensive
	UN summer–fall offensive

DECORATIONS

Presidential Unit Citation (Army), Streamer embroidered ST. VITH (634th Antiaircraft Artillery Automatic Weapons Battalion cited; WD GO 108, 1945)

1st BATTALION, 61st AIR DEFENSE ARTILLERY

RA
(inactive)

LINEAGE

Constituted 12 April 1808 in the Regular Army as a company in the Regiment of Light Artillery. Organized in 1808 as Capt. Nathan Estabrook's Company of Light Artillery, Regiment of Light Artillery. Redesignated 1 March 1811 as Capt. Robert H. MacPherson's Company of Light Artillery, Regiment of Light Artillery. Redesignated in 1812 as Capt. Luther Leonard's Company of Light Artillery, Regiment of Light Artillery. Redesignated in 1815 as Capt. Gabriel Manigault's Company of Light Artillery, Regiment of Light Artillery. Redesignated 22 May 1816 as Company B, Regiment of Light Artillery. Redesignated 1 June 1821 as Company G, 1st Regiment of Artillery.

Reorganized and redesignated 13 February 1901 as the 6th Company, Coast Artillery, Artillery Corps. Redesignated 2 February 1907 as the 6th Company, Coast Artillery Corps. Redesignated in July 1916 as the 6th Company, Fort Monroe [Virginia]. Redesignated 31 August 1917 as the 6th Company, Coast Defenses of Chesapeake Bay.

Reorganized and redesignated 23 December 1917 as Battery E, 60th Artillery (Coast Artillery Corps). Demobilized 24 February 1919 at Fort Washington, Maryland.

Reconstituted 1 June 1922 in the Regular Army; concurrently consolidated with Battery A, 1st Antiaircraft Battalion (organized 1 July 1921 in the Regular Army at Fort Monroe, Virginia), and consolidated unit redesignated as Battery A, 61st Artillery Battalion (Antiaircraft) (concurrently additionally designated as the 6th Company, Coast Artillery Corps; additional designation abolished 1 July 1924). Redesignated 1 July 1924 as Battery A, 61st Coast Artillery. Consolidated 16 October 1936 with Battery A, 61st Artillery (Coast Artillery Corps) (constituted 9 March 1918 in the Regular Army and organized at Fort Moultrie, South Carolina; demobilized 28 February 1919 at Camp Upton, New York), and consolidated unit designated as Battery A, 61st Coast Artillery.

Inactivated 10 August 1943 at Honiton, England; personnel concurrently transferred to Battery A, 184th Antiaircraft Artillery Gun Battalion (constituted 25 February 1943 in the Army of the United States and activated 10 August 1943 at Honiton, England). Battery A, 184th Antiaircraft Artillery Gun Battalion, inactivated 4 December 1945 at Camp Myles Standish, Massachusetts. Consolidated 28 June 1950 with Battery A, 61st Coast Artillery (disbanded 14 June 1944 and reconstituted 28 June 1950 in the Regular Army), and consolidated unit redesignated as Battery A, 61st Antiaircraft Artillery Battalion. Redesignated 21 August 1950 as Battery A, 61st Antiaircraft Artillery Automatic Weapons Battalion, an element of the 6th Armored Division. Activated 5 September 1950 at Fort Leonard Wood, Missouri. Inactivated 16 March 1956 at Fort

Leonard Wood, Missouri, and relieved from assignment to the 6th Armored Division.

Redesignated 12 August 1958 as Headquarters and Headquarters Battery, 1st Missile Battalion, 61st Artillery (organic elements concurrently constituted). Battalion activated 1 September 1958 at Travis Air Force Base, California. Redesignated 20 December 1965 as the 1st Battalion, 61st Artillery. Redesignated 1 September 1971 as the 1st Battalion, 61st Air Defense Artillery. Inactivated 30 August 1974 at Travis Air Force Base, California.

Campaign Participation Credit

War of 1812
  *Canada

Indian Wars
  *Seminoles

Mexican War
  *Cerro Gordo
  *Contreras
  *Churubusco
  *Chapultepec
  *Vera Cruz 1847
  *Mexico 1847

Civil War
  *Bull Run
  *Peninsula
  *Manassas
  *Antietam
  *Fredericksburg
  *Chancellorsville
  *Gettysburg
  *Wilderness
  *Spotsylvania

*Cold Harbor
*Virginia 1863
*Virginia 1864
*West Virginia 1863

World War I
  *St. Mihiel
  *Meuse-Argonne

World War II
  *Normandy
  *Northern France
  *Rhineland
  Ardennes-Alsace
  *Central Europe
  *Iceland 1942
  *England 1944

Korean War
  CCF intervention
  First UN counteroffensive
  CCF spring offensive
  UN summer–fall offensive

Decorations

Presidential Unit Citation (Army), Streamer embroidered ST. VITH
  *Belgian Fourragere 1940 (184th Antiaircraft Artillery Gun Battalion cited; DA GO 43, 1950)

  *Cited in the Order of the Day of the Belgian Army for action in defense of ANTWERP (184th Antiaircraft Artillery Gun Battalion cited; DA GO 43, 1950)

  *Cited in the Order of the Day of the Belgian Army for action in defense of ANTWERP HARBOR (184th Antiaircraft Artillery Gun Battalion cited; DA GO 43, 1950)

2d BATTALION, 61st AIR DEFENSE ARTILLERY

RA
(2d Infantry Division)

LINEAGE

Organized 30 May 1917 in the Regular Army at Fort Monroe, Virginia, as the 13th Company, Fort Monroe [Virginia]. Redesignated 31 August 1917 as the 5th Company, Coast Defenses of Chesapeake Bay.

Reorganized and redesignated 1 July 1921 as Battery B, 1st Antiaircraft Battalion. Redesignated 1 June 1922 as Battery B, 61st Artillery Battalion (Antiaircraft) (concurrently additionally designated as the 257th Company, Coast Artillery Corps; additional designation abolished 1 July 1924). Redesignated 1 July 1924 as Battery B, 61st Coast Artillery.

Inactivated 10 August 1943 at Honiton, England; personnel concurrently transferred to Battery B, 184th Antiaircraft Artillery Gun Battalion (constituted 25 February 1943 in the Army of the United States and activated 10 August 1943 at Honiton, England). Battery B, 184th Antiaircraft Artillery Gun Battalion, inactivated 4 December 1945 at Camp Myles Standish, Massachusetts. Consolidated 28 June 1950 with Battery B, 61st Coast Artillery (disbanded 14 June 1944 and reconstituted 28 June 1950 in the Regular Army), and consolidated unit redesignated as Battery B, 61st Antiaircraft Artillery Battalion. Redesignated 21 August 1950 as Battery B, 61st Antiaircraft Artillery Automatic Weapons Battalion, an element of the 6th Armored Division. Activated 5 September 1950 at Fort Leonard Wood, Missouri. Inactivated 16 March 1956 at Fort Leonard Wood, Missouri, and relieved from assignment to the 6th Armored Division.

Redesignated 7 August 1958 as Headquarters and Headquarters Battery, 2d Gun Battalion, 61st Artillery (organic elements concurrently constituted). Battalion activated 1 September 1958 on Okinawa. Reorganized and redesignated 25 March 1959 as the 2d Missile Battalion, 61st Artillery. Redesignated 30 June 1968 as the 2d Battalion, 61st Artillery. Inactivated 1 May 1970 on Okinawa. Redesignated 1 September 1971 as the 2d Battalion, 61st Air Defense Artillery. Assigned 13 September 1972 to the 2d Infantry Division and activated in Korea.

CAMPAIGN PARTICIPATION CREDIT

World War I
   Streamer without inscription

World War II
   *Normandy
   *Northern France
   *Rhineland
   Ardennes-Alsace

*Central Europe
*Iceland 1942
*England 1944

Korean War
   CCF intervention
   First UN counteroffensive
   CCF spring offensive
   UN summer–fall offensive

DECORATIONS

Presidential Unit Citation (Army), Streamer embroidered ST. VITH

*Belgian Fourragere 1940 (184th Antiaircraft Artillery Gun Battalion cited; DA GO 43, 1950)

*Cited in the Order of the Day of the Belgian Army for action in defense of ANTWERP (184th Antiaircraft Artillery Gun Battalion cited; DA GO 43, 1950)

*Cited in the Order of the Day of the Belgian Army for action in defense of ANTWERP HARBOR (184th Antiaircraft Artillery Gun Battalion cited; DA GO 43, 1950)

3d BATTALION, 61st AIR DEFENSE ARTILLERY

RA
(3d Armored Division)

LINEAGE

Constituted 1 July 1924 in the Regular Army as Battery D, 61st Coast Artillery. Activated 18 November 1939 at Fort Sheridan, Illinois.

Inactivated 10 August 1943 at Honiton, England; personnel concurrently transferred to Battery D, 184th Antiaircraft Artillery Gun Battalion (constituted 25 February 1943 in the Army of the United States and activated 10 August 1943 at Honiton, England). Battery D, 184th Antiaircraft Artillery Gun Battalion, inactivated 4 December 1945 at Camp Myles Standish, Massachusetts. Consolidated 28 June 1950 with Battery D, 61st Coast Artillery (disbanded 14 June 1944 and reconstituted 28 June 1950 in the Regular Army), and consolidated unit redesignated as Battery D, 61st Antiaircraft Artillery Battalion. Redesignated 21 August 1950 as Battery D, 61st Antiaircraft Artillery Automatic Weapons Battalion, an element of the 6th Armored Division. Activated 5 September 1950 at Fort Leonard Wood, Missouri. Inactivated 16 March 1956 at Fort Leonard Wood, Missouri, and relieved from assignment to the 6th Armored Division.

Redesignated 12 August 1958 as Headquarters and Headquarters Battery, 3d Missile Battalion, 61st Artillery (organic elements concurrently constituted). Battalion activated 1 September 1958 at Loring Air Force Base, Maine. Inactivated 25 June 1966 at Loring Air Force Base, Maine. Redesignated 9 March 1970 as the 3d Battalion, 61st Artillery and activated at Fort Bliss, Texas. Assigned 2 September 1970 to the 3d Armored Division. Redesignated 1 September 1971 as the 3d Battalion, 61st Air Defense Artillery.

CAMPAIGN PARTICIPATION CREDIT

World War I
    Streamer without inscription

World War II
    *Normandy
    *Northern France
    *Rhineland
    Ardennes-Alsace

    *Central Europe
    *Iceland 1942
    *England 1944

Korean War
    CCF intervention
    First UN counteroffensive
    CCF spring offensive
    UN summer–fall offensive

DECORATIONS

Presidential Unit Citation (Army), Streamer embroidered ST. VITH
*Belgian Fourragere 1940 (184th Antiaircraft Artillery Gun Battalion cited; DA GO 43, 1950)

*Cited in the Order of the Day of the Belgian Army for action in defense of ANTWERP (184th Antiaircraft Artillery Gun Battalion cited; DA GO 43, 1950)

*Cited in the Order of the Day of the Belgian Army for action in defense of ANTWERP HARBOR (184th Antiaircraft Artillery Gun Battalion cited; DA GO 43, 1950)

4th BATTALION, 61st AIR DEFENSE ARTILLERY

RA
(4th Infantry Division)

LINEAGE

Constituted 2 November 1907 in the Regular Army as the 168th Company, Coast Artillery Corps. Organized 20 November 1907 at Fort Monroe, Virginia. Redesignated 1 July 1916 as the 8th Company, Fort Monroe [Virginia]. Redesignated 31 August 1917 as the 8th Company, Coast Defenses of Chesapeake Bay.

Reorganized and redesignated 23 December 1917 as Headquarters Company, 60th Artillery (Coast Artillery Corps). Demobilized 24 February 1919 at Fort Monroe, Virginia.

Reconstituted 1 June 1922 in the Regular Army; concurrently consolidated with Battery C, 1st Antiaircraft Battalion (organized 1 July 1921 in the Regular Army at Fort Monroe, Virginia), and consolidated unit redesignated as Battery C, 61st Artillery Battalion (Antiaircraft) (concurrently additionally designated as the 168th Company, Coast Artillery Corps; additional designation abolished 1 July 1924). Redesignated 1 July 1924 as Battery E, 61st Coast Artillery.

Inactivated 10 August 1943 at Honiton, England; personnel concurrently transferred to Battery A, 634th Antiaircraft Artillery Automatic Weapons Battalion (constituted 25 February 1943 in the Army of the United States and activated 10 August 1943 at Honiton, England). Battery A, 634th Antiaircraft Artillery Automatic Weapons Battalion, inactivated 6 October 1945 at Camp Kilmer, New Jersey. Consolidated 28 June 1950 with Battery E, 61st Coast Artillery (disbanded 14 June 1944 and reconstituted 28 June 1950 in the Regular Army), and Battery A, 39th Antiaircraft Artillery Automatic Weapons Battalion (active) (*see* ANNEX), and consolidated unit designated as Battery A, 39th Antiaircraft Artillery Automatic Weapons Battalion, Mobile. Redesignated 31 July 1950 as Battery A, 39th Antiaircraft Artillery Battalion. Inactivated 17 June 1957 in England.

Redesignated 12 August 1958 as Headquarters and Headquarters Battery, 4th Missile Battalion, 61st Artillery (organic elements concurrently constituted). Battalion activated 1 September 1958 at San Francisco, California. Inactivated 25 March 1966 at Robins Air Force Base, Georgia. Redesignated 3 January 1969 as the 4th Battalion, 61st Artillery, and activated at Fort Bliss, Texas. Assigned (less Batteries C and D) 14 August 1969 to the 5th Infantry Division (Batteries C and D concurrently assigned to the 4th Infantry Division). Relieved (less Batteries C and D) 15 December 1970 from assignment to the 5th Infantry Division and assigned to the 4th Infantry Division. Redesignated 1 September 1971 as the 4th Battalion, 61st Air Defense Artillery.

ANNEX

Constituted 25 February 1943 in the Army of the United States as

Battery A, 788th Coast Artillery Battalion. Activated 20 April 1943 at Camp Hulen, Texas. Redesignated 30 April 1943 as Battery A, 788th Antiaircraft Artillery Automatic Weapons Battalion. Inactivated 29 June 1946 in France. Redesignated 13 October 1948 as Battery A, 39th Antiaircraft Artillery Automatic Weapons Battalion, Mobile, and allotted to the Regular Army. Activated 15 January 1949 at Fort Bliss, Texas.

CAMPAIGN PARTICIPATION CREDIT

World War I
   *St. Mihiel
   *Meuse-Argonne

World War II
   *Normandy
   *Northern France
   *Rhineland
   *Ardennes-Alsace

*Central Europe
*Iceland 1942
*England 1944

Korean War
   CCF intervention
   First UN counteroffensive
   CCF spring offensive
   UN summer–fall offensive

DECORATIONS

Presidential Unit Citation (Army), Streamer embroidered ST. VITH (634th Antiaircraft Artillery Automatic Weapons Battalion cited; WD GO 108, 1945)

HEADQUARTERS AND HEADQUARTERS BATTERY 5th BATTALION, 61st AIR DEFENSE ARTILLERY

RA
(inactive)

LINEAGE

Constituted 1 July 1924 in the Regular Army as Battery C, 61st Coast Artillery. Activated 18 November 1939 at Fort Sheridan, Illinois.

Inactivated 10 August 1943 at Honiton, England; personnel concurrently transferred to Battery C, 184th Antiaircraft Artillery Gun Battalion (constituted 25 February 1943 in the Army of the United States and activated 10 August 1943 at Honiton, England). Battery C, 184th Antiaircraft Artillery Gun Battalion, inactivated 4 December 1945 at Camp Myles Standish, Massachusetts. Consolidated 28 June 1950 with Battery C, 61st Coast Artillery (disbanded 14 June 1944 and reconstituted 28 June 1950 in the Regular Army), and consolidated unit redesignated as Battery C, 61st Antiaircraft Artillery Battalion. Redesignated 21 August 1950 as Battery C, 61st Antiaircraft Artillery Automatic Weapons Battalion, an element of the 6th Armored Division. Activated 5 September 1950 at Fort Leonard Wood, Missouri. Inactivated 16 March 1956 at Fort Leonard Wood, Missouri, and relieved from assignment to the 6th Armored Division.

Redesignated 12 August 1958 as Battery C, 61st Artillery. Activated 1 September 1958 at Fort Bliss, Texas. Inactivated 25 April 1959 at Fort Bliss, Texas. Redesignated 25 August 1961 as Headquarters and Headquarters Battery, 5th Battalion, 61st Artillery. Redesignated 1 September 1971 as Headquarters and Headquarters Battery, 5th Battalion, 61st Air Defense Artillery.

CAMPAIGN PARTICIPATION CREDIT

World War I
  Streamer without inscription

World War II
  *Normandy
  *Northern France
  *Rhineland
  Ardennes-Alsace
  *Central Europe

*Iceland 1942
*England 1944

Korean War
  CCF intervention
  First UN counteroffensive
  CCF spring offensive
  UN summer–fall offensive

DECORATIONS

Presidential Unit Citation (Army), Streamer embroidered ST. VITH
  *Belgian Fourragere 1940 (184th Antiaircraft Artillery Gun Battalion cited; DA GO 43, 1950)
    *Cited in the Order of the Day of the Belgian Army for action in defense of ANTWERP (184th Antiaircraft Artillery Gun Battalion cited; DA GO 43, 1950)
    *Cited in the Order of the Day of the Belgian Army for action in defense of ANTWERP HARBOR (184th Antiaircraft Artillery Gun Battalion cited; DA GO 43, 1950)

6th BATTALION, 61st AIR DEFENSE ARTILLERY

RA
(inactive)

LINEAGE

Constituted 9 March 1918 in the Regular Army as Headquarters, 1st Battalion, 61st Artillery (Coast Artillery Corps), and organized at Fort Moultrie, South Carolina. Demobilized 28 February 1919 at Camp Upton, New York. Reconstituted 1 July 1924 in the Regular Army and redesignated as Headquarters and Headquarters Battery and Combat Train, 1st Battalion, 61st Coast Artillery. Activated 18 November 1939 at Fort Sheridan, Illinois, as Headquarters and Headquarters Battery, 1st Battalion, 61st Coast Artillery.

Inactivated 10 August 1943 at Honiton, England; personnel concurrently transferred to Headquarters and Headquarters Battery, 184th Antiaircraft Artillery Gun Battalion (constituted 25 February 1943 in the Army of the United States and activated 10 August 1943 at Honiton, England). Headquarters and Headquarters Battery, 184th Antiaircraft Artillery Gun Battalion, inactivated 4 December 1945 at Camp Myles Standish, Massachusetts. Consolidated 28 June 1950 with Headquarters and Headquarters Battery, 1st Battalion, 61st Coast Artillery (disbanded 14 June 1944 and reconstituted 28 June 1950 in the Regular Army), and consolidated unit redesignated as Headquarters and Headquarters Battery, 61st Antiaircraft Artillery Battalion. Redesignated 21 August 1950 as Headquarters and Headquarters Battery, 61st Antiaircraft Artillery Automatic Weapons Battalion, an element of the 6th Armored Division. Activated 5 September 1950 at Fort Leonard Wood, Missouri. Inactivated 16 March 1956 at Fort Leonard Wood, Missouri, and relieved from assignment to the 6th Armored Division.

Redesignated 16 February 1961 as Headquarters and Headquarters Battery, 6th Missile Battalion, 61st Artillery (organic elements concurrently constituted). Battalion activated 25 March 1961 at Fort Bliss, Texas. Redesignated 25 August 1965 as the 6th Battalion, 61st Artillery. Redesignated 1 September 1971 as the 6th Battalion, 61st Air Defense Artillery. Inactivated 13 September 1972 at Fort Bliss, Texas.

CAMPAIGN PARTICIPATION CREDIT

World War I
  *Streamer without inscription

World War II
  *Normandy
  *Northern France
  *Rhineland
  Ardennes-Alsace

*Central Europe
*Iceland 1942
*England 1944

Korean War
  CCF intervention
  First UN counteroffensive
  CCF spring offensive
  UN summer–fall offensive

DECORATIONS

Presidential Unit Citation (Army), Streamer embroidered ST. VITH

*Belgian Fourragere 1940 (184th Antiaircraft Artillery Gun Battalion cited; DA GO 43, 1950)

*Cited in the Order of the Day of the Belgian Army for action in defense of ANTWERP (184th Antiaircraft Artillery Gun Battalion cited; DA GO 43, 1950)

*Cited in the Order of the Day of the Belgian Army for action in defense of ANTWERP HARBOR (184th Antiaircraft Artillery Gun Battalion cited; DA GO 43, 1950)

7th BATTALION, 61st AIR DEFENSE ARTILLERY

RA
(inactive)

LINEAGE

Constituted 1 July 1924 in the Regular Army as Headquarters and Headquarters Battery and Combat Train, 2d Battalion, 61st Coast Artillery. Activated 28 November 1939 at Fort Sheridan, Illinois, as Headquarters and Headquarters Battery, 2d Battalion, 61st Coast Artillery.

Inactivated 10 August 1943 at Honiton, England; personnel concurrently transferred to Headquarters and Headquarters Battery, 634th Antiaircraft Artillery Automatic Weapons Battalion (constituted 25 February 1943 in the Army of the United States and activated 10 August 1943 at Honiton, England). Headquarters and Headquarters Battery, 634th Antiaircraft Artillery Automatic Weapons Battalion, inactivated 6 October 1945 at Camp Kilmer, New Jersey. Consolidated 28 June 1950 with Headquarters and Headquarters Battery, 2d Battalion, 61st Coast Artillery (disbanded 14 June 1944 and reconstituted 28 June 1950 in the Regular Army), and Headquarters and Headquarters Battery, 39th Antiaircraft Artillery Automatic Weapons Battalion, Mobile (active) (*see* ANNEX), and consolidated unit designated as Headquarters and Headquarters Battery, 39th Antiaircraft Artillery Automatic Weapons Battalion, Mobile. Redesignated 31 July 1950 as Headquarters and Headquarters Battery, 39th Antiaircraft Artillery Battalion. Inactivated 17 June 1957 in England.

Redesignated 25 August 1961 as Headquarters and Headquarters Battery, 7th Battalion, 61st Artillery. Activated 10 November 1969 at Fort Bliss, Texas (organic elements concurrently constituted and activated). Redesignated 1 September 1971 as the 7th Battalion, 61st Air Defense Artillery. Inactivated 13 September 1972 in Germany.

ANNEX

Constituted 25 February 1943 in the Army of the United States as Headquarters and Headquarters Battery, 788th Coast Artillery Battalion. Activated 20 April 1943 at Camp Hulen, Texas. Redesignated 30 April 1943 as Headquarters and Headquarters Battery, 788th Antiaircraft Artillery Automatic Weapons Battalion. Inactivated 29 June 1946 in France. Redesignated 13 October 1948 as Headquarters and Headquarters Battery, 39th Antiaircraft Artillery Automatic Weapons Battalion, Mobile, and allotted to the Regular Army. Activated 15 January 1949 at Fort Bliss, Texas.

Campaign Participation Credit

World War I
    Streamer without inscription

World War II
    *Normandy
    *Northern France
    *Rhineland
    *Ardennes-Alsace
    *Central Europe

*Iceland 1942
*England 1944

Korean War
    CCF intervention
    First UN counteroffensive
    CCF spring offensive
    UN summer–fall offensive

Decorations

*Presidential Unit Citation (Army), Streamer embroidered ST. VITH (634th Antiaircraft Artillery Automatic Weapons Battalion cited; WD GO 108, 1945)

8th BATTALION, 61st AIR DEFENSE ARTILLERY

RA
(inactive)

LINEAGE

Constituted 9 October 1942 in the Regular Army as Headquarters and Headquarters Battery, 3d Battalion, 61st Coast Artillery. Activated 8 January 1943 at Reykjavik, Iceland.

Inactivated 10 August 1943 at Honiton, England; personnel concurrently transferred to Headquarters and Headquarters Battery, 635th Antiaircraft Artillery Automatic Weapons Battalion (constituted 25 February 1943 in the Army of the United States and activated 10 August 1943 at Honiton, England). Headquarters and Headquarters Battery, 635th Antiaircraft Artillery Automatic Weapons Battalion, inactivated 27 March 1946 at Camp Kilmer, New Jersey. Consolidated 28 June 1950 with Headquarters and Headquarters Battery, 3d Battalion, 61st Coast Artillery (disbanded 14 June 1944 and reconstituted 28 June 1950 in the Regular Army), and consolidated unit redesignated as Headquarters and Headquarters Battery, 52d Antiaircraft Artillery Battalion. Redesignated 20 October 1950 as Headquarters and Headquarters Battery, 52d Antiaircraft Artillery Automatic Weapons Battalion, and activated at Fort Lewis, Washington. Inactivated 10 November 1951 in Korea. Redesignated 19 November 1952 as Headquarters and Headquarters Battery, 52d Antiaircraft Artillery Automatic Weapons Battalion, Mobile. Activated 26 November 1952 at Camp Roberts, California. Redesignated 31 March 1953 as Headquarters and Headquarters Battery, 52d Antiaircraft Artillery Battalion. Inactivated 15 June 1957 at Castle Air Force Base, California.

Redesignated 25 August 1961 as Headquarters and Headquarters Battery, 8th Battalion, 61st Artillery. Activated 6 September 1970 at Fort Bliss, Texas (organic elements concurrently constituted and activated). Redesignated 1 September 1971 as the 8th Battalion, 61st Air Defense Artillery, and assigned to the 2d Infantry Division. Inactivated 13 September 1972 in Korea and relieved from assignment to the 2d Infantry Division.

CAMPAIGN PARTICIPATION CREDIT

World War I
    Streamer without inscription

World War II
    *Normandy
    *Northern France
    *Rhineland
    *Ardennes-Alsace
    *Central Europe

*Iceland 1942
*England 1944

Korean War
    *CCF intervention
    *First UN counteroffensive
    *CCF spring offensive
    *UN summer–fall offensive

DECORATIONS

Presidential Unit Citation (Army), Streamer embroidered ST. VITH

*Republic of Korea Presidential Unit Citation, Streamer embroidered KOREA (52d Antiaircraft Artillery Automatic Weapons Battalion cited; DA GO 41, 1955)

12th DETACHMENT, 61st AIR DEFENSE ARTILLERY

AR
(inactive)

LINEAGE

Constituted 9 October 1942 in the Regular Army as Battery K, 61st Coast Artillery. Activated 8 January 1943 at Reykjavik, Iceland.

Inactivated 10 August 1943 at Honiton, England; personnel concurrently transferred to Battery B, 635th Antiaircraft Artillery Automatic Weapons Battalion. Battery B, 635th Antiaircraft Artillery Automatic Weapons Battalion, inactivated 27 March 1946 at Camp Kilmer, New Jersey. Consolidated 28 June 1950 with Battery K, 61st Coast Artillery (disbanded 14 June 1944 and reconstituted 28 June 1950 in the Regular Army), and consolidated unit redesignated as Battery B, 52d Antiaircraft Artillery Battalion. Redesignated 20 October 1950 as Battery B, 52d Antiaircraft Artillery Automatic Weapons Battalion, and activated at Fort Lewis, Washington. Inactivated 10 November 1951 in Korea. Redesignated 19 November 1952 as Battery B, 52d Antiaircraft Artillery Automatic Weapons Battalion, Mobile. Activated 26 November 1952 at Camp Roberts, California. Redesignated 31 March 1953 as Battery B, 52d Antiaircraft Artillery Battalion. Inactivated 15 June 1957 at Castle Air Force Base, California.

Redesignated 24 July 1959 as the 12th Detachment, 61st Artillery; concurrently withdrawn from the Regular Army, allotted to the Army Reserve, and assigned to the Fifth United States Army. Activated 1 September 1959 at Lafayette, Indiana. Inactivated 31 January 1963 at Lafayette, Indiana. Redesignated 1 September 1971 as the 12th Detachment, 61st Air Defense Artillery.

CAMPAIGN PARTICIPATION CREDIT

World War II–EAME
Normandy
Northern France
Rhineland
Ardennes-Alsace
Central Europe
England 1944

Korean War
CCF intervention
First UN counteroffensive
CCF spring offensive
UN summer–fall offensive

DECORATIONS

Republic of Korea Presidential Unit Citation, Streamer embroidered KOREA (52d Antiaircraft Artillery Automatic Weapons Battalion cited; DA GO 41, 1955)

16th DETACHMENT, 61st AIR DEFENSE ARTILLERY

RA
(inactive)

LINEAGE

Constituted 9 October 1942 in the Regular Army as Battery I, 61st Coast Artillery. Activated 8 January 1943 at Reykjavik, Iceland.

Inactivated 10 October 1943 at Honiton, England; personnel concurrently transferred to Battery A, 635th Antiaircraft Artillery Automatic Weapons Battalion. Battery A, 635th Antiaircraft Artillery Automatic Weapons Battalion, inactivated 27 March 1946 at Camp Kilmer, New Jersey. Consolidated 28 June 1950 with Battery I, 61st Coast Artillery (disbanded 14 June 1944 and reconstituted 28 June 1950 in the Regular Army), and consolidated unit redesignated as Battery A, 52d Antiaircraft Artillery Battalion. Redesignated 20 October 1950 as Battery A, 52d Antiaircraft Artillery Automatic Weapons Battalion, and activated at Fort Lewis, Washington. Inactivated 10 November 1951 in Korea. Redesignated 19 November 1952 as Battery A, 52d Antiaircraft Artillery Automatic Weapons Battalion, Mobile. Activated 26 November 1952 at Camp Roberts, California. Redesignated 31 March 1953 as Battery A, 52d Antiaircraft Artillery Battalion. Inactivated 15 June 1957 at Castle Air Force Base, California.

Redesignated 5 August 1958 as the 16th Detachment, 61st Artillery. Activated 1 September 1958 at Camp Haven, Wisconsin. Inactivated 1 July 1962 at Fort Stewart, Georgia. Redesignated 1 September 1971 as the 16th Detachment, 61st Air Defense Artillery.

CAMPAIGN PARTICIPATION CREDIT

World War II–EAME
Normandy
Northern France
Rhineland
Ardennes-Alsace
Central Europe
England 1944

Korean War
CCF intervention
First UN counteroffensive
CCF spring offensive
UN summer–fall offensive

DECORATIONS

Republic of Korea Presidential Unit Citation, Streamer embroidered KOREA (52d Antiaircraft Artillery Automatic Weapons Battalion cited; DA GO 41, 1955)

61ST AIR DEFENSE ARTILLERY BIBLIOGRAPHY

Aaron, John S. "24th Division Antiaircraft Artillery." *Antiaircraft Artillery Journal* 95 (January–February 1952):18–20. Contains information about the 52d Antiaircraft Artillery Battalion.

"Activities of the 35th Antiaircraft Artillery Brigade." *Antiaircraft Artillery Journal* 93 (July 1950):31–32. Contains information about the 39th Antiaircraft Artillery Battalion.

Dyer, Frederick. "1st Regiment of Artillery." *A Compendium of the War of the Rebellion.* New York: Thomas Yoseloff, 1959. Contains information about the current 1st Battalion, 61st Air Defense Artillery.

Gill, Burgo D. "The '61st Coast Artillery' Mechanized Force." *Quartermaster Review* 20 (January 1941):39–41, 81–84.

Haskin, William Lawrence. "The First Regiment of Artillery, 1821–1876." *The Army of the United States.* Edited by Theophilus F. Rodenbough and William L. Haskin, 301–11. New York: Maynard, Merrill and Company, 1896. Originally published in the *Journal of the Military Service Institution of the United States* 15 (1894):1321–31. Contains information about the current 1st Battalion, 61st Air Defense Artillery.

———. *The History of the First Regiment of Artillery; From Organization in 1821 to January 1st, 1876.* Portland, Maine: B. Thurston and Company, 1879. Contains information about the current 1st Battalion, 61st Air Defense Artillery.

History of the 184th AAA Gun Battalion, 1943–1945. Fulda, Germany: Parzeller and Company, 1945.

Marquat, William F. "Automatic Artillery in Korea." *Antiaircraft Artillery Journal* 93 (November–December 1950):2–9; 94 (January–February 1951):2–12; (March–April 1951):2–5; (May–June 1951):2–6; (July–August 1951):2–9; (September–October 1951):2–5; (November–December 1951):2–6; 95 (January–February 1952):2–5; (March–April 1952):8–10; (May–June 1952):12–15. Contains information about the 52d Antiaircraft Artillery Battalion.

Sprague, John T. *The Origin, Progress, and Conclusion of the Florida War.* New York: D. Appleton and Company, 1848. Reprint. Gainesville, Fla.: University of Florida Press, 1964. Contains information about the current 1st Battalion, 61st Air Defense Artillery.

39th AAA, AW Battalion (M), Fort Bliss, Texas, 1949. Baton Rouge: Army and Navy Publishing Company, 1949.

"View From the Field: Clear the Sky." *Air Defense Magazine* (April–June 1973):19–21. Pertains to the 2d Battalion, 61st Air Defense Artillery.

Wilson, William H., John B. McClure, and John McLaren. *A History of the Sixth Company, Coast Artillery, Late Battery "G," First Untied States Artillery, 1808–1906.* Hampton: Houston Printing Company, 1906. Pertains to the current 1st Battalion, 61st Air Defense Artillery.

62d AIR DEFENSE ARTILLERY

Heraldic items

Coat of Arms

Shield: Gyronny of six embattled azure and gules, a circle of sixteen mullets argent.

Crest: On a wreath of the colors, argent and azure, on a saltire azure fimbriated argent two arrows of the last, all entwined with a serpent vert.

Motto: *Nitimur in Alta* (We Aim at High Things).

Symbolism: The six embattled sectors symbolize participation in six wars by units of the 62d Coast Artillery, from which the 62d Air Defense Artillery is descended—the War of 1812, Indian Wars, Mexican War, Civil War, War With Spain, and the Philippine Insurrection. The blue and red and the sixteen mullets commemorate the date (1798) one element of the regiment was organized; the uniforms worn by artillery soldiers were dark blue faced with scarlet and there were sixteen states in the Union.

The saltire, alluding to the flag of the Confederacy, is blue to indicate that service of elements of the regiment during the Civil War was with the Union Army. The two arrows represent the Indian Wars and the serpent the Mexican War.

Distinctive Insignia

The distinctive insignia is the shield of the coat of arms.

Lineage and Honors

Lineage

Constituted 1 August 1921 in the Regular Army as the 2d Antiaircraft Artillery Battalion. Organized 4 September 1921 at Fort Totten, New York, from existing units. Redesignated 1 June 1922 as the 62d Artillery Battalion (Antiaircraft).

Reorganized and redesignated 14 September 1922 as the 62d Artillery (Antiaircraft) (Coast Artillery Corps). Redesignated 1 July 1924 as the 62d Coast Artillery. Regiment broken up 24 March 1944 and its elements reorganized and redesignated as follows: Headquarters and Headquarters Battery, 80th Antiaircraft Artillery Group; 1st Battalion as the 62d Antiaircraft Artillery Gun Battalion; 2d Battalion as the 893d Antiaircraft Artillery Automatic Weapons Battalion; and 3d Battalion as the 331st Antiaircraft Artillery Searchlight Battalion.

Headquarters and Headquarters Battery, 80th Antiaircraft Artillery Group, inactivated 14 December 1945 in Germany. Activated 20 December 1948 at Fort Bliss, Texas. Redesignated 20 March 1958 as Headquarters and Headquarters Battery, 80th Artillery Group. Inactivated 24 June 1961 at Fort Wadsworth, New York.

62d Antiaircraft Artillery Gun Battalion inactivated 13 March 1946 at Camp Kilmer, New Jersey. Redesignated 9 December 1948 as the 62d Antiaircraft Artillery Automatic Weapons Battalion. Activated 15 January 1949 at Fort Bliss, Texas. Assigned 4 November 1949 to the 2d Armored Division. Relieved 20 October 1950 from assignment to the 2d Armored Division. Redesignated 1 October 1953 as the 62d Antiaircraft Artillery Battalion. Inactivated 15 September 1958 in Germany.

893d Antiaircraft Artillery Automatic Weapons Battalion inactivated 14 December 1945 in Germany. Redesignated 13 October 1948 as the 50th Antiaircraft Artillery Automatic Weapons Battalion. Activated 8 June 1949 at Fort Bliss, Texas. Redesignated 20 March 1953 as the 50th Antiaircraft Artillery Battalion. Inactivated 25 June 1958 in Korea.

331st Antiaircraft Artillery Searchlight Battalion disbanded 4 December 1944 in Italy. Reconstituted 5 August 1958 in the Regular Army.

Headquarters and Headquarters Battery, 80th Artillery Group; 62d and 50th Antiaircraft Artillery Battalions; and 331st Antiaircraft Artillery Searchlight Battalion consolidated, reorganized, and redesignated 24 June 1961 as the 62d Artillery, a parent regiment under the Combat Arms Regimental System. Redesignated 1 September 1971 as the 62d Air Defense Artillery.

CAMPAIGN PARTICIPATION CREDIT

War of 1812
Streamer without inscription

Mexican War
Vera Cruz
Cerro Gordo
Contreras
Churubusco
Molino del Rey
Chapultepec
Puebla 1847

Indian Wars
Seminoles
Washington 1858

Civil War
Peninsula
Antietam
Fredericksburg
Chancellorsville
Gettysburg
Wilderness
Spotsylvania
Shenandoah
Virginia 1863

War With Spain
Manila

Philippine Insurrection
Manila
Malolos
Luzon 1899

World War II
Algeria-French Morocco
Tunisia
Sicily
Rome-Arno
Southern France
Rhineland
Ardennes-Alsace
Central Europe

Korean War
UN defensive
UN offensive
CCF intervention
First UN counteroffensive
CCF spring offensive
UN summer-fall offensive
Second Korean winter
Korea, summer-fall 1952
Third Korean winter
Korea, summer 1953

DECORATIONS

Presidential Unit Citation (Navy), Streamer embroidered INCHON (50th Antiaircraft Artillery Automatic Weapons Battalion cited; DA GO 63, 1952)

1st BATTALION, 62d AIR DEFENSE ARTILLERY

RA
(25th Infantry Division)

LINEAGE

Constituted 27 April 1798 in the Regular Army as a company in the 2d Regiment of Artillerists and Engineers. Organized in 1798 near Philadelphia, Pennsylvania, as Capt. Callender Irvine's Company, 2d Regiment of Artillerists and Engineers. Redesignated 3 March 1799 as Capt. Callender Irvine's Company, 2d Battalion, 2d Regiment of Artillerists and Engineers. Consolidated 28 October 1800 with Capt. William Steele's Company, 2d Regiment of Artillerists and Engineers (constituted 27 April 1798 in the Regular Army and organized near Philadelphia, Pennsylvania, as Capt. Walter L. Cochran's Company, 2d Regiment of Artillerists and Engineers; redesignated in 1800 as Capt. William Steele's Company, 2d Regiment of Artillerists and Engineers), and consolidated unit designated as Capt. Callender Irvine's Company, 2d Battalion, 2d Regiment of Artillerists and Engineers. Redesignated 20 May 1801 as Capt. George W. Carmichael's Company, 2d Battalion, 2d Regiment of Artillerists and Engineers. Consolidated 1 April 1802 with Capt. William A. Barron's Company, 2d Regiment of Artillerists and Engineers (constituted 27 April 1798 in the Regular Army and organized at Fort Jay, New York), and Capt. William Deveaux's Company, 2d Regiment of Artillerists and Engineers (constituted 27 April 1798 in the Regular Army and organized at Fort Jay, New York, as Capt. Francis K. Huger's Company, 2d Regiment of Artillerists and Engineers; redesignated in 1801 as Capt. William Deveaux's Company, 2d Regiment of Artillerists and Engineers), and consolidated unit redesignated as Capt. George Ingersoll's Company, Regiment of Artillerists. Redesignated 8 July 1802 as Capt. John W. Livingston's Company, Regiment of Artillerists. Redesignated in July 1804 as Capt. Richard Whiley's Company, Regiment of Artillerists. Redesignated 11 January 1812 as Capt. James R. Hanham's Company, 1st Regiment of Artillery. Redesignated 12 May 1814 as Capt. James R. Hanham's Company, Corps of Artillery. Redesignated in April 1815 as Capt. Richard L. Howell's Company, Corps of Artillery. Redesignated 17 May 1815 as Capt. Richard L. Howell's Company, Corps of Artillery, Northern Division. Redesignated 17 June 1816 as Company K, 4th Battalion, Corps of Artillery, Northern Division. Redesignated 1 June 1821 as Company G, 2d Regiment of Artillery.

Reorganized and redesignated 13 February 1901 as the 17th Company, Coast Artillery, Artillery Corps. Redesignated 2 February 1907 as the 17th Company, Coast Artillery Corps. Redesignated 5 August 1916 as the 4th Company, Fort Mills [Philippine Islands]. Redesignated 31 August 1917 as the 4th Company, Coast Defenses of Manila and Subic Bays. Redesignated 30 June 1922 as the 17th Company, Coast Artillery Corps.

Reorganized and redesignated 14 September 1922 as Battery B, 62d Artillery (Antiaircraft) (Coast Artillery Corps) (concurrently additionally designated as the 17th Company, Coast Artillery Corps; additional designation abolished 1 July 1924). Redesignated 1 July 1924 as Battery B, 62d Coast Artillery.

Reorganized and redesignated 24 March 1944 as Battery B, 62d Antiaircraft Artillery Gun Battalion. Inactivated 13 March 1946 at Camp Kilmer, New Jersey. Redesignated 9 December 1948 as Battery B, 62d Antiaircraft Artillery Automatic Weapons Battalion. Activated 15 January 1949 at Fort Bliss, Texas. (62d Antiaircraft Artillery Automatic Weapons Battalion assigned 4 November 1949 to the 2d Armored Division; relieved 20 October 1950 from assignment to the 2d Armored Division.) Redesignated 1 October 1953 as Battery B, 62d Antiaircraft Artillery Battalion. Inactivated 15 September 1958 in Germany.

Redesignated 16 September 1958 as Headquarters and Headquarters Battery, 1st Automatic Weapons Battalion, 62d Artillery (organic elements concurrently constituted). Battalion activated 1 June 1959 at St. Louis, Missouri. Redesignated 20 December 1965 as the 1st Battalion, 62d Artillery. Inactivated 15 January 1969 at Scott Air Force Base, Illinois. Activated 15 March 1971 at Fort Bliss, Texas. Redesignated 1 September 1971 as the 1st Battalion, 62d Air Defense Artillery. Assigned 6 January 1972 to the 25th Infantry Division.

CAMPAIGN PARTICIPATION CREDIT

War of 1812
  *Streamer without inscription

Mexican War
  *Monterey
  *Vera Cruz
  *Cerro Gordo
  *Contreras
  *Churubusco
  *Molino del Rey
  *Chapultepec
  *Puebla 1847

Indian Wars
  *Seminoles
   Washington 1858

Civil War
  *Bull Run
  *Peninsula
  *Antietam
  *Fredericksburg
  *Chancellorsville
  *Gettysburg
  *Wilderness
  *Spotsylvania
   Shenandoah
  *Cold Harbor
  *Virginia 1861
  *Virginia 1862
  *Virginia 1863

War With Spain
  Manila

Philippine Insurrection
  Manila
  Malolos
  Luzon 1899

World War II
  *Algeria-French Morocco
  *Tunisia
  *Sicily
  *Rome-Arno
  *Southern France
  *Rhineland
  *Ardennes-Alsace
  *Central Europe

Korean War
  UN defensive
  UN offensive
  CCF intervention
  First UN counteroffensive
  CCF spring offensive
  UN summer-fall offensive
  Second Korean winter
  Korea, summer-fall 1952
  Third Korean winter
  Korea, summer 1953

Decorations

  Presidential Unit Citation (Navy), Streamer embroidered INCHON

2d BATTALION, 62d AIR DEFENSE ARTILLERY

RA
(nondivisional)

LINEAGE

Constituted 12 April 1808 in the Regular Army as a company in the Regiment of Light Artillery. Organized in 1808 as Capt. George Peter's Company of Light Artillery, Regiment of Light Artillery. Redesignated in 1809 as Capt. Joseph G. Telfair's Company of Light Artillery, Regiment of Light Artillery. Redesignated in 1811 as Capt. William Campbell's Company of Light Artillery, Regiment of Light Artillery. Redesignated in 1812 as Capt. James Gibson's Company of Light Artillery, Regiment of Light Artillery. Redesignated in 1813 as Capt. Arthur W. Thornton's Company of Light Artillery, Regiment of Light Artillery. Redesignated 22 May 1816 as Company F, Regiment of Light Artillery. Redesignated 1 June 1821 as Company H, 3d Regiment of Artillery.

Reorganized and redesignated 13 February 1901 as the 30th Company, Coast Artillery, Artillery Corps. Redesignated 2 February 1907 as the 30th Company, Coast Artillery Corps. Redesignated in 1916 as the 1st Company, Fort Worden [Washington]. Redesignated 31 August 1917 as the 1st Company, Coast Defenses of Puget Sound. Redesignated 1 June 1922 as the 30th Company, Coast Artillery Corps.

Reorganized and redesignated 14 September 1922 as Battery E, 62d Artillery (Antiaircraft) (Coast Artillery Corps) (concurrently additionally designated as the 30th Company, Coast Artillery Corps; additional designation abolished 1 July 1924). Redesignated 1 July 1924 as Battery E, 62d Coast Artillery.

Reorganized and redesignated 24 March 1944 as Battery A, 893d Antiaircraft Artillery Automatic Weapons Battalion. Inactivated 14 December 1945 in Germany. Redesignated 13 October 1948 as Battery A, 50th Antiaircraft Artillery Automatic Weapons Battalion. Activated 8 June 1949 at Fort Bliss, Texas. Redesignated 20 March 1953 as Battery A, 50th Antiaircraft Artillery Battalion. Inactivated 25 June 1958 in Korea.

Redesignated 12 August 1958 as Headquarters and Headquarters Battery, 2d Missile Battalion, 62d Artillery (organic elements concurrently constituted). Battalion activated 1 September 1958 at Lancaster, New York. Inactivated 15 December 1961 at Lancaster, New York. Redesignated 1 September 1971 as the 2d Missile Battalion, 62d Air Defense Artillery. Redesignated 13 September 1972 as the 2d Battalion, 62d Air Defense Artillery, and activated in Germany.

CAMPAIGN PARTICIPATION CREDIT

War of 1812
  *Canada

Mexican War
  *Vera Cruz
  *Cerro Gordo
  *Contreras
  *Churubusco
   Molino del Rey
  *Chapultepec
   Puebla 1847

Indian Wars
  *Seminoles
   Washington 1858
  *Nevada 1860

Civil War
   Peninsula
   Antietam
   Fredericksburg
   Chancellorsville
   Gettysburg
   Wilderness
   Spotsylvania
   Shenandoah
   Virginia 1863

War With Spain
  *Manila

Philippine Insurrection
  *Manila
  *Malolos
  *Luzon 1899

World War II
  *Algeria-French Morocco (with arrowhead)
   Tunisia
   Sicily
  *Rome-Arno
  *Southern France
  *Rhineland
   Ardennes-Alsace
  *Central Europe

Korean War
  *UN defensive
  *UN offensive
  *CCF intervention
  *First UN counteroffensive
  *CCF spring offensive
  *UN summer-fall offensive
  *Second Korean winter
  *Korea, summer-fall 1952
  *Third Korean winter
  *Korea, summer 1953

DECORATIONS

*Presidential Unit Citation (Navy), Streamer embroidered INCHON (50th Antiaircraft Artillery Automatic Weapons Battalion cited; DA GO 63, 1952)

*Republic of Korea Presidential Unit Citation, Streamer embroidered INCHON-SEOUL-HUNGNAM (50th Antiaircraft Artillery Automatic Weapons Battalion cited; DA GO 8, 1952)

*Republic of Korea Presidential Unit Citation, Streamer embroidered KOREA 1950–1952 (50th Antiaircraft Artillery Automatic Weapons Battalion cited; DA GO 41, 1955)

*Republic of Korea Presidential Unit Citation, Streamer embroidered DEFENSE OF KOREA (50th Antiaircraft Artillery Automatic Weapons Battalion cited; DA GO 51, 1957)

3d BATTALION, 62d AIR DEFENSE ARTILLERY

RA
(inactive)

LINEAGE

Organized in 1812 in the Regular Army at Fort Independence, Massachusetts, as a detachment, 2d Regiment of Artillery, under the command of 2d Lt. William Smith. Expanded and redesignated in November 1812 as Capt. John Goodall's Company, 2d Regiment of Artillery. Redesignated 12 May 1814 as Capt. John Goodall's Company, Corps of Artillery. Redesignated 17 May 1815 as Capt. John Goodall's Company, Corps of Artillery, Southern Division. Redesignated 21 August 1816 as Company P, 2d Battalion, Corps of Artillery, Southern Division. Redesignated 1 June 1821 as Company G, 3d Regiment of Artillery.

Reorganized and redesignated 13 February 1901 as the 29th Company, Coast Artillery, Artillery Corps. Redesignated 2 February 1907 as the 29th Company, Coast Artillery Corps. Redesignated 20 July 1916 as the 9th Company, Fort Winfield Scott [California]. Redesignated 31 August 1917 as the 9th Company, Coast Defenses of San Francisco. Redesignated 1 June 1922 as the 29th Company, Coast Artillery Corps.

Reorganized and redesignated 14 September 1922 as Battery C, 62d Artillery (Antiaircraft) (Coast Artillery Corps) (concurrently additionally designated as the 29th Company, Coast Artillery Corps; additional designation abolished 1 July 1924). Redesignated 1 July 1924 as Battery C, 62d Coast Artillery.

Reorganized and redesignated 24 March 1944 as Battery C, 62d Antiaircraft Artillery Gun Battalion. Inactivated 13 March 1946 at Camp Kilmer, New Jersey. Redesignated 9 December 1948 as Battery C, 62d Antiaircraft Artillery Automatic Weapons Battalion. Activated 15 January 1949 at Fort Bliss, Texas. (62d Antiaircraft Artillery Automatic Weapons Battalion assigned 4 November 1949 to the 2d Armored Division; relieved 20 October 1950 from assignment to the 2d Armored Division.) Redesignated 1 October 1953 as Battery C, 62d Antiaircraft Artillery Battalion.

Reorganized and redesignated 3 March 1958 as Headquarters and Headquarters Battery, 3d Automatic Weapons Battalion, 62d Artillery (organic elements concurrently constituted and activated). Inactivated 25 September 1961 at Fort Bragg, North Carolina. Redesignated 21 December 1965 as the 3d Battalion, 62d Artillery. Activated 1 February 1966 at Fort Bliss, Texas. Inactivated 30 June 1971 at Fort Bliss, Texas. Redesignated 1 September 1971 as the 3d Battalion, 62d Air Defense Artillery.

CAMPAIGN PARTICIPATION CREDIT

War of 1812
  *Streamer without inscription

Mexican War
  *Vera Cruz
  *Cerro Gordo
  *Contreras
  *Churubusco
  *Molino del Rey
  *Chapultepec
  *Puebla 1847

Indian Wars
  *Creeks
  *Seminoles
  *Washington 1858

Civil War
  *Peninsula
  *Antietam
   Fredericksburg
   Chancellorsville
   Gettysburg
  *Wilderness
   Spotsylvania
   Shenandoah
   Virginia 1863

War With Spain
  *Manila

Philippine Insurrection
  *Manila
  *Malolos
  *Luzon 1899
  *Luzon 1900

World War II
  *Algeria-French Morocco (with arrowhead)
   Tunisia
  *Sicily
  *Rome-Arno
  *Southern France
  *Rhineland
  *Ardennes-Alsace
  *Central Europe

Korean War
   UN defensive
   UN offensive
   CCF intervention
   First UN counteroffensive
   CCF spring offensive
   UN summer–fall offensive
   Second Korean winter
   Korea, summer–fall 1952
   Third Korean winter
   Korea, summer 1953

DECORATIONS

Presidential Unit Citation (Navy), Streamer embroidered INCHON

4th BATTALION, 62d AIR DEFENSE ARTILLERY

RA
(inactive)

LINEAGE

Constituted 5 July 1838 in the Regular Army as Company K, 3d Regiment of Artillery. Organized in August 1838 at Fort Monroe, Virginia.

Reorganized and redesignated 13 February 1901 as the 32d Company, Coast Artillery, Artillery Corps. Redesignated 2 February 1907 as the 32d Company, Coast Artillery Corps. Redesignated 20 July 1916 as the 3d Company, Fort Baker [California]. Redesignated 31 August 1917 as the 12th Company, Coast Defenses of San Francisco. Reorganized and redesignated 25 October 1918 as Battery A, 18th Artillery (Coast Artillery Corps). Reorganized and redesignated 2 December 1918 as the 12th Company, Coast Defenses of San Francisco. Inactivated 16 September 1921 at Fort Winfield Scott, California. Redesignated 1 June 1922 as the 32d Company, Coast Artillery Corps.

Redesignated 14 September 1922 as Battery F, 62d Artillery (Antiaircraft) (Coast Artillery Corps), and activated at Fort Totten, New York (concurrently additionally designated as the 32d Company, Coast Artillery Corps; additional designation abolished 1 July 1924). Redesignated 1 July 1924 as Battery F, 62d Coast Artillery.

Reorganized and redesignated 24 March 1944 as Battery B, 893d Antiaircraft Artillery Automatic Weapons Battalion. Inactivated 14 December 1945 in Germany. Redesignated 13 October 1948 as Battery B, 50th Antiaircraft Artillery Automatic Weapons Battalion. Activated 8 June 1949 at Fort Bliss, Texas. Redesignated 20 March 1953 as Battery B, 50th Antiaircraft Artillery Battalion. Inactivated 25 June 1958 in Korea.

Redesignated 12 August 1958 as Headquarters and Headquarters Battery, 4th Missile Battalion, 62d Artillery (organic elements concurrently constituted). Battalion activated 1 September 1958 at Fort MacArthur, California. Redesignated 14 June 1965 as the 4th Battalion, 62d Artillery. Redesignated 1 September 1971 as the 4th Battalion, 62d Air Defense Artillery. Inactivated 30 September 1979 at Fort Bliss, Texas.

Campaign Participation Credit

War of 1812
    Streamer without inscription

Mexican War
    Vera Cruz
    *Cerro Gordo
    *Contreras
    *Churubusco
    *Molino del Rey
    *Chapultepec
    *Puebla 1847

Indian Wars
    *Seminoles
    *Washington 1858

Civil War
    *Peninsula
    Antietam
    *Fredericksburg
    *Chancellorsville
    *Gettysburg
    *Spotsylvania
    *Petersburg
    *Shenandoah
    *Virginia 1861
    *Virginia 1863

War With Spain
    *Manila

Philippine Insurrection
    *Manila
    *Malolos
    *Luzon 1899

World War II
    *Algeria-French Morocco
    Tunisia
    Sicily
    *Rome-Arno
    *Southern France
    *Rhineland
    Ardennes-Alsace
    *Central Europe

Korean War
    *UN defensive
    *UN offensive
    *CCF intervention
    *First UN counteroffensive
    *CCF spring offensive
    *UN summer–fall offensive
    *Second Korean winter
    *Korea, summer–fall 1952
    *Third Korean winter
    *Korea, summer 1953

Decorations

*Presidential Unit Citation (Navy), Streamer embroidered INCHON (50th Antiaircraft Artillery Automatic Weapons Battalion cited; DA GO 63, 1952)

*Republic of Korea Presidential Unit Citation, Streamer embroidered INCHON-SEOUL-HUNGNAM (50th Antiaircraft Artillery Automatic Weapons Battalion cited; DA GO 8, 1952)

*Republic of Korea Presidential Unit Citation, Streamer embroidered KOREA 1950–1952 (50th Antiaircraft Artillery Automatic Weapons Battalion cited; DA GO 41, 1955)

*Republic of Korea Presidential Unit Citation, Streamer embroidered DEFENSE OF KOREA (50th Antiaircraft Artillery Automatic Weapons Battalion cited; DA GO 51, 1957)

6th BATTALION, 62d AIR DEFENSE ARTILLERY

RA
(inactive)

LINEAGE

Constituted 3 March 1847 in the Regular Army as Company L, 3d Regiment of Artillery. Organized 1 October 1847.

Reorganized and redesignated 13 February 1901 as the 33d Company, Coast Artillery, Artillery Corps. Redesignated 2 February 1907 as the 33d Company, Coast Artillery Corps. Redesignated 5 August 1916 as the 14th Company, Fort Mills [Philippine Islands]. Redesignated 31 August 1917 as the 14th Company, Coast Defenses of Manila and Subic Bays. Redesignated 30 June 1922 as the 33d Company, Coast Artillery Corps.

Reorganized and redesignated 14 September 1922 as Battery D, 62d Artillery (Antiaircraft) (Coast Artillery Corps) (concurrently additionally designated as the 33d Company, Coast Artillery Corps; additional designation abolished 1 July 1924). Redesignated 1 July 1924 as Battery D, 62d Coast Artillery.

Reorganized and redesignated 24 March 1944 as Battery D, 62d Antiaircraft Artillery Gun Battalion. Inactivated 13 March 1946 at Camp Kilmer, New Jersey. Redesignated 9 December 1948 as Battery D, 62d Antiaircraft Artillery Automatic Weapons Battalion. Activated 15 January 1949 at Fort Bliss, Texas. (62d Antiaircraft Artillery Automatic Weapons Battalion assigned 4 November 1949 to the 2d Armored Division; relieved 20 October 1950 from assignment to the 2d Armored Division.) Redesignated 1 October 1953 as Battery D, 62d Antiaircraft Artillery Battalion. Inactivated 15 September 1958 in Germany.

Redesignated 21 March 1961 as Headquarters and Headquarters Battery, 6th Missile Battalion, 62d Artillery (organic elements concurrently constituted). Battalion activated 19 April 1961 at Fort Bliss, Texas. Redesignated 20 August 1965 as the 6th Battalion, 62d Artillery. Redesignated 1 September 1971 as the 6th Battalion, 62d Air Defense Artillery. Inactivated 13 September 1972 in Germany.

CAMPAIGN PARTICIPATION CREDIT

War of 1812
    Streamer without inscription

Mexican War
    Vera Cruz
    Cerro Gordo
    Contreras
    Churubusco
    Molino del Rey
    Chapultepec
    Puebla 1847

Indian Wars
    Seminoles
    *Washington 1856
    Washington 1858

Civil War
    *Mississippi River
    *Peninsula
    *Antietam
    *Fredericksburg
    Chancellorsville
    Gettysburg
    *Wilderness
    Spotsylvania
    Shenandoah
    Virginia 1863
    *Mississippi 1863
    *Tennessee 1863
    *Tennessee 1864

War With Spain
    *Manila

Philippine Insurrection
    *Manila
    *Malolos
    *Luzon 1899

World War II
    *Algeria-French Morocco
    *Tunisia
    *Sicily
    *Rome-Arno
    *Southern France
    *Rhineland
    *Ardennes-Alsace
    *Central Europe

Korean War
    UN defensive
    UN offensive
    CCF intervention
    First UN counteroffensive
    CCF spring offensive
    UN summer-fall offensive
    Second Korean winter
    Korea, summer-fall 1952
    Third Korean winter
    Korea, summer 1953

DECORATIONS

Presidential Unit Citation (Navy), Streamer embroidered INCHON

12th DETACHMENT, 62d AIR DEFENSE ARTILLERY

RA
(inactive)

LINEAGE

Constituted 27 May 1942 in the Regular Army as Headquarters and Headquarters Battery, 3d Battalion, 62d Coast Artillery. Activated 15 June 1942 near Fort Totten, New York.

Reorganized and redesignated 24 March 1944 as Headquarters and Headquarters Battery, 331st Antiaircraft Artillery Searchlight Battalion. Disbanded 4 December 1944 in Italy.

Reconstituted 5 August 1948 in the Regular Army and redesignated as the 12th Detachment, 62d Artillery. Activated 15 September 1958 at Elmendorf Air Force Base, Alaska. Inactivated 15 September 1960 at Elmendorf Air Force Base, Alaska. Redesignated 1 September 1971 as the 12th Detachment, 62d Air Defense Artillery.

CAMPAIGN PARTICIPATION CREDIT

World War II–EAME
    Algeria-French Morocco
    Rome-Arno

DECORATIONS

None.

16th DETACHMENT, 62d AIR DEFENSE ARTILLERY

RA
(inactive)

LINEAGE

Constituted 27 May 1942 in the Regular Army as Battery I, 62d Coast Artillery. Activated 15 June 1942 near Fort Totten, New York.

Reorganized and redesignated 24 March 1944 as Battery A, 331st Antiaircraft Artillery Searchlight Battalion. Disbanded 4 December 1944 in Italy.

Reconstituted 5 August 1958 in the Regular Army and redesignated as the 16th Detachment, 62d Artillery. Activated 1 September 1958 at Fort Bliss, Texas. Inactivated 23 September 1960 at Fort Bliss, Texas. Redesignated 1 September 1971 as the 16th Detachment, 62d Air Defense Artillery.

CAMPAIGN PARTICIPATION CREDIT

World War II–EAME
    Algeria-French Morocco
    Rome-Arno

DECORATIONS

None.

62D AIR DEFENSE ARTILLERY BIBLIOGRAPHY

Anderson, Robert. *An Artillery Officer in the Mexican War, 1846–7*. New York and London: G.P. Putnam's Sons, 1911. Contains information about the current 2d, 3d, 4th, and 6th Battalions, 62d Air Defense Artillery.

Birkhimer, William E., et al. "Historical Sketch of the Second United States Artillery." *Journal of the Military Service Institution of the United States* 14 (1893): 1042. Contains information about the current 1st Battalion, 62d Air Defense Artillery.

————. "The Third Regiment of Artillery." *The Army of the United States.* Edited by Theophilus F. Rodenbough and William L. Haskin, 328–50. New York: Maynard, Merrill and Company, 1896. Originally published in the *Journal of the Military Service Institution of the United States* 14 (1893):458–90. Contains information about the current 2d, 3d, 4th, and 6th Battalions, 62d Air Defense Artillery.

Dyer, Frederick. "2d and 3d Regiments of Artillery." *A Compendium of the War of the Rebellion.* New York: Thomas Yoseloff, 1959. Contains information about the current 1st, 2d, 3d, 4th, and 6th Battalions, 62d Air Defense Artillery.

Mahon, John K. *History of the Second Seminole War, 1835–1842*. Gainesville, Fla.: University of Florida Press, 1967. Contains information about the current 1st, 2d, 3d, 4th, and 6th Battalions, 62d Air Defense Artillery.

Marquat, William F. "Automatic Artillery in Korea." *Antiaircraft Artillery Journal* 93 (November–December 1950):2–9; 94 (January–February 1951):2–12; (March–April 1951):2–5; (May–June 1951):2–6; (July–August 1951):2–9; (September–October 1951):2–5; (November–December 1951):2–6; 95 (January–February 1952):2–5; (March–April 1952):8–10; (May–June 1952):12–15. Contains information about the 50th Antiaircraft Artillery Automatic Weapons Battalion.

O'Malley, Charles S. "The 50th Antiaircraft Artillery Automatic Weapons Battalion in Korea." *Antiaircraft Artillery Journal* 94 (January 1951):20–23.

Simpson, W.A. "The Second Regiment of Artillery." *The Army of the United States.* Edited by Theophilus F. Rodenbough and William L. Haskin, 312–27. New York: Maynard, Merrill and Company, 1896. Contains information about the current 1st Battalion, 62d Air Defense Artillery.

62nd AAA, AW Battalion (SP), Fort Bliss, Texas. Baton Rouge: Army and Navy Publishing Company, 1949.

Sprague, John T. *The Origin, Progress, and Conclusion of the Florida War.* New York: D. Appleton and Company, 1948. Reprint. Gainesville, Fla.: University of Florida Press, 1964. Contains information about the current 1st, 2d, 3d, and 4th Battalions, 64th Air Defense Artillery.

242nd AAA Group. London: Montgomery, 1953. Contains information about the 62d Antiaircraft Artillery Automatic Weapons Battalion.

Weaver, Erasmus M. "History of the 2d Artillery." *Journal of the Military Service Institution of the United States* 14 (1893):1258–60. Contains information about the current 1st Battalion, 62d Air Defense Artillery.

65th AIR DEFENSE ARTILLERY

Heraldic Items

Coat of Arms

Shield: Gules, six piles or, from chief terminating at the nombril point, over all a strangler fig tree (*Ficus specia*) standing on a plot of ground, all proper.

Crest: On a wreath of the colors, or and gules, an ocelot rampant or, spotted sable.

Motto: *Sursum* (Upwards).

Symbolism: The shield is red for artillery; the yellow rays represent the direction of antiaircraft fire; the six yellow rays and the five red spaces between also represent the number of the regiment. The strangler fig tree is peculiar to tropical America and indicates the location of the regiment when it was reorganized in 1924.

      The crest is an ocelot, a native of Panama; it further signifies the character of the unit in that it usually climbs trees and fights upwards for its prey.

Distinctive Insignia

The distinctive insignia is the crest of the coat of arms without wreath.

Lineage and Honors

Lineage

Constituted 26 December 1917 in the Regular Army as the 65th Artillery (Coast Artillery Corps) and organized (less 1st Battalion) at Fort Stevens, Oregon, from existing Regular Army companies and a National Guard company from California. (1st Battalion organized 1 January 1918 at Fort Rosecrans, California.) Demobilized 28 February 1919 at Camp Lewis, Washington.

Reconstituted 1 July 1924 in the Regular Army as the 65th Coast Artillery and organized (less 3d Battalion) in the Canal Zone. (3d Battalion activated 31 July 1926 at Fort Randolph, Canal Zone.) Inactivated 15 April 1932 at Fort Amador, Canal Zone. Activated (less 2d and 3d Battalions) 1 June 1938 at Fort Winfield Scott, California. (2d Battalion activated 11 October 1939 at Fort Winfield Scott, California; 3d Battalion activated 15 June 1942 at Inglewood, California.) Regiment broken up 10 May 1943 and its elements reorganized and redesignated as follows: Headquarters and Headquarters Battery as Headquarters and Headquarters Battery, 65th Antiaircraft Artillery Group; 1st Battalion as the 65th

Antiaircraft Artillery Gun Battalion; 2d Battalion as the 255th Antiaircraft Artillery Automatic Weapons Battalion; 3d Battalion as the 245th Antiaircraft Artillery Searchlight Battalion.

Headquarters and Headquarters Battery, 65th Antiaircraft Artillery Group, inactivated 29 February 1944 at Adak, Alaska. Disbanded 26 October 1944. Reconstituted 18 December 1946 in the Regular Army. Activated 15 January 1947 at Fort Amador, Canal Zone. Inactivated 26 December 1957 at Fort Clayton, Canal Zone.

65th Antiaircraft Artillery Gun Battalion inactivated (less Batteries B, C, and D) 26 January 1945 at Camp Hood, Texas (Batteries B, C, and D redesignated 1 May 1945 as the 247th, 428th, and 429th Antiaircraft Artillery Gun Batteries—see below). 65th Antiaircraft Artillery Gun Battalion activated 1 May 1949 (with new Batteries B, C, and D) on Okinawa. Inactivated 1 September 1958 in Japan.

427th Antiaircraft Artillery Gun Battery inactivated 4 December 1945 at Fort Lawton, Washington. Redesignated 3 October 1946 as the 427th Antiaircraft Artillery Searchlight Battery. Activated 1 November 1946 at Camp Hood, Texas. Inactivated 27 December 1948 at Camp Hood, Texas. Redesignated 2 December 1954 as the 427th Airborne Antiaircraft Artillery Battery. Activated 1 January 1955 at Camp Campbell, Kentucky. Inactivated 22 March 1957 at Camp Campbell, Kentucky.

428th Antiaircraft Artillery Gun Battery reorganized and redesignated 1 November 1945 as the 428th Coast Artillery Battery. Reorganized and redesignated 9 November 1946 as the 428th Antiaircraft Artillery Gun Battery. Inactivated 5 January 1947 at Adak, Alaska. Redesignated 6 May 1953 as the 428th Antiaircraft Artillery Battery. Activated 8 June 1953 at Fort Bliss, Texas. Inactivated 15 May 1958 at Thule, Greenland.

429th Antiaircraft Artillery Gun Battery inactivated 30 November 1945 at Fort Lewis, Washington. Redesignated 6 May 1953 as the 429th Antiaircraft Artillery Battery. Activated 8 June 1953 at Fort Bliss, Texas. Inactivated 15 May 1958 at Thule, Greenland.

255th Antiaircraft Artillery Automatic Weapons Battalion disbanded 3 February 1945 at Camp Earle, Alaska. Reconstituted 28 June 1950 in the Regular Army; concurrently consolidated with the 40th Antiaircraft Artillery Gun Battalion (*see* ANNEX), and consolidated unit designated as the 40th Antiaircraft Artillery Gun Battalion. Activated 15 March 1953 in Germany. Redesignated 1 October 1953 as the 40th Antiaircraft Artillery Battalion. Inactivated 10 April 1958 in Germany.

245th Antiaircraft Artillery Searchlight Battalion inactivated 12 June 1944 at Camp Haan, California. Disbanded 26 June 1944. Reconstituted 5 August 1958 in the Regular Army.

Headquarters and Headquarters Battery, 65th Antiaircraft Artillery Group; 65th and 40th Antiaircraft Artillery Battalions; 427th Airborne Antiaircraft Artillery Battery; 428th and 429th Antiaircraft Artillery Batteries; and 245th Antiaircraft Artillery Searchlight Battalion consolidated, reorganized, and redesignated 31 July 1959 as the 65th Artillery, a parent regiment under the Combat Arms Regimental System. Redesignated 1 September 1971 as the 65th Air Defense Artillery.

ANNEX

Constituted 8 February 1943 in the Army of the United States as the 116th Coast Artillery Battalion. Activated 20 March 1943 at Camp Davis, North Carolina. Redesignated 28 June 1943 as the 116th Antiaircraft Artillery Gun Battalion. Inactivated 6 October 1945 in Germany. Redesignated 13 October 1948 as the 40th Antiaircraft Artillery Gun Battalion and allotted to the Regular Army.

CAMPAIGN PARTICIPATION CREDIT

World War I
St. Mihiel
Meuse-Argonne
Lorraine 1918

World War II
Normandy (with arrowhead)
Northern France
Rhineland
Ardennes-Alsace
Central Europe
Aleutian Islands

Vietnam
Counteroffensive, Phase II
Counteroffensive, Phase III
Tet Counteroffensive
Counteroffensive, Phase IV
Counteroffensive, Phase V
Counteroffensive, Phase VI
Tet 69/Counteroffensive
Summer–fall 1969
Winter–spring 1970
Sanctuary Counteroffensive
Counteroffensive, Phase VII
Consolidation I
Consolidation II

DECORATIONS

Presidential Unit Citation (Navy), Streamer embroidered VIETNAM 1966–1967 (Battery G, 65th Artillery, cited; DA GO 32, 1973)

Valorous Unit Award, Streamer embroidered QUANG TRI–THUA THIEN (Battery G, 65th Artillery, cited; DA GO 48, 1968)

Valorous Unit Award, Streamer embroidered QUANG TIN PROVINCE (Battery G, 65th Artillery, cited; DA GO 39, 1970)

Meritorious Unit Commendation, Streamer embroidered FLORIDA 1962–1963 (6th Missile Battalion, 65th Artillery, cited; DA GO 33, 1963)

1st BATTALION, 65th AIR DEFENSE ARTILLERY

RA
(nondivisional)

LINEAGE

Constituted 14 August 1901 in the Regular Army as the 116th Company, Coast Artillery, Artillery Corps. Organized 17 August 1901 at Fort Screven, Georgia. Redesignated 2 February 1907 as the 116th Company, Coast Artillery Corps. Redesignated in July 1916 as the 4th Company, Fort Grant [Canal Zone]. Redesignated 31 August 1917 as the 4th Company, Coast Defenses of Balboa. Redesignated 30 June 1922 as the 116th Company, Coast Artillery Corps.

Reorganized and redesignated 1 July 1924 as Battery A, 65th Coast Artillery. Inactivated 15 April 1932 at Fort Amador, Canal Zone. Activated 1 June 1938 at Fort Winfield Scott, California.

Reorganized and redesignated 10 May 1943 as Battery A, 65th Antiaircraft Artillery Gun Battalion. Inactivated 26 January 1945 at Camp Hood, Texas. Activated 1 May 1949 on Okinawa. Redesignated 23 February 1955 as Battery A, 65th Antiaircraft Artillery Battalion.

Reorganized and redesignated 1 September 1958 as Headquarters and Headquarters Battery, 1st Gun Battalion, 65th Artillery (organic elements constituted 7 August 1958 and activated 1 September 1958). (Headquarters and Headquarters Battery, 1st Gun Battalion, 65th Artillery, consolidated 1 October 1958 with Battery B, 49th Antiaircraft Artillery Missile Battalion [*see* ANNEX], and consolidated unit designated as Headquarters and Headquarters Battery, 1st Gun Battalion, 65th Artillery.) Reorganized and redesignated 25 March 1959 as the 1st Missile Battalion, 65th Artillery. Redesignated 30 June 1968 as the 1st Battalion, 65th Artillery. Inactivated 1 May 1970 on Okinawa. Redesignated 1 September 1971 as the 1st Battalion, 65th Air Defense Artillery. Activated 13 September 1972 at Key West, Florida.

ANNEX

Constituted 14 August 1901 in the Regular Army as the 115th Company, Coast Artillery, Artillery Corps. Organized 23 August 1901 at San Diego, California. Redesignated 2 February 1907 as the 115th Company, Coast Artillery Corps. Redesignated in July 1916 as the 2d Company, Fort Rosecrans [California]. Redesignated 31 August 1917 as the 2d Company, Coast Defenses of San Diego.

Reorganized and redesignated 1 January 1918 as Battery A, 65th Artillery (Coast Artillery Corps). Demobilized 28 February 1919 at Camp Lewis, Washington.

Reconstituted 1 June 1922 in the Regular Army; concurrently consolidated with the 2d Company, Coast Defenses of San Diego (organized 31 May 1921 at San Diego, California) and consolidated unit redesignated as the 115th Company, Coast Artillery Corps. Inactivated 9 November 1922 at San Diego, California.

Redesignated 1 July 1924 as Battery I, 14th Coast Artillery. Activated 4 June 1941 at Fort Worden, Washington. Inactivated 8 May 1944 at Camp Barkeley, Texas. Disbanded 18 October 1944.

Reconstituted 28 June 1950 in the Regular Army and redesignated as Battery B, 49th Antiaircraft Artillery Battalion. Redesignated 21 April 1952 as Battery B, 49th Antiaircraft Artillery Gun Battalion. Activated 13 May 1952 at Fort Sheridan, Illinois. Redesignated 24 July 1953 as Battery B, 49th Antiaircraft Artillery Battalion. Reorganized and redesignated 10 November 1956 as Battery B, 49th Antiaircraft Artillery Missile Battalion. Inactivated 1 September 1958 at Chicago, Illinois.

CAMPAIGN PARTICIPATION CREDIT

World War I	World War II
*St. Mihiel	Normandy (with arrowhead)
*Meuse-Argonne	Northern France
Lorraine 1918	Rhineland
	Ardennes-Alsace
	Central Europe
	*Aleutian Islands

DECORATIONS

None.

2d BATTALION, 65th AIR DEFENSE ARTILLERY

RA
(inactive)

LINEAGE

Constituted 28 February 1901 in the Regular Army as the 87th Company, Coast Artillery, Artillery Corps. Organized in 1901 at Fort Slocum, New York. Redesignated 2 February 1907 as the 87th Company, Coast Artillery Corps. Redesignated in July 1916 as the 2d Company, Fort Grant [Canal Zone]. Redesignated 31 August 1917 as the 2d Company, Coast Defenses of Balboa. Redesignated 30 June 1922 as the 87th Company, Coast Artillery Corps.

Reorganized and redesignated 1 July 1924 as Battery B, 65th Coast Artillery. Inactivated 15 April 1932 at Fort Amador, Canal Zone. Activated 1 June 1938 at Fort Winfield Scott, California.

Reorganized and redesignated 10 May 1943 as Battery B, 65th Antiaircraft Artillery Gun Battalion. Reorganized and redesignated 1 May 1945 as the 427th Antiaircraft Artillery Gun Battery. Inactivated 4 December 1945 at Fort Lawton, Washington. Redesignated 3 October 1946 as the 427th Antiaircraft Artillery Searchlight Battery. Activated 1 November 1946 at Camp Hood, Texas. Inactivated 27 December 1948 at Camp Hood, Texas. Redesignated 28 December 1954 as the 427th Airborne Antiaircraft Artillery Battery. Activated 1 January 1955 at Fort Campbell, Kentucky. Inactivated 22 March 1957 at Fort Campbell, Kentucky.

Redesignated 12 August 1958 as Headquarters and Headquarters Battery, 2d Missile Battalion, 65th Artillery (organic elements concurrently constituted). Battalion activated 1 September 1958 at Camp Kilmer, New Jersey. Inactivated 26 July 1960 at Camp Kilmer, New Jersey. Redesignated 1 September 1971 as the 2d Missile Battalion, 65th Air Defense Artillery. Redesignated 13 September 1972 as the 2d Battalion, 65th Air Defense Artillery, and activated at Van Nuys, California. Inactivated 30 September 1974 at Van Nuys, California.

CAMPAIGN PARTICIPATION CREDIT

World War I
St. Mihiel
Meuse-Argonne
Lorraine 1918

World War II
Normandy (with arrowhead)
Northern France
Rhineland
Ardennes-Alsace
Central Europe
*Aleutian Islands

DECORATIONS

None.

3d BATTALION, 65th AIR DEFENSE ARTILLERY

RA
(inactive)

LINEAGE

Constituted 7 October 1901 in the Regular Army as the 124th Company, Coast Artillery, Artillery Corps. Organized 15 October 1901 at Fort Wadsworth, New York. Redesignated 2 February 1907 as the 124th Company, Coast Artillery Corps. Redesignated in July 1916 as the 2d Company, Fort Sherman [Canal Zone]. Redesignated 31 August 1917 as the 2d Company, Coast Defenses of Cristobal. Redesignated 30 June 1922 as the 124th Company, Coast Artillery Corps.

Consolidated 1 July 1924 with Battery D, 65th Artillery (Coast Artillery Corps) (constituted 26 December 1917 in the Regular Army and organized at Fort Stevens, Oregon; demobilized 28 February 1919 at Camp Lewis, Washington; reconstituted 1 July 1924 in the Regular Army), and consolidated unit reorganized and redesignated as Battery D, 65th Coast Artillery. Inactivated 15 April 1932 at Fort Randolph, Canal Zone. Activated 11 October 1939 at Fort Winfield Scott, California.

Reorganized and redesignated 10 May 1943 as Battery D, 65th Antiaircraft Artillery Gun Battalion. Reorganized and redesignated 1 May 1945 as the 429th Antiaircraft Artillery Gun Battery. Inactivated 30 November 1945 at Fort Lewis, Washington. Redesignated 6 May 1953 as the 429th Antiaircraft Artillery Battery. Activated 8 June 1953 at Fort Bliss, Texas. Inactivated 15 May 1958 at Thule, Greenland.

Redesignated 12 August 1958 as Headquarters and Headquarters Battery, 3d Missile Battalion, 65th Artillery (organic elements concurrently constituted). Battalion activated 1 September 1958 at Cleveland, Ohio. Redesignated 20 December 1965 as the 3d Battalion, 65th Artillery. Inactivated 30 June 1971 at Cleveland, Ohio. Redesignated 1 September 1971 as the 3d Battalion, 65th Air Defense Artillery.

CAMPAIGN PARTICIPATION CREDIT

World War I
  *St. Mihiel
  *Meuse-Argonne
  Lorraine 1918

World War II
  Normandy (with arrowhead)
  Northern France
  Rhineland
  Ardennes-Alsace
  Central Europe
  *Aleutian Islands

DECORATIONS

None.

4th BATTALION, 65th AIR DEFENSE ARTILLERY

RA
(inactive)

LINEAGE

Constituted 28 February 1901 in the Regular Army as the 89th Company, Coast Artillery, Artillery Corps. Organized 5 April 1901 at Fort Banks, Massachusetts. Redesignated 2 February 1907 as the 89th Company, Coast Artillery Corps. Redesignated in July 1916 as the 4th Company, Fort Williams [Maine].

Reorganized and redesignated 21 July 1917 as Battery F, 6th Provisional Regiment, Coast Artillery Corps. Redesignated 5 February 1918 as Battery F, 51st Artillery (Coast Artillery Corps). Redesignated 7 August 1918 as Battery C, 57th Artillery (Coast Artillery Corps). Demobilized 30 June 1921 at Camp Lewis, Washington.

Reconstituted 1 June 1922 in the Regular Army; concurrently consolidated with the 3d Company, Coast Defenses of San Diego (organized 23 May 1917 in the Regular Army as the 3d Company, Fort Rosecrans [California]; redesignated 31 August 1917 as the 3d Company, Coast Defenses of San Diego), and consolidated unit reorganized and redesignated as the 89th Company, Coast Artillery Corps.

Consolidated 1 July 1924 with Battery F, 65th Artillery (Coast Artillery Corps) (constituted 26 December 1917 in the Regular Army and organized at Fort Casey, Washington; demobilized 28 February 1919 at Camp Lewis, Washington; reconstituted 1 July 1924 in the Regular Army); consolidated unit redesignated as Battery F, 65th Coast Artillery, and inactivated at San Diego, California. Activated 31 July 1926 at Fort Randolph, Canal Zone. Inactivated 15 April 1932 at Fort Amador, Canal Zone. Activated 11 October 1939 at Fort Winfield Scott, California.

Reorganized and redesignated 10 May 1943 as Battery B, 255th Antiaircraft Artillery Automatic Weapons Battalion. Disbanded 3 February 1945 at Camp Earle, Alaska. Reconstituted 28 June 1950 in the Regular Army; concurrently consolidated with Battery B, 40th Antiaircraft Artillery Gun Battalion (see ANNEX), and consolidated unit designated as Battery B, 40th Antiaircraft Artillery Gun Battalion. Activated 15 March 1953 in Germany. Redesignated 1 October 1953 as Battery B, 40th Antiaircraft Artillery Battalion. Inactivated 10 April 1958 in Germany.

Redesignated 12 August 1958 as Headquarters and Headquarters Battery, 4th Missile Battalion, 65th Artillery (organic elements concurrently constituted). Battalion activated 1 September 1958 at Los Angeles, California. Redesignated 20 December 1965 as the 4th Battalion, 65th Artillery. Redesignated 1 September 1971 as the 4th Battalion, 65th Air Defense Artillery. Inactivated 13 September 1972 at Van Nuys, California.

Constituted 8 February 1943 in the Army of the United States as Battery B, 116th Coast Artillery Battalion. Activated 20 March 1943 at Camp Davis, North Carolina. Redesignated 28 June 1943 as Battery B, 116th Antiaircraft Artillery Gun Battalion. Inactivated 6 October 1945 in Germany. Redesignated 13 October 1948 as Battery B, 40th Antiaircraft Artillery Gun Battalion, and allotted to the Regular Army.

CAMPAIGN PARTICIPATION CREDIT

World War I
St. Mihiel
Meuse-Argonne
*Lorraine 1918

World War II
*Normandy (with arrowhead)
*Northern France
*Rhineland
*Ardennes-Alsace
*Central Europe
*Aleutian Islands

DECORATIONS

None.

6th BATTALION, 65th AIR DEFENSE ARTILLERY

RA
(inactive)

LINEAGE

Organized 1 June 1917 in the Regular Army at Fort Grant, Canal Zone, as the 7th Company, Fort Grant [Canal Zone]. Redesignated 31 August 1917 as the 7th Company, Coast Defenses of Balboa. Redesignated 30 June 1922 as the 195th Company, Coast Artillery Corps.

Consolidated 1 July 1924 with Battery E, 65th Artillery (Coast Artillery Corps) (constituted 26 December 1917 in the Regular Army and organized at Fort Stevens, Oregon; demobilized 28 February 1919 at Camp Lewis, Washington; reconstituted 1 July 1924 in the Regular Army); consolidated unit redesignated as Battery E, 65th Coast Artillery, and inactivated in the Canal Zone. Activated 31 July 1926 at Fort Randolph, Canal Zone. Inactivated 15 April 1932 at Fort Amador, Canal Zone. Activated 1 June 1938 at Fort Winfield Scott, California.

Reorganized and redesignated 10 May 1943 as Battery A, 255th Antiaircraft Artillery Automatic Weapons Battalion. Disbanded 3 February 1945 at Camp Earle, Alaska. Reconstituted 28 June 1950 in the Regular Army; concurrently consolidated with Battery A, 40th Antiaircraft Artillery Gun Battalion (*see* ANNEX), and consolidated unit designated as Battery A, 40th Antiaircraft Artillery Gun Battalion. Activated 15 March 1953 in Germany. Redesignated 1 October 1953 as Battery A, 40th Antiaircraft Artillery Battalion. Inactivated 10 April 1958 in Germany.

Redesignated 31 July 1959 as Headquarters and Headquarters Battery, 6th Battalion, 65th Artillery. Redesignated 11 October 1961 as Headquarters and Headquarters Battery, 6th Missile Battalion, 65th Artillery (organic elements concurrently constituted). Battalion activated 22 December 1961 at Fort Bliss, Texas. Redesignated 20 December 1965 as the 6th Battalion, 65th Artillery. Redesignated 1 September 1971 as the 6th Battalion, 65th Air Defense Artillery. Inactivated 13 September 1972 at Key West, Florida.

ANNEX

Constituted 8 February 1943 in the Army of the United States as Battery A, 116th Coast Artillery Battalion. Activated 20 March 1943 at Camp Davis, North Carolina. Redesignated 28 June 1943 as Battery A, 116th Antiaircraft Artillery Gun Battalion. Inactivated 6 October 1945 in Germany. Redesignated 13 October 1948 as Battery A, 40th Antiaircraft Artillery Gun Battalion, and allotted to the Regular Army.

Campaign Participation Credit

World War I
    St. Mihiel
    Meuse-Argonne
    *Lorraine 1918

World War II
    *Normandy (with arrowhead)
    *Northern France
    *Rhineland
    *Ardennes-Alsace
    *Central Europe
    *Aleutian Islands

Decorations

*Meritorious Unit Commendation, Streamer embroidered FLORIDA 1962–1963 (6th Missile Battalion, 65th Artillery, cited; DA GO 33, 1963)

BATTERY G, 65th AIR DEFENSE ARTILLERY

RA
(inactive)

LINEAGE

Organized 1 June 1917 in the Regular Army at Fort de Lesseps, Canal Zone, as the 1st Company, Fort de Lesseps [Canal Zone]. Redesignated 31 August 1917 as the 6th Company, Coast Defenses of Cristobal. Inactivated 15 September 1921 at Fort de Lesseps, Canal Zone. Redesignated 30 June 1922 as the 193d Company, Coast Artillery Corps.

Redesignated 1 July 1924 as Battery G, 65th Coast Artillery. Activated 11 October 1939 at Fort Winfield Scott, California.

Reorganized and redesignated 10 May 1943 as Battery C, 255th Antiaircraft Artillery Automatic Weapons Battalion. Disbanded 3 February 1945 at Camp Earle, Alaska. Reconstituted 28 June 1950 in the Regular Army; concurrently consolidated with Battery C, 40th Antiaircraft Artillery Gun Battalion (see ANNEX), and consolidated unit designated as Battery C, 40th Antiaircraft Artillery Gun Battalion. Activated 15 March 1953 in Germany. Redesignated 1 October 1953 as Battery C, 40th Antiaircraft Artillery Battalion. Inactivated 10 April 1958 in Germany.

Redesignated 31 July 1959 as Headquarters and Headquarters Battery, 7th Battalion, 65th Artillery. Redesignated 30 December 1965 as Battery G, 65th Artillery. Activated 1 March 1966 at Fort Bliss, Texas. Redesignated 1 September 1971 as Battery G, 65th Air Defense Artillery. Inactivated 26 December 1971 in Vietnam.

ANNEX

Constituted 8 February 1943 in the Army of the United States as Battery C, 116th Coast Artillery Battalion. Activated 20 March 1943 at Camp Davis, North Carolina. Redesignated 28 June 1943 as Battery C, 116th Antiaircraft Artillery Gun Battalion. Inactivated 6 October 1945 in Germany. Redesignated 13 October 1948 as Battery C, 40th Antiaircraft Artillery Gun Battalion, and allotted to the Regular Army.

CAMPAIGN PARTICIPATION CREDIT

World War II–EAME
  Normandy (with arrowhead)
  Northern France
  Rhineland
  Ardennes-Alsace
  Central Europe

World War II–AP
  Aleutian Islands

Vietnam
  Counteroffensive, Phase II
  Counteroffensive, Phase III

Tet Counteroffensive
Counteroffensive, Phase IV
Counteroffensive, Phase V
Counteroffensive, Phase VI
Tet 69/Counteroffensive
Summer–fall 1969
Winter–spring 1970
Sanctuary Counteroffensive
Counteroffensive, Phase VII
Consolidation I
Consolidation II

DECORATIONS

Presidential Unit Citation (Navy), Streamer embroidered VIETNAM 1966–1967 (Battery G, 65th Artillery, cited; DA GO 32, 1973)

Valorous Unit Award, Streamer embroidered QUANG TRI–THUA THIEN (Battery G, 65th Artillery, cited; DA GO 48, 1968)

Valorous Unit Award, Streamer embroidered QUANG TIN PROVINCE (Battery G, 65th Artillery, cited; DA GO 39, 1970)

Republic of Vietnam Cross of Gallantry with Palm, Streamer embroidered VIETNAM 1971 (Battery G, 65th Artillery, cited; DA GO 6, 1974)

12th DETACHMENT, 65th AIR DEFENSE ARTILLERY

AR
(inactive)

LINEAGE

Constituted 22 April 1929 in the Regular Army as Battery I, 65th Coast Artillery. Activated 15 June 1942 at Inglewood, California.

Reorganized and redesignated 10 May 1943 as Battery A, 245th Anti-aircraft Artillery Searchlight Battalion. Inactivated 12 June 1944 at Camp Haan, California. Disbanded 26 June 1944.

Reconstituted 30 April 1959 in the Army Reserve; concurrently redesignated as the 12th Detachment, 65th Artillery, and assigned to the Second United States Army. Activated 1 June 1959 at Clarion, Pennsylvania. Inactivated 11 February 1963 at Clarion, Pennsylvania. Redesignated 1 September 1971 as the 12th Detachment, 65th Air Defense Artillery.

CAMPAIGN PARTICIPATION CREDIT

None.

DECORATIONS

None.

16th DETACHMENT, 65th AIR DEFENSE ARTILLERY

RA
(inactive)

LINEAGE

Constituted 27 May 1942 in the Regular Army as Headquarters and Headquarters Battery, 3d Battalion, 65th Coast Artillery. Activated 15 June 1942 at Inglewood, California.

Reorganized and redesignated 10 May 1943 as Headquarters and Headquarters Battery, 245th Antiaircraft Artillery Searchlight Battalion. Inactivated 12 June 1944 at Camp Haan, California. Disbanded 26 June 1944.

Reconstituted 5 August 1958 in the Regular Army and redesignated as the 16th Detachment, 65th Artillery. Activated 1 September 1958 at Camp Irwin, California. Inactivated 2 July 1962 at Camp Irwin, California. Redesignated 1 September 1971 as the 16th Detachment, 65th Air Defense Artillery.

CAMPAIGN PARTICIPATION CREDIT

None.

DECORATIONS

None.

65TH AIR DEFENSE ARTILLERY BIBLIOGRAPHY

The 116th AAA Gun Bn. Mobile. Frankfurt am Main: Franz Jos. Heinrich, 1945.

Verga, S.J., et al. "The 65th Antiaircraft Artillery Group, Bulwark of Canal Zone Defense." *Antiaircraft Artillery Journal* 93 (July 1950):33–34.

67th AIR DEFENSE ARTILLERY

HERALDIC ITEMS

COAT OF ARMS

Shield: Gules, a chevron vairé or and vert, in dexter chief a crescent of the second.

Crest: On a wreath of the colors, or and gules, seven bird-bolts to chief six in saltire, three and three and one in pale vert barbed, flighted and banded argent, surmounted by a Roman shield of the second bearing a cross pattée gold within a border silver.

Motto: *Memor et Fidelis* (Mindful and Faithful).

Symbolism: The shield is red for artillery. The chevron is taken from the arms of General James Oglethorpe, the founder of the colony of Georgia, and the crescent is from the flag displayed on the fort in South Carolina by Col. William Moultrie.

The Roman shield bearing a cross adapted from the coat of arms of Rome refers to the organization's service in Italy for which an element of the regiment was awarded the French Croix de Guerre with Palm embroidered "Road to Rome." The bird-bolts, a type of arrow used to bring down birds, allude to the antiaircraft designation of the organization during World War II. The bolts are seven in number in reference to the seven campaigns in which the unit participated in World War II. Red and green allude to the colors of the French Croix de Guerre; and red, white, and green to the national colors of Italy.

DISTINCTIVE INSIGNIA

The distinctive insignia is the shield and motto of the coat of arms.

LINEAGE AND HONORS

LINEAGE

Constituted 2 May 1918 in the Regular Army as the 67th Artillery (Coast Artillery Corps). Organized 21 May 1918 at Fort Winfield Scott, California, from existing Regular Army companies and National Guard companies from California. Demobilized 23 April 1919 at the Presidio of San Francisco, California. Reconstituted 22 January 1926 in the Regular Army as the 67th Coast Artillery. (1st Battalion activated 1 July 1940 at Fort Bragg, North Carolina.) Regiment (less 1st Battalion) activated

351

10 February 1941 at Fort Bragg, North Carolina. Regiment broken up 23 May 1944 and its elements reorganized and redesignated as follows: Headquarters and Headquarters Battery as Headquarters and Headquarters Battery, 91st Antiaircraft Artillery Group; 1st Battalion as the 67th Antiaircraft Artillery Gun Battalion; 2d Battalion as the 894th Antiaircraft Artillery Automatic Weapons Battalion; 3d Battalion disbanded in Italy.

Headquarters and Headquarters Battery, 91st Antiaircraft Artillery Group, inactivated 1 June 1946 in Germany. Activated 8 June 1949 at Fort Bliss, Texas. Inactivated 22 August 1949 at Fort Bliss, Texas. Redesignated 28 June 1950 as Headquarters and Headquarters Battery, 67th Antiaircraft Artillery Group. Activated 1 May 1955 at Fort Stewart, Georgia. Redesignated 20 March 1958 as Headquarters and Headquarters Battery, 67th Artillery Group. Inactivated 25 August 1961 at Cleveland, Ohio.

67th Antiaircraft Artillery Gun Battalion inactivated 25 November 1945 at Camp Shanks, New York. Activated 31 January 1949 at Fort Bliss, Texas. Redesignated 1 October 1953 as the 67th Antiaircraft Artillery Battalion. Redesignated 1 November 1957 as the 67th Antiaircraft Artillery Missile Battalion. Inactivated 1 September 1958 in Germany.

894th Antiaircraft Artillery Automatic Weapons Battalion inactivated 14 December 1945 in Germany. Redesignated 13 October 1948 as the 5th Antiaircraft Artillery Automatic Weapons Battalion, Mobile. Activated 15 January 1949 at Fort Bliss, Texas. Redesignated 30 May 1955 as the 5th Antiaircraft Artillery Battalion. Inactivated 15 June 1958 in Germany.

3d Battalion, 67th Coast Artillery, reconstituted 5 August 1958 in the Regular Army.

Headquarters and Headquarters Battery, 67th Artillery Group; 67th Antiaircraft Artillery Missile Battalion; 5th Antiaircraft Artillery Battalion; and 3d Battalion, 67th Coast Artillery, consolidated, reorganized, and redesignated 25 August 1961 as the 67th Artillery, a parent regiment under the Combat Arms Regimental System. Redesignated 1 September 1971 as the 67th Air Defense Artillery.

CAMPAIGN PARTICIPATION CREDIT

World War I
    Streamer without inscription

World War II
    Tunisia
    Naples-Foggia

Rome-Arno
Southern France
Rhineland
Ardennes-Alsace
Central Europe

DECORATIONS

None.

1st BATTALION, 67th AIR DEFENSE ARTILLERY

RA
(9th Infantry Division)

LINEAGE

Organized in February 1917 in the Regular Army at Fort Baker, California, as the 4th Company, Fort Baker [California]. Redesignated 31 August 1917 as the 13th Company, Coast Defenses of San Francisco.

Reorganized and redesignated 21 May 1918 as Battery A, 67th Artillery (Coast Artillery Corps). Demobilized 23 April 1919 at the Presidio of San Francisco, California. Reconstituted 22 January 1926 in the Regular Army as Battery A, 67th Coast Artillery. Activated 1 July 1940 at Fort Bragg, North Carolina.

Reorganized and redesignated 23 May 1944 as Battery A, 67th Antiaircraft Artillery Gun Battalion. Inactivated 25 November 1945 at Camp Shanks, New York. Activated 31 January 1949 at Fort Bliss, Texas. Redesignated 1 October 1953 as Battery A, 67th Antiaircraft Artillery Battalion. Redesignated 1 November 1957 as Battery A, 67th Antiaircraft Artillery Missile Battalion.

Reorganized and redesignated 1 September 1958 as Headquarters and Headquarters Battery, 1st Missile Battalion, 67th Artillery (organic elements constituted 12 August 1958 and activated 1 September 1958). Redesignated 20 August 1965 as the 1st Battalion, 67th Artillery. Inactivated 26 December 1969 in Germany. Redesignated 1 September 1971 as the 1st Battalion, 67th Air Defense Artillery. Assigned 13 September 1972 to the 9th Infantry Division. Activated 21 November 1972 at Fort Bliss, Texas.

CAMPAIGN PARTICIPATION CREDIT

World War I
    *Streamer without inscription

World War II
    *Tunisia
    *Naples-Foggia

*Rome-Arno
*Southern France
*Rhineland
*Ardennes-Alsace
*Central Europe

DECORATIONS

*French Croix de Guerre with Palm, World War II, Streamer embroidered ROAD TO ROME (67th Antiaircraft Artillery Gun Battalion cited; DA GO 43, 1950)

2d BATTALION, 67th AIR DEFENSE ARTILLERY

RA
(1st Infantry Division)

LINEAGE

Constituted 22 January 1926 in the Regular Army as Battery B, 67th Coast Artillery. Activated 1 July 1940 at Fort Bragg, North Carolina.

Reorganized and redesignated 23 May 1944 as Battery B, 67th Antiaircraft Artillery Gun Battalion. Inactivated 25 November 1945 at Camp Shanks, New York. Activated 31 January 1949 at Fort Bliss, Texas. Redesignated 1 October 1953 as Battery B, 67th Antiaircraft Artillery Battalion. Redesignated 1 November 1957 as Battery B, 67th Antiaircraft Artillery Missile Battalion.

Reorganized and redesignated 1 September 1958 as Headquarters and Headquarters Battery, 2d Missile Battalion, 67th Artillery (organic elements constituted 12 August 1958 and activated 1 September 1958). Battalion inactivated 25 August 1961 at Ellsworth Air Force Base, South Dakota. Redesignated 1 September 1971 as the 2d Missile Battalion, 67th Air Defense Artillery. Redesignated 13 September 1972 as the 2d Battalion, 67th Air Defense Artillery, assigned to the 1st Infantry Division, and activated at Fort Riley, Kansas.

CAMPAIGN PARTICIPATION CREDIT

World War I
  Streamer without inscription

World War II
  *Tunisia
  *Naples-Foggia

*Rome-Arno
*Southern France
*Rhineland
*Ardennes-Alsace
*Central Europe

DECORATIONS

*French Croix de Guerre with Palm, World War II, Streamer embroidered ROAD TO ROME (67th Antiaircraft Artillery Gun Battalion cited; DA GO 43, 1950)

3d BATTALION, 67th AIR DEFENSE ARTILLERY

RA
(3d Infantry Division)

LINEAGE

Organized in December 1917 in the Regular Army at the Presidio of San Francisco, California, as the 45th Company, Coast Defenses of San Francisco. Redesignated in January 1918 as the 7th Company, Coast Defenses of San Francisco.

Reorganized and redesignated 21 May 1918 as Battery C, 67th Artillery (Coast Artillery Corps). Demobilized 23 April 1919 at the Presidio of San Francisco, California. Reconstituted 22 January 1926 in the Regular Army as Battery C, 67th Coast Artillery. Activated 1 July 1940 at Fort Bragg, North Carolina.

Reorganized and redesignated 23 May 1944 as Battery C, 67th Antiaircraft Artillery Gun Battalion. Inactivated 25 November 1945 at Camp Shanks, New York. Activated 31 January 1949 at Fort Bliss, Texas. Redesignated 1 October 1953 as Battery C, 67th Antiaircraft Artillery Battalion. Redesignated 1 November 1957 as Battery C, 67th Antiaircraft Artillery Missile Battalion.

Reorganized and redesignated 1 September 1958 as Headquarters and Headquarters Battery, 3d Missile Battalion, 67th Artillery (organic elements constituted 12 August 1958 and activated 1 September 1958). Battalion inactivated 25 August 1961 at Milwaukee, Wisconsin. Redesignated 1 September 1971 as the 3d Missile Battalion, 67th Air Defense Artillery. Redesignated 13 September 1972 as the 3d Battalion, 67th Air Defense Artillery, assigned to the 3d Infantry Division, and activated in Germany.

CAMPAIGN PARTICIPATION CREDIT

World War I
  *Streamer without inscription

World War II
  *Tunisia
  *Naples-Foggia
*Rome-Arno
*Southern France
*Rhineland
*Ardennes-Alsace
*Central Europe

DECORATIONS

*French Croix de Guerre with Palm, World War II, Streamer embroidered ROAD TO ROME (67th Antiaircraft Artillery Gun Battalion cited; DA GO 43, 1950)

4th MISSILE BATTALION, 67th AIR DEFENSE ARTILLERY

RA
(inactive)

LINEAGE

Constituted 22 January 1926 in the Regular Army as Battery D, 67th Coast Artillery. Activated 10 February 1941 at Fort Bragg, North Carolina.

Reorganized and redesignated 23 May 1944 as Battery D, 67th Antiaircraft Artillery Gun Battalion. Inactivated 25 November 1945 at Camp Shanks, New York. Activated 31 January 1949 at Fort Bliss, Texas. Redesignated 1 October 1953 as Battery D, 67th Antiaircraft Artillery Battalion. Redesignated 1 November 1957 as Battery D, 67th Antiaircraft Artillery Missile Battalion.

Reorganized and redesignated 1 September 1958 as Headquarters and Headquarters Battery, 4th Missile Battalion, 67th Artillery (organic elements constituted 12 August 1958 and activated 1 September 1958). Battalion inactivated 28 June 1963 at San Pablo, California. Redesignated 1 September 1971 as the 4th Missile Battalion, 67th Air Defense Artillery.

CAMPAIGN PARTICIPATION CREDIT

World War I
    Streamer without inscription

World War II
    *Tunisia
    *Naples-Foggia

*Rome-Arno
*Southern France
*Rhineland
*Ardennes-Alsace
*Central Europe

DECORATIONS

*French Croix de Guerre with Palm, World War II, Streamer embroidered ROAD TO ROME (67th Antiaircraft Artillery Gun Battalion cited; DA GO 43, 1950)

5th BATTALION, 67th AIR DEFENSE ARTILLERY

RA
(inactive)

LINEAGE

Organized in January 1918 in the Regular Army at Fort Barry, California, as the 14th Company, Coast Defenses of San Francisco.

Reorganized and redesignated 21 May 1918 as Battery E, 67th Artillery (Coast Artillery Corps). Demobilized 23 April 1919 at the Presidio of San Francisco, California. Reconstituted 22 January 1926 in the Regular Army as Battery E, 67th Coast Artillery. Activated 10 February 1941 at Fort Bragg, North Carolina.

Reorganized and redesignated 23 May 1944 as Battery A, 894th Antiaircraft Artillery Automatic Weapons Battalion. Inactivated 14 December 1945 in Germany. Redesignated 13 October 1948 as Battery A, 5th Antiaircraft Artillery Automatic Weapons Battalion, Mobile. Activated 15 January 1949 at Fort Bliss, Texas. Redesignated 30 May 1955 as Battery A, 5th Antiaircraft Artillery Battalion. Inactivated 15 June 1958 in Germany.

Redesignated 31 July 1959 as Headquarters and Headquarters Battery, 5th Battalion, 67th Artillery. Activated 1 August 1968 at Fort Bliss, Texas (organic elements concurrently constituted and activated). Redesignated 1 September 1971 as the 5th Battalion, 67th Air Defense Artillery. Inactivated 13 September 1972 at Fort Bliss, Texas.

CAMPAIGN PARTICIPATION CREDIT

World War I
  *Streamer without inscription

World War II
  *Tunisia
  *Naples-Foggia

*Rome-Arno
*Southern France
*Rhineland
*Ardennes-Alsace
*Central Europe

DECORATIONS

None.

6th BATTALION, 67th AIR DEFENSE ARTILLERY

RA
(inactive)

LINEAGE

Organized in February 1917 in the Regular Army at Fort Barry, California, as the 3d Company, Fort Barry [California]. Redesignated 31 August 1917 as the 17th Company, Coast Defenses of San Francisco.

Reorganized and redesignated 21 May 1918 as Battery F, 67th Artillery (Coast Artillery Corps). Demobilized 23 April 1919 at the Presidio of San Francisco, California. Reconstituted 22 January 1926 in the Regular Army as Battery F, 67th Coast Artillery. Activated 10 February 1941 at Fort Bragg, North Carolina.

Reorganized and redesignated 23 May 1944 as Battery B, 894th Anti-aircraft Artillery Automatic Weapons Battalion. Inactivated 14 December 1945 in Germany. Redesignated 13 October 1948 as Battery B, 5th Anti-aircraft Artillery Automatic Weapons Battalion, Mobile. Activated 15 January 1949 at Fort Bliss, Texas. Redesignated 30 May 1955 as Battery B, 5th Antiaircraft Artillery Battalion. Inactivated 15 June 1958 in Germany.

Redesignated 31 July 1959 as Headquarters and Headquarters Battery, 6th Battalion, 67th Artillery. Redesignated 5 April 1960 as Battery F, 67th Artillery. Activated 22 April 1960 at Fort Bliss, Texas. Inactivated 10 September 1960 at Fort Amador, Canal Zone. Redesignated 7 October 1968 as Headquarters and Headquarters Battery, 6th Battalion, 67th Artillery, and activated at Fort Bliss, Texas (organic elements concurrently constituted and activated). Battalion assigned 30 June 1969 to the 24th Infantry Division. Relieved 15 April 1970 from assignment to the 24th Infantry Division and assigned to the 1st Infantry Division. Redesignated 1 September 1971 as the 6th Battalion, 67th Air Defense Artillery. Inactivated 13 September 1972 at Fort Riley, Kansas, and relieved from assignment to the 1st Infantry Division.

CAMPAIGN PARTICIPATION CREDIT

World War I
    *Streamer without inscription

World War II
    *Tunisia
    *Naples-Foggia

*Rome-Arno
*Southern France
*Rhineland
*Ardennes-Alsace
*Central Europe

DECORATIONS

None.

7th BATTALION, 67th AIR DEFENSE ARTILLERY

RA
(inactive)

LINEAGE

Constituted 22 January 1926 in the Regular Army as Battery G, 67th Coast Artillery. Activated 10 February 1941 at Fort Bragg, North Carolina.

Reorganized and redesignated 23 May 1944 as Battery C, 894th Antiaircraft Artillery Automatic Weapons Battalion. Inactivated 14 December 1945 in Germany. Redesignated 13 October 1948 as Battery C, 5th Antiaircraft Artillery Automatic Weapons Battalion, Mobile. Activated 15 January 1949 at Fort Bliss, Texas. Redesignated 30 May 1955 as Battery C, 5th Antiaircraft Artillery Battalion. Inactivated 15 June 1958 in Germany.

Redesignated 31 July 1959 as Headquarters and Headquarters Battery, 7th Battalion, 67th Artillery. Activated 7 July 1969 at Fort Bliss, Texas (Batteries A and B concurrently constituted and activated; Batteries C and D constituted and activated 1 September 1969). Battalion assigned 3 March 1970 to the 3d Infantry Division. Redesignated 1 September 1971 as the 7th Battalion, 67th Air Defense Artillery. Inactivated 13 September 1972 in Germany and relieved from assignment to the 3d Infantry Division.

CAMPAIGN PARTICIPATION CREDIT

World War I
  Streamer without inscription

World War II
  *Tunisia
  *Naples-Foggia

*Rome-Arno
*Southern France
*Rhineland
*Ardennes-Alsace
*Central Europe

DECORATIONS

None.

16th DETACHMENT, 67th AIR DEFENSE ARTILLERY

RA
(inactive)

LINEAGE

Constituted 27 May 1942 in the Regular Army as Battery I, 67th Coast Artillery. Activated 15 June 1942 at Paterson, New Jersey. Inactivated 24 May 1943 at Norfolk, Virginia. Disbanded 23 May 1944.

Reconstituted 5 August 1958 in the Regular Army and redesignated as the 16th Detachment, 67th Artillery. Activated 1 September 1958 at the Erie Ordnance Depot, Ohio. Inactivated 10 May 1963 at Fort Knox, Kentucky. Redesignated 1 September 1971 as the 16th Detachment, 67th Air Defense Artillery.

CAMPAIGN PARTICIPATION CREDIT

None.

DECORATIONS

None.

67TH AIR DEFENSE ARTILLERY BIBLIOGRAPHY

"Activities of the 35th Antiaircraft Artillery Brigade," *Antiaircraft Artillery Journal* 93 (July 1950):31–32. Contains information about the 5th Antiaircraft Artillery Automatic Weapons Battalion, Mobile.

894th AAA Bn. History, 1940–1945. N.p., 1945.

5th AAA AW Bn, 1861–1954. Darmstadt, Germany: Stars and Stripes, 1954.

Gibbs, Gerald G. "Activities of the 45th Antiaircraft Artillery Brigade." *Coast Artillery Journal* 90 (November–December 1947):3–9. Contains information about the 91st Antiaircraft Artillery Group.

67th AAA, Gun Battalion, Fort Bliss, Texas, 1949. Baton Rouge: Army and Navy Publishing Company, 1949.

67th Coast Artillery (AA), Fort Bragg. Baton Rouge: Army and Navy Publishing Company, 1941.

242nd AAA Group. London: Montgomery, 1953. Contains information about the 67th Antiaircraft Artillery Battalion.

68th AIR DEFENSE ARTILLERY

Heraldic Items

Coat of Arms

Shield: Azure, a pile or.
Crest: On a wreath of the colors, or and gules, a fleur-de-lis gules.
Motto: *Lolamy* (Can Do).
Symbolism: The design of the shield represents a searchlight beam in the sky, which alludes to the antiaircraft activity of the regiment.

The fleur-de-lis is red, the color of artillery, and indicates the service of the 68th Artillery (Coast Artillery Corps) in France during World War I. The motto is taken from the Navajo Indian language.

Distinctive Insignia

The distinctive insignia is the shield, crest, and motto of the coat of arms.

Lineage and Honors

Lineage

Constituted 1 June 1918 in the Regular Army as the 68th Artillery (Coast Artillery Corps) and organized at Fort Terry, New York. Demobilized 1 March 1919 at Fort Wadsworth, New York. Reconstituted 22 January 1926 in the Regular Army as the 68th Coast Artillery. Activated (less 1st Battalion) 4 November 1939 at Fort Williams, Maine. (1st Battalion activated 15 November 1939 at Fort Williams, Maine. 3d Battalion constituted 27 May 1942 in the Regular Army; activated 15 June 1942 at Boston, Massachusetts.) Regiment broken up 4 June 1944 and its elements reorganized and redesignated as follows: Headquarters and Headquarters Battery as Headquarters and Headquarters Battery, 68th Antiaircraft Artillery Group; 1st Battalion as the 68th Antiaircraft Artillery Gun Battalion; 2d Battalion as the 895th Antiaircraft Artillery Automatic Weapons Battalion; 3d Battalion disbanded in Italy.

Headquarters and Headquarters Battery, 68th Antiaircraft Artillery Group, inactivated 22 December 1945 at Camp Kilmer, New Jersey. Activated 1 November 1948 at Fort Bliss, Texas. Inactivated 16 December 1957 at Fort Richardson, Alaska.

68th Antiaircraft Artillery Gun Battalion inactivated 5 April 1946 at Camp Kilmer, New Jersey. Activated 1 August 1946 at Fort Bliss, Texas. Redesignated 25 January 1955 as the 68th Antiaircraft Artillery Battalion. Inactivated 25 March 1958 in Korea.

895th Antiaircraft Artillery Automatic Weapons Battalion inactivated 6 January 1946 at Camp Kilmer, New Jersey. Redesignated 13 October 1948 as the 8th Antiaircraft Artillery Automatic Weapons Battalion. Activated 13 January 1949 at Fort Bliss, Texas. Consolidated 28 June 1950 with the 1st Battalion, 8th Coast Artillery (*see* ANNEX), and consolidated unit designated as the 8th Antiaircraft Artillery Automatic Weapons Battalion. Redesignated 3 January 1951 as the 8th Antiaircraft Artillery Battalion. Inactivated 1 September 1958 at Camp Lucas, Michigan.

Headquarters and Headquarters Battery, 68th Antiaircraft Artillery Group; 68th and 8th Antiaircraft Artillery Battalions; and 3d Battalion, 68th Coast Artillery (reconstituted 5 August 1958 in the Regular Army), consolidated, reorganized, and redesignated 31 July 1959 as the 68th Artillery, a parent regiment under the Combat Arms Regimental System. Redesignated 1 September 1971 as the 68th Air Defense Artillery.

ANNEX

Constituted 1 July 1924 in the Regular Army as the 1st Battalion, 8th Coast Artillery. Activated 10 February 1941 in the Harbor Defenses of Portland, Maine. Inactivated (less Battery B) 18 April 1944 at Camp Shelby, Mississippi. (Battery B inactivated 20 May 1944 at Camp Shelby, Mississippi.) Disbanded 31 May 1944. Reconstituted 28 June 1950 in the Regular Army.

CAMPAIGN PARTICIPATION CREDIT

World War I
    Streamer without inscription

World War II
    Sicily
    Naples-Foggia
    Anzio (with arrowhead)
    Rome-Arno
    Southern France (with arrowhead)
    Rhineland
    Ardennes-Alsace
    Central Europe

Korean War
    UN defensive
    UN offensive
    CCF intervention
    First UN counteroffensive
    CCF spring offensive
    UN summer–fall offensive
    Second Korean winter
    Korea, summer–fall 1952
    Third Korean winter
    Korea, summer 1953

DECORATIONS

None.

1st BATTALION, 68th AIR DEFENSE ARTILLERY

RA
(1st Cavalry Division)

LINEAGE

Constituted 1 June 1918 in the Regular Army as Battery A, 68th Artillery (Coast Artillery Corps), and organized at Fort Terry, New York. Demobilized 1 March 1919 at Fort Wadsworth, New York. Reconstituted 22 January 1926 in the Regular Army as Battery A, 68th Coast Artillery. Activated 15 November 1939 at Fort Williams, Maine.

Reorganized and redesignated 4 June 1944 as Battery A, 68th Antiaircraft Artillery Gun Battalion. Inactivated 5 April 1946 at Camp Kilmer, New Jersey. Activated 1 August 1946 at Fort Bliss, Texas. Redesignated 25 January 1955 as Battery A, 68th Antiaircraft Artillery Battalion. Inactivated 25 March 1958 in Korea.

Redesignated 12 August 1958 as Headquarters and Headquarters Battery, 1st Missile Battalion, 68th Artillery (organic elements concurrently constituted). Battalion activated 1 September 1958 at Cleveland, Ohio. Inactivated 25 August 1961 at Cleveland, Ohio. (Maintenance Platoon, 1st Missile Battalion, 68th Artillery, activated 17 June 1963 at Redstone Arsenal, Alabama.) Redesignated 8 August 1963 as the 1st Battalion, 68th Artillery. Activated (less Maintenance Platoon) 15 October 1963 at Fort Sill, Oklahoma. Battalion inactivated 23 June 1970 in Germany. Redesignated 1 September 1971 as the 1st Battalion, 68th Air Defense Artillery. Assigned 13 September 1972 to the 1st Cavalry Division and activated at Fort Hood, Texas.

CAMPAIGN PARTICIPATION CREDIT

World War I
  *Streamer without inscription

World War II
  *Sicily
  *Naples-Foggia
  *Anzio (with arrowhead)
  *Rome-Arno
  *Southern France (with arrowhead)
  *Rhineland
   Ardennes-Alsace
  *Central Europe

Korean War
  *UN defensive
  *UN offensive
  *CCF intervention
  *First UN counteroffensive
  *CCF spring offensive
  *UN summer–fall offensive
  *Second Korean winter
  *Korea, summer–fall 1952
  *Third Korean winter
  *Korea, summer 1953

DECORATIONS

*Republic of Korea Presidential Unit Citation, Streamer embroidered KOREA 1950–1952 (68th Antiaircraft Artillery Gun Battalion cited; DA GO 41, 1955)

*Republic of Korea Presidential Unit Citation, Streamer embroidered DEFENSE OF KOREA (68th Antiaircraft Artillery Gun Battalion cited; DA GO 51, 1957)

2d GUN BATTALION, 68th AIR DEFENSE ARTILLERY

RA
(inactive)

LINEAGE

Constituted 1 June 1918 in the Regular Army as Battery B, 68th Artillery (Coast Artillery Corps), and organized at Fort Terry, New York. Demobilized 1 March 1919 at Fort Wadsworth, New York. Reconstituted 22 January 1926 in the Regular Army as Battery B, 68th Coast Artillery. Activated 15 November 1939 at Fort Williams, Maine.

Reorganized and redesignated 4 June 1944 as Battery B, 68th Antiaircraft Artillery Gun Battalion. Inactivated 5 April 1946 at Camp Kilmer, New Jersey. Activated 1 August 1946 at Fort Bliss, Texas. Redesignated 25 January 1955 as Battery B, 68th Antiaircraft Artillery Battalion. Inactivated 25 March 1958 in Korea.

Redesignated 12 August 1958 as Headquarters and Headquarters Battery, 2d Gun Battalion, 68th Artillery (organic elements concurrently constituted). Battalion activated 1 September 1958 at Camp Lucas, Michigan. Inactivated 15 June 1960 at Camp Lucas, Michigan. Redesignated 1 September 1971 as the 2d Gun Battalion, 68th Air Defense Artillery.

CAMPAIGN PARTICIPATION CREDIT

World War I
  *Streamer without inscription

World War II
  *Sicily
  *Naples-Foggia
  *Anzio (with arrowhead)
  *Rome-Arno
  *Southern France (with arrowhead)
  *Rhineland
   Ardennes-Alsace
  *Central Europe

Korean War
  *UN defensive
  *UN offensive
  *CCF intervention
  *First UN counteroffensive
  *CCF spring offensive
  *UN summer-fall offensive
  *Second Korean winter
  *Korea, summer–fall 1952
  *Third Korean winter
  *Korea, summer 1953

DECORATIONS

*Republic of Korea Presidential Unit Citation, Streamer embroidered KOREA 1950–1952 (68th Antiaircraft Artillery Gun Battalion cited; DA GO 41, 1955)

*Republic of Korea Presidential Unit Citation, Streamer embroidered DEFENSE OF KOREA (68th Antiaircraft Artillery Gun Battalion cited; DA GO 51, 1957)

3d BATTALION, 68th AIR DEFENSE ARTILLERY

RA
(nondivisional)

LINEAGE

Constituted 1 June 1918 in the Regular Army as Battery C, 68th Artillery (Coast Artillery Corps), and organized at Fort Terry, New York. Demobilized 1 March 1919 at Fort Wadsworth, New York. Reconstituted 22 January 1926 in the Regular Army and redesignated as Battery C, 68th Coast Artillery. Activated 15 November 1939 at Fort Williams, Maine.

Reorganized and redesignated 4 June 1944 as Battery C, 68th Anti-aircraft Artillery Gun Battalion. Inactivated 5 April 1946 at Camp Kilmer, New Jersey. Activated 1 August 1946 at Fort Bliss, Texas. Redesignated 25 January 1955 as Battery C, 68th Antiaircraft Artillery Battalion. Inactivated 25 March 1958 in Korea.

Redesignated 12 August 1958 as Headquarters and Headquarters Battery, 3d Automatic Weapons Battalion, 68th Artillery (organic elements concurrently constituted). Battalion activated 1 September 1958 in Germany. Inactivated 20 November 1958 in Germany. Redesignated 1 May 1959 as the 3d Missile Battalion, 68th Air Defense Artillery. Activated 1 June 1959 at Minneapolis, Minnesota. Redesignated 20 December 1965 as the 3d Battalion, 68th Artillery. Inactivated 30 June 1971 at Fort Snelling, Minnesota. Redesignated 1 September 1971 as the 3d Battalion, 68th Air Defense Artillery, and activated at Homestead Air Force Base, Florida.

CAMPAIGN PARTICIPATION CREDIT

World War I
  *Streamer without inscription

World War II
  *Sicily
  *Naples-Foggia
  *Anzio (with arrowhead)
  *Rome-Arno
  *Southern France (with arrowhead)
  *Rhineland
   Ardennes-Alsace
  *Central Europe

Korean War
  *UN defensive
  *UN offensive
  *CCF intervention
  *First UN counteroffensive
  *CCF spring offensive
  *UN summer-fall offensive
  *Second Korean winter
  *Korea, summer–fall 1952
  *Third Korean winter
  *Korea, summer 1953

DECORATIONS

*Republic of Korea Presidential Unit Citation, Streamer embroidered KOREA 1950–1952 (68th Antiaircraft Artillery Gun Battalion cited; DA GO 41, 1955)

*Republic of Korea Presidential Unit Citation, Streamer embroidered DEFENSE OF KOREA (68th Antiaircraft Artillery Gun Battalion cited; DA GO 51, 1957)

4th MISSILE BATTALION, 68th AIR DEFENSE ARTILLERY

RA
(inactive)

LINEAGE

Constituted 1 June 1918 in the Regular Army as Battery D, 68th Artillery (Coast Artillery Corps), and organized at Fort Terry, New York. Demobilized 1 March 1919 at Fort Wadsworth, New York. Reconstituted 22 January 1926 in the Regular Army and redesignated as Battery D, 68th Coast Artillery. Activated 15 November 1939 at Fort Williams, Maine.

Reorganized and redesignated 4 June 1944 as Battery D, 68th Anti-aircraft Artillery Gun Battalion. Inactivated 5 April 1946 at Camp Kilmer, New Jersey. Activated 1 August 1946 at Fort Bliss, Texas. Redesignated 25 January 1955 as Battery D, 68th Antiaircraft Artillery Battalion. Inactivated 25 March 1958 in Korea.

Redesignated 12 August 1958 as Headquarters and Headquarters Battery, 4th Missile Battalion, 68th Artillery (organic elements concurrently constituted). Battalion activated 1 September 1958 at Coventry, Rhode Island. Inactivated 15 December 1961 at Coventry, Rhode Island. Redesignated 1 September 1971 as the 4th Missile Battalion, 68th Air Defense Artillery.

CAMPAIGN PARTICIPATION CREDIT

World War I
  *Streamer without inscription

World War II
  *Sicily
  *Naples-Foggia
  *Anzio (with arrowhead)
  *Rome-Arno
  *Southern France (with arrowhead)
  *Rhineland
   Ardennes-Alsace
  *Central Europe

Korean War
  *UN defensive
  *UN offensive
  *CCF intervention
  *First UN counteroffensive
  *CCF spring offensive
  *UN summer-fall offensive
  *Second Korean winter
  *Korea, summer–fall 1952
  *Third Korean winter
  *Korea, summer 1953

DECORATIONS

*Republic of Korea Presidential Unit Citation, Streamer embroidered KOREA 1950–1952 (68th Antiaircraft Artillery Gun Battalion cited; DA GO 41, 1955)

*Republic of Korea Presidential Unit Citation, Streamer embroidered DEFENSE OF KOREA (68th Antiaircraft Artillery Gun Battalion cited; DA GO 51, 1957)

6th BATTALION, 68th AIR DEFENSE ARTILLERY

RA
(inactive)

LINEAGE

Constituted 10 July 1907 in the Regular Army as the 155th Company, Coast Artillery Corps. Organized 20 August 1907 at Fort Williams, Maine. Redesignated 30 June 1916 as the 1st Company, Fort Williams [Maine]. Redesignated 31 August 1917 as the 3d Company, Coast Defenses of Portland. Disbanded in 1921 at Fort Williams, Maine. Reconstituted in March 1921 in the Regular Army. Redesignated 1 June 1922 as the 155th Company, Coast Artillery Corps.

Redesignated 1 July 1924 as Battery B, 8th Coast Artillery. Activated 10 February 1941 in the Harbor Defenses of Portland, Maine. Inactivated 20 May 1944 at Camp Shelby, Mississippi. Disbanded 31 May 1944. Reconstituted 28 June 1950 in the Regular Army; concurrently consolidated with Battery B, 8th Antiaircraft Artillery Automatic Weapons Battalion (active) (*see* ANNEX), and consolidated unit designated as Battery B, 8th Antiaircraft Artillery Automatic Weapons Battalion. Redesignated 3 January 1951 as Battery B, 8th Antiaircraft Artillery Battalion. Inactivated 1 September 1958 at Camp Lucas, Michigan.

Redesignated 31 July 1959 as Headquarters and Headquarters Battery, 6th Battalion, 68th Artillery. Activated 10 May 1971 at Fort Bliss, Texas (organic elements concurrently constituted and activated). Redesignated 1 September 1971 as the 6th Battalion, 68th Air Defense Artillery. Assigned 5 July 1972 to the 1st Cavalry Division. Inactivated 13 September 1972 at Fort Hood, Texas, and relieved from assignment to the 1st Cavalry Division.

ANNEX

Constituted 1 June 1918 in the Regular Army as Battery F, 68th Artillery (Coast Artillery Corps), and organized at Fort Terry, New York. Demobilized 1 March 1919 at Fort Wadsworth, New York. Reconstituted 22 January 1926 in the Regular Army as Battery F, 68th Coast Artillery. Activated 4 November 1939 at Fort Williams, Maine.

Reorganized and redesignated 4 June 1944 as Battery B, 895th Antiaircraft Artillery Automatic Weapons Battalion. Inactivated 6 January 1946 at Camp Kilmer, New Jersey. Redesignated 13 October 1948 as Battery B, 8th Antiaircraft Artillery Automatic Weapons Battalion. Activated 13 January 1949 at Fort Bliss, Texas.

CAMPAIGN PARTICIPATION CREDIT

World War I
  *Streamer without inscription

World War II
  *Tunisia
  *Sicily
  *Naples-Foggia
  *Anzio (with arrowhead)
  *Rome-Arno
  *Southern France (with arrowhead)
  *Rhineland
  *Ardennes-Alsace
  *Central Europe

Korean War
  UN defensive
  UN offensive
  CCF intervention
  First UN counteroffensive
  CCF spring offensive
  UN summer-fall offensive
  Second Korean winter
  Korea, summer–fall 1952
  Third Korean winter
  Korea, summer 1953

DECORATIONS

None.

BATTERY G, 68th AIR DEFENSE ARTILLERY

RA
(inactive)

LINEAGE

Constituted 1 June 1918 in the Regular Army as Headquarters, 1st Battalion, 68th Artillery (Coast Artillery Corps), and organized at Fort Terry, New York. Demobilized 1 March 1919 at Fort Wadsworth, New York. Reconstituted 22 January 1926 in the Regular Army and redesignated as Headquarters and Headquarters Battery, 1st Battalion, 68th Coast Artillery. Activated 15 November 1939 at Fort Williams, Maine.

Reorganized and redesignated 4 June 1944 as Headquarters and Headquarters Battery, 68th Antiaircraft Artillery Gun Battalion. Inactivated 5 April 1946 at Camp Kilmer, New Jersey. Activated 1 August 1946 at Fort Bliss, Texas. Redesignated 25 January 1955 as Headquarters and Headquarters Battery, 68th Antiaircraft Artillery Battalion. Inactivated 25 March 1958 in Korea.

Redesignated 31 July 1959 as Headquarters and Headquarters Battery, 7th Battalion, 68th Artillery. Redesignated 21 December 1965 as Battery G, 68th Artillery. Activated 1 February 1966 at Fort Bliss, Texas. Redesignated 1 September 1971 as Battery G, 68th Air Defense Artillery. Inactivated 27 December 1971 at Fort Bliss, Texas.

CAMPAIGN PARTICIPATION CREDIT

World War II–EAME
  Sicily
  Naples-Foggia
  Anzio (with arrowhead)
  Rome-Arno
  Southern France (with arrowhead)
  Rhineland
  Central Europe

Korean War
  UN defensive
  UN offensive

CCF intervention
First UN counteroffensive
CCF spring offensive
UN summer-fall offensive
Second Korean winter
Korea, summer–fall 1952
Third Korean winter
Korea, summer 1953

DECORATIONS

Republic of Korea Presidential Unit Citation, Streamer embroidered KOREA 1950–1952 (68th Antiaircraft Artillery Gun Battalion cited; DA GO 41, 1955)

Republic of Korea Presidential Unit Citation, Streamer embroidered DEFENSE OF KOREA (68th Antiaircraft Artillery Gun Battalion cited; DA GO 51, 1957)

16th DETACHMENT, 68th AIR DEFENSE ARTILLERY

RA
(inactive)

LINEAGE

Constituted 27 May 1942 in the Regular Army as Headquarters and Headquarters Battery, 3d Battalion, 68th Coast Artillery. Activated 15 June 1942 at Boston, Massachusetts. Disbanded 4 June 1944 at Foggia, Italy.

Reconstituted 5 August 1958 in the Regular Army and redesignated as the 16th Detachment, 68th Artillery. Activated 1 September 1958 at Camp Lucas, Michigan. Inactivated 1 June 1960 at Camp Lucas, Michigan. Redesignated 1 September 1971 as the 16th Detachment, 68th Air Defense Artillery.

CAMPAIGN PARTICIPATION CREDIT

World War II–EAME
    Sicily
    Naples-Foggia

DECORATIONS

None.

68TH AIR DEFENSE ARTILLERY BIBLIOGRAPHY

Brooks, Arthur C. "From Pusan to Unsan With the 10th Antiaircraft Artillery Group." *Antiaircraft Artillery Journal* 94 (January 1951):13–15. Contains information about the 68th Antiaircraft Artillery Gun Battalion.

Brown, William F. "Chongchon Withdrawal." *Antiaircraft Artillery Journal* 94 (March 1951):18–20. Contains information about the 68th Antiaircraft Artillery Gun Battalion.

Cheal, Raymond C. "Ack-Ack on the Naktong." *Antiaircraft Artillery Journal* 94 (May 1951):9–10. Contains information about the 68th Antiaircraft Artillery Gun Battalion.

———. "The 68th in Korea." *Antiaircraft Artillery Journal* 94 (March 1951):13–14.

"Colonel Hennig and the 10th Antiaircraft Artillery Group." *Antiaircraft Artillery Journal* 95 (March 1952):7. Contains information about the 68th Antiaircraft Artillery Gun Battalion.

8th AAA, AW Battalion (SP), Fort Bliss, Texas, 1949. Baton Rouge: Army and Navy Publishing Company, 1949.

Glaenzer, Charles F. *History of Battery "E," 68th Artillery, Coast Artillery Corps, Over Here and Over There, 1918–1919*. N.p., 1919.

Historical Division, War Department. *Anzio Beachhead (22 January–25 May 1944)*. American Forces in Action. Washington: Government Printing Office, 1947.

Marquat, William F. "Automatic Artillery in Korea." *Antiaircraft Artillery Journal* 93 (November–December 1950):2–9; 94 (January–February 1951):2–12; (March–April 1951):2–5; (May–June 1951):2–6; (July–August 1951):2–9; (September–October 1951):2–5; (November–December 1951):2–6; 95 (January–February 1952):2–5; (March–April 1952):8–10; (May–June 1952):12–15. Contains information about the 68th Antiaircraft Artillery Gun Battalion.

71st AIR DEFENSE ARTILLERY

HERALDIC ITEMS

COAT OF ARMS

Shield: Gules, five high-explosive projectiles palewise in chevron surmounted by three chevronels or.

Crest: On a wreath of the colors, or and gules, a fixed searchlight sable, glass or charged with a fleur-de-lis gules.

Motto: *Undique Venimus* (We Come From All Parts).

Symbolism: Scarlet and yellow are the colors used for artillery. The three chevronels from the coat of arms of John Winthrop, the founder of the Boston colony, allude to Boston, the area in which the unit was originally constituted and organized in 1918. The five projectiles are symbolic of the unit's five battle honors awarded for service in World War II. They also commemorate the mission of the battalion to attack and destroy enemy aircraft.

The fixed searchlight used in seacoast defense refers to the former mission of the regiment as coast artillery. The fleur-de-lis is for service in World War I.

DISTINCTIVE INSIGNIA

The distinctive insignia is the shield and motto of the coat of arms.

LINEAGE AND HONORS

LINEAGE

Constituted 2 May 1918 in the Regular Army as the 71st Artillery (Coast Artillery Corps). Organized 12 May 1918 in the Coast Defenses of Boston with Headquarters at Fort Strong, Massachusetts. Demobilized 6 March 1919 at Camp Devens, Massachusetts. Reconstituted 1 July 1940 in the Regular Army as the 71st Coast Artillery (1st Battalion concurrently activated at Fort Story, Virginia). Regiment (less 1st Battalion) activated 3 January 1941 at Fort Story, Virginia. Regiment broken up 1 September 1943 and its elements reorganized and redesignated as follows: Headquarters and Headquarters Battery as Headquarters and Headquarters Battery, 71st Antiaircraft Artillery Group; 1st Battalion as the 71st Antiaircraft Artillery Gun Battalion; 2d Battalion as the 384th Antiaircraft Artillery Automatic Weapons Battalion; 3d Battalion as the 241st Antiaircraft Artillery Searchlight Battalion.

Headquarters and Headquarters Battery, 71st Antiaircraft Artillery Group, inactivated 25 March 1946 at Munich, Germany. Redesignated

15 September 1949 as Headquarters and Headquarters Battery, 71st Antiaircraft Artillery Gun Battalion. Activated 30 September 1949 at Fort Bliss, Texas, with organic batteries of the former 71st Antiaircraft Artillery Gun Battalion (see below). Redesignated 22 July 1953 as the 71st Antiaircraft Artillery Battalion. Redesignated 6 July 1954 as the 71st Antiaircraft Artillery Missile Battalion. Inactivated 1 September 1958 in the Washington-Baltimore Defense Area.

71st Antiaircraft Artillery Gun Battalion reorganized with new batteries and redesignated 10 January 1945 as the 526th Antiaircraft Artillery Composite Battalion. Reorganized and redesignated 1 September 1945 as the 526th Antiaircraft Artillery Gun Battalion. Redesignated 3 August 1953 as the 526th Antiaircraft Artillery Battalion. Redesignated 13 February 1954 as the 526th Antiaircraft Artillery Missile Battalion. Inactivated 1 September 1958 at Fort Hancock, New Jersey.

384th Antiaircraft Artillery Automatic Weapons Battalion inactivated 18 August 1944 at Camp Pickett, Virginia. Disbanded 26 October 1944. Reconstituted 23 April 1946 in the Regular Army and redesignated as the 384th Antiaircraft Artillery Gun Battalion. Activated 8 May 1946 at Fort Bliss, Texas. Disbanded 31 January 1949 at Fort Bliss, Texas. Reconstituted 28 June 1950 in the Regular Army; concurrently consolidated with the 41st Antiaircraft Artillery Gun Battalion (active) (*see* ANNEX), and consolidated unit designated as the 41st Antiaircraft Artillery Gun Battalion. Redesignated 3 August 1953 as the 41st Antiaircraft Artillery Battalion. Inactivated 20 December 1957 at Fort Totten, New York.

241st Antiaircraft Artillery Searchlight Battalion inactivated 5 August 1944 at Camp Shelby, Mississippi. Disbanded 4 September 1944. Reconstituted 5 August 1958 in the Regular Army.

71st and 526th Antiaircraft Artillery Missile Battalions, 41st Antiaircraft Artillery Battalion, and 241st Antiaircraft Artillery Searchlight Battalion consolidated, reorganized, and redesignated 31 July 1959 as the 71st Artillery, a parent regiment under the Combat Arms Regimental System. Redesignated 1 September 1971 as the 71st Air Defense Artillery.

ANNEX

Constituted 25 February 1943 in the Army of the United States as the 119th Coast Artillery Battalion. Activated 2 April 1943 at Camp Haan, California. Redesignated 28 June 1943 as the 119th Antiaircraft Artillery Gun Battalion. Inactivated 17 December 1945 at Camp Kilmer, New Jersey. Redesignated 13 October 1948 as the 41st Antiaircraft Artillery Gun Battalion and allotted to the Regular Army. Activated 8 June 1949 at Fort Bliss, Texas.

Campaign Participation Credit

World War I
Streamer without inscription

World War II
Normandy
Northern France
Rhineland
Ardennes-Alsace
Central Europe

Vietnam
Defense
Counteroffensive
Counteroffensive, Phase II

Counteroffensive, Phase III
Tet Counteroffensive
Counteroffensive, Phase IV
Counteroffensive, Phase V
Counteroffensive, Phase VI
Tet 69/Counteroffensive
Summer–fall 1969
Winter–spring 1970
Sanctuary Counteroffensive
Counteroffensive, Phase VII
Consolidation I
Consolidation II

Decorations

Valorous Unit Award, Streamer embroidered VIETNAM 1968–1969 (Battery D, 71st Artillery, cited; DA GO 43, 1970)

Meritorious Unit Commendation, Streamer embroidered VIETNAM 1965–1966 (6th Battalion, 71st Artillery, cited; DA GO 17, 1968)

Meritorious Unit Commendation, Streamer embroidered VIETNAM 1967–1968 (Battery D, 71st Artillery, cited; DA GO 60, 1969)

Air Force Outstanding Unit Award, Streamer embroidered KOREA 1978–1982 (2d Battalion, 71st Air Defense Artillery, cited; DA GO 8, 1982, to be amended)

1st MISSILE BATTALION, 71st AIR DEFENSE ARTILLERY

RA
(inactive)

LINEAGE

Constituted 2 May 1918 in the Regular Army as Battery A, 71st Artillery (Coast Artillery Corps). Organized 12 May 1918 at Fort Strong, Massachusetts. Demobilized 6 March 1919 at Camp Devens, Massachusetts. Reconstituted 1 July 1940 in the Regular Army as Battery A, 71st Coast Artillery, and activated at Fort Story, Virginia.

Reorganized and redesignated 1 September 1943 as Battery A, 71st Antiaircraft Artillery Gun Battalion. Inactivated 26 December 1944 at Camp Gruber, Oklahoma. Activated 30 September 1949 at Fort Bliss, Texas. Redesignated 22 July 1953 as Battery A, 71st Antiaircraft Artillery Battalion. Redesignated 1 August 1956 as Battery D, 602d Antiaircraft Artillery Missile Battalion.

Reorganized and redesignated 1 September 1958 as Headquarters and Headquarters Battery, 1st Missile Battalion, 71st Artillery (organic elements constituted 12 August 1958 and activated 1 September 1958). Battalion inactivated in 1965 at Suitland, Maryland. Redesignated 1 September 1971 as the 1st Missile Battalion, 71st Air Defense Artillery.

CAMPAIGN PARTICIPATION CREDIT

World War I
  *Streamer without inscription

World War II
  Normandy
  Northern France

Rhineland
Ardennes-Alsace
Central Europe

DECORATIONS

None.

2d BATTALION, 71st AIR DEFENSE ARTILLERY

RA
(inactive)

LINEAGE

Constituted 2 May 1918 in the Regular Army as Battery B, 71st Artillery (Coast Artillery Corps). Organized 12 May 1918 at Fort Strong, Massachusetts. Demobilized 6 March 1919 at Camp Devens, Massachusetts. Reconstituted 1 July 1940 in the Regular Army as Battery B, 71st Coast Artillery, and activated at Fort Story, Virginia.

Reorganized and redesignated 1 September 1943 as Battery B, 71st Antiaircraft Artillery Gun Battalion. Inactivated 26 December 1944 at Camp Gruber, Oklahoma. Activated 30 September 1949 at Fort Bliss, Texas. Redesignated 22 July 1953 as Battery B, 71st Antiaircraft Artillery Battalion. Redesignated 6 July 1954 as Battery B, 71st Antiaircraft Artillery Missile Battalion.

Reorganized and redesignated 28 August 1958 as Headquarters and Headquarters Battery, 2d Missile Battalion, 71st Artillery (organic elements concurrently constituted and activated). Battalion inactivated 15 August 1959 on Taiwan. Activated 1 March 1960 at Fort Bliss, Texas. Redesignated 10 January 1966 as the 2d Battalion, 71st Artillery. Redesignated 1 September 1971 as the 2d Battalion, 71st Air Defense Artillery. Inactivated 20 July 1982 in Korea.

CAMPAIGN PARTICIPATION CREDIT

World War I
   *Streamer without inscription

World War II
   Normandy
   Northern France

Rhineland
Ardennes-Alsace
Central Europe

DECORATIONS

*Air Force Outstanding Unit Award, Streamer embroidered KOREA 1978–1982 (2d Battalion, 71st Air Defense Artillery, cited; DA GO 8, 1982, to be amended)

3d BATTALION, 71st AIR DEFENSE ARTILLERY

RA
(nondivisional)

LINEAGE

Constituted 2 May 1918 in the Regular Army as Battery C, 71st Artillery (Coast Artillery Corps). Organized 12 May 1918 at Fort Andrews, Massachusetts. Demobilized 6 March 1919 at Camp Devens, Massachusetts. Reconstituted 1 July 1940 in the Regular Army as Battery C, 71st Coast Artillery, and activated at Fort Story, Virginia.

Reorganized and redesignated 1 September 1943 as Battery C, 71st Antiaircraft Artillery Gun Battalion. Inactivated 26 December 1944 at Camp Gruber, Oklahoma. Activated 30 September 1949 at Fort Bliss, Texas. Redesignated 22 July 1953 as Battery C, 71st Antiaircraft Artillery Battalion. Redesignated 6 July 1954 as Battery C, 71st Antiaircraft Artillery Missile Battalion.

Reorganized and redesignated 1 September 1958 as Headquarters and Headquarters Battery, 3d Missile Battalion, 71st Artillery (organic elements constituted 12 August 1958 and activated 1 September 1958). Redesignated 20 August 1965 as the 3d Battalion, 71st Artillery. Redesignated 1 September 1971 as the 3d Battalion, 71st Air Defense Artillery.

CAMPAIGN PARTICIPATION CREDIT

World War I
*Streamer without inscription

World War II
Normandy
Northern France

Rhineland
Ardennes-Alsace
Central Europe

DECORATIONS

None.

BATTERY D, 71st AIR DEFENSE ARTILLERY

RA
(inactive)

LINEAGE

Constituted 2 May 1918 in the Regular Army as Battery D, 71st Artillery (Coast Artillery Corps). Organized 12 May 1918 at Fort Andrews, Massachusetts. Demobilized 6 March 1919 at Camp Devens, Massachusetts. Reconstituted 1 July 1940 in the Regular Army as Battery D, 71st Coast Artillery, and activated at Fort Story, Virginia.

Reorganized and redesignated 1 September 1943 as Battery D, 71st Antiaircraft Artillery Gun Battalion. Reorganized and redesignated 10 January 1945 as Battery A, 526th Antiaircraft Artillery Composite Battalion. Redesignated 3 August 1953 as Battery A, 526th Antiaircraft Artillery Battalion. Redesignated 13 February 1954 as Battery A, 526th Antiaircraft Artillery Missile Battalion.

Reorganized and redesignated 1 September 1958 as Headquarters and Headquarters Battery, 4th Missile Battalion, 71st Artillery (organic elements constituted 12 August 1958 and activated 1 September 1958). Battalion inactivated 19 June 1964 at Fort Hancock, New Jersey. Headquarters and Headquarters Battery, 4th Missile Battalion, 71st Artillery, redesignated 25 April 1966 as Battery D, 71st Artillery. Activated 1 June 1966 at Fort Bliss, Texas. Inactivated 25 June 1971 in Vietnam. Redesignated 1 September 1971 as Battery D, 71st Air Defense Artillery. Activated 15 September 1971 in Vietnam. Inactivated 20 March 1972 in Vietnam.

CAMPAIGN PARTICIPATION CREDIT

Vietnam

Counteroffensive, Phase II	Tet 69/Counteroffensive
Counteroffensive, Phase III	Summer–fall 1969
Tet Counteroffensive	Winter–spring 1970
Counteroffensive, Phase IV	Sanctuary Counteroffensive
Counteroffensive, Phase V	Counteroffensive, Phase VII
Counteroffensive, Phase VI	Consolidation I
	Consolidation II

DECORATIONS

Valorous Unit Award, Streamer embroidered VIETNAM 1968–1969 (Battery D, 71st Artillery, cited; DA GO 43, 1970)

Meritorious Unit Commendation, Streamer embroidered VIETNAM 1967–1968 (Battery D, 71st Artillery, cited; DA GO 70, 1969)

Republic of Vietnam Cross of Gallantry with Palm, Streamer embroidered VIETNAM 1967–1969 (Battery D, 71st Artillery, cited; DA GO 60, 1969)

Republic of Vietnam Cross of Gallantry with Palm, Streamer embroidered VIETNAM 1969–1970 (Battery D, 71st Artillery, cited; DA GO 5, 1973)

Republic of Vietnam Civil Action Honor Medal, First Class, Streamer embroidered VIETNAM 1966–1971 (Battery D, 71st Artillery, cited; DA GO 51, 1971)

6th BATTALION, 71st AIR DEFENSE ARTILLERY

RA
(inactive)

LINEAGE

Constituted 2 May 1918 in the Regular Army as Battery F, 71st Artillery (Coast Artillery Corps). Organized 12 May 1918 at Fort Banks, Massachusetts. Demobilized 6 March 1919 at Camp Devens, Massachusetts. Reconstituted 1 July 1940 in the Regular Army as Battery F, 71st Coast Artillery. Activated 3 January 1941 at Fort Story, Virginia.

Reorganized and redesignated 1 September 1943 as Battery B, 384th Antiaircraft Artillery Automatic Weapons Battalion. Inactivated 18 August 1944 at Camp Pickett, Virginia. Disbanded 26 October 1944. Reconstituted 23 April 1946 in the Regular Army and redesignated as Battery B, 384th Antiaircraft Artillery Gun Battalion. Activated 8 May 1946 at Fort Bliss, Texas. Disbanded 31 January 1949 at Fort Bliss, Texas. Reconstituted 28 June 1950 in the Regular Army; concurrently consolidated with Battery B, 41st Antiaircraft Artillery Gun Battalion (active) (*see* ANNEX), and consolidated unit designated as Battery B, 41st Antiaircraft Artillery Gun Battalion. Redesignated 3 August 1953 as Battery B, 41st Antiaircraft Artillery Battalion. Inactivated 20 December 1957 at New York, New York.

Redesignated 31 July 1959 as Headquarters and Headquarters Battery, 6th Battalion, 71st Artillery. Redesignated 18 January 1962 as Headquarters and Headquarters Battery, 6th Missile Battalion, 71st Artillery (organic elements concurrently constituted). Battalion activated 2 June 1962 at Fort Bliss, Texas. Redesignated 14 June 1965 as the 6th Battalion, 71st Artillery. Inactivated 31 March 1970 at Fort Bliss, Texas. Redesignated 1 September 1971 as the 6th Battalion, 71st Air Defense Artillery.

ANNEX

Constituted 25 February 1943 in the Army of the United States as Battery B, 119th Coast Artillery Battalion. Activated 2 April 1943 at Camp Haan, California. Redesignated 28 June 1943 as Battery B, 119th Antiaircraft Artillery Gun Battalion. Inactivated 17 December 1945 at Camp Kilmer, New Jersey. Redesignated 13 October 1948 as Battery B, 41st Antiaircraft Artillery Gun Battalion, and allotted to the Regular Army. Activated 8 June 1949 at Fort Bliss, Texas.

CAMPAIGN PARTICIPATION CREDIT

World War I
  *Streamer without inscription

World War II
  *Normandy
  *Northern France
  *Rhineland
  *Ardennes-Alsace
  *Central Europe

Vietnam
  *Defense
  *Counteroffensive
  *Counteroffensive, Phase II
  *Counteroffensive, Phase III
  *Tet Counteroffensive
  *Counteroffensive, Phase IV
  *Counteroffensive, Phase V

DECORATIONS

*Meritorious Unit Commendation, Streamer embroidered VIETNAM 1965–1966 (6th Battalion, 71st Artillery, cited; DA GO 17, 1968)

16th DETACHMENT, 71st AIR DEFENSE ARTILLERY

RA
(inactive)

LINEAGE

Constituted 27 May 1942 in the Regular Army as Headquarters and Headquarters Battery, 3d Battalion, 71st Coast Artillery. Activated 15 June 1942 at Washington, D.C.

Reorganized and redesignated 1 September 1943 as Headquarters and Headquarters Battery, 241st Antiaircraft Artillery Searchlight Battalion. Inactivated 5 August 1944 at Camp Shelby, Mississippi. Disbanded 4 September 1944.

Reconstituted 5 August 1958 in the Regular Army and redesignated as the 16th Detachment, 71st Artillery. Activated 1 September 1958 at Fort Bliss, Texas. Inactivated 17 September 1962 at Fort Bliss, Texas. Redesignated 1 September 1971 as the 16th Detachment, 71st Air Defense Artillery.

CAMPAIGN PARTICIPATION CREDIT

None.

DECORATIONS

None.

71ST AIR DEFENSE ARTILLERY BIBLIOGRAPHY

Elder, Bowman. *An Illustrated History of the 71st Artillery (Coast Artillery Corps)*. Indianapolis: William B. Burford, 1920?

Pictorial History, "The Rollin' Seventy-First," 71st Coast Artillery (AA), 1941. Baton Rouge: Army and Navy Publishing Company, 1941.

Pictorial Review. Atlanta: Albert Love Enterprises, 1944.

Robinson, James L. *Combat Diary, Battery D, 119th AAA Gun Battalion (Mobile)*. Regensburg: Friedrich Pustet, 1945.

Weichel, Frederick P. "The Last to Leave." *Air Defense Magazine* (July–September 1982):32–32. Pertains to the 2d Battalion, 71st Air Defense Artillery.

111th AIR DEFENSE ARTILLERY

HERALDIC ITEMS

COAT OF ARMS

Shield: Gules, on a cross or voided of the field, a saltire in fess gray fimbriated of the second between two fleurs-de-lis of the like.

Crest: That for the regiments and separate battalions of the Virginia Army National Guard: On a wreath of the colors, or and gules, Virtus, the genius of the commonwealth dressed as an Amazon, resting on a spear with one hand and holding a sword in the other; and treading on Tyranny, represented by a man prostrate, a crown falling from his head, a broken chain in his left hand and a scourge in his right, all proper.

Motto: Glory and Honor.

Symbolism: Scarlet and yellow are the colors used for artillery. The voided cross of St. George refers to the English colonization and development of Virginia and commemorates Grimes' battery, formed at Portsmouth in 1809, and now an element of the organization; it also refers to the War of 1812. The saltire is for Confederate service in the Civil War. The two fleur-de-lis are for service in France and Central Europe, World War II, and also allude to the award of the French Croix de Guerre with Palm (World War II) for participation in the invasion of Normandy.

DISTINCTIVE INSIGNIA

The distinctive insignia is the shield and motto of the coat of arms.

LINEAGE AND HONORS

ARNG
(Virginia)

LINEAGE

Constituted 2 July 1946 in the Virginia National Guard as the 691st Antiaircraft Artillery Automatic Weapons Battalion. Organized in southwestern Virginia from new and existing units; Headquarters federally recognized 13 December 1946 at Portsmouth. Redesignated 1 February 1949 as the 129th Antiaircraft Artillery Automatic Weapons Battalion and assigned to the 29th Infantry Division. Redesignated 1 October 1954 as the 129th Antiaircraft Artillery Battalion.

Reorganized and redesignated 1 June 1959 as the 3d Automatic Weapons Battalion, 111th Artillery, and relieved from assignment to the 29th Infantry Division. Redesignated 1 November 1965 as the 3d Battalion, 111th Artillery.

Consolidated 1 May 1972 with the 4th Battalion, 111th Artillery (*see* ANNEX), and consolidated unit reorganized and redesignated as the 111th Artillery, a parent regiment under the Combat Arms Regimental System, to consist of the 3d and 4th Battalions. Redesignated 1 November 1972 as the 111th Air Defense Artillery. Reorganized 30 September 1974 to consist of the 3d Battalion. Reorganized 1 August 1975 to consist of the 3d Battalion, an element of the 28th Infantry Division.

ANNEX

Constituted 26 July 1954 in the Virginia Army National Guard as the 615th Antiaircraft Artillery Battalion. Organized 1954–1955 in southwestern Virginia; Headquarters federally recognized 13 September 1954 at South Norfolk. Reorganized and redesignated 15 February 1958 as the 615th Missile Battalion.

Reorganized and redesignated 1 June 1959 as the 4th Missile Battalion, 111th Artillery. Redesignated 1 January 1966 as the 4th Battalion, 111th Artillery.

CAMPAIGN PARTICIPATION CREDIT

Headquarters Battery (Portsmouth), 3d Battalion, entitled to the following:

War of 1812
    Virginia 1813

Civil War—Confederate service
    Peninsula
    Second Manassias
    Sharpsburg
    Fredricksburg
    Gettysburg
    Cold Harbor
    Petersburg
    Appomattox
    Virginia 1861

Virginia 1863
Virginia 1864
North Carolina 1864

World War I
    Meuse-Argonne
    Alsace 1918

World War II–EAME
    Normandy (with arrowhead)
    Northern France
    Rhineland
    Central Europe

Battery C (Grimes' Battery, Portsmouth), 3d Battalion, entitled to the following:

War of 1812
    Virginia 1813

Civil War—Confederate service
    Peninsula
    Second Manassas
    Sharpsburg
    Virginia 1861
    Virginia 1862
    North Carolina 1862

World War II–EAME
    Normandy (with arrowhead)
    Northern France
    Rhineland
    Central Europe

DECORATIONS

Headquarters Battery (Portsmouth) and Battery C (Grimes' Battery, Portsmouth), 3d Battalion, each entitled to French Croix de Guerre with Palm, World War II, Streamer embroidered BEACHES OF NORMANDY (111th Field Artillery Battalion cited; DA GO 43, 1950)

111TH AIR DEFENSE ARTILLERY BIBLIOGRAPHY

No published histories.

174th AIR DEFENSE ARTILLERY

HERALDIC ITEMS

COAT OF ARMS

Shield: Per bend gules and barry wavy of eight or and of the first, in chief a pineapple of the second.

Crest: That for the regiments and separate battalions of the Ohio Army National Guard: On a wreath of the colors, or and gules, a sheaf of seventeen arrows argent bound by a sprig of buckeye (*Aesculus glabra*) fructed proper (two leaves with bursting burr).

Motto: *Caveat Oppugnator* (Let the Oppressor [Hostile One] Beware).

Symbolism: Red and yellow are the colors used for artillery. The pineapple is used to show service in Hawaii. The barry wavy, symbolizing the Pacific Ocean, represents service in the Western Pacific during World War II.

DISTINCTIVE INSIGNIA

The distinctive insignia is the shield and motto of the coat of arms.

LINEAGE AND HONORS

ARNG
(Ohio)

LINEAGE

Constituted 19 May 1944 in the Army of the United States as the 180th Coast Artillery Battalion. Activated 31 May 1944 at Fort Ruger, Hawaii. Inactivated 13 December 1945 in the Mariana Islands. Redesignated 1 March 1951 as the 180th Antiaircraft Artillery Gun Battalion and allotted to the Ohio Army National Guard. Organized and federally recognized 29 May 1951 with Headquarters at Dayton. Redesignated 1 October 1953 as the 180th Antiaircraft Artillery Battalion.

Reorganized and redesignated 1 September 1959 as the 174th Artillery, a parent regiment under the Combat Arms Regimental System, to consist of the 1st Gun Battalion, the 2d Automatic Weapons Battalion, and the 3d Detachment. Reorganized 1 April 1963 to consist of the 1st and 2d Automatic Weapons Battalions and the 3d Detachment. Reorganized 15 February 1968 to consist of the 1st and 2d Battalions. Reorganized 1 February 1972 to consist of the 2d Battalion. Redesignated 1 November 1972 as the 174th Air Defense Artillery. Reorganized 1 August 1975 to consist of the 2d Battalion, an element of the 38th Infantry Division.

CAMPAIGN PARTICIPATION CREDIT

World War II
> Western Pacific

Headquarters Battery (Athens), 2d Battalion, additionally entitled to the following:

World War II–AP
> New Guinea

DECORATIONS

None.

174TH AIR DEFENSE ARTILLERY BIBLIOGRAPHY

No published histories.

200th AIR DEFENSE ARTILLERY
(First New Mexico)

COAT OF ARMS

Shield: Or, an Avanyu sable. (The Avanyu is a Pueblo Indian device not unlike the device of the Isle of Man conventionalized, which is blazoned three legs embowed conjoined at the thighs, the three arms of the Avanyu each ending in a triangular head bearing five points.)

Crest: That for the regiments and separate battalions of the New Mexico Army National Guard: On a wreath of the colors, or and sable, a coiled rattlesnake proper.

Motto: *Pro Civitate et Patria* (For State and Country).

Symbolism: The Avanyu device used by the Pueblo Indians is another form of the triskelion, a lucky talisman and symbolic of energy, motion, and victory. It is also emblematic of "the whirling sun" and "lightning in air" which allude to the firepower and air defense mission of the unit.

DISTINCTIVE INSIGNIA

The distinctive insignia is the shield, crest, and motto of the coat of arms.

LINEAGE AND HONORS

LINEAGE

Organized 1 September 1880 in the New Mexico Volunteer Militia in west-central New Mexico from independent companies as the 1st Regiment. Expanded 18 February 1882 to form the 1st Regiment with Headquarters at Socorro and the 2d Regiment with Headquarters at Albuquerque.

1st Regiment expanded 25 April 1883 to form the 1st Regiment and the 2d Cavalry Battalion (1st Regiment—hereafter separate lineage). 2d Cavalry Battalion reorganized and redesignated 14 September 1883 as the 1st Regiment of Cavalry (less 3d Battalion—see below). Reorganized 10 November 1885 as the 1st Regiment of Cavalry. Disbanded 29 December 1893 and two remaining troops attached to the 1st Regiment of Infantry. Reorganized 12 September 1896 in the New Mexico Volunteer Militia as the 1st Battalion of Cavalry with Headquarters at Santa Fe. (New Mexico Volunteer Militia redesignated 17 March 1897 as the New Mexico National Guard.) Redesignated in 1897 as the 1st Squadron of Cavalry. While remaining in state service the 1st Squadron of Cavalry additionally formed the 2d Squadron, 1st United States Volunteer Cavalry, also known as the Rough Riders (mustered into federal service 6–7 May 1898 at Santa Fe; mustered out of federal service 15 September 1898 at Montauk Point, New York). Troop A attached 5 February 1908 to the 1st Regiment of Infantry (see below); remainder of squadron concurrently disbanded.

2d Regiment expanded 25 April 1883 to form the 2d Regiment and the 1st Cavalry Battalion. 2d Regiment redesignated 10 November 1885 as the 1st Regiment of Infantry with Headquarters at Santa Fe. Location of Headquarters changed 16 August 1886 to Albuquerque.

1st Cavalry Battalion reorganized and redesignated 14 September 1883 as the 3d Battalion, 1st Regiment of Cavalry. Expanded, reorganized, and redesignated 10 November 1885 as the 2d Regiment of Cavalry.

1st Regiment of Infantry and elements of the 2d Regiment of Cavalry consolidated 24 December 1890 and consolidated unit designated as the 1st Regiment of Infantry. 1st Regiment of Infantry consolidated in 1909 with Troop A (see above) and consolidated unit designated as the 1st Regiment of Infantry. Mustered into federal service 16 July 1916 at Albuquerque for service on the Mexican border; mustered out of federal service 5 April 1917 at Columbus. Called into federal service 21 April 1917; mustered into federal service 11 June 1917 at Albuquerque. Drafted into federal service 5 August 1917. Regiment broken up 19–24 October 1917 and its elements reorganized and redesignated as elements of the 115th Train Headquarters and Military Police and the 143d and 144th Machine Gun Battalions, elements of the 40th Division.

Military Police section of 115th Train Headquarters and Military Police reorganized and redesignated 27 October 1918 as the 40th Military Police Company, an element of the 40th Division; 115th Train Headquarters and Military Police currently reorganized and redesignated as the 115th Train Headquarters. 40th Military Police Company demobilized 2 May 1919 at Camp Kearny, California; 115th Train Headquarters demobilized 25 April 1919 at Camp Kearny, California.

143d and 144th Machine Gun Battalions demobilized 30 April 1919 at Camp Grant, Illinois.

Former 1st Regiment of Infantry reconstituted 16 July 1919 in the New Mexico National Guard as a separate squadron of cavalry and organized with Troops A and B at Albuquerque and Carlsbad, respectively. Expanded, reorganized, and redesignated 3 December 1920 as the 1st Cavalry. Redesignated 2 May 1922 as the 111th Cavalry. Headquarters federally recognized 4 May 1924 at Sante Fe. Assigned 5 November 1923 to the 23d Cavalry Division. Relieved 15 March 1929 from assignment to the 23d Cavalry Division. Converted and redesignated 26 April 1940 as the 207th Coast Artillery. Redesignated 1 July 1940 as the 200th Coast Artillery. Inducted into federal service 6 January 1941 at home stations. Surrendered 9 April 1942 to the Japanese *14th Army*. Inactivated 2 April

1946 at Fort Mills, Philippine Islands.

Headquarters, 200th Coast Artillery, redesignated 31 May 1946 as Headquarters and Headquarters Battery, 200th Antiaircraft Artillery Group. Headquarters, 200th Antiaircraft Artillery Group, organized and federally recognized 25 September 1947 at Roswell (Headquarters Battery organized and federally recognized 10 October 1947 at Las Cruces—hereafter separate lineage). Reorganized and redesignated 1 September 1959 as Headquarters, 200th Artillery Group. Consolidated 15 December 1967 with the 200th Artillery and consolidated unit designated as the 200th Artillery, a parent regiment under the Combat Arms Regimental System (see below).

Headquarters Battery, 200th Coast Artillery, redesignated 31 May 1946 as the 716th Antiaircraft Artillery Gun Battalion. Reorganized and federally recognized 27 September 1947 in southwestern New Mexico with Headquarters at Silver City. Ordered into active federal service 14 August 1950 at home stations; released 13 August 1952 from active federal service and reverted to state control. Redesignated 1 October 1953 as the 716th Antiaircraft Artillery Battalion.

1st Battalion (less Battery C), 200th Coast Artillery, redesignated 31 May 1946 as the 717th Antiaircraft Artillery Gun Battalion. Reorganized and federally recognized 23 June 1947 in northwestern New Mexico with Headquarters at Albuquerque. Ordered into active federal service 1 May 1951 at home stations; released 28 February 1953 from active federal service and reverted to state control. Redesignated 1 October 1953 as the 717th Antiaircraft Artillery Battalion.

Battery C, 200th Coast Artillery, redesignated 31 May 1946 as the 726th Antiaircraft Artillery Searchlight Battalion. Reorganized and federally recognized 23 June 1947 in north-central New Mexico with Headquarters at Albuquerque. Reorganized and redesignated 1 December 1947 as the 726th Antiaircraft Artillery Gun Battalion. Location of Headquarters changed 1 July 1948 to Sante Fe. Ordered into active federal service 14 August 1950 at home stations; released 13 May 1952 from active federal service and reverted to state control. Redesignated 1 October 1953 as the 726th Antiaircraft Artillery Battalion.

2d Battalion, 200th Coast Artillery, redesignated 31 May 1946 as the 697th Antiaircraft Artillery Automatic Weapons Battalion. Reorganized and federally recognized 2 November 1947 in southeastern New Mexico with Headquarters at Roswell. Redesignated 1 October 1953 as the 697th Antiaircraft Artillery Battalion.

716th, 717th, 726th, and 697th Antiaircraft Artillery Battalions; Headquarters, 515th Antiaircraft Artillery Group (see ANNEX 1); 502d Field Artillery Battalion (organized and federally recognized 21 September 1956 in eastern New Mexico with Headquarters at Clovis); 120th Antiaircraft Artillery Battalion (see ANNEX 2); and 804th Antiaircraft Artillery Battalion (see ANNEX 3) consolidated 1 September 1959 and consolidated unit reorganized and redesignated as the 200th Artillery, a parent regiment under the Combat Arms Regimental System, to consist of the 1st Automatic Weapons Battalion; the 2d, 3d, 4th, 5th, and 6th Gun Battalions; and the 7th Detachment. Reorganized 1 February 1962 to consist of the 1st Automatic Weapons Battalion; the 2d, 3d, 4th, 5th, and 6th Gun Battalions; and the 7th and 8th Detachments. Reorganized 1 April 1962 to consist of the 1st, 2d, 3d, 4th, 5th, and 6th Automatic Weapons Battalions and the 7th and 8th Detachments. Consolidated 15 December 1967 with Headquarters, 200th Artillery Group (see above), and consolidated unit designated as the 200th Artillery, a parent regiment under the Combat Arms Regimental System, to consist of the 1st, 2d, 3d, and 4th Battalions. Redesignated 1 November 1972 as the 200th Air Defense Artillery. Reorganized 1 September 1975 to consist of the 1st Battalion, an element of the 49th Armored Division; the 2d Battalion, an element of the 47th Infantry Division; the 3d Battalion, an element of the 50th Armored Division; and the 4th Battalion, an element of the 40th Infantry Division.

ANNEX 1

Constituted in July 1923 in the Organized Reserves as the 515th Coast Artillery. Organized in November 1924 with Headquarters at Topeka, Kansas. Withdrawn 19 December 1941 from the Organized Reserves and allotted to the Regular Army; concurrently activated at Manila, Philippine Islands, with personnel of the 200th Coast Artillery. Surrendered 9 April 1942 to the Japanese *14th Army.* Inactivated 2 April 1946 at Fort Mills, Philippine Islands. Redesignated 1 August 1946 as the 515th Coast Artillery Battery and activated at Fort Winfield Scott, California. Inactivated 25 November 1946 at Fort Winfield Scott, California.

Redesignated 23 April 1947 as Headquarters and Headquarters Battery, 515th Antiaircraft Artillery Group; concurrently withdrawn from the Regular Army and allotted to the New Mexico National Guard. Headquarters organized and federally recognized 25 September 1947 at Roswell (Headquarters Battery organized and federally recognized 23 June 1947 at Sante Fe—hereafter separate lineage). Location changed 16 April 1955 to Albuquerque.

ANNEX 2

Constituted 30 November 1920 in the New Mexico National Guard as an engineer regiment (less one battalion allotted to the Oklahoma National Guard). Organized 3 June–17 August 1921 as the 1st Engineers (2d Battalion allotted to the Oklahoma National Guard); Headquarters federally recognized 8 June 1924 at Las Cruces. Redesignated 2 May 1922 as the 137th Engineers. Reorganized and redesignated 23 February 1923 as the 120th Engineers and assigned to the 47th Division (1st Battalion allotted to the Oklahoma National Guard). Inducted into federal service 16 September 1940 at home stations. Reorganized and redesignated (less 1st Battalion and Band) 20 February 1942 as the 120th Engineer Battalion, an element of the 45th Infantry Division (1st Battalion and Band concurrently reorganized and redesignated as the 1st Battalion and Band, 176th Engineers—hereafter separate lineages). Reorganized and redesignated 1 August 1942 as the 120th Engineer Combat Battalion. Inactivated 26 November 1945 at Camp Bowie, Texas.

Converted and redesignated 31 May 1946 as the 3630th Ordnance Maintenance Company and relieved from assignment to the 45th Infantry Division. Reorganized and federally recognized 5 October 1947 at Roswell. Converted and redesignated 12 May 1949 as Headquarters and Headquarters Battery, 120th Antiaircraft Artillery Gun Battalion (organic elements concurrently organized from new and existing units). Redesignated 1 October 1953 as the 120th Antiaircraft Artillery Battalion.

ANNEX 3

Constituted 30 August 1940 in the New Mexico National Guard as the 104th Antitank Battalion. Organized September–November 1940 from new and existing units; Headquarters federally recognized 5 November 1940 at Roswell. Inducted into Federal service 6 January 1941 at home stations. Redesignated 24 July 1941 as the 104th Infantry Battalion, Antitank. Redesignated 15 December 1941 as the 804th Tank Destroyer Battalion. Inactivated 10 December 1945 at Camp Hood, Texas. Converted and redesignated 31 May 1946 as the 804th Antiaircraft Artillery Automatic Weapons Battalion. Reorganized and federally recognized 3 October 1947 with Headquarters at Tucumcari. Redesignated 1 October 1953 as the 804th Antiaircraft Artillery Battalion.

CAMPAIGN PARTICIPATION CREDIT

Indian Wars	Naples-Foggia (with arrowhead)
New Mexico 1881	Anzio
New Mexico 1882	Rome-Arno
War With Spain	Southern France (with arrowhead)
Santiago	North Apennines
	Rhineland
World War I	Ardennes-Alsace
Streamer without inscription	Central Europe
World War II	Po Valley
Sicily (with arrowhead)	Philippine Islands

Battery A (Roswell), 1st Battalion, additionally entitled to the following:

World War I	St. Mihiel
Champagne-Marne	Meuse-Argonne
Aisne-Marne	Champagne 1918

DECORATIONS

Presidential Unit Citation (Army), Streamer embroidered CLARK FIELD (200th Coast Artillery cited; WD GO 14, 1942)

Presidential Unit Citation (Army), Streamer embroidered MANILA 1941 (515th Coast Artillery cited; WD GO 14, 1942)

Presidential Unit Citation (Army), Streamer embroidered BATAAN (200th and 515th Coast Artillery cited; WD GO 14, 1942)

Presidential Unit Citation (Army), Streamer embroidered DEFENSE OF THE PHILIPPINES (Military and naval forces of the United States engaged in the defense of the Philippines cited; WD GO 22, 1942, as amended by DA GO 46, 1948)

Philippine Presidential Unit Citation, Streamer embroidered 7 DECEMBER 1941 TO 10 MAY 1942 (200th and 515th Coast Artillery cited; DA GO 47, 1950)

Battery A (Roswell), 1st Battalion, and Headquarters Battery (Tucumcari), 4th Battalion, each additionally entitled to French Croix de Guerre with Palm, World War II, Streamer embroidered CENTRAL ITALY (804th Tank Destroyer Battalion cited; DA GO 43, 1950)

Battery C (Socorro), 2d Battalion, additionally entitled to Presidential Unit Citation (Army), Streamer embroidered BLIES RIVER (Company B, 120th Engineer Combat Battalion, cited; WD GO 84, 1945), and French Croix de Guerre with Palm, World War II, Streamer embroidered ACQUAFONDATA (120th Engineer Combat Battalion cited; DA GO 43, 1950)

Headquarters Battery (Albuquerque), 3d Battalion, additionally entitled to French Croix de Guerre with Palm, World War II, Streamer embroidered ACQUAFONDATA (120th Engineer Combat Battalion cited; DA GO 43, 1950)

200TH AIR DEFENSE ARTILLERY BIBLIOGRAPHY

Adams, Clarence S. "ADA Guardsmen Train at Bliss." *Air Defense Magazine* (October–December 1978):14–15.

Azoy, A.C.M. *Charge: The Story of the Battle of San Juan Hill.* New York: Longmans, Green, and Company, 1961.

Ball, Larry D. "Militia Posses: The Territorial Militia in Civil Law Enforcement in New Mexico Territory, 1883–1887." *New Mexico Historical Review* (January 1980):47–69.

Blumenson, Martin. *Salerno to Cassino.* United States Army in World War II. Washington: Government Printing Office, 1969. Contains information about the 120th Engineer Combat Battalion.

Case, Blair. "Clark Field: Air Defense Debacle in the Philippines." *Air Defense Magazine* (July–September 1982):4–7.

Fisher, Ernest F., Jr. *Cassino to the Alps.* United States Army in World War II. Washington: Government Printing Office, 1977. Contains information about the 804th Tank Destroyer Battalion.

"Heroes of Bataan." *The National Guardsman* 17 (March 1963): back cover.

Historical Division, War Department. *Salerno: American Operations From the Beaches to the Volturno (9 Sepember–6 October 1943).* American Forces in Action. Washington: Government Printing Office, 1944. Contains information about the 120th Engineer Combat Battalion.

————. *Small Unit Actions*. American Forces in Action. Washington: Government Printing Office, 1946. Contains information about the 804th Tank Destroyer Battalion.

"I Bowed Briefly on Grim Corregidor." *The Push Pin Post* 8 (November 1978):4.

Maddox, Robert J. "Teddy Roosevelt and the Rough Riders." *American History Illustrated* 12 (November 1977):8–19.

Marshall, Edward. *The Story of the Rough Riders, 1st U.S. Volunteer Cavalry: The Regiment in Camp and on the Battlefield*. New York: G.W. Dillingham Company, Publishers, 1899.

Mellnik, Stephen M. "The Life and Death of the 200th Coast Artillery (AA)." *Coast Artillery Journal* 90 (March–April 1947):2–7.

Morton, Louis. *The Fall of the Philippines*. United States Army in World War II. Washington: Government Printing Office, 1953.

Pico, Susan. "ADA in New Mexico National Guard." *Air Defense Magazine* (October–December 1979):20–22.

Roosevelt, Theodore. *The Rough Riders*. New York: Charles Scribner's Sons, 1899.

Westermeir, Clifford R. *Who Rush to Glory: The Cavalry Volunteers of 1898*. Caldwell, Idaho: The Caxton Printers, 1958.

263d AIR DEFENSE ARTILLERY

HERALDIC ITEMS

COAT OF ARMS

Shield: Gules, on a cross of the field fimbriated or two cannon in pale of the last.

Crest: That for the regiments and separate battalions of the South Carolina Army National Guard: On a wreath of the colors, or and gules, upon a mount vert a palmetto tree proper charged with a crescent argent.

Motto: Unsurrendered.

Symbolism: The shield is red for artillery. The red cross of Saint George symbolizes the origin of the regiment prior to the War of the American Revolution. The two cannon are old trophies of the regiment.

DISTINCTIVE INSIGNIA

The distinctive insignia is the shield and motto of the coat of arms.

LINEAGE AND HONORS

ARNG
(South Carolina)

LINEAGE

Organized in 1756 at Charles Town as the Artillery Company of Charles Town, commanded by Capt. Christopher Gadsden. Chartered 31 July 1760 by the colony of South Carolina. Expanded, reorganized, and redesignated in 1775 as the Charles Town Battalion of Artillery. Surrendered 12 May 1780 to the British forces at Charles Town. Reconstituted in 1783 as the Charleston Battalion of Artillery and organized at Charleston. Attached 17 December 1794 to the 7th Brigade, 2d Division, South Carolina Militia. Expanded, reorganized, and redesignated 16 December 1797 as the 1st Regiment of Artillery. Provisional battalion from the 1st Regiment of Artillery, commanded by Maj. John P. Felder, mustered into federal service 6 November 1814 at Charleston; mustered out of federal service 3 March 1815 at Charleston. Elements of the 1st Regiment of Artillery mustered into federal service 10 March 1836 at Charleston; mustered out of federal service 6–7 April 1836 at Charleston. While remaining in state service during the Civil War the 1st Regiment of Artillery furnished personnel for the German Artillery Battery and the Washington Artillery, volunteer units in the Confederate States Army. German Artillery Battery disbanded in April 1865 at Camden, South

397

Carolina; remaining artillery units surrendered 26 April 1865 at Greensboro, North Carolina, with the Army of the Tennessee.

Reorganized in 1878 in the South Carolina Volunteer Troops at Charleston as the 1st Regiment of Artillery. Reorganized in 1883 as the German Artillery and Lafayette Artillery.

Lafayette Artillery consolidated 1 May 1892 with the Beaufort Volunteer Artillery (*see* ANNEX) and the Chicora Rifles (organized 22 February 1890 at Mount Pleasant, as Company F, 1st Battalion of Infantry) to form the Naval Battalion; concurrently withdrawn from the South Carolina Volunteer Troops and allotted to the South Carolina Naval Militia. South Carolina Naval Militia called into active federal service 8 April 1917 at home stations to serve on patrol duty with the United States Navy off the coast of South Carolina; personnel demobilized in 1919.

Reorganized 21 July 1923 in the South Carolina National Guard as the 1st Coast Defense Command, Coast Artillery Corps, with Headquarters at Beaufort. Redesignated 25 March 1924 as the 1st Separate Battalion, Coast Artillery Corps. Redesignated 31 July 1925 as the 263d Coast Artillery Battalion. Expanded, reorganized, and redesignated 10 June 1930 as the 263d Coast Artillery. Headquarters federally recognized 14 June 1930 at Beaufort. (3d Battalion, 263d Coast Artillery, reorganized and redesignated 10 December 1940 as the 107th Separate Battalion, Coast Artillery—see below.)

263d Coast Artillery inducted into federal service 13 January 1941 at home stations. Regiment broken up 1 October 1944 and its elements reorganized and redesignated as follows: Headquarters and Headquarters Battery and Batteries C, D, and E as Headquarters and Headquarters Battery and Batteries A, B, and C, respectively, Harbor Defense of Charleston; Headquarters and Headquarters Batteries, 1st and 2d Battalions; Battery F, and Searchlight Battery disbanded (Batteries A and B as the 248th and 249th Coast Artillery Batteries, respectively—hereafter separate lineages).

Harbor Defense of Charleston redesignated 30 June 1945 as the 263d Coast Artillery and inactivated at Fort Moultrie, South Carolina.

1st Battalion, 263d Coast Artillery, reorganized and federally recognized 4 April 1947 as the 713th Antiaircraft Artillery Gun Battalion with Headquarters at Lancaster. Ordered into active federal service 15 August 1950 at home stations; released 14 June 1952 from active federal service and reverted to state control. Redesignated 1 October 1953 as the 713th Antiaircraft Artillery Battalion.

2d Battalion, 263d Coast Artillery, reorganized and federally recognized 15 April 1947 as the 678th Antiaircraft Artillery Automatic Weapons Battalion with Headquarters at Anderson. Redesignated 1 October 1953 as the 678th Antiaircraft Artillery Battalion.

107th Separate Battalion, Coast Artillery, inducted into federal service 10 February 1941 at home stations. Reorganized and redesignated 13 November 1943 as the 107th Antiaircraft Artillery Automatic Weapons Battalion. Inactivated 5 December 1944 in Italy. Reorganized and federally recognized 10 February 1947 with Headquarters at Newberry. Redesignated 1 October 1953 as the 107th Antiaircraft Artillery Battalion.

Headquarters and Headquarters Battery, 263d Coast Artillery, and the 713th, 678th, and 107th Antiaircraft Artillery Battalions consolidated 1 April 1959 and consolidated unit reorganized and redesignated as the 263d Artillery, a parent regiment under the Combat Arms Regimental System, to consist of the 1st, 2d, and 3d Automatic Weapons Battalions and the 4th Detachment. Reorganized 1 April 1963 to consist of the 1st and 2d Automatic Weapons Battalions and the 4th Detachment. Reorganized 1 January 1968 to consist of the 2d Battalion. Redesignated 1 November 1972 as the 263d Air Defense Artillery. Reorganized 1 August 1975 to consist of the 2d Battalion, an element of the 26th Infantry Division.

ANNEX

Organized 21 February 1776 at Beaufort as the Beaufort Volunteer Artillery. Assigned 18 October 1776 to the 4th South Carolina Regiment (Continental) (Artillery). Surrendered 12 May 1780 to the British forces at Charles Town. Reorganized in 1800 in the South Carolina Militia at Beaufort as the Beaufort Volunteer Artillery; incorporated 20 December 1820. Consolidated about 1843 with the Beaufort Volunteer Guards (incorporated 18 December 1824 at Beaufort) and consolidated unit redesignated as the Beaufort Volunteer Company of Artillery. Mustered into Confederate service 14 March 1862 at Beaufort. Surrendered April 1865 near Greensboro, North Carolina, with the Army of the Tennessee. Reorganized 12 March 1878 in the South Carolina Volunteer Troops at Beaufort.

CAMPAIGN PARTICIPATION CREDIT

Revolutionary War
    Charleston
    Savannah
    South Carolina 1775
    South Carolina 1779

War of 1812
    Streamer without inscription

Civil War–Confederate service
    Sumter
    South Carolina 1862

    South Carolina 1863
    South Carolina 1864
    South Carolina 1865
    North Carolina 1865

World War II
    Tunisia
    Sicily (with arrowhead)
    Rome-Arno
    Southern France (with arrowhead)

Battery B (Easley), 2d Battalion, additionally entitled to the following:

World War II–EAME
    Northern France
    Rhineland

DECORATIONS

None.

263D AIR DEFENSE ARTILLERY BIBLIOGRAPHY

Cureton, Charles, and Fitzhugh McMaster. "The Charleston Battalion of Artillery, 1778–1797." *Military Collector and Historian* 30 (Spring 1978):25.

Davis, Nora Marshall. *History of the 263rd Coast Artillery (HD) Regiment, SCNG.* Columbia, 1938.

McMaster, Fitzhugh. "Colonial Cannon, South Carolina Artillery, 1670–1813." *Field Artillery Journal* 45 (September–October 1977):47–50.

107th Separate Coast Artillery Battalion (AA), Camp Stewart. Baton Rouge: Army and Navy Publishing Company, 1941.

Todd, Frederick P. "Notes on the Organization and Uniforms of South Carolina Military Forces, 1860–1861." *Military Collector and Historian* 3 (September 1951):53–62.

265th AIR DEFENSE ARTILLERY

HERALDIC ITEMS

COAT OF ARMS

Shield: Gules, on the bend nebuly or between a bezent bearing a mullet of four points azure and a roundel barry wavy of six of the second and of the last, a lightning flash of the third.

Crest: That for the regiments and separate battalions of the Florida Army National Guard: On a wreath of the colors, or and gules, an alligator statant proper.

Motto: Home and Country.

Symbolism: The colors scarlet and yellow are used for artillery. The unit's service in Alaska during World War II is denoted by the bezent, symbol for gold, and the four-pointed polar star. The diagonal stripe with the nebuly edges, heraldic symbol for clouds, bearing a lightning flash signifies the air defense artillery mission. The barry wavy roundel alludes to water and refers to the former coast artillery service. Additionally, it indicates the organization's location in Florida and alludes to the legendary "Fountain of Youth" sought by Ponce de Leon, the discoverer of Florida.

DISTINCTIVE INSIGNIA

The distinctive insignia is the shield and motto of the coat of arms.

LINEAGE AND HONORS

ARNG
(Florida)

LINEAGE

Constituted 19 October 1923 in the Florida National Guard as the 1st Separate Battalion, Coast Artillery Corps. Organized and federally recognized 14 November 1923 with Headquarters at Jacksonville. Redesignated 4 April 1924 as the 1st Separate Battalion, Coast Artillery. Redesignated 22 July 1925 as the 265th Coast Artillery Battalion. Expanded, reorganized, and redesignated 20 November 1929 as the 265th Coast Artillery. Inducted into federal service 6 January 1941 at home stations. Disbanded 31 July 1944 in Alaska. Reconstituted 25 August 1945 in the Florida National Guard.

Headquarters and 1st Battalion, 265th Coast Artillery, reorganized and federally recognized 5 December 1946 as the 692d Antiaircraft Artillery Automatic Weapons Battalion, an element of the 48th Infantry Division (later redesignated as the 48th Armored Division), with Headquarters at Jacksonville. Redesignated 1 February 1949 as the 148th Antiaircraft Artillery Automatic Weapons Battalion. Redesignated 1 October 1953 as the 148th Antiaircraft Artillery Battalion.

2d Battalion reorganized and federally recognized 17 December 1946 as the 712th Antiaircraft Artillery Gun Battalion with Headquarters at Miami. Ordered into active federal service 1 May 1951 at home stations; released 30 April 1953 from active federal service and reverted to state control. Location of Headquarters changed 22 June 1953 to Sarasota. Redesignated 1 October 1953 as the 712th Antiaircraft Artillery Battalion.

(Headquarters Battery reorganized and federally recognized 15 September 1946 at Jacksonville as Headquarters and Headquarters Battery, 227th Antiaircraft Artillery Group—hereafter separate lineage.)

148th and 712th Antiaircraft Artillery Battalions consolidated 15 April 1959 and consolidated unit reorganized and redesignated as the 265th Artillery, a parent regiment under the Combat Arms Regimental System, to consist of the 1st Automatic Weapons Battalion and the 2d Howitzer Battalion. Reorganized 15 February 1963 to consist of the 1st and 2d Automatic Weapons Battalions and the 16th and 17th Detachments. Reorganized 20 January 1968 to consist of the 1st Battalion.

CAMPAIGN PARTICIPATION CREDIT

World War II
    Asiatic-Pacific Theater, Streamer
        without inscription

DECORATIONS

None.

265TH AIR DEFENSE ARTILLERY BIBLIOGRAPHY

Historical Annual, National Guard of the State of Florida. Baton Rouge: Army and Navy Publishing Company, 1939.

517th AIR DEFENSE ARTILLERY

HERALDIC ITEMS

COAT OF ARMS

Shield: Gules, on a bezant a bomber, nose to base, sable.
Crest: None approved.
Motto: We Sweep the Sky.
Symbolism: The scarlet shield and the yellow disc charged with the diving bomber symbolize the antiaircraft nature of the organization.

DISTINCTIVE INSIGNIA

The distinctive insignia is the shield and motto of the coat of arms.

LINEAGE AND HONORS

LINEAGE

Constituted in July 1923 in the Organized Reserves as the 517th Coast Artillery. Organized in August 1925. Inactivated 1 January 1938; concurrently withdrawn from the Organized Reserves and allotted to the Regular Army. Redesignated 1 August 1940 as the 78th Coast Artillery (1st Battalion concurrently activated at March Field, California). Regiment (less 1st Battalion) activated 10 February 1941 at Camp Haan, California. (3d Battalion activated 15 June 1942 at Long Beach, California; reorganized and redesignated 10 September 1943 as the 248th Antiaircraft Artillery Searchlight Battalion—hereafter separate lineage). Regiment broken up 7 February 1944 and its elements reorganized and redesignated as follows: Headquarters and Headquarters Battery as Headquarters and Headquarters Battery, 78th Antiaircraft Artillery Group; 1st Battalion as the 78th Antiaircraft Artillery Gun Battalion; 2d Battalion as the 591st Antiaircraft Artillery Automatic Weapons Battalion.

Headquarters and Headquarters Battery, 78th Antiaircraft Artillery Group, disbanded 3 February 1945 at Camp Earle, Alaska. Reconstituted 10 January 1949 in the Organized Reserve Corps, redesignated as Headquarters and Headquarters Battery, 328th Antiaircraft Artillery Group, and assigned to the Fifth Army. Activated 1 February 1949 at Great Bend, Kansas. (Organized Reserve Corps redesignated 9 July 1952 as the Army Reserve.) Inactivated 1 December 1955 at Great Bend, Kansas. Withdrawn 31 July 1959 from the Army Reserve and allotted to the Regular Army.

78th Antiaircraft Artillery Gun Battalion inactivated 31 October 1945 at Fort Bliss, Texas. Activated 15 January 1949 at Fort Bliss, Texas. Inactivated 24 June 1955 in Korea. Redesignated 13 September 1955 as the 78th Antiaircraft Artillery Missile Battalion. Activated 10 October 1955 at Fort Sheridan, Illinois. Inactivated 6 September 1958 at Libertyville, Illinois.

591st Antiaircraft Artillery Automatic Weapons Battalion inactivated 26 January 1945 at Camp Hood, Texas. Redesignated 28 June 1950 as the 99th Antiaircraft Artillery Battalion. Redesignated 14 May 1952 as the 99th Antiaircraft Artillery Gun Battalion. Activated 3 August 1952 at Fort Custer, Michigan. Redesignated 24 July 1953 as the 99th Antiaircraft Artillery Battalion. Inactivated 15 June 1957 at Detroit, Michigan.

Headquarters and Headquarters Battery, 328th Antiaircraft Artillery Group; 78th Antiaircraft Artillery Missile Battalion; and 99th Antiaircraft Artillery Battalion consolidated, reorganized, and redesignated 31 July 1959 as the 517th Artillery, a parent regiment under the Combat Arms Regimental System. Redesignated 1 September 1971 as the 517th Air Defense Artillery.

CAMPAIGN PARTICIPATION CREDIT

World War II
Aleutian Islands (with arrowhead)

Korean War
UN defensive
UN offensive
CCF intervention
First UN counteroffensive
CCF spring offensive
UN summer–fall offensive
Second Korean winter
Korea, summer–fall 1952
Third Korean winter
Korea, summer 1953

DECORATIONS

None.

1st MISSILE BATTALION, 517th AIR DEFENSE ARTILLERY

RA
(inactive)

LINEAGE

Constituted in July 1923 in the Organized Reserves as Battery A, 517th Coast Artillery. Organized in August 1925. Inactivated 1 January 1938; concurrently withdrawn from the Organized Reserves and allotted to the Regular Army. Redesignated 1 August 1940 as Battery A, 78th Coast Artillery, and activated at March Field, California.

Reorganized and redesignated 7 February 1944 as Battery A, 78th Antiaircraft Artillery Gun Battalion. Reorganized and redesignated 1 September 1945 as Battery C, 526th Antiaircraft Artillery Composite Battalion. Reorganized and redesignated 3 August 1953 as Battery C, 526th Antiaircraft Artillery Battalion. Reorganized and redesignated 13 February 1954 as Battery C, 526th Antiaircraft Artillery Missile Battalion.

Consolidated 1 September 1958 with Battery A, 78th Antiaircraft Artillery Missile Battalion (*see* ANNEX), and consolidated unit reorganized and redesignated as Headquarters and Headquarters Battery, 1st Missile Battalion, 517th Artillery (organic elements constituted 12 August 1958 and activated 1 September 1958). Battalion inactivated 23 December 1960 at Mundeloin, Illinois. Redesignated 1 September 1971 as the 1st Missile Battalion, 517th Air Defense Artillery.

ANNEX

Constituted 9 December 1948 in the Regular Army as Battery A, 78th Antiaircraft Artillery Gun Battalion. Activated 15 January 1949 at Fort Bliss, Texas. Inactivated 24 June 1955 in Korea. Redesignated 13 September 1955 as Battery A, 78th Antiaircraft Artillery Missile Battalion. Activated 10 October 1955 at Fort Sheridan, Illinois.

CAMPAIGN PARTICIPATION CREDIT

World War II
  *Aleutian Islands (with arrowhead)

Korean War
  *UN defensive
  *UN offensive
  *CCF intervention
  *First UN counteroffensive

*CCF spring offensive
*UN summer–fall offensive
*Second Korean winter
*Korea, summer–fall 1952
*Third Korean winter
*Korea, summer 1953

DECORATIONS

*Republic of Korea Presidential Unit Citation, Streamer embroidered DEFENSE OF KOREA (78th Antiaircraft Artillery Gun Battalion cited; DA GO 51, 1957)

2d MISSILE BATTALION, 517th AIR DEFENSE ARTILLERY

RA
(inactive)

LINEAGE

Constituted in July 1923 in the Organized Reserves as Battery B, 517th Coast Artillery. Organized in August 1925. Inactivated 1 January 1938; concurrently withdrawn from the Organized Reserves and allotted to the Regular Army. Redesignated 1 August 1940 as Battery B, 78th Coast Artillery, and activated at March Field, California.

Reorganized and redesignated 7 February 1944 as Battery B, 78th Antiaircraft Artillery Gun Battalion. Inactivated 31 October 1945 at Fort Bliss, Texas. Activated 15 January 1949 at Fort Bliss, Texas. Inactivated 24 June 1955 in Korea. Redesignated 13 September 1955 as Battery B, 78th Antiaircraft Artillery Missile Battalion. Activated 10 October 1955 at Fort Sheridan, Illinois.

Reorganized and redesignated 1 September 1958 as Headquarters and Headquarters Battery, 2d Missile Battalion, 517th Artillery (organic elements constituted 12 August 1958 and activated 1 September 1958). Battalion inactivated 8 February 1963 at Carleton, Michigan. Redesignated 1 September 1971 as the 2d Missile Battalion, 517th Air Defense Artillery.

CAMPAIGN PARTICIPATION CREDIT

World War II
  *Aleutian Islands (with arrowhead)

Korean War
  *UN defensive
  *UN offensive
  *CCF intervention

*First UN counteroffensive
*CCF spring offensive
*UN summer–fall offensive
*Second Korean winter
*Korea, summer–fall 1952
*Third Korean winter
*Korea, summer 1953

DECORATIONS

*Republic of Korea Presidential Unit Citation, Streamer embroidered DEFENSE OF KOREA (78th Antiaircraft Artillery Gun Battalion cited; DA GO 51, 1957)

3d BATTALION, 517th AIR DEFENSE ARTILLERY

RA
(inactive)

LINEAGE

Constituted in July 1923 in the Organized Reserves as Battery C, 517th Coast Artillery. Organized in August 1925. Inactivated 1 January 1938; concurrently withdrawn from the Organized Reserves and allotted to the Regular Army. Redesignated 1 August 1940 as Battery C, 78th Coast Artillery, and activated at March Field, California.

Reorganized and redesignated 7 February 1944 as Battery C, 78th Antiaircraft Artillery Gun Battalion. Inactivated 31 October 1945 at Fort Bliss, Texas. Activated 15 January 1949 at Fort Bliss, Texas. Inactivated 24 June 1955 in Korea. Redesignated 13 September 1955 as Battery C, 78th Antiaircraft Artillery Missile Battalion. Activated 10 October 1955 at Fort Sheridan, Illinois.

Reorganized and redesignated 1 September 1958 as Headquarters and Headquarters Battery, 3d Missile Battalion, 517th Artillery (organic elements constituted 12 August 1958 and activated 1 September 1958). Redesignated 20 December 1965 as the 3d Battalion, 517th Artillery. Redesignated 1 September 1971 as the 3d Battalion, 517th Air Defense Artillery. Inactivated 13 September 1972 at Selfridge Air Force Base, Michigan.

CAMPAIGN PARTICIPATION CREDIT

World War II
　　Aleutian Islands (with arrowhead)

Korean War
　　UN defensive
　　*UN offensive
　　*CCF intervention

*First UN counteroffensive
*CCF spring offensive
*UN summer–fall offensive
*Second Korean winter
*Korea, summer–fall 1952
*Third Korean winter
*Korea, summer 1953

DECORATIONS

*Republic of Korea Presidential Unit Citation, Streamer embroidered DEFENSE OF KOREA (78th Antiaircraft Artillery Gun Battalion cited; DA GO 51, 1957)

4th BATTALION, 517th AIR DEFENSE ARTILLERY

RA

(inactive)

LINEAGE

Constituted in July 1923 in the Organized Reserves as Battery D, 517th Coast Artillery. Organized in August 1925. Inactivated 1 January 1938; concurrently withdrawn from the Organized Reserves and allotted to the Regular Army. Redesignated 1 August 1940 as Battery D, 78th Coast Artillery, and activated at March Field, California.

Reorganized and redesignated 7 February 1944 as Battery D, 78th Antiaircraft Artillery Gun Battalion. Reorganized and redesignated 1 September 1945 as Battery D, 526th Antiaircraft Artillery Composite Battalion. Reorganized and redesignated 3 August 1953 as Battery D, 526th Antiaircraft Artillery Battalion. Reorganized and redesignated 13 February 1954 as Battery D, 526th Antiaircraft Artillery Missile Battalion.

Consolidated 1 September 1958 with Battery D, 86th Antiaircraft Artillery Missile Battalion (*see* ANNEX), and consolidated unit reorganized and redesignated as Headquarters and Headquarters Battery, 4th Gun Battalion, 517th Artillery (organic elements constituted 8 August 1958 and activated 1 September 1958). Reorganized and redesignated 10 September 1960 as the 4th Missile Battalion, 517th Artillery. Redesignated 20 May 1968 as the 4th Battalion, 517th Artillery. Inactivated 31 March 1970 at Fort Clayton, Canal Zone. Redesignated 1 September 1971 as the 4th Battalion, 517th Air Defense Artillery.

ANNEX

Constituted 9 December 1948 in the Regular Army as Battery D, 78th Antiaircraft Artillery Gun Battalion. Activated 15 January 1949 at Fort Bliss, Texas. Inactivated 24 June 1955 in Korea. Redesignated 13 September 1955 as Battery D, 78th Antiaircraft Artillery Missile Battalion. Activated 10 October 1955 at Fort Sheridan, Illinois. Redesignated 15 September 1956 as Battery D, 86th Antiaircraft Artillery Missile Battalion.

CAMPAIGN PARTICIPATION CREDIT

World War II
  *Aleutian Islands (with arrowhead)

Korean War
  UN defensive
  *UN offensive
  *CCF intervention

*First UN counteroffensive
*CCF spring offensive
*UN summer–fall offensive
*Second Korean winter
*Korea, summer–fall 1952
*Third Korean winter
*Korea, summer 1953

DECORATIONS

*Republic of Korea Presidential Unit Citation, Streamer embroidered DEFENSE OF KOREA (78th Antiaircraft Artillery Gun Battalion cited; DA GO 51, 1957)

5th MISSILE BATTALION, 517th AIR DEFENSE ARTILLERY

RA
(inactive)

LINEAGE

Constituted in July 1923 in the Organized Reserves as Battery E, 517th Coast Artillery. Organized in August 1925. Inactivated 1 January 1938; concurrently withdrawn from the Organized Reserves and allotted to the Regular Army. Redesignated 1 August 1940 as Battery E, 78th Coast Artillery. Activated 10 February 1941 at Camp Haan, California.

Reorganized and redesignated 7 February 1944 as Battery A, 591st Antiaircraft Artillery Automatic Weapons Battalion. Inactivated 26 January 1945 at Camp Hood, Texas. Redesignated 28 June 1950 as Battery A, 99th Antiaircraft Artillery Battalion. Redesignated 14 May 1952 as Battery A, 99th Antiaircraft Artillery Gun Battalion. Activated 3 August 1952 at Fort Custer, Michigan. Redesignated 24 July 1953 as Battery A, 99th Antiaircraft Artillery Battalion. Inactivated 15 June 1957 at Hazel Park, Michigan.

Redesignated 18 June 1959 as Headquarters and Headquarters Battery, 5th Missile Battalion, 517th Artillery. Activated 15 March 1960 at Dyess Air Force Base, Texas (organic elements constituted 1 February 1960 and activated 15 March 1960). Battalion inactivated 25 June 1966 at Dyess Air Force Base, Texas. Redesignated 1 September 1971 as the 5th Missile Battalion, 517th Air Defense Artillery.

CAMPAIGN PARTICIPATION CREDIT

World War II
  *Aleutian Islands (with arrowhead)

Korean War
  UN defensive
  UN offensive
  CCF intervention

First UN counteroffensive
CCF spring offensive
UN summer–fall offensive
Second Korean winter
Korea, summer–fall 1952
Third Korean winter
Korea, summer 1953

DECORATIONS

None.

6th BATTALION, 517th AIR DEFENSE ARTILLERY

RA
(inactive)

LINEAGE

Constituted in July 1923 in the Organized Reserves as Battery F, 517th Coast Artillery. Organized in August 1925. Inactivated 1 January 1938; concurrently withdrawn from the Organized Reserves and allotted to the Regular Army. Redesignated 1 August 1940 as Battery F, 78th Coast Artillery. Activated 10 February 1941 at Camp Haan, California.

Reorganized and redesignated 7 February 1944 as Battery B, 591st Antiaircraft Artillery Automatic Weapons Battalion. Inactivated 26 January 1945 at Camp Hood, Texas. Redesignated 28 June 1950 as Battery B, 99th Antiaircraft Artillery Battalion. Redesignated 14 May 1952 as Battery B, 99th Antiaircraft Artillery Gun Battalion. Activated 3 August 1952 at Fort Custer, Michigan. Redesignated 24 July 1953 as Battery B, 99th Antiaircraft Artillery Battalion. Inactivated 15 June 1957 at Detroit, Michigan.

Redesignated 31 July 1959 as Headquarters and Headquarters Battery, 6th Battalion, 517th Artillery. Redesignated 18 January 1962 as Headquarters and Headquarters Battery, 6th Missile Battalion, 517th Artillery (organic elements concurrently consolidated). Battalion activated 12 March 1962 at Fort Bliss, Texas. Redesignated 20 August 1965 as the 6th Battalion, 517th Artillery. Redesignated 1 September 1971 as the 6th Battalion, 517th Air Defense Artillery. Inactivated 28 September 1972 in Germany.

CAMPAIGN PARTICIPATION CREDIT

World War II
  *Aleutian Islands (with arrowhead)

Korean War
  UN defensive
  UN offensive
  CCF intervention

First UN counteroffensive
CCF spring offensive
UN summer–fall offensive
Second Korean winter
Korea, summer–fall 1952
Third Korean winter
Korea, summer 1953

DECORATIONS

*Presidential Unit Citation (Army), Streamer embroidered CHICHAGOF HARBOR, ATTU (Battery F, 78th Coast Artillery, cited; WD GO 10, 1944)

16th DETACHMENT, 517th AIR DEFENSE ARTILLERY

RA
(inactive)

LINEAGE

Constituted in July 1923 in the Organized Reserves as Headquarters and Headquarters Battery, 3d Battalion, 517th Coast Artillery. Organized in August 1925. Inactivated 1 January 1938; concurrently withdrawn from the Organized Reserves and allotted to the Regular Army. Redesignated 1 August 1940 as Headquarters and Headquarters Battery, 3d Battalion, 78th Coast Artillery. Activated 15 June 1942 at Long Beach, California.

Reorganized and redesignated 10 September 1943 as Headquarters and Headquarters Battery, 248th Antiaircraft Artillery Searchlight Battalion. Inactivated 4 November 1944 at Camp Howze, Texas. Disbanded 28 June 1950.

Reconstituted 5 August 1958 in the Regular Army and redesignated as the 16th Detachment, 517th Artillery. Activated 1 September 1958 at Fort Bliss, Texas. Inactivated 23 September 1960 at Fort Bliss, Texas. Redesignated 1 September 1971 as the 16th Detachment, 517th Air Defense Artillery.

CAMPAIGN PARTICIPATION CREDIT

None.

DECORATIONS

None.

517TH AIR DEFENSE ARTILLERY BIBLIOGRAPHY

Ackert, Thomas W. "Operation 'We Go.' " *Antiaircraft Artillery Journal* 94 (March–April 1951):7–11. Pertains to the 78th Antiaircraft Artillery Battalion.

Brooks, Arthur C. "From Pusan to Unsan With the 10th Antiaircraft Artillery Group." *Antiaircraft Artillery Journal* 94 (January–February 1951):13–15. Contains information about the 78th Antiaircraft Artillery Battalion.

Brown, William F. "Chongchon Withdrawal." *Antiaircraft Artillery Journal* 94 (March–April 1951):18–20. Contains information about the 78th Antiaircraft Artillery Battalion.

"Colonel Henning and the 10th Antiaircraft Artillery Group." *Antiaircraft Artillery Journal* 95 (March–April 1952):7. Contains information about the 78th Antiaircraft Artillery Battalion.

Gooding, Earl Robert. "78th Antiaircraft Artillery Gun Battalion." *Antiaircraft Artillery Journal* 96 (September–October 1953):9–11.

Marquat, William F. "Automatic Artillery in Korea." *Antiaircraft Artillery Journal* 93 (November–December 1950):2–9; 94 (January–February 1951):2–12; (March–April 1951):2–5; (May–June 1951):2–6; (July–August 1951):2–9; (September–October 1951):2–5; (November–December 1951):2–6; 95 (January–February 1952):2–5; (March–April 1952):8–10; (May–June 1952):12–15. Contains information about the 78th Antiaircraft Artillery Battalion.

78th AAA Gun Battalion (90 mm), Fort Bliss, Texas. Baton Rouge: Army and Navy Publishing Company, 1949.

78th Coast Artillery, Antiaircraft, Camp Haan, California, First Anniversary Number, 1941. Los Angeles: Times-Mirror, 1941.

562d AIR DEFENSE ARTILLERY

HERALDIC ITEMS

COAT OF ARMS

Shield: Gules, a pile bendwise or, a dragon passant counterchanged pierced by an arrow bend sinisterwise sable.

Crest: None approved.

Motto: *Tuebor* (I Will Defend).

Symbolism: The red field indicates artillery. The pile represents the searchlight beam playing on the enemy in the sky, symbolized by the dragon. The black arrow signifies the gun and machine-gun fire from the ground.

DISTINCTIVE INSIGNIA

The distinctive insignia is the shield and motto of the coat of arms.

LINEAGE AND HONORS

LINEAGE

Constituted 5 September 1928 in the Organized Reserves as the 562d Coast Artillery. Redesignated 30 November 1928 as the 917th Coast Artillery. Organized in 1929 with Headquarters at Roanoke, Virginia. Inactivated 1 October 1933; concurrently withdrawn from the Organized Reserves and allotted to the Regular Army. Redesignated 4 November 1939 as the 70th Coast Artillery and activated at Fort Monroe, Virginia. Regiment broken up 10 November 1943 and its elements reorganized and redesignated as follows: Headquarters and Headquarters Battery as Headquarters and Headquarters Battery, 70th Antiaircraft Artillery Group; 1st Battalion as the 70th Antiaircraft Artillery Gun Battalion; 2d Battalion as the 925th Antiaircraft Artillery Automatic Weapons Battalion; 3d Battalion disbanded on Guadalcanal.

Headquarters and Headquarters Battery, 70th Antiaircraft Artillery Group, inactivated 15 May 1947 on Luzon, Philippine Islands. Activated 11 April 1949 in Japan. Inactivated 26 June 1950 in Japan.

70th Antiaircraft Artillery Gun Battalion inactivated 30 May 1947 on Luzon, Philippine Islands. Activated 15 January 1949 at Fort Bliss, Texas. Redesignated 15 May 1953 as the 70th Antiaircraft Artillery Battalion. Inactivated 20 December 1957 at Bailey's Cross Roads, Virginia.

925th Antiaircraft Artillery Automatic Weapons Battalion inactivated 31 August 1946 on Luzon, Philippine Islands. Redesignated 13 October 1948 as the 21st Antiaircraft Artillery Automatic Weapons Battalion.

Activated 8 June 1949 at Fort Bliss, Texas. Assigned 14 November 1951 to the 25th Infantry Division. Redesignated 15 April 1953 as the 21st Antiaircraft Artillery Battalion. Relieved 1 February 1957 from assignment to the 25th Infantry Division. Inactivated 14 December 1957 in Hawaii.

Headquarters and Headquarters Battery, 70th Antiaircraft Artillery Group, and the 70th and 21st Antiaircraft Artillery Battalions consolidated, reorganized, and redesignated 31 July 1959 as the 562d Artillery, a parent regiment under the Combat Arms Regimental System. Redesignated 1 September 1971 as the 562d Air Defense Artillery.

CAMPAIGN PARTICIPATION CREDIT

World War II
  Northern Solomons
  Bismarck Archipelago
  Leyte
  Luzon (with arrowhead)

Korean War
  CCF intervention

First UN counteroffensive
CCF spring offensive
UN summer–fall offensive
Second Korean winter
Korea, summer–fall 1952
Third Korean winter
Korea, summer 1953

DECORATIONS

Presidential Unit Citation (Navy), Streamer embroidered WONJU-HWACHON (21st Antiaircraft Artillery Automatic Weapons Battalion cited; DA GO 38, 1957)

Navy Unit Commendation, Streamer embroidered PANMUNJOM (21st Antiaircraft Artillery Automatic Weapons Battalion cited; DA GO 38, 1957)

Philippine Presidential Unit Citation, Streamer embroidered 17 OCTOBER 1944 TO 4 JULY 1945 (Headquarters and Headquarters Battery, 70th Antiaircraft Artillery Group; 70th Antiaircraft Artillery Gun Battalion; and 925th Antiaircraft Artillery Automatic Weapons Battalion cited; DA GO 47, 1950)

1st MISSILE BATTALION, 562d AIR DEFENSE ARTILLERY

RA
(inactive)

LINEAGE

Constituted 5 September 1928 in the Organized Reserves as Battery A, 562d Coast Artillery. Redesignated 30 September 1928 as Battery A, 917th Coast Artillery. Organized in 1929 in Virginia. Inactivated 1 October 1933; concurrently withdrawn from the Organized Reserves and allotted to the Regular Army. Redesignated 4 November 1939 as Battery A, 70th Coast Artillery, and activated at Fort Monroe, Virginia.

Reorganized and redesignated 10 November 1943 as Battery A, 70th Antiaircraft Artillery Gun Battalion. Inactivated 30 May 1947 on Luzon, Philippine Islands. Activated 15 January 1949 at Fort Bliss, Texas. Redesignated 15 May 1953 as Battery A, 70th Antiaircraft Artillery Battalion. Inactivated 20 December 1957 in northern Virginia.

Redesignated 12 August 1958 as Headquarters and Headquarters Battery, 1st Missile Battalion, 562d Artillery (organic elements concurrently constituted). Battalion activated 1 September 1958 at Fort George G. Meade, Maryland. Inactivated 11 December 1962 at Fort George G. Meade, Maryland. Redesignated 1 September 1971 as the 1st Missile Battalion, 562d Air Defense Artillery.

CAMPAIGN PARTICIPATION CREDIT

World War II
  *Northern Solomons
  Bismarck Archipelago
  Leyte
  *Luzon (with arrowhead)

Korean War
  CCF intervention

First UN counteroffensive
CCF spring offensive
UN summer–fall offensive
Second Korean winter
Korea, summer–fall 1952
Third Korean winter
Korea, summer 1953

DECORATIONS

Presidential Unit Citation (Navy), Streamer embroidered WONJU-HWACHON

Navy Unit Commendation, Streamer embroidered PANMUNJOM

*Philippine Presidential Unit Citation, Streamer embroidered 17 OCTOBER 1944 TO 4 JULY 1945 (70th Antiaircraft Artillery Gun Battalion cited; DA GO 47, 1950)

2d BATTALION, 562d AIR DEFENSE ARTILLERY

RA
(inactive)

LINEAGE

Constituted 5 September 1928 in the Organized Reserves as Battery B, 562d Coast Artillery. Redesignated 30 November 1928 as Battery B, 917th Coast Artillery. Organized in 1929 in Virginia. Inactivated 1 October 1933; concurrently withdrawn from the Organized Reserves and allotted to the Regular Army. Redesignated 4 November 1939 as Battery B, 70th Coast Artillery, and activated at Fort Monroe, Virginia.

Reorganized and redesignated 10 November 1943 as Battery B, 70th Antiaircraft Artillery Gun Battalion. Inactivated 30 May 1947 on Luzon, Philippine Islands. Activated 15 January 1949 at Fort Bliss, Texas. Redesignated 15 May 1953 as Battery B, 70th Antiaircraft Artillery Battalion. Inactivated 20 December 1957 at Annandale, Virginia.

Redesignated 5 August 1958 as Headquarters and Headquarters Battery, 2d Gun Battalion, 562d Artillery (organic elements concurrently constituted). Battalion activated 15 September 1958 in Alaska. Reorganized and redesignated 15 May 1959 as the 2d Missile Battalion, 562d Artillery. Redesignated 31 March 1968 as the 2d Battalion, 562d Artillery. Inactivated 30 June 1971 at Ladd Air Force Base, Alaska. Redesignated 1 September 1971 as the 2d Battalion, 562d Air Defense Artillery.

CAMPAIGN PARTICIPATION CREDIT

World War II
    Northern Solomons
    Bismarck Archipelago
    Leyte
    *Luzon (with arrowhead)

Korean War
    CCF intervention

First UN counteroffensive
CCF spring offensive
UN summer–fall offensive
Second Korean winter
Korea, summer–fall 1952
Third Korean winter
Korea, summer 1953

DECORATIONS

Presidential Unit Citation (Navy), Streamer embroidered WONJU-HWACHON

Navy Unit Commendation, Streamer embroidered PANMUNJOM

*Philippine Presidential Unit Citation, Streamer embroidered 17 OCTOBER 1944 TO 4 JULY 1945 (70th Antiaircraft Artillery Gun Battalion cited; DA GO 47, 1950)

Headquarters Battery additionally entitled to Air Force Outstanding Unit Award, Streamer embroidered FAIRBANKS, ALASKA (Headquarters Battery, 2d Missile Battalion, 562d Artillery, cited; DA GO 21, 1968)

3d MISSILE BATTALION, 562d AIR DEFENSE ARTILLERY

RA
(inactive)

LINEAGE

Constituted 5 September 1928 in the Organized Reserves as Battery C, 562d Coast Artillery. Redesignated 30 November 1928 as Battery C, 917th Coast Artillery. Organized in 1929 in Virginia. Inactivated 1 October 1933; concurrently withdrawn from the Organized Reserves and allotted to the Regular Army. Redesignated 4 November 1939 as Battery C, 70th Coast Artillery, and activated at Fort Monroe, Virginia.

Reorganized and redesignated 10 November 1943 as Battery C, 70th Antiaircraft Artillery Gun Battalion. Inactivated 30 May 1947 on Luzon, Philippine Islands. Activated 15 January 1949 at Fort Bliss, Texas. Redesignated 15 May 1953 as Battery C, 70th Antiaircraft Artillery Battalion. Inactivated 20 December 1957 at Gun Springs, Virginia.

Redesignated 12 August 1958 as Headquarters and Headquarters Battery, 3d Missile Battalion, 562d Artillery (organic elements concurrently constituted). Battalion activated 1 September 1958 at Croom, Maryland. Inactivated 15 December 1961 at Suitland, Maryland. Redesignated 1 September 1971 as the 3d Missile Battalion, 562d Air Defense Artillery.

CAMPAIGN PARTICIPATION CREDIT

World War II
  *Northern Solomons
  Bismarck Archipelago
  Leyte
  *Luzon (with arrowhead)

Korean War
  CCF intervention

First UN counteroffensive
CCF spring offensive
UN summer–fall offensive
Second Korean winter
Korea, summer–fall 1952
Third Korean winter
Korea, summer 1953

DECORATIONS

Presidential Unit Citation (Navy), Streamer embroidered WONJU-HWACHON

Navy Unit Commendation, Streamer embroidered PANMUNJOM

*Philippine Presidential Unit Citation, Streamer embroidered 17 OCTOBER 1944 TO 4 JULY 1945 (70th Antiaircraft Artillery Gun Battalion cited; DA GO 47, 1950)

4th BATTALION, 562d AIR DEFENSE ARTILLERY

RA
(inactive)

LINEAGE

Constituted 5 September 1928 in the Organized Reserves as Battery D, 562d Coast Artillery. Redesignated 30 November 1928 as Battery D, 917th Coast Artillery. Organized in 1929 in Virginia. Inactivated 1 October 1933; concurrently withdrawn from the Organized Reserves and allotted to the Regular Army. Redesignated 4 November 1938 as Battery D, 70th Coast Artillery, and activated at Fort Monroe, Virginia.

Reorganized and redesignated 10 November 1943 as Battery D, 70th Antiaircraft Artillery Gun Battalion. Inactivated 30 May 1947 on Luzon, Philippine Islands. Activated 15 January 1949 at Fort Bliss, Texas. Redesignated 15 May 1953 as Battery D, 70th Antiaircraft Artillery Battalion. Inactivated 20 December 1957 at Forrestville, Virginia.

Redesignated 1 May 1959 as Headquarters and Headquarters Battery, 4th Missile Battalion, 562d Artillery (organic elements concurrently constituted). Battalion activated 15 June 1959 at Dallas, Texas. Redesignated 20 December 1965 as the 4th Battalion, 562d Artillery. Inactivated 10 February 1969 at Duncanville, Texas. Redesignated 1 September 1971 as the 4th Battalion, 562d Air Defense Artillery.

CAMPAIGN PARTICIPATION CREDIT

World War II
　*Northern Solomons
　Bismarck Archipelago
　Leyte
　*Luzon (with arrowhead)

Korean War
　CCF intervention

First UN counteroffensive
CCF spring offensive
UN summer–fall offensive
Second Korean winter
Korea, summer–fall 1952
Third Korean winter
Korea, summer 1953

DECORATIONS

Presidential Unit Citation (Navy), Streamer embroidered WONJU-HWACHON

Navy Unit Commendation, Streamer embroidered PANMUNJOM

*Philippine Presidential Unit Citation, Streamer embroidered 17 OCTOBER 1944 TO 4 JULY 1945 (70th Antiaircraft Artillery Gun Battalion cited; DA GO 47, 1950)

5th BATTALION, 562d AIR DEFENSE ARTILLERY

RA
(inactive)

LINEAGE

Constituted 5 September 1928 in the Organized Reserves as Battery E, 562d Coast Artillery. Redesignated 30 November 1928 as Battery E, 917th Coast Artillery. Organized in 1929 in Virginia. Inactivated 1 October 1933; concurrently withdrawn from the Organized Reserves and allotted to the Regular Army. Redesignated 4 November 1939 as Battery E, 70th Coast Artillery, and activated at Fort Monroe, Virginia.

Reorganized and redesignated 10 November 1943 as Battery A, 925th Antiaircraft Artillery Automatic Weapons Battalion. Inactivated 31 August 1946 on Luzon, Philippine Islands. Redesignated 13 October 1948 as Battery A, 21st Antiaircraft Artillery Automatic Weapons Battalion. Activated 8 June 1949 at Fort Bliss, Texas. (21st Antiaircraft Artillery Automatic Weapons Battalion assigned 14 November 1951 to the 25th Infantry Division.) Redesignated 15 April 1953 as Battery A, 21st Antiaircraft Artillery Battalion. (21st Antiaircraft Artillery Battalion relieved 1 February 1957 from assignment to the 25th Infantry Division.) Inactivated 14 December 1957 in Hawaii.

Redesignated 18 June 1959 as Headquarters and Headquarters Battery, 5th Missile Battalion, 562d Artillery. Activated 17 March 1960 at Barksdale Air Force Base, Louisiana (organic elements constituted 1 February 1960 and activated 17 March 1960). Battalion inactivated 25 March 1966 at Barksdale Air Force Base, Louisiana. Redesignated 1 September 1971 as the 5th Missile Battalion, 562d Air Defense Artillery. Redesignated 1 May 1972 as the 5th Battalion, 562d Air Defense Artillery, and activated at Fort Campbell, Kentucky. Inactivated 13 September 1972 at Fort Campbell, Kentucky.

CAMPAIGN PARTICIPATION CREDIT

World War II
 *Northern Solomons
 *Bismarck Archipelago
 *Leyte
  Luzon (with arrowhead)

Korean War
 *CCF intervention

*First UN counteroffensive
*CCF spring offensive
*UN summer–fall offensive
*Second Korean winter
*Korea, summer–fall 1952
*Third Korean winter
*Korea, summer 1953

DECORATIONS

*Presidential Unit Citation (Navy), Streamer embroidered WONJU-HWACHON (21st Antiaircraft Artillery Automatic Weapons Battalion cited; DA GO 38, 1957)

*Navy Unit Commendation, Streamer embroidered PANMUNJOM (21st Antiaircraft Artillery Automatic Weapons Battalion cited; DA GO 38, 1957)

*Philippine Presidential Unit Citation, Streamer embroidered 17 OCTOBER 1944 TO 4 JULY 1945 (925th Antiaircraft Artillery Automatic Weapons Battalion cited; DA GO 47, 1950)

*Republic of Korea Presidential Unit Citation, Streamer embroidered MUNSAN-NI (21st Antiaircraft Artillery Automatic Weapons Battalion cited; DA GO 19, 1955)

6th BATTALION, 562d AIR DEFENSE ARTILLERY

RA
(inactive)

LINEAGE

Constituted 5 September 1928 in the Organized Reserves as Battery F, 562d Coast Artillery. Redesignated 30 November 1928 as Battery E, 917th Coast Artillery. Organized in 1929 in Virginia. Inactivated 1 October 1933; concurrently withdrawn from the Organized Reserves and allotted to the Regular Army. Redesignated 4 November 1939 as Battery F, 70th Coast Artillery, and activated at Fort Monroe, Virginia.

Reorganized and redesignated 10 November 1943 as Battery B, 925th Antiaircraft Artillery Automatic Weapons Battalion. Inactivated 31 August 1946 on Luzon, Philippine Islands. Redesignated 13 October 1948 as Battery B, 21st Antiaircraft Artillery Automatic Weapons Battalion. Activated 8 June 1949 at Fort Bliss, Texas. (21st Antiaircraft Artillery Automatic Weapons Battalion assigned 14 November 1951 to the 25th Infantry Division.) Redesignated 15 April 1953 as Battery B, 21st Antiaircraft Artillery Battalion. (21st Antiaircraft Artillery Battalion relieved 1 February 1957 from assignment to the 25th Infantry Division.) Inactivated 14 December 1957 in Hawaii.

Redesignated 31 July 1959 as Headquarters and Headquarters Battery, 6th Battalion, 562d Artillery. Redesignated 18 January 1962 as Headquarters and Headquarters Battery, 6th Missile Battalion, 562d Artillery (organic elements concurrently constituted). Battalion activated 7 May 1962 at Fort Bliss, Texas. Redesignated 20 August 1965 as the 6th Battalion, 562d Artillery. Redesignated 1 September 1971 as the 6th Battalion, 562d Air Defense Artillery. Inactivated 13 September 1972 in Germany.

CAMPAIGN PARTICIPATION CREDIT

World War II
  *Northern Solomons
  *Bismarck Archipelago
  *Leyte
    Luzon (with arrowhead)

Korean War
  *CCF intervention

*First UN counteroffensive
*CCF spring offensive
*UN summer–fall offensive
*Second Korean winter
*Korea, summer–fall 1952
*Third Korean winter
*Korea, summer 1953

DECORATIONS

*Presidential Unit Citation (Navy), Streamer embroidered WONJU-HWACHON (21st Antiaircraft Artillery Automatic Weapons Battalion cited; DA GO 38, 1957)

*Navy Unit Commendation, Streamer embroidered PANMUNJOM (21st Antiaircraft Artillery Automatic Weapons Battalion cited; DA GO 38, 1957)

*Philippine Presidential Unit Citation, Streamer embroidered

17 OCTOBER 1944 TO 4 JULY 1945 (925th Antiaircraft Artillery Automatic Weapons Battalion cited; DA GO 47, 1950)

*Republic of Korea Presidential Unit Citation, Streamer embroidered MUNSAN-NI (21st Antiaircraft Artillery Automatic Weapons Battalion cited; DA GO 19, 1955)

12th DETACHMENT, 562d AIR DEFENSE ARTILLERY

RA
(inactive)

LINEAGE

Constituted 5 September 1928 in the Organized Reserves as Headquarters Battery, 562d Coast Artillery. Redesignated 30 November 1928 as Headquarters Battery, 917th Coast Artillery. Organized in 1929 in Virginia. Inactivated 1 October 1933; concurrently withdrawn from the Organized Reserves and allotted to the Regular Army. Redesignated 4 November 1939 as Headquarters Battery, 70th Coast Artillery, and activated at Fort Monroe, Virginia.

Reorganized and redesignated 10 November 1943 as Headquarters Battery, 70th Antiaircraft Artillery Group. Inactivated 15 May 1947 on Luzon, Philippine Islands. Activated 11 April 1949 in Japan. Inactivated 26 June 1950 in Japan.

Redesignated 5 September 1957 as the 12th Detachment, 562d Artillery, and activated at Fort George G. Meade, Maryland. Inactivated 23 January 1959 at Fort George G. Meade, Maryland. Redesignated 1 September 1971 as the 12th Detachment, 562d Air Defense Artillery.

CAMPAIGN PARTICIPATION CREDIT

World War II—AP
    Northern Solomons
    Luzon

DECORATIONS

Philippine Presidential Unit Citation, Streamer embroidered 17 OCTOBER 1944 TO 4 JULY 1945 (Headquarters and Headquarters Battery, 70th Antiaircraft Artillery Group, cited; DA GO 47, 1950)

16th DETACHMENT, 562d AIR DEFENSE ARTILLERY

RA
(inactive)

LINEAGE

Constituted 5 September 1928 in the Organized Reserves as Battery I, 562d Coast Artillery. Redesignated 30 November 1928 as Battery I, 917th Coast Artillery. Organized in 1929 in Virginia. Inactivated 1 October 1933; concurrently withdrawn from the Organized Reserves and allotted to the Regular Army. Redesignated 4 November 1939 as Battery I, 70th Coast Artillery, and activated at Fort Monroe, Virginia.

Reorganized and redesignated 15 November 1943 as the 725th Antiaircraft Artillery Searchlight Battery. Inactivated 5 June 1948 on Guam. Redesignated 8 May 1956 as the 725th Antiaircraft Artillery Battery. Activated 15 May 1956 at Fort Bliss, Texas. Inactivated 1 October 1957 at Fort Bliss, Texas.

Redesignated 5 August 1958 as the 16th Detachment, 562d Artillery. Activated 1 September 1958 at Fort Bliss, Texas. Inactivated 17 September 1962 at Fort Bliss, Texas. Redesignated 1 September 1971 as the 16th Detachment, 562d Air Defense Artillery.

CAMPAIGN PARTICIPATION CREDIT

World War II—AP
    Bismarck Archipelago

DECORATIONS

Philippine Presidential Unit Citation, Streamer embroidered 17 OCTOBER 1944 TO 4 JULY 1945 (725th Antiaircraft Artillery Searchlight Battery cited; DA GO 47, 1950)

562D AIR DEFENSE ARTILLERY BIBLIOGRAPHY

Aaron, John S. "24th Division Antiaircraft Artillery." *Antiaircraft Artillery Journal* 95 (January–February 1952):18–20. Contains information about the 21st Antiaircraft Artillery Battalion.

"Activities of the 35th Antiaircraft Artillery Brigade." *Antiaircraft Artillery Journal* 93 (July 1950):31–32. Contains information about the 70th Antiaircraft Artillery Battalion.

Bennett, Karl F. "With the 21st on a Task Force." *Antiaircraft Artillery Journal* 94 (November–December 1951):13–15.

History of the 21st Antiaircraft Artillery Automatic Weapons Battalion (Self-Propelled). New York: Thompson Litho Associates, 1953.

Keeling, William O. "The A-B-C's for Ground Support." *Antiaircraft Artillery Journal* 94 (November–December 1951):9–11. Pertains to the 21st Antiaircraft Artillery Battalion.

Marquat, William F. "Automatic Artillery in Korea." *Antiaircraft Artillery Journal* 93 (November–December 1950):2–9; 94 (January–February 1951):2–12; (March–April 1951):2–5; (May–June 1951):2–6; (July–August 1951):2–9; (September–October 1951):2–5; (November–December 1951):2–6; 95 (January–February 1952):2–5; (March–April 1952):8–10; (May–June 1952):12–15. Contains information about the 21st Antiaircraft Artillery Battalion.

Morrison, Robert C. "The Wolfhounds Fangs." *Antiaircraft Artillery Journal* 94 (November–December 1951):7–9. Pertains to the 21st Antiaircraft Artillery Battalion.

Popovics, John. "Baker Battery Supports the 'Wolfhounds.' " *Antiaircraft Artillery Journal* 95 (January–February 1952):12–14. Pertains to the 21st Antiaircraft Artillery Battalion.

70th AAA Gun Battalion (90 mm), Fort Bliss, Texas, 1949. Baton Rouge: Army and Navy Publishing Company, 1949.

"The 21st Antiaircraft Artillery Automatic Weapons Battalion (SP) in Combat." *Antiaircraft Artillery Journal* 94 (July–August 1951):16–20.

Williams, Daniel B. "The Missions of 'Quad Lightning.' " *Antiaircraft Artillery Journal* 96 (March–April 1953):17–18. Pertains to the 21st Antiaircraft Artillery Battalion.

Glossary of Lineage Terms

ACTIVATE. To bring into being or establish a unit that has been constituted. Usually personnel and equipment are assigned at this time; however, a unit may be active at zero strength, that is, without personnel or equipment. This term was not used before 1921. It is never used when referring to Army National Guard units, and only since World War II has it been used in connection with Army Reserve units. (See also ORGANIZE.)

ALLOT. To assign a unit to one of the components of the United States Army. The present components of the Army are the Regular Army (RA), the Army National Guard (ARNG), and the Army Reserve (AR), which was formerly known as the Organized Reserves and the Organized Reserve Corps. During World War I units were also allotted to the National Army, and during World War II to the Army of the United States. A unit may be withdrawn from any component except the Army National Guard and allotted to another. The new allotment, however, does not change the history, lineage, and honors of the unit.

ASSIGN. To make a unit part of a larger organization and place it under that organization's command and control until it is relieved from the assignment. As a rule, only divisional and separate brigade assignments are shown in unit lineages.

CONSOLIDATE. To merge or combine two or more units into one new unit. The new unit may retain the designation of one of the original units or it may have a new designation, but it inherits the history, lineage, and honors of all of the units affected by the merger. In the nineteenth century, consolidation was frequently a merger of several understrength units to form one full-strength unit. At the present time, in the Regular Army and the Army Reserve, units are usually consolidated when they are inactive or when only one of the units is active; therefore, personnel and equipment are seldom involved. In the Army National Guard, on the other hand, active units are often consolidated, and their personnel are combined in the new unit.

CONSTITUTE. To place the designation of a new unit on the official rolls of the Army.

CONVERT. To transfer a unit from one branch of the Army to another, for example, from infantry to armor. Such a move always requires a redesignation, with the unit adopting the name of its new branch; however, there is no break in the historical continuity of the unit. If the unit is active, it must also be reorganized under a new table of organization and equipment (TOE).

DEMOBILIZE. To remove the designation of a unit from the official rolls of the Army. If the unit is active, it must also be inactivated. This term is used in unit lineages only when referring to the period during and immediately after World War I. (For other periods, see DISBAND.)

DESIGNATION. The official title of a unit, consisting usually of a number and a name.

DISBAND. To remove the designation of a unit from the official rolls of the Army. If the unit is active, it must also be inactivated.

427

ELEMENT. A unit that is assigned to or part of a larger organization. (See also
   ORGANIC ELEMENT.)

INACTIVATE. To place a unit that is not currently needed in an inoperative status
   without assigned personnel or equipment. The unit's designation, however, is
   retained on the rolls of the Army, and it can be reactivated whenever needed.
   Its personnel and equipment are reassigned to one or more active units, but its
   organizational properties and trophies are put in storage. When the unit is
   activated again, it is assigned new personnel and equipment, but it keeps its old
   history, honors, and organizational properties and trophies. This term has
   been used only since 1921. Before that time, units either remained active or
   were removed from the rolls of the Army.

ORDER INTO ACTIVE MILITARY SERVICE. To place an Army Reserve unit on full-
   time active duty usually during a war or a major crisis, such as the Berlin crisis
   of 1961–62. After completing its active duty, the unit may be inactivated or it
   may be released from active military service, reverting to reserve status. This
   phrase does not apply to Army Reserve units on annual active duty training.

ORGANIC ELEMENT. A unit that is an integral part of a larger organization, for
   example, a lettered company of a battalion or regiment.

ORGANIZE. To assign personnel and equipment to a unit and make it operative,
   that is, capable of performing its mission.

RECONSTITUTE. To restore to the official rolls of the Army a unit that has been
   disbanded or demobilized. The reconstituted unit may have a new designation,
   but it retains its former history, lineage, and honors.

REDESIGNATE. To change a unit's official name or number or both. Redesignation
   is a change of title only; the unit's history, lineage, and honors remain the same.
   Active as well as inactive units can be redesignated, but personnel and equipment of an active unit are not changed unless it is reorganized at the same time.

REORGANIZE. To change the structure of a unit in accordance with a new table of
   organization and equipment (TOE), or to change from one type of unit to
   another within the same branch of the Army, for example, from mechanized to
   airborne infantry. (For reorganizations involving a new branch, see CONVERT.)
   When referring to the Army National Guard, however, this term also means to
   organize an active unit again.

TRANSFER LESS PERSONNEL AND EQUIPMENT. To move a unit from one place to
   another without its personnel and equipment. The transfer is, therefore,
   merely a move on paper. The unit is usually reorganized at its new location with
   newly assigned personnel and equipment, but it retains its own lineage, honors,
   and organizational properties and trophies. The original personnel and equipment are reassigned to one or more units.

The U.S. Army Center of Military History

The Center of Military History prepares and publishes histories as required by the U.S. Army. It coordinates Army historical matters, including historical properties, and supervises the Army museum system. It also maintains liaison with public and private agencies and individuals to stimulate interest and study in the field of military history. The Center is located at 20 Massachusetts Avenue, N.W., Washington, D.C. 20314–0200.

Department of the Army Historical Advisory Committee

Roger A. Beaumont, Texas A&M University
Maj. Gen. Quinn H. Becker, Deputy Surgeon General, U.S. Army
Maj. Gen. John B. Blount, U.S. Army Training and Doctrine Command
Brig. Gen. Dallas C. Brown, Jr., U.S. Army War College
Richard D. Challener, Princeton University
Col. Roy K. Flint, U.S. Military Academy
John H. Hatcher, The Adjutant General Center
Archer Jones, North Dakota State University
Jamie W. Moore, The Citadel
James C. Olson, University of Missouri
James O'Neill, National Archives and Records Service
Charles P. Roland, University of Kentucky
John Shy, University of Michigan
Col. William A. Stofft, U.S. Army Command and General Staff College

Date Due

PRINTED IN U.S.A.   CAT. NO. 24 161   BRO DART